American Historical Press
Sun Valley, California

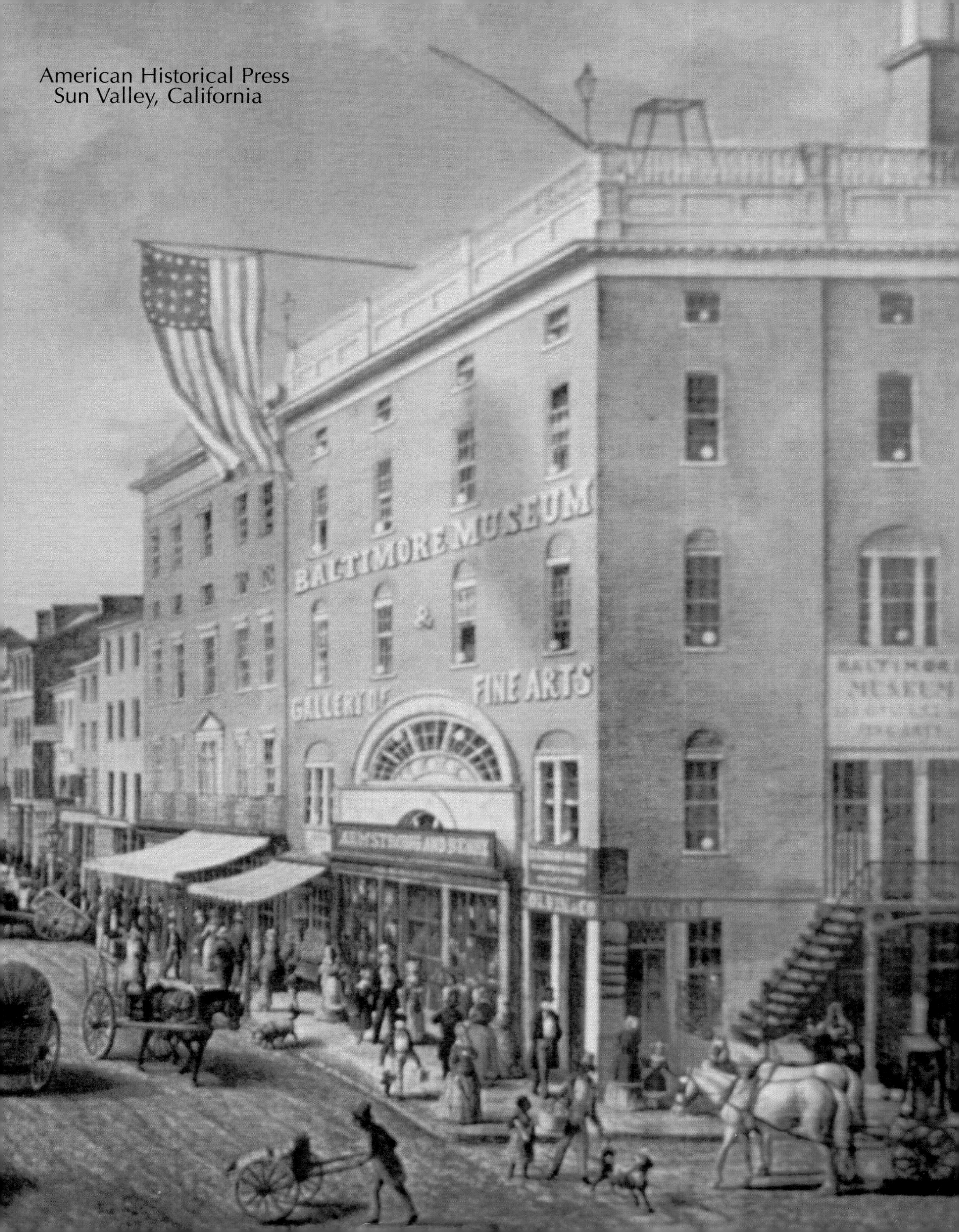

Previous page:
This 1859 view of Baltimore Street looking east from Calvert Street shows the wide variety of people and vehicles along the city's main business thoroughfare.

Published 2000
Printed in the United States of America

Library of Congress Catalogue Card Number: 00-108139
ISBN: 1-892724-11-1

Bibliography: p. 356
Includes Index

Contents

A lithograph of the Pimlico
Race Course taken from an
1875 drawing by Conrad
Ludloff.

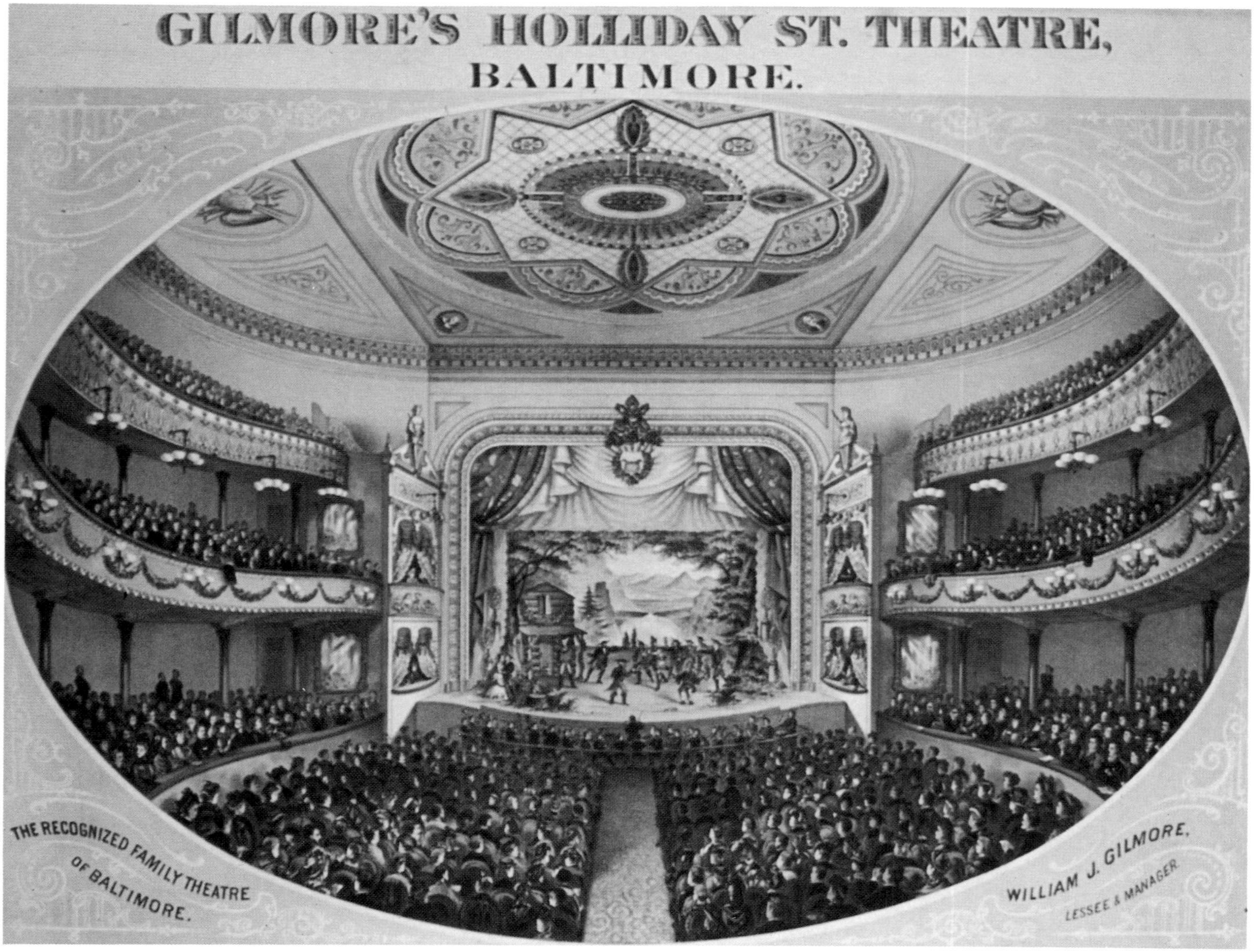

A View of Gilmore's Holliday Street Theatre taken from an 1876 lithograph.

In 1880 carriages such as these for sale on North Howard Street provided private transportation for the wealthier Baltimoreans

Preface

Baltimore is a great city to live in and to write about. It has been a joy and a delight, as well as a lot of hard work, to bring readers this history of Baltimore. The book is written for general readers, for all Baltimoreans and others who would like to know about the city. This history includes all facets of the life of the city, the wonderful diversity of people in Baltimore, and the sort of interpretive analysis that professional historians are trained to do. The photos make the history come alive in ways that mere words cannot. In many cases, the photos illustrate trends and specific points made in the text. In the preface to an earlier version of Baltimore's history, I wrote: "When this book was proposed, I felt a sense of sheer excitement at the prospect of writing the first comprehensive history of Baltimore in many decades....One major conclusion of this comparatively brief study is that many episodes mentioned here deserve more comprehensive treatment in the future." I am happy to report that during the last few decades a lot of fine work has been done. Some recent books are listed in the further reading section and I recommend them highly.

I am greatly indebted to a large number of people who helped in the creation of this history: people who allowed me to use their unpublished manuscripts and who lent me photographs and rare books; fellow scholars; members of museum, archives and library staffs who went out of their way to aid the effort; and many others. Many individuals' names are listed in the bibliography and among the picture credits. To those names I add with gratitude: Kim Donahue, Frederick Douglass, Jack Goellner, Donna Tyler Hollie, Kathy Hudson, Mary Valladares Jurkiewicz, Timothy Kim, Jeff Korman, Barbara Lamb, A. Jay McCullough, James Moody, Greg Otto, David Prencipe, John "Rocky" Rockefeller, Jean Russo, Rob Schoeberlein, Jay Sherman, Eva Slezak, and Jeff Walstrum. I cannot miss the opportunity to reflect on how lucky I am to be able to include many new photos by Middleton Evans, whose work is very highly thought of in Baltimore. And I would like to list again the names of persons I thanked in the earlier preface whose contributions remain: Muriel Berkeley, Gary Browne, Dean Esslinger, John Hankey, Ronald Hoffman, James Kramer, F. Pierce Linaweaver, Etta Lyles, Edward C. Papenfuse, and Constance Platt. I would like to thank Carolyn Martin and the staff at the American Historical Press for proposing this new edition and for their hard work on putting the book together. Every book I have ever worked on has been the effort of many people, and this one is no exception. I would also like to thank my colleagues at Morgan State University and my good friends who have understood my hectic schedule and the ways in which this history has impinged on my day-to-day life. Most of all, I wish to thank my two fine assistants, Jennifer Greene and Jean Wittich, whose help has been enormous. Lastly, I wish to thank all the people who have worked hard to make Baltimore a better place to live. You will see many of their names in the pages of this book.

I dedicate this book with love to Jenny, Duncan, Amanda, Mike, and Suzannah.

Suzanne Ellery Greene Chapelle
Baltimore, August 2000

The Waterloo Inn, the first inn along the main road south from Baltimore, was a typical stage coach stop during the eighteenth century. It provided a respite from the very rough and dirty roads, as well as meals and lodging

Beginnings

1608-1773

I

Only one house stood on the land that would soon be Baltimore, when Maryland's colonial General Assembly passed the enabling act for the erection of a town on the north side of the Patapsco River. By 1773, when the annexation of eighty acres of Fells Point marked the pinnacle of a series of territorial additions, Baltimore had been transformed into a flourishing port city with a cosmopolitan population and a wide range of urban amenities. Despite the periodic flooding of the Jones Falls and the malarial marshes which had to be drained, many natural advantages boosted the growth of Baltimore Town. The safe and deep harbor facilitated shipping. Rapid streams from the northern and western hills provided abundant water power for milling. The fertile soil rendered the back country wealthy in agricultural produce. Fine forests which surrounded the town furnished timber for building material and fuel. Stone of good quality and mines rich with iron ore lay within easy hauling distance. The moderate climate spared the settlers the rigors of the harsh northern winters and the pestilences of the southern heat. Into this setting came several generations of pioneers who made a city out of the wilderness.

Captain John Smith recorded the first known description of the site of Baltimore Town in his journal of explorations of the Chesapeake Bay in 1608. Sailing up the bay from the mouth of the Patuxent River, he noted: "Thirtie leagues Northward is a river not inhabited, yet navigable; for the red clay resembling *bole Armoniack* we called it Bolus. At the end of the Bay where it is 6 or 7 myles in breadth, it divides it selfe into 4 branches, the best commeth Northwest from among the mountaines." His map shows the spot. The clumps of red clay along the river banks reminded Smith of the medicinal Armenian Bole used in Europe. By the time George Alsop drew his map in 1666, common parlance had restored the Indian name Patapsco to the river that flowed into the Chesapeake Bay.

Most of the Indian place names along the western shore of the Chesapeake Bay came from the Algonquin dialect spoken by the Piscataway Indians who lived south of the site of Baltimore. It is agreed that Chesapeake meant "great shellfish bay." The meaning of Patapsco is uncertain, but the heaviest evidence points to a reference to the water's "penetrating a ledge of rock" as it flowed. Another opinion gives "back water," or "tide-water covered with froth" as the translation for Patapsco.

The place that became Baltimore had no permanent Indian settlements in the seventeenth century. The area did lie within the hunting grounds of the Susquehannocks whose villages were located further north, along the Susquehanna River, the "smooth-flowing stream." Game was abundant throughout Maryland and bears were especially plentiful on the site of Baltimore. The Susquehannocks ate their meat and used the hides, often whole, for clothing. They were tall and strong and presented an awesome picture attired in a bear skin with the neck hole cut below the animal's face. Susquehannock warriors were feared by the Piscataway and also the Eastern Shore Nanticokes on whom they made war, generally victoriously. Colonial settlers and the Susquehannocks experienced only minor conflicts until the Senecas began to push southward into Susquehannock territory. Squeezed between the attackers and the white settlers, the Susquehannocks sometimes fell upon the colonists.

Before the end of the 17th century, however, smallpox and tuberculosis, diseases new to America, had weakened the Susquehannocks so greatly that the few survivors, who moved to the area around Lancaster, Pennsylvania, became tributaries of the Senecas.

Beginnings 1608-1773

By 1700, only a few hundred Indians lived in any part of Maryland.

Baltimore County was established in 1659. At that time it stood on the frontier of Maryland, the proprietary colony of the Calvert family, granted by King Charles I to George Calvert, the first Lord of Baltimore, in 1632. Maryland's first settlers, who landed in the *Ark* and the *Dove* in 1634, had built their town, St. Mary's City, in southern Maryland at the junction of the Potomac River and the Chesapeake Bay.

At a time when many colonies and nations promulgated one official religion to which all citizens were supposed to adhere, Maryland had a Roman Catholic proprietor and passed the Toleration Act of 1649, which specifically allowed the practice of all Christian religions. Catholics, Protestants and Quakers all began to move to Baltimore County frontier area which included all of today's Harford and Carroll Counties and parts of Anne Arundel, Howard and Frederick Counties.

The General Assembly appointed county commissioners and people began to take out patents on the land. A few pioneering settlers came to the vicinity of the Patapsco River. In February, 1661, Charles Gorsuch, a Quaker, patented fifty acres at Whetstone Point, where Fort McHenry now stands. He agreed to pay the proprietor, Cecilius Calvert, son of Charles, 61 pounds per year for the use of the land. In June of the same year, David Jones hired Peter Carroll to survey 380 acres along the stream later named the Jones Falls in his honor. He built a house and is said to have been Baltimore's first settler. In 1663 Alexander Mountenay took up two hundred acres along Harford Run, where Central Avenue now lies, which he called "Mountenay's Neck." Later this same land was surveyed for William Fell. In 1668 Thomas Cole patented 550 acres that stretched from Harford Run on the east to what became Howard Street on the west and Madison Street on the north. "Cole's Harbor" became "Todd's Range," when purchased by James Todd, and finally was sold to Charles and Daniel Carroll of Annapolis, who bought that land and more, totalling 1000 acres, in 1696. Also in 1668, "Timber Neck," lying between the current Howard, Paca and Eutaw Streets, was patented by John Howard. In 1706 Whetstone Point was made a port of entry by act of the legislature. Although a few ships loaded cargo there, it never grew into a town. In 1711, Charles Carroll sold 31 acres to Jonathan Hanson, who erected a mill, probably the first along the Jones Falls.

Life was very primitive in the country surrounding the future town of Baltimore. The best transportation was by water. A few narrow roads traversed the woods. A law of 1704 required that enough trees be cut down to widen the main roads to twenty feet and that roads be marked. The marking system consisted of cutting slashes in tree trunks: one vertical slash on trees beside a road leading to a church and three horizontal lines, two close together and one a bit higher, on roads leading to a county courthouse.

Courts were convened in every county. In 1715 the legislature authorized the Baltimore County court to hold sessions four times a year, on the first Tuesday of March, June, August and November. Court business must have been slight.

Little hard money circulated, either English or provincial silver. In trade with local Indians, some colonists used *peake* and *roanoke*, wampum made from shells. Most trade was conducted by barter or by using tobacco as currency.

In Baltimore County, most farmers rolled hogsheads of tobacco to either Joppa or Elkridge Landing for shipment and these towns grew, but slowly. Annapolis was the one city of wealth and

George Calvert, the first lord of Baltimore and first proprietor of Maryland, received the grant from King Charles I in 1632, almost a century before the establishment of Baltimore Town. Many generations of Calverts ruled the colony during the century and a half before independence. The coat of arms of the Calvert family provided the inspiration for Maryland's state flag

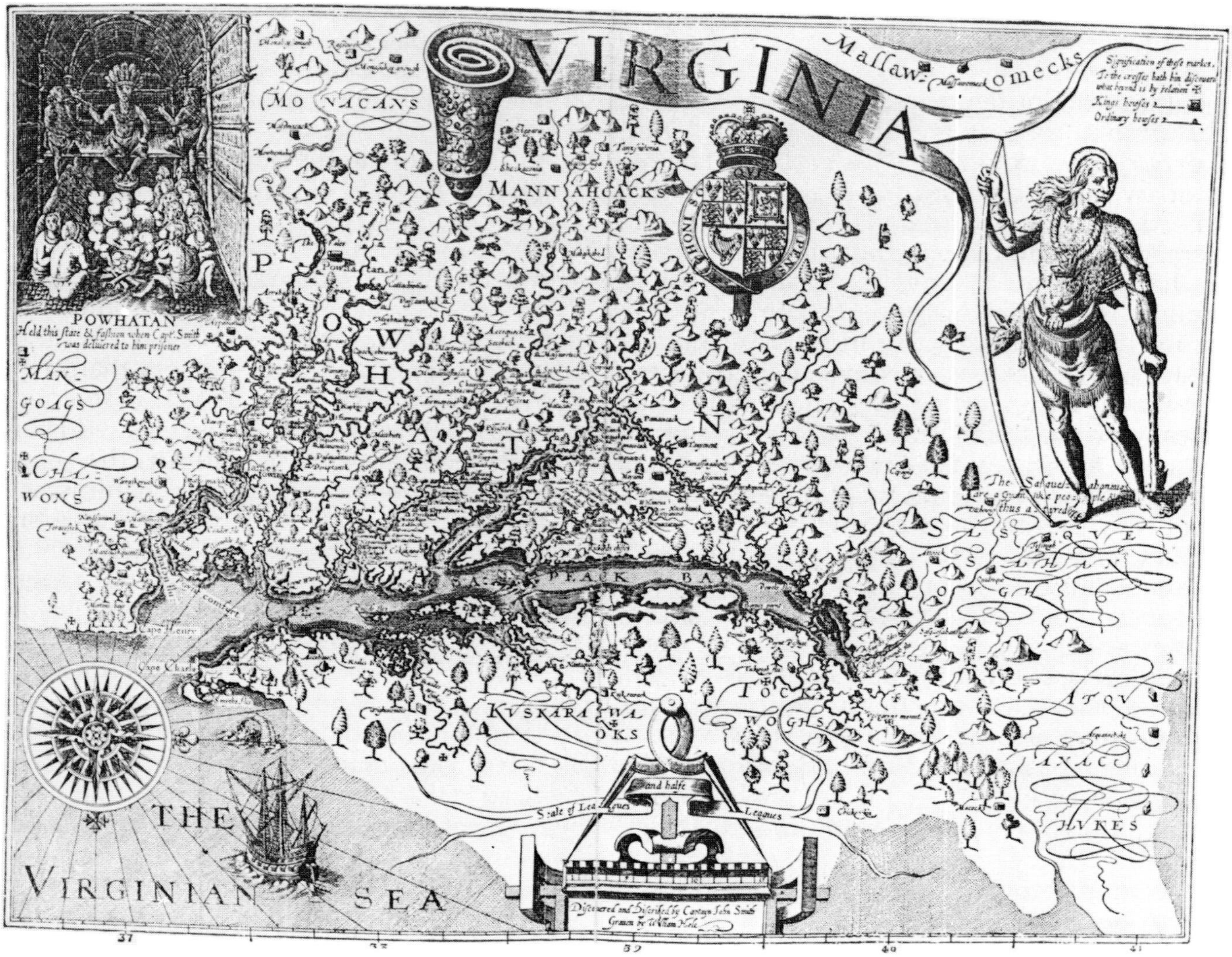

Left:
In his journal John Smith wrote the first known description of the site of Baltimore

Above:
In the exploration of the Chesapeake Bay and its tributaries in 1608, Captain John Smith sailed up "a river not inhabited, yet navigable," which he named the Bolus Flu. Indians who hunted in the region called it the Patapsco

status on the western shore of the Chesapeake Bay.

As more people settled along the Patapsco, the need for a town there became apparent. Thus in 1729, a group of leading citizens petitioned the legislature for the establishment of a town. The original plan called for the purchase of the land along the middle branch of the Patapsco belonging to John Moale, a merchant from Devonshire. Moale objected, because he believed that valuable iron ore was located there. Daniel and Charles Carroll then consented to the use of a portion of "Cole's Harbor" on the northwest branch of the river. The sole known resident was John Fleming, a tenant of the Carrolls', whose house stood near what is now the southeast corner of Charles and Lombard Streets.

According to the enabling legislation, sixty acres of land were to be divided into one-acre lots, to be bought in fee simple. The Carrolls would receive 40 shillings an acre in currency or tobacco at the rate of one penny per pound. The buyer of each lot would have to build a house of 400 square feet within 18 months or forfeit his land.

Commissioners were appointed to supervise the design of the town and the sale of lots. The act stated that these town commissioners were to hold their office for life and gave the group the power to fill vacancies as they occurred. The appointed commissioners were "gentlemen of consequence," including county justices of the peace and delegates to the General Assembly. Their names were specified in the act: Thomas Tolley, William Hamilton, William Buckner, Dr. George Walker, Richard Gist, Dr. George Buchanan, and William Hammond. The fathers of Gist and Hammond had apparently settled in Baltimore County in the late 1600s. Dr. Buchanan and Dr. Walker both practiced medicine.

County surveyor Philip Jones laid out the town. Three streets were built: Calvert Street; Forest Street, now Charles; and Long Street, which became Market, then Baltimore Street. Nine narrow alleys ran between the three streets. Lots were divided and numbered. On January 14, 1730, Charles Carroll, who, as owner of the property had first choice, selected Lot 49 at the corner of Calvert Street and the harbor basin. Philip Jones, with second choice, picked Lot 37, on the basin at the foot of Charles Street. Sixteen other men took up lots that first day, many along the waterfront. The process continued over the next few years with some of the claimants forfeiting their land because of failure to build within eighteen months. Ten years later, some of the forfeited lots were still in the hands of the commissioners. Baltimore was not an instant boom town. Its growth resulted rather from the ingenuity of its citizens and half a century of hard work.

Steiger's Meadows and Harrison's Marsh had separated Baltimore Town and the earlier settlement on the other side of the falls. In 1726, Richard Gist made a survey of the area for Edward Fell and reported three dwelling houses, several tobacco houses, an orchard, and a mill, Jonathan Hanson's, which stood by the Falls at the present Holliday Street. Edward Fell built a store. He found the area so favorable that he convinced his brother William, a carpenter, to leave Lancashire and join him. William arrived in 1730, and purchased "Copus Harbor," a 100-acre piece of land on Long Island Point. Here William built a house and a shipyard in the vicinity of Lancaster Street, establishing the industry that would bring prosperity and fame to the area later called Fells Point.

Settlers began to build on the land between Hanson's mill and Edward Fell's store, and in 1732 they petitioned the General Assembly to establish a town called Jones's Town. This was

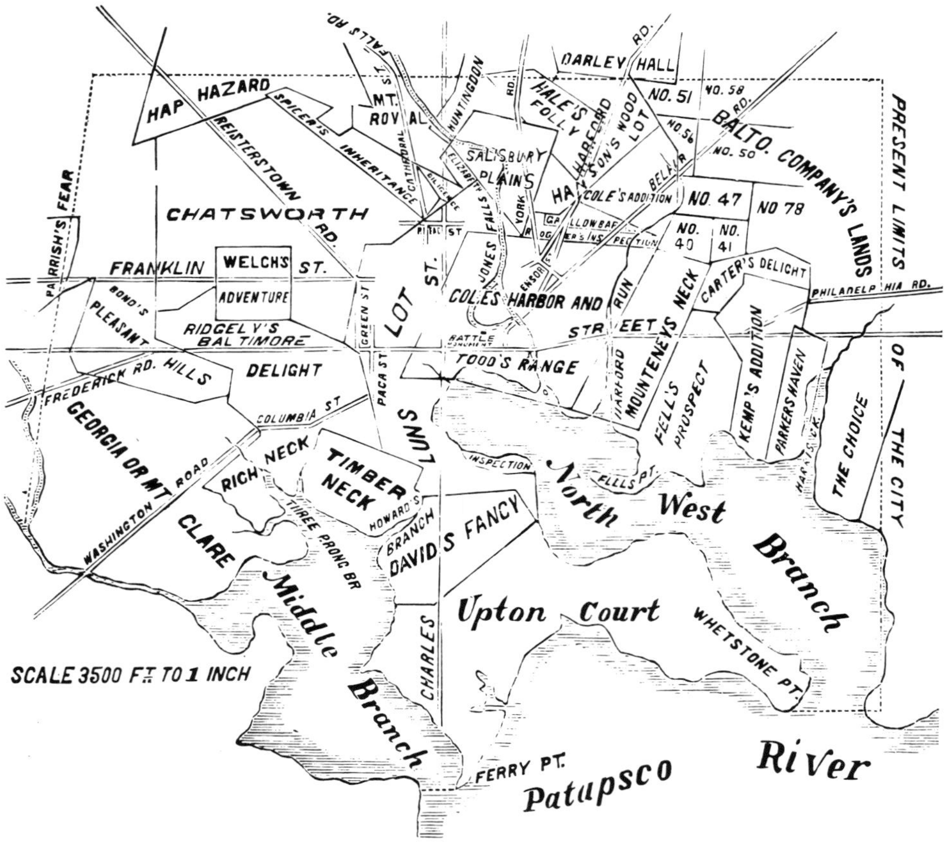

Above:
Charles Carroll of Annapolis and Daniel Carroll, his brother, agreed to sell part of their land to be divided into lots for the building of Baltimore Town

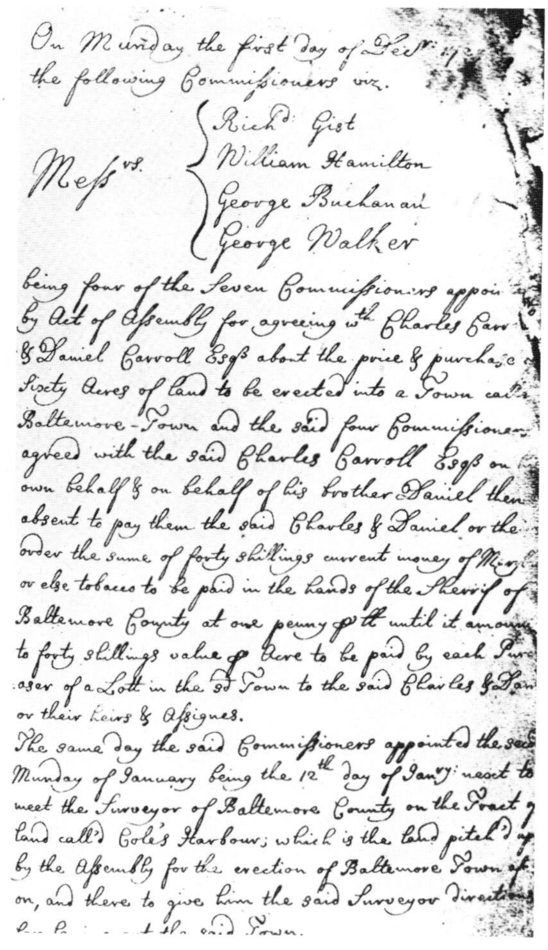

On Munday the first day of Decr. 1729
the following Commissioners viz.

Messrs. Richd. Gist, William Hamilton, George Buchanan, George Walker

being four of the Seven Commissioners appointed by Act of Assembly for agreeing wth. Charles Carroll & Daniel Carroll Esqs about the price & purchase of Sixty Acres of land to be erected into a Town call'd Baltemore-Town and the said four Commissioners agreed with the said Charles Carroll Esqs on his own behalf & on behalf of his brother Daniel then absent to pay them the said Charles & Daniel or their order the sume of forty shillings current money of Maryd. or else tobacco to be paid in the hands of the Sherif of Baltemore County at one penny p lb until it amounts to forty shillings value p Acre to be paid by each Purchaser of a Lott in the sd Town to the said Charles & Daniel or their heirs & Assignes.
The same day the said Commissioners appointed the second Munday of January being the 12th day of Janry. next to meet the Surveyor of Baltemore County on the Tract of land call'd Cole's Harbour; which is the land pitch'd upon by the Assembly for the erection of Baltemore Town and on, and there to give him the said Surveyor directions for laying out the said Town.

Above:
This map shows the original tracts of land granted in central Baltimore. Alexander Mountenay patented "Mountenay's Neck" in 1663. It was later sold to William Fell. Thomas Cole took up "Cole's Harbor" in 1668. This became "Todd's Range" when sold to James Todd. Later still, Charles and Daniel Carroll bought the land and then sold it for the building of Baltimore Town

Left:
Four of the commissioners of the newly authorized town met with Charles and Daniel Carroll on December 1, 1729. They agreed that the selling price for the land would be 40 shillings an acre, or tobacco at the rate of one penny per pound

done in August and lifetime self-perpetuating commissioners were once again appointed to lay out the lots, which were to be sold subject to a ground rent. Like the first commissioners of Baltimore, these men were well established citizens and landowners. Major Thomas Sheridan had taken up land in the county in 1721. Captain Robert North, one of the original lot owners in Baltimore Town, commanded the ship *Content* in which he carried freight as early as 1723. Thomas Todd was the son and heir of Captain Thomas Todd who had purchased land in North Point in 1664. John Cockey (whose brother Thomas settled in the Limestone Valley on York Road and gave his name to Cockeysville) purchased land near the Patapsco in 1728. John Boring was a merchant whose father had bought land on Patapsco Neck in 1679.

The commissioners had Philip Jones lay out 10 acres into 20 lots along four streets. Three streets ran parallel with the Jones Falls, one alongside the water and the marsh. The only cross street, now Gay Street, was named Bridge Street after the citizens of the two towns built a bridge across the stream and marsh which divided them. A major civic undertaking for two eighteenth century villages, this bridge could bear the weight of carts and wagons as well as horses and men on foot. More than any other single factor, the bridge made the two towns one. A stipulation of the act of consolidation was that the bridge be public and be maintained by the county.

The merger of Baltimore Town and Jones's Town (also known as Old Town) officially took place on September 28, 1745 by an act that proclaimed "the same Towns, now called Baltimore and Jones's Town be incorporated into one entire town, and for the future be called and known by the name of Baltimore Town and by no other name."

Even before the merger, the small number of people who dwelt along both sides of the Jones Falls began to build the institutions and join in the physical development that would make Baltimore a leading American city in just a few decades.

The first institutional building project began with the vestry of St. Paul's Parish, who purchased Lot 19, the most elevated point of land in Baltimore Town, following an act of the Assembly passed in June, 1730, moving the seat of the parish to the new town from its former location eight miles east. After the return of Protestant monarchs to the British throne with the crowning of William and Mary, the Church of England had become established in Maryland in 1692. This meant that it was supported by tax money. Furthermore, at this time, the vestries were elected by all the voters in each parish. It is worth noting that the only other elected officials in the colony were the delegates to the lower house of the General Assembly.

The building project, directed by the rector, the Rev. William Tibbs, and his successor, the Rev. Joseph Hooper, continued until 1739, when the new church finally stood complete at Charles and Saratoga Streets. It was constructed with the first bricks manufactured in Baltimore — 100,000 of them — made by Charles Wells for 90 pounds. The early church must have been less than resplendant as William Tibbs complained in one of his reports that St. Paul's owned neither "Surplice, pulpit Cloth, Cushion, nor Plate for the Communion Service but Pewter." Time and money improved the situation. The growth of the parish also resulted in the opening of a school at St. Paul's under the supervision of the rector.

After St. Paul's was built, residents began to use brick to construct houses as well. Edward Fottrell, who came from Ireland and bought the land belonging to Jonathan Hanson and George Walker in 1741, built the first brick house in

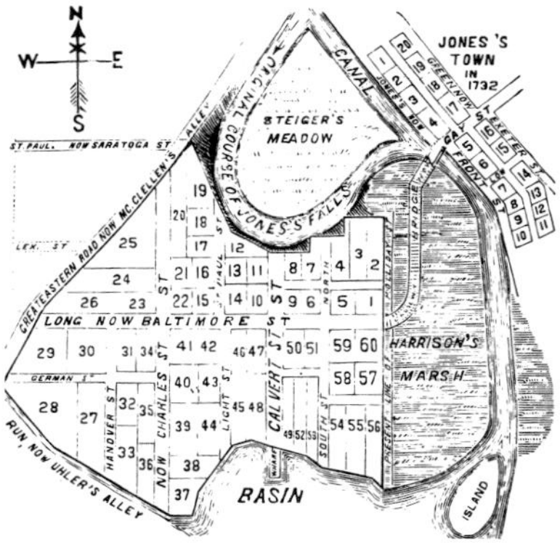

Baltimore Town was divided into lots in 1730, and Jones's Town was divided in 1732. Charles Carroll, who had the first choice, selected lot 49. Philip Jones, with second choice, took lot 37. Richard Gist chose lot 48 across Calvert Street from Carroll's land. Captain Robert North selected lot 10. In Jones's Town, Edward Fell took up lot 4, William Fell lot 6, and Thomas Boone lot 5

Above:
County surveyor Philip Jones laid out the town in 1730. Beginning at an oak tree located at the present corner of Charles and Camden Streets, he surveyed sixty acres and divided them into lots

Right:
The vestry of St. Paul's Church in 1731 purchased lot 19, the most elevated point of land. It took eight years to complete the town's first church, constructed with the first bricks manufactured locally

town. It had freestone corners and was the first to reach two stories without a hip-roof. The house stood at the location of the northwest corner of Calvert and Fayette Streets. Before Fottrell's arrival, all the houses and commercial structures were built of wood. This was the case in almost all colonial towns and resulted in one of the greatest common dangers: fire.

A number of fledgling towns were wiped out by fires that swept from building to building and could not be stopped. The wooden structures burned rapidly and fire equipment was almost non-existent. Baltimore's first attempt at dealing with this problem came in a 1747 regulation, promulgated by the commissioners, which stated that housekeepers would be subject to a 10 shilling fine if they did not "keep a ladder high enough to extend to the top of the roof of such house, or if their chimnies blazed out at top." If a fire did break out, all the townspeople grabbed a bucket and rushed to the burning structure. At night, two men led the way; one carrying a torch, the other blowing a fog horn. This system of fire protection left much to be desired. Baltimore pioneered an improvement when a group of volunteer firemen who had organized themselves into the Mechanical Company in 1763 six years later discovered a hand fire engine on board a Dutch ship that was anchored in the harbor. They bought the machine for 99 pounds (or $264) and named it the "Dutchman." The city could boast that it had a fire engine ten years before Boston and thirty years before Paris.

The other major problem faced by all colonial towns was filth. Early streets were unpaved, dusty on dry days and muddy on wet ones. Horses drew vehicles through the streets. Most animals roamed at will through the towns. Often hogs served as the only garbage collectors. Baltimore's first attempt to clean up the streets took the form of a law included in the act for the merger of Baltimore Town and Jones's Town. Section 11 required that, "None shall keep or raise any swine, geese, or sheep within the said town, unless they be inclosed within some lot or pen." A further sanitary regulation of 1751 revealed another problem: " . . . whereas several persons permit stinking fish, dead creatures or carron to lie on their Lotts or in the Streets near their Doors which are very offensive Nusances and contrary to act of Assembly the Commissioners therefore Order the Clerk to put up advertisements to inform such Persons that they are to remove them . . ."

The animals apparently continued to roam in and out of town. In 1746 the commissioners hired Captain Robert North to build a fence around the area that was formerly Jones Town. Then in 1748 the townsfolk generally took up a subscription to build a post and rail fence around all of Baltimore Town and to keep it in repair. Although many people said later that the fence was to keep out Indians, the subscription paper specifically referred to the prohibition on raising hogs or geese in town. Robert North, William Hammond, Thomas Chase, Richard Chase, Darby Lux, William Rogers and William Lyon all contributed 10 pounds while others joined them with smaller amounts. By 1750, the fence was complete. Two gates, one at the west end of Market Street and one at the upper part of Bridge Street, permitted vehicular entry. A smaller portal, at the top of Charles Street, near St. Paul's Church, opened for foot passengers. Protection against intruders, whether human or animal, apparently was of less concern to people than the cold winters. Within several years most of the fence had disappeared for use as kindling in local fireplaces. The town commissioners tried to prosecute the offenders but found that they had no legal authority to do so and therefore in November 1752 ordered the rest of the wood sold before it, too, disappeared.

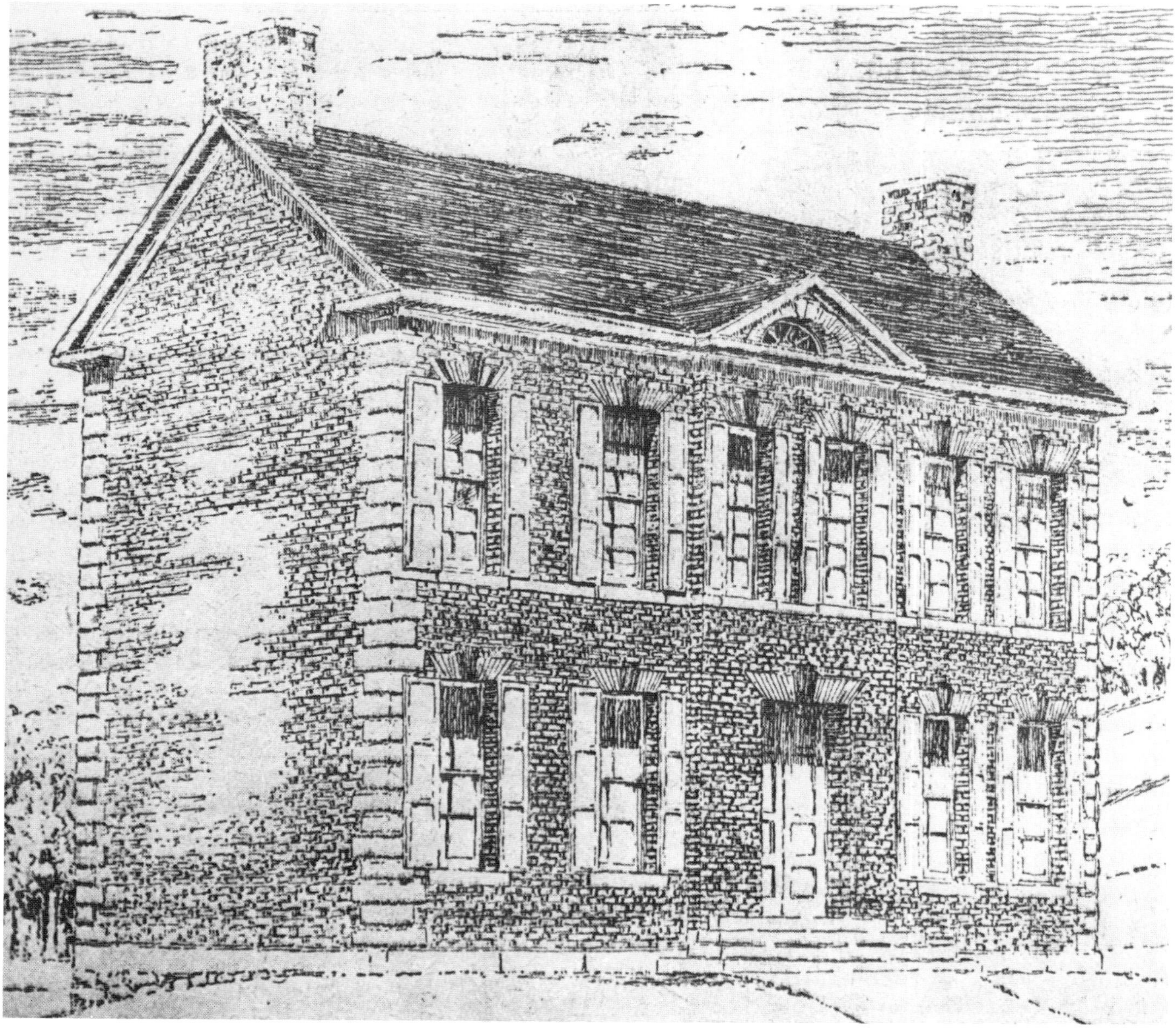

The first brick house with freestone corners, and the first which was two stories without a hip roof, was erected by Edward Fottrell on the hill close to where the Battle Monument now stands. It is said that Fottrell returned to his homeland, Ireland, before the Revolution, when his property was confiscated and sold to pay off a gambling debt

As the population grew, Baltimore Town could support a growing variety of industries and businesses. The success of Hanson's mill led to the establishment of other mills and soon bakeries. The manufacturing of bricks continued. In 1743, Captain Darby Lux opened the first tannery in town, on Exeter Street, and produced leather goods like harnesses, saddles, and buckets. In 1746 Dr. William Lyon and Mr. Brian Philpot joined as partners in the town's first drug store, located at Market and Calvert Streets.

In the late 1740s, Germans began to immigrate from Pennsylvania. The influx led to the opening of establishments for the spinning of wool and flax and the weaving of linens and wool, as well as the manufacture of leather goods. In 1748, two German brothers who moved to Baltimore Town from York, Leonard and Daniel Barnetz, erected the Town's first brewery, located at the southwest corner of Baltimore and Hanover Streets.

Most manufactured goods still were imported from England. The most common export was tobacco. Regular shipments of tobacco from Baltimore began in 1742. Farmers from throughout the area rolled their hogsheads of tobacco along the "rolling roads" to the harbor. By the year 1747 seven ships called at the port of Baltimore. In 1748, fifteen arrived, all bound for London. In 1750, residents built a tobacco inspection warehouse on the west side of Charles Street and began the construction of a public wharf. Individuals had been encouraged to build structures along the harbor by a section of the 1745 merger act which provided that "all Improvements of what kind soever, Either Wharves, Houses, or other Buildings, that have, or shall be made out of the Water, or where it usually flows, as an Encouragement to such improvers be forever deemed the Right, Title, and Inheritance of such Improver or Improvers, their Heirs and Assigns for ever." Most early builders of wharves benefitted from this provision and added water territory to their holdings free of cost while at the same time increasing the town's capacity for trade.

Before beginning a chronicle of the phenomenal economic growth of the young town, it is worth pausing to look at Baltimore in 1752. A drawing and several documents from that year provide a good picture of the small town just before a major spurt of growth transformed Baltimore into a major city.

A boyhood drawing by John Moale, son of the man who declined to sell his land for the erection of the town, depicts each structure in the original Baltimore Town. The drawing does not include most of the former Jones Town or nearby settlements like Fells Point. In his sketch, John Moale showed twenty-five houses, four made of brick. St. Paul's, the only church, stands high on the hill. Two taverns, Payne's and Kaminsky's, hosted by William Rogers, lie closer to the harbor. The traditional gathering places for all colonial communities were the churches and taverns. It is fair to assume that Baltimore Town's two taverns and one church served that function here. Taverns especially provided a meeting place for people of high and low class, all religions, permanent residents and travellers bearing news. Of all the structures in Moale's picture, Kaminsky's Tavern stood the longest. The sketch also shows the Barnetz brothers' brewery, the tobacco inspection house, a barber shop and an insurance office.

Craftsmen generally ran their businesses from their houses. An early listing of the heads of household indicates the variety of services already available only 23 years after the founding of the town. This record of 1752 is considered one of the earliest census accounts put together in any American town. It tantalizes as much as it contributes but is, in any case, worth including. Thirty names appear, some with descriptions:

John Moale in 1752 made a drawing of Baltimore Town. This more recent version is based on his original sketch

Baltimoreans built a tobacco inspection warehouse and paid an inspector to assure the consistent good quality of the town's first major export

This small wharf, Baltimore's first, was constructed at the foot of Calvert Street in 1750. The brig belonged to Nicholas Rogers

"Capt. Lucas, Wm. Rogers, Nich. Rogers, Dr. Wm. Lyon, Thomas Harrison, Alex. Lawson, Bryan Philpot, Nick Ruxton Gay, James Cary (innkeeper), Parson Chase, Mr. Paine, Chris Carnan, Dame Hughes (the only midwife among English folk), Chs. Constable, Mr. Ferguson, Mr. Goldsmith, Mr. Jno. Moore, Mr. Sheppard (tailor), Bill Adams (barber), Geo. Strebeck (only wagoner, drove a single team), Jake Keeports (carpenter), Conrad Smith, Captain Dunlop, Jack Crosby (carpenter), Bob Lance (cooper), Philip Littig (whose wife was *accoucheuse* among the German population), John Wood, Hilt Stanwitch (laborer), Nancy Low, Mr. Gwinn."

People whose names do not appear in this census would include wives and children of the men listed, black slaves, and servants and convict workers who came from Ireland, Scotland and England. Although in the 1600s some Africans came with indentures or contracts to work a limited number of years, by the 1750s most were slaves for life unless they were legally manumitted. Convict workers, often prisoners because of their political opposition to the English government or refugees from debtors' prison, had limited terms after which they became free. Many servants, under a 1638 law, worked for four years and then received 50 acres of land and a year's provision of corn. Slaves and servants frequently ran away. The advertisements for runaways printed in the Annapolis *Maryland Gazette,* the nearest newspaper, show that many such workers were not content with their lot and left to seek their fortunes elsewhere. No count of servants and slaves exists for Baltimore Town, but one such listing for the entire county in 1752 is presented by J. Thomas Scharf in his *Chronicles of Baltimore.* He enumerated: free whites, 11,345; white servants and convicts, 1,501; black and mulatto slaves, 4,143; free blacks and mulattos, 204. The population in town thus included a wide range of people, many born in America and many immigrants of varied nationalities. The town's wealthier leaders shared English, Scottish and Irish backgrounds. Servants and convict workers came from those same countries. Slaves were of African ancestry. An increasing number of craftsmen and manufacturers were Germans, many of them recent immigrants from Pennsylvania.

By 1752 Baltimore Town was lucky enough to have a school, not as common an occurrence in towns south of Philadelphia as it was further north, especially in New England. Scharf wrote that the school was located at South and Water Streets and was kept by Mr. James Gardner. Either the demand for education was greater than Mr. Gardner could meet or something caused the need for a new teacher. In February and March 1752, the *Maryland Gazette* ran a notice: "*Wanted* Person of a good sober Character, who understands Teaching English, Writing, and Arithmetic, and will undertake a School. Such a Person well recommended, will meet with very good Encouragement from the Inhabitants of Baltimore Town." Any school in Baltimore during this period would have been limited to white children whose parents were able to pay tuition sufficient to support the teacher and maintain the building.

In 1752, Baltimore seemed little different from many small colonial towns with a church, a school, several taverns, and craft shops increasing as rapidly as the population could support them. The difference is that Baltimore grew into a city while hundreds of others remained small towns or faded into oblivion. The colonial towns that did succeed, like Philadelphia, New York, Boston and Baltimore, shared several characteristics. Their wealth was based on trade. All were situated on good natural harbors. All drew on productive hinterlands to which good access was estab-

Kaminsky's Tavern, one of the oldest meeting places in Baltimore

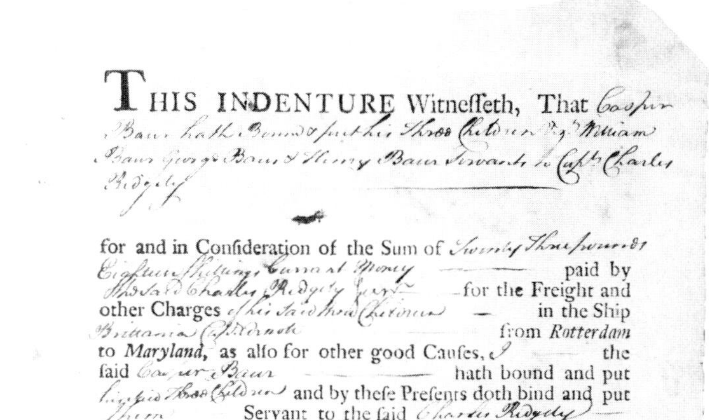

THIS INDENTURE Witnesseth, That Caspar Baur hath Bound & put his Three Children Viz: William Baur George Baur & Henry Baur Servants to Capt. Charles Ridgely

for and in Consideration of the Sum of Twenty Three pounds Eighteen Shillings Current Money paid by the said Charles Ridgely Esqr. for the Freight and other Charges of his said three Children in the Ship Brittania Capt. [illegible] from *Rotterdam* to *Maryland*, as also for other good Causes, I the said Caspar Baur hath bound and put his said three Children and by these Presents doth bind and put them Servant to the said Charles Ridgely to serve him his Executors, and Assigns from the Day of the Date hereof, for and during the full Term of their Arrival at the Age of twenty one years each from thence next ensuing. During all which Term, the said Servant their said Master his Executors or Assigns, faithfully shall serve, and that honestly and obediently in all Things, as a good and dutiful Servant ought to do. AND the said Charles Ridgely his Executors and Assigns, during the said Term, shall find and provide for the said Servants sufficient Meat, Drink, Apparell Washing and Lodging, And at the Expiration of their Servitude to give them the Customary freedom Dues. William Baur being six years Old the Eleventh Day of September Last George Baur being four years Old the [illegible] Day of November Next, & Henry Baur being two years Old the Ninth day of May Next.

AND for the true Performance hereof, both the said Parties bind themselves firmly unto each other by these Presents. *In Witness whereof* they have hereunto interchangeably set their Hands and Seals. Dated the Twenty Sixth Day of October in the Fifth Year of his Majesty's Reign, *Annoque Domini*, 1765

Sealed and Delivered in Presence of us,

Johann Caspar Baur

[illegible]

[illegible]

Charles Ridgely

This documents the 1765 indenture by Casper Baur of his three children, ages two, four, and six, to Charles Ridgley. The children were indentured until they reached the age of twenty-one. Many parents sent their children to serve such apprenticeships so they could learn a marketable trade

lished early. And all enjoyed the leadership of a group of merchants and other citizens who recognized the potential and knew how to make it work, for their own profit as well as that of the town as a whole. This mercantile leadership in Baltimore represented both descendants of early settlers and new immigrants. Some began with money, some with just a skill and an idea. The town and the surrounding countryside depended on each other for their growth. The hinterland produced the raw products which were either transformed into some saleable item or taken into town for shipment to another colony or to England. The countryside also provided a market for manufactured goods imported by the town's merchants and goods and services sold by its craftsmen and business people.

Baltimore's earliest trade, like that of much of Maryland, depended on tobacco. The real boom came because of the realization that another product, for which demand was even greater, could be shipped through Baltimore. That product was wheat, which was grown by farmers in Western Maryland and Pennsylvania. A Scotch-Irish Presbyterian who immigrated from Londonderry in 1745, Dr. John Stevenson, first recognized the potential. He and Captain Benjamin North joined forces and in 1758 shipped 1000 bushels of wheat to New York. Their small schooner, *Sharp Packet,* also carried one hogshead of tobacco, 15 barrels of flour, 16 barrels of bread, and one barrel of beeswax. A week after its return from the first voyage, the *Sharp Packet* sailed for Newport, Rhode Island with 900 bushels of wheat. William Lux, John Ridgely and others quickly joined in the profitable new export trade and Baltimore boomed. Soon ships sailed for the West Indies and Great Britain carrying wheat and locally milled flour and baked ship's bread. Mills sprung up rapidly, along both Jones's Falls and Gwynn's Falls, to meet the rising demand. Jonathan Hanson's original mill site, sold to Edward Fell, passed into the hands of William Moore and thence to Joseph Ellicott in partnership with

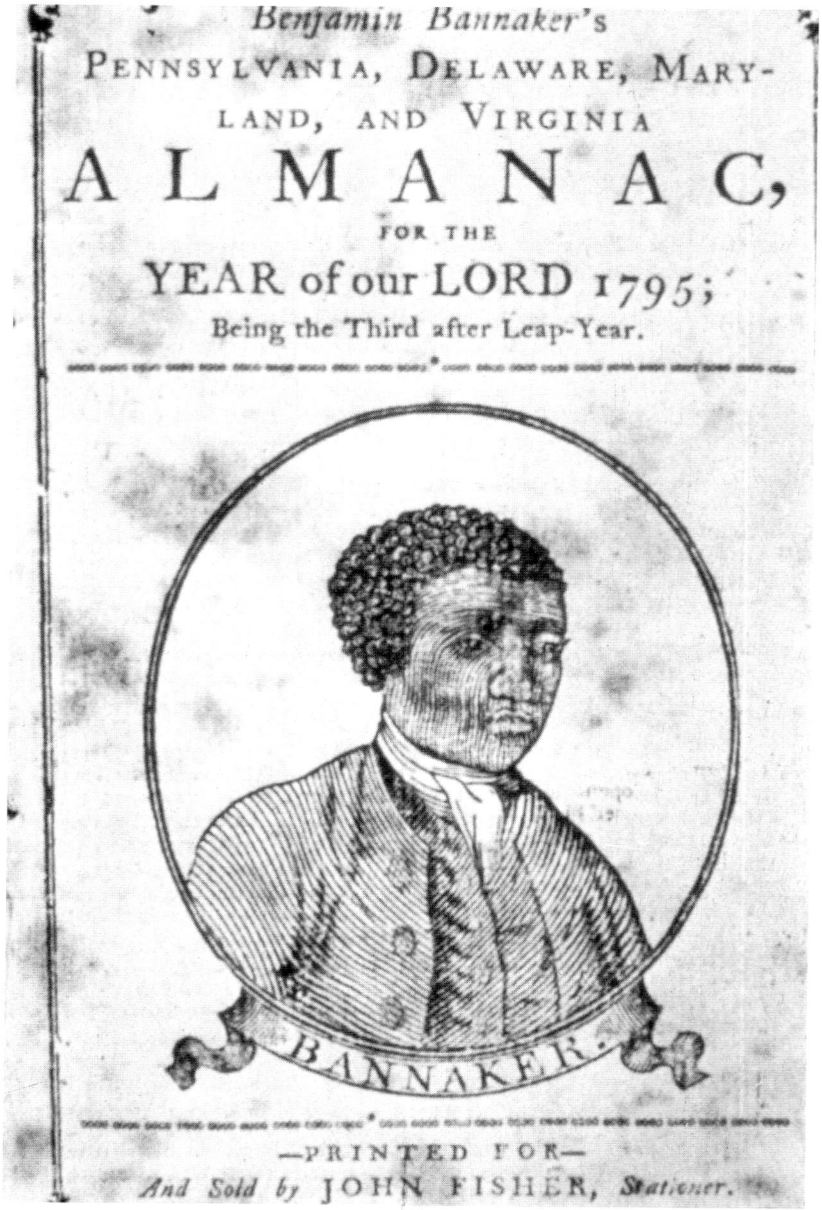

Benjamin Bannaker's
PENNSYLVANIA, DELAWARE, MARY-
LAND, AND VIRGINIA
ALMANAC,
FOR THE
YEAR of our LORD 1795;
Being the Third after Leap-Year.

BANNAKER.

—PRINTED FOR—
And Sold by JOHN FISHER, Stationer.

One of the best known African American residents of colonial Baltimore County is Benjamin Banneker, born in 1731. His family history sheds light on the life of servants and slaves in the earliest years. Banneker's grandmother was Molly Welsh, an indentured servant who came from England in the 1680s. After she completed her term of service, she acquired land and began to farm it. She bought two African slaves, whom she later freed. She and one of them, a man named Banneky, married. They had four daughters. The eldest daughter, Mary, married Robert, a former slave who was born in Guinea, on the west coast of Africa. Robert and Mary bought additional land, which they farmed. Their son, Benjamin, became widely known as a self-taught scientist, inventor, and musician. In his later years, he helped survey the land for the nation's new capital and produced an almanac, which was circulated in states from Pennsylvania to Virginia.

John and Hugh Burgess. Joseph Ellicott returned to Pennsylvania but moved to the area again in 1772 and along with his brothers, John and Andrew, established the very successful Ellicott's Mills on the Patapsco River upstream from Baltimore.

The real secret to the success of the milling and shipping of grain and its products lay in the opening of roads between Baltimore and western Maryland and central and eastern Pennsylvania. The early roads made it easier and faster for the farmers to sell their grain through the port of Baltimore than through Philadelphia which was reached by a longer and more strenuous journey. From its earliest days, Baltimore was in communication with Annapolis and Philadelphia by the Great Eastern Road and the northern route of the post road used for inter-colonial mail. In 1745, citizens of Baltimore and York, Pennsylvania completed a wagon road connecting their two cities. In that same decade, roads were built from Baltimore to Reisterstown and on up to Gettysburg and Hanover, Pennsylvania. Later in the century a road was built going eastward, through Bel Air and Rising Sun in Maryland and Oxford, Pennsylvania. More and more farmers, many of them Germans, settled in the areas opened up by the new road system and shipped their products through Baltimore. Countryside and city prospered together.

Letters from contemporary residents and visitors written to friends and relatives attest to the success. After Governor Horatio Sharp visited Baltimore in February 1754 amid a great celebration of parades, a dance and fireworks, he reported to Lord Baltimore that the town "has the Appearance of the most increasing Town in the Province." William Otley wrote from Baltimore in 1761 to John Cook in Northumberland encouraging him to emigrate: " . . . this place is excellently situated for Trade . . . and the Country about well adapted for Farming and Grasing, the Land in General Producing good Wheat and without Manure . . . and the demand for Wheat is Large, a good Quantity of Oats and Barley might be sold. Green peas might be Introduced for feeding Hogs Instead of Indian Corn which is the Bane of the Land . . ." Edward Cook, joining the effort to convince his brother to move to Baltimore, wrote that there were: "All sorts of Mechanicks . . . Masons, Brickmakers, Brick layers, Carpenters, Wheelwrights, Shoemakers, Barbers, Gardners, Sadlers, Watchmakers, Butchers . . . ," and that "Building is going fast on and [the town] cannot get workmen." He added that "Horses [are] dear, servants very scarce." Edward Cook noted some interesting figures: that seven years' service of a convict sold for 12-15 pounds and black slaves sold for 40-60 pounds, sometimes more. Compare to this a few consumer prices he recorded: wheat for 3 pence a bushel, beef and mutton for 2 to 3 pence a pound, and hay for 50 pence a ton.

William Eddis, the Royal Collector of the Port of Annapolis, wrote to friends in London ten years later in 1771: "This place, which is named Baltimore, in compliment to the Proprietary's family, is situated on the northern branch of the river Patapsco . . . Within these few years some scattered cottages were only to be found on this spot, occupied by obscure storekeepers, merely for the supply of the adjacent plantations. But the peculiar advantages it possesses, with respect to the trade of the frontier counties of Virginia, Pennsylvania, and Maryland, so strongly impressed the mind of Mr. John Stevenson, an Irish gentleman who had settled in the vicinity in a medical capacity, that he first conceived the important project of rendering this port the grand emporium of Maryland commerce . . . Persons of a commercial and enterprising spirit emigrated from all

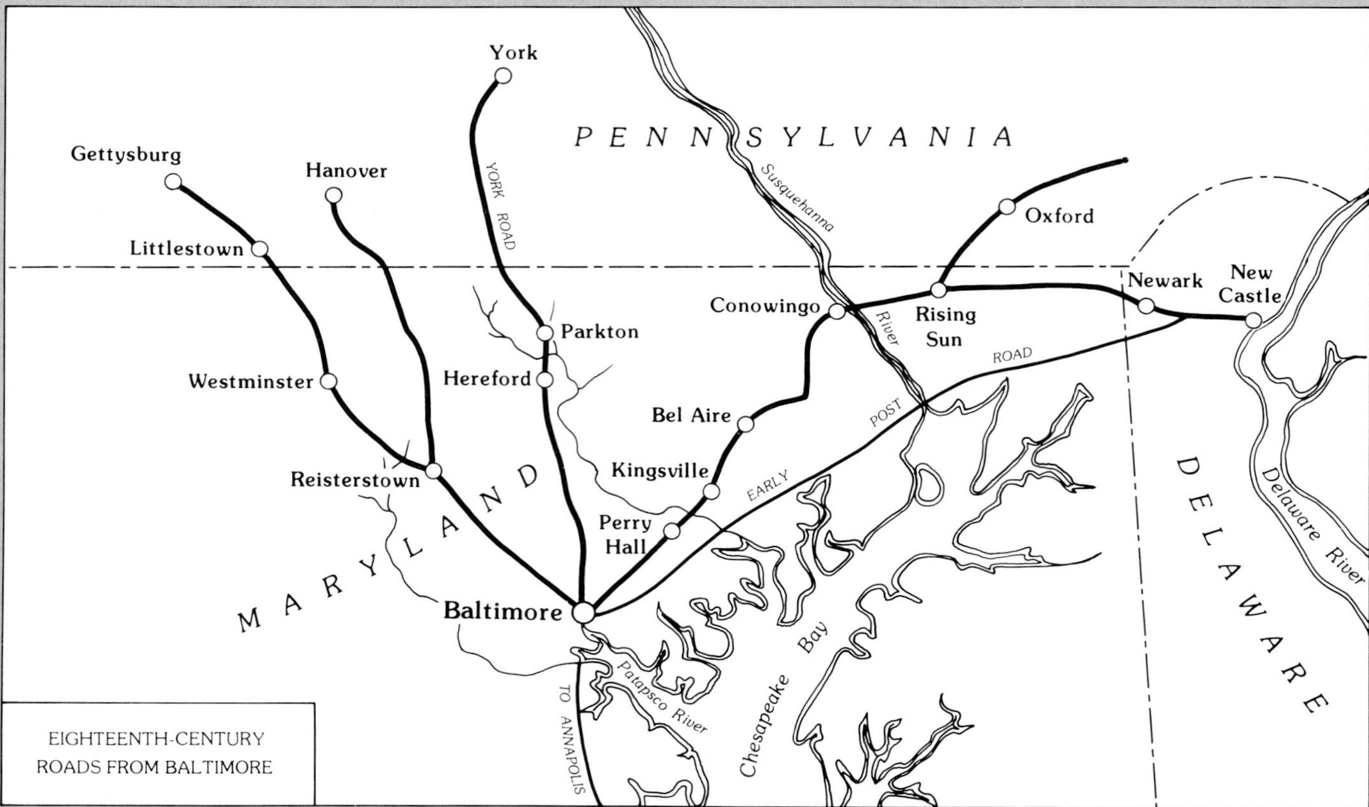

Roads leading north and west out of Baltimore opened up a hinterland rich in grain, which local entrepreneurs began to buy for export. The milling and shipping of grain quickly became the town's major source of prosperity

quarters to this new and promising scene of industry. Wharfs were constructed; elegant and convenient habitations were rapidly erected; marshes were drained; spacious fields were occupied for the purposes of general utility; and within forty years from its first commencement, Baltimore became not only *the* most wealthy and populous town in the Province, but inferior to few on this Continent."

The town certainly did thrive, and not just because of the wheat trade. Baltimore also became a center of a growing iron industry. The area's first successful smelting enterprise, the Principio Company based in Cecil County, was founded in 1715 by a group of British iron-masters, merchants, and investors. The firm eventually bought 30,000 acres of land to supply wood for its furnaces and needed the labor of over 100 slaves. In 1731, a group of influential Marylanders, among them Daniel Dulany, the elder, Benjamin Tasker, Sr., Dr. Charles Carroll, Charles Carroll, Esq., and Daniel Carroll, established the Baltimore Ironworks Company. Ironworks expanded and the products exported through the ports of Baltimore and Fells Point proliferated.

Fells Point was laid off as a town in 1763, and divided into streets with English names like Thames and Shakespeare and alleys called Strawberry, Apple, Happy and Petticoat. Fells Point proved a formidable rival and major shipbuilding center. Following William Fell's example and determined to benefit from the combined advantages of the natural harbor and the nearby supplies of wood and iron, other men flocked to open more shipyards and to build wharves and warehouses. Benjamin Griffith, a shipwright from Cecil County, purchased a waterfront lot as did Captain Charles Ridgely. Samuel Purviance, who came from Ireland by way of Philadelphia, erected a distillery in Baltimore and bought a waterfront lot in Fells Point. The shipbuilding industry and Fells Point prospered together and eventually made a major contribution to Baltimore's growth.

A group of new immigrants helped foster the shipbuilding industry. Many ship carpenters and mariners were among the Acadians who arrived in Baltimore in 1756. These French-speaking refugees from Nova Scotia left their homes in the Canadian maritime province when the British wrested control from the French. They were forcibly dispersed throughout the colonies. Longfellow wrote their tale in his narrative poem *Evangeline.*

The Acadians, having been forced to leave most of their possessions behind, arrived in Baltimore almost destitute. A public subscription was taken up to provide aid. Some of the refugees were sheltered in private homes and a large number stayed at the two-story brick house abandoned by Edward Fottrell when he returned to Ireland. Eventually many of the Acadians settled along South Charles Street near Lombard in an area that Baltimoreans began to call French Town. Many built primitive cabins of mud and mortar, which they gradually replaced with frame houses.

Another group of refugees that swelled Baltimore's population in the mid-1750s came from Western Maryland following the defeat of British General Edward Braddock in the French and Indian War. Indian allies of the French pushed past Fort Cumberland and Fort Frederick to within 50 miles of the city, driving many fleeing settlers before them. Some Baltimoreans panicked fearing that they too would be subject to attack and boarded ships in the harbor, but the attack never materialized. Instead, Baltimore gained settlers who left the west or were prevented from moving westward and it grew accordingly as a market. The war effort occasioned a rather peculiar tax that remained in effect from 1756 to 1762. All bachelors 25 years

An Acadian woman in a costume which originated in Normandy

When the Acadians first arrived, many built primitive cabins of brick and mortar, which they replaced gradually with sturdier houses like this one

Priests who accompanied the refugees may have said mass in Baltimore for the first time

of age and over had to pay, 5 shillings a year if they had property worth 100-300 pounds, 20 shillings if worth over 300.

The growth in population spurred the increase of institutions and services that required the support of the greater number of residents. Churches, particularly, proliferated as various groups grew large enough to form a congregation and undertake a building project. In view of the large number of German immigrants, it is not surprising that they built the second church in town.

The first German Reformed congregation was founded around 1750. In 1756 they invited the Rev. John Christian Faber to become their pastor and began the building of a church just north of St. Paul's on Charles Street. The local Lutherans worshipped with them; then they built their own church in 1758 on Fish Street (now Saratoga Street). This congregation, the only Lutheran one until 1824, later built the church on Gay Street, the original Zion Lutheran Church, where services in German are still held. The church opened a school in 1769 where courses were taught in the German language.

When the Acadians arrived in Baltimore in 1756, the nearest Catholic priest resided 15 miles away at the Carrolls' Doughoregan Manor. They converted a room of Edward Fottrell's house into a chapel and the Rev. John Ashton came once a month to celebrate Mass for a congregation of 20 to 40 French and a few Irish Catholics. Around 1770, Baltimore Catholics determined to build a church on a lot at Charles and Saratoga donated by Charles Carroll. St. Peter's was not completed until 1783 because of financial difficulties and the intervention of the Revolutionary War.

In 1763, a group of Scotch-Irish Presbyterians, including Drs. John and Henry Stevenson, Robert Purviance, John Brown, Benjamin Griffith and William Spear, leased two lots at the corner of Fayette and Gay Streets and erected a small log meeting house. Several years later they purchased a lot at Fayette and North and built a larger structure.

Ministers of the fervently emotional evangelical Great Awakening conducted revival meetings in Baltimore. George Whitefield preached here in 1740. New denominations like Methodists and Baptists grew out of this movement away from Calvinist coldness and from the formality and corruption of the Church of England. Methodist leader Francis Asbury preached in Fells Point in 1772 and in the following year a group which included Richard Moale, Jesse Hollingsworth and George Wells built the first Methodist meeting house in Strawberry Alley in Fells Point. The Baptists also erected their first meeting house in 1773. It stood at Front and Fayette Streets. Quakers had lived in the area of Baltimore since its beginnings, but until 1781 their log meeting house stood outside the town limits on Harford Road.

Not only churches but large homes and a variety of public structures began to proliferate from the 1750s on, transforming Baltimore from a town to the city it had become on the eve of the Revolutionary War. In 1753, Baltimoreans, including John Stevenson, Richard Chase, John Moale, William and Nicholas Rogers, John Ridgely, Nicholas Ruxton Gay, William Lux and Brian Philpot, managed a lottery to raise money to build a public wharf. In 1754, great effort went into rebuilding after the Jones Falls flooded and washed away the bridge and most of the mills. The same year saw the erection of several famous mansions, among them Mount Clare by Charles Carroll the Barrister (a cousin of Charles Carroll of Carrollton) and Parnassus by Dr. Henry Stevenson (brother of John) along York Road. According to legend, this house was called "Stevenson's Folly" by townspeople jealous of

Bookplate of Charles Carroll, Barrister. From the library at Mt. Clare

Photograph of Mr. Clare painting on a chairback, probably done by John Findley, between 1800 and 1810. Begun in 1754, it is the only colonial mansion still standing in the area. It was the home of Charles Carroll, Barrister, and his wife, Margaret Tilghman.

Charles Carroll, Barrister, a distant cousin of Charles Carroll of Carrollton, was a major investor in the Baltimore Iron Works and later a prominent leader in the protest against England. He served as one of Maryland's delegates to the Continental Congress and is credited with drawing up the Maryland Declaration of Rights and much of the state's first constitution. Painting by Charles Willson Peale

its elegance.

In 1769, Baltimoreans had cause to be thankful, when Dr. Henry Stevenson turned "Parnassus" into a smallpox hospital and began innoculating local citizens. Smallpox was one of the scourges of colonial settlements, capable of wiping out large numbers of people in one epidemic. Those who could, often fled rather than trust their fate to the as yet unproven vaccinations. In 1757, a smallpox epidemic in Annapolis had driven the members of the legislature to Baltimore to hold their sessions. In 1771, Dr. Stevenson advertised in *The Maryland Gazette* that: "he continued Innoculations the Year round after the most improved *American* Manner: his Patients are not at all confined to the House, nor disagreeably restrained in their Diet. Those who incline to put themselves under his Care, are requested not to alter their Way of living before they come to be innoculated, as a long Course of successful Practise has shown it hurtful instead of beneficial. Negroes are insured at five percent on their value." He noted further that twenty-two people who had been innoculated had recently been exposed to smallpox without contracting the disease.

Another edifice which served the city well was its first market, erected in 1763 with 3000 pounds raised by a lottery. An effort, in 1751, to raise funds by subscription had failed, so it was not until twelve years later that a majority of town commissioners, including William Lyon, Nicholas Gay, John Moale, and Archibald Buchanan, leased the land at the northwest corner of Baltimore and Gay Streets from Thomas Harrison and oversaw the construction of the two-story market house. Many colonial markets were built with a large hall on the second floor to be used for public meetings, dances, travelling shows and other entertainments. Baltimore followed this pattern. An ordinance of 1773 set the market days as Wednesday and Saturday from early morning till twelve noon.

One event that signaled the success of the town was the removal of the county seat from Joppa to Baltimore in 1768. When the move was announced, the townsfolk collected 900 pounds to pay for building the new courthouse. Court was held in the room over the market house until the new two-story brick building with a tall lookout and spire was erected high on Calvert Street, where the Battle Monument now stands. A whipping post, pillory and stocks stood in front of the courthouse and a jail was built a bit further out from town. The citizens of Joppa resented their town's loss in status and resisted Alexander Lawson's removal of the records with some violence. Despite that, Baltimore Town became the county seat.

The growth in population and status not withstanding, formal amusements remained scant until after the Revolution. Horse races were always popular and easy to arrange since they required neither a building nor special equipment. At least as early as 1745 fairs were held in Baltimore at which the main events were races. Once the market house had been constructed, indoor events could be planned. One William Johnson advertised in July, 1764; "For the Entertainment of the Curious, Will be Exhibited at the Market House in Baltimore Town, a Course of Experiments in that instructive and entertaining Branch of Natural Philosophy, called Electricity. To be accompanied with Lectures on the Nature and Property of the Electric Fire." This sort of spectacular lecture and also travelling exhibitions of oddities and freaks of nature provided a common form of entertainment during the colonial period.

The first known regular theatrical performance was produced by the British touring company of Lewis Hallam in a large warehouse at the corner of Baltimore and Frederick Streets.

Above Left:
Miniature of Henry Stevenson, M.D., 1721-1814. Born in Londonderry and educated at Oxford, he and his brother John arrived in Baltimore around 1745. He established a medical practice and introduced smallpox inoculation to Maryland

Left:
As the town grew, public buildings proliferated. Baltimoreans collected 900 pounds sterling to pay for a new courthouse when the county seat was moved from Joppa to their town in 1768. The courthouse stood high on Calvert Street, at the current location of Battle Monument

Above
Parnassus, the home begun by Dr. Henry Stevenson in 1763, stood near the northwest corner of what is now Eager Street and Greenmount Avenue. Often called "Stevenson's Folly" because of its size and pretentious appearance, the house was used as a smallpox inoculation hospital

Baltimore received the theatricals with such enthusiasm that the company constructed a small theater at the corner of King George's (now Lombard) Street and Albemarle. The repertory companies that toured the colonies produced standard British theatrical fare, plays by Shakespeare, Addison, Farquhar, Sheridan and others. Maryland never had the prohibitions against dramatic productions that the Puritan and Quaker colonies further north did and thus both Annapolis, quite early, and Baltimore later became centers of theatrical performance.

Colonial towns did not escape consumer fads and marketing ventures. Scharf in his *Chronicles* made the following notation for 1772: "In this year the first efforts were made in Baltimore to introduce the use of umbrellas as a defence from the sun and rain. They were then scouted as ridiculous effeminacy. On the other hand, the physicians recommended them to keep off vertigos, epilepsies, sore-eyes, fevers, etc. Finally, as the doctors were their chief patrons, they were generally adopted. They were of oiled linen, very coarse and clumsy, with rattan sticks, and were imported from India by way of England . . ."

In 1773 Baltimore grew both territorially and economically with the annexation of 80 acres of Fells Point. The unification of the two towns helped end their rivalry and joined their resources to the eventual profit of both. By the outbreak of the Revolution, Baltimore had become one of the colonies' foremost cities. Before beginning to trace the conflict which finally led to the War for Independence, it is worth pausing to look at Baltimore in 1773. The year was marked by "firsts" that signaled the continuing growth of the town.

In November 1773, the Assembly established the first Alms House and an adjoining Work House for Baltimore Town and County. Refugees from the frontier areas, widows and children, men without jobs and disabled persons had grown in number to the point where they were a burden on the town. The Alms House and Work House provided refuge for both white and black people who had nowhere else to go. The hope was always that temporary relief would allow the recipients of the public support to become self-sustaining soon again. The buildings were constructed on land bought from William Lux for 350 pounds (property values were going up), located on the square bounded by Howard, Eutaw, Biddle and Garden Streets.

The Assembly appointed a group of leading citizens as trustees: Charles Ridgely, William Lux, John Moale, William Smith, and Samuel Purviance of Baltimore Town, and Andrew Buchanan and Harry Dorsey Gough of the County. It is interesting to note the overlapping directorates that existed even before the Revolution.

A major first for Baltimore in 1773 was the establishment of the town's own newspaper, the *Maryland Journal and Baltimore Advertiser*. Publisher William Goddard brought out the first issue on Friday, August 20. The paper appeared weekly thereafter and provided Baltimore with a source of news and communication far preferable in terms of local matters to the copies of the *Maryland Gazette* previously imported from Annapolis. Goddard had printed the *Pennsylvania Chronicle* in Philadelphia from 1767 to 1773, when he was forced to cease publication because of his pro-Tory leanings. In Baltimore Goddard opened up shop on Market Street, set up his presses, and began producing his journal. The papers carried world and local news, features including kitchen helps and poetry, and a lot of advertising. Goddard travelled frequently and when he did, Mary Katherine Goddard, his sister, edited and published the newspaper. She later became the Postmistress of Baltimore, a job she held for 15

Baltimore's first post office on Front Street near Exeter typifies the small wooden structures built during the eighteenth century

Umbrellas were introduced in Baltimore in 1772. Physicians recommended them to ward off vertigos, epilepsies, sore-eyes, fevers, and various other ailments

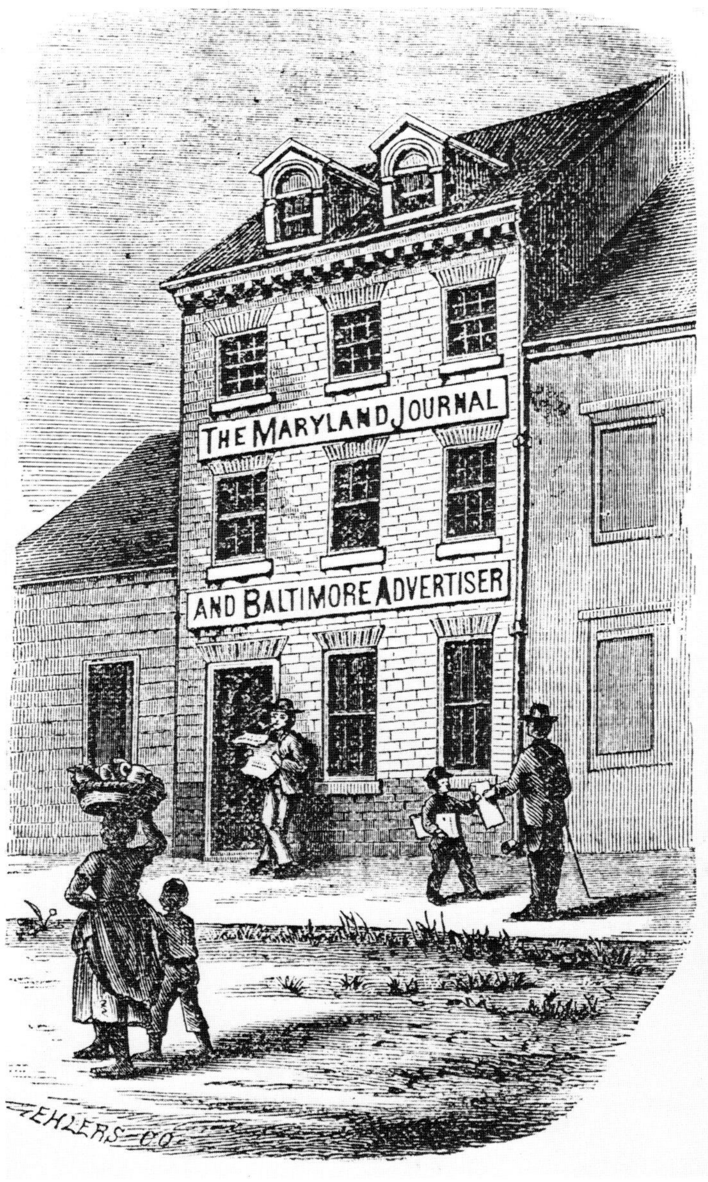

When the Goddards arrived in Baltimore, they set up shop on Market Street, near South Lane

years.

Perusal of the early issues of the *Maryland Journal and Baltimore Advertiser* gives a good indication of what life was like just before the conflict with Britain. In the two decades since 1752, life had obviously became easier in terms of the availability of goods and services attainable locally. Benjamin Levy, for example, advertised that his store carried imported wines, spices, corks for bottles, tea, coffee, chocolate, buckets, pails, fine pickled salmon, Irish beef, rose blankets, English cloth, rugs, felt hats, silk, cloth umbrellas, and sundry other articles. Another shopkeeper, John Flanagan, advertised port wine from London, Lisbon wine, Malaga wine, West India and New England rum, tea, coffee, chocolate, allspice, ginger, raisins, sugar, indigo, cotton, soap, etc. Although weavers made cloth locally, Baltimore merchants continued to import cloth. In September 1773, Clark's Warehouse featured a newly arrived shipment of Yorkshire broadcloths which brought from 3 to 15 shillings a yard. Hugh Young was selling Irish linens for 10 pence to 3 shillings a yard.

Frequently the *Maryland Journal and Baltimore Advertiser* published lists of prices current in Baltimore. These included food products like wheat at 6 shillings 6 pence a bushel, corn at 2 shillings 9 pence a dozen, superfine flour at 20 shillings, West Indian rum at 3 shillings 6 pence a gallon, salt at 2 shillings a bushel, pork at 85 shillings a barrel, 100 feet of pine board for 7 shillings 6 pence, and cotton at 18 pence per pound.

Skilled craftsmen sold both services and products to the townspeople. Watchmaker Jacob Mohler maintained a shop on South Street. Christopher Hughes and Company, Goldsmiths and Jewelers, sold tea pots, flatware, buckles, rings, chains and combs in a shop at Market and Gay Streets. Francis Sanderson, a coppersmith, sold his own goods as well as

[AUGUST, M.DCC.LXXIII] (1) [NUMB. I.]

THE

MARYLAND JOURNAL, AND BALTIMORE ADVERTISER.

Containing the FRESHEST ADVICES, both FOREIGN and DOMESTIC.

Omne tulit punctum qui miscuit utile dulci.

Lectorem delectando, pariterque monendo. HOR.

FRIDAY, AUGUST 20, 1773. [VOL. I.]

To the PUBLIC.

THE great Difficulty and experience of Speedily obtaining a proper Assortment of Printing Materials, an inadequate Number of Subscribers to defray the Charge of printing a weekly News-Paper, added to several unfortunate Events which have happened to me, have been the Reasons why the MARYLAND JOURNAL and BALTIMORE ADVERTISER, *so long expected, hath not before made its appearance. This, I flatter myself, will be considered an ample Apology, in the Minds of the Candid, for the long Delay in publishing it.—Many Gentlemen, however, encouraging me to hope for a considerable Addition to my List of Subscribers, I now venture to send the first* Number *abroad; and while I solicit the further Encouragement of the Public, I humbly bespeak a candid Reception for* this Beginning, *which, I am sensible, must appear under many Disadvantages, as I have not yet been able to establish a special Post from this Place to* Philadelphia, *for the Purpose of bringing down, in due Season, the latest Papers.*

I was aware when it was first proposed to me to undertake a News-Paper in this Town, that although it possessed many Advantages in Point of Situation, yet it was impracticable to print such a one as would suit this Part of the Country, without establishing a RIDER *from* Baltimore *to* Philadelphia, *to set out from the last-mentioned Place early on* Monday Morning, *and to arrive here on* Tuesday Evening, *whereby I should receive the* Massachusetts, Connecticut, New-York, Pennsylvania, *and sometimes the* British *and* Irish *Papers, and be enabled to publish the* JOURNAL, *with the freshest Advices, deliver it to the Customers in Town, and forward it to* Annapolis *and the* Lower Counties, *on* Thursday Morning, *several Hours before the Arrival of the King's Post.—This was a Plan I had contemplated (in order to render this Paper of great and extensive Utility) and had determined some Time ago, with the Assistance of the Public-spirited, to have carried it into Execution; but I have been prevented making the necessary Trial by a severe Indisposition.—I have not, however, given over my Scheme, but shall persevere to the utmost to accomplish it, knowing that on the Success of it depends the* Credit*—and indeed the very* Existence *of this Paper.*

After what I have already published touching the Plan I propose to pursue in conducting this Paper, little I think, need be added.—I shall content myself, therefore, with assuring the Public that I am determined that nothing shall induce me to depart from the Engagements I have made in my Proposals—and, in short, that it is my Resolution to continue the MARYLAND JOURNAL, &c., *in the following Manner—viz.*

First.—*That the Paper shall be published every* Thursday *(unless another Day should prove more agreeable to the Customers) and shall contain not only the Public News, which I shall collect and compile with the greatest Care, but on Failure of Anecdotes of that Sort, I will supply the Room with such moral Pieces, from the best Writers, as will conduce most to inculcate good Principles and humane Behaviour, and now and then with Pieces of Wit and Humour, that tend both to amuse and instruct.*

Second.—*That I shall always publish with Pleasure whatever is sent me in Favour of Liberty and the Rights of Mankind, provided the Language is decent and compatible with good Government; but I am resolved that my Paper shall be FREE and of NO PARTY. And as Agriculture and every Branch of Husbandry ought, in this Country, to be a primary Object of Attention, and forasmuch as printed Books on such Subjects, adapted to Climates different from ours, are apt to mislead rather than instruct, our own Experiments in these Matters, on which alone we can rely with Safety, may be better communicated, and the Knowledge thereof spread amongst us by the Channel of a weekly News-Paper than by any other, wherefore I shall always be careful to find a place a Place in my Paper for whatever may be sent me that is* new *and* useful *on such Subjects.*

While these several Matters are attended to, the Arrival and Departure of Ships, the Course of Exchange, and Prices Current of Goods, &c., shall not be neglected.

Having entered upon a very arduous and expensive *Undertaking, I must now earnestly entreat the* immediate *Assistance of* every *Subscriber, in advancing the* Entrance Money *agreeable to* Contract; *without which the Life of this Paper will be but of very short Duration.—All who wish well to the Institution, I am persuaded, will chearfully comply with my Request,* without Delay*—and I hope they will dispense with a personal Application, which were it* practicable, *would be very* painful, *and send the Money to the Printing Office, from whence Receipts (for whatever they may be disposed to advance for the Encouragement of the Work) shall be returned to them.*

I cannot conclude without returning my most grateful Acknowledgments to all those who have kindly assisted me in taking in Subscriptions for this Paper, and otherwise promoting my Interest in this Province; and particularly to those public-spirited Gentlemen who exerted themselves in a remarkable Manner for the Establishment of this Paper and the Printing-Business in the Town of Baltimore.

I am the Public's
Devoted humble Servant,
W. GODDARD.

PRINTING OFFICE, BALTIMORE, AUGUST 20, 1773.

A Letter from the Bishop of C. to the Earl of Bellamont, on his late duel with Lord Townshend.

MY LORD,

THOUGH I presume to address myself to your Lordship on a subject in which you are unfortunately but too much interested, it is not my intention, by any means, to wound the sensibility of your temper, or to question the benevolence of your heart. I am sure you are a brave man, and I hear you are as good a man as any to be found among the youth of condition in this kingdom; yet, pardon me, my Lord, if I say that our youth of condition do not want advice upon any point so much as upon the point of honour, with which they fancy themselves so intimately acquainted; and let me inform you, a father of the Church now begs your most serious attention, that, through your Lordship, he may communicate a few observations to the world, no less necessary to maintain the laws of his country than to enforce the commandments of his God.

Be not, however, terrified, my Lord, though an old man, and that man of some ecclesiastical consequence too, breaks this abruptly on your retirement: He will talk to you as fashionably as if he did not think religiously, and make (the better to answer his purpose) a serious question in morals, an object of polite investigation. To drop the third person, my Lord, I know experimentally what the passions are at your time of life; young men prefer any criminality with which meanness is not connected, to the slightest idea of dishonour; they do not fear to commit a flagitious action so much as to be concerned in a foolish one; and there are particular crimes, such as duelling, for instance, in which custom has made it glory, not only to sacrifice every dictate of our reason, but every impulse of our humanity.

I have said, my Lord, that I know experimentally with what a vehemence the passions, especially where the point of honour is concerned, rage in the bosom of a young man. In the early part of life, I received an insult which I thought myself indispensibly bound to resent, and of course either a submission or a meeting in the field became the only alternative I could propose to the party by whom I supposed myself injured. He chose the latter; and your Lordship can easily conceive my affliction. My own personal safety was no more than an atom in the scale of consideration; but I agonized at the suspicion of ruin the which I was probably going to pull down upon my whole family, as well as upon the family of my antagonist. I was an only son, the sole heir of an ancient house, and in a fortnight to marry a woman on whom I doated to distraction. The man whom I challenged, besides was circumstanced almost similarly, and had lived with me in an uninterrupted course of friendship for many years. These reflections occurred to me incessantly; yet my pride (your Lordship will excuse me) steeled me against the salutary counsels they suggested. Reason, no less than Religion, pointed out the various horrors of my situation in the most forcible light, my pride, however, taught me to oppose the influence of both; and I determined to act like a man of *spirit*, let the consequence be never so fatal, either to my temporal peace or to my eternal felicity.

Not to trespass unnecessarily on your Lordship's patience, I repaired with a heavy heart to the place of appointment, and waited scarce a second for the appearance of my enemy. His looks sufficiently bespoke the anguish of his mind; but he was equally biggotted with myself to the heresy of that Moloch, modern honour, and equally resolved to worship him with blood. We could both of us, I am confident, have embraced with the utmost cordiality; yet, to behave *spiritedly*, it was indispensably requisite to attack each other's lives. Our courage might be suspected if we hesitated, even a moment, at a fashionable murder, and we therefore fired to purchase the good opinion of the world, though at the absolute expense of our own. My ball, thanks to the mercy of God, did no mischief; my antagonist's was more effectual; I received a wound so as to be in a state of the greatest danger for three months; and, in less than twelve, saw the father whom I reverenced, and the woman whom I adored, carried to the grave, in consequence of what they suffered during the afflicting interval of my cure. Oh, my Lord, the scorn of a thousand worlds would have been elysium to what I felt on that dreadful occasion! How often did I wish that nature had formed me with a disposition the most dastardly that ever fell to the lot of her meanest sons! If I flew to reason for comfort, she told me that I had despised her best advice; if I turned to religion, she bid me remember how I had trampled on her gravest admonitions. Pride only appeared with a gleam of seeming consolation; she told me that I had acted as became a man of honour, and had spiritedly demanded satisfaction for an unpardonable affront. It was true, I had *demanded* satisfaction; yet what satisfaction had I *received?* If I was grossly insulted at first, I was now irreparably injured, and clearly saw that, though I might have behaved very gallantly, the behaviour was nevertheless madness, which could think lasting misery an effectual remedy for imaginary disgrace.

In the superstitious ages of the world, my Lord, when men absurdly believed that Providence interposed immediately in favor of the party injured, a decision of a dispute by personal combat was not altogether ridiculous; but in these more enlightened times, when the sun of science has rapidly dispelled the clouds of enthusiasm, a continuation of so Gothic a custom is a scandal upon the human understanding. No preternatural interposition is now expected to give a certain triumph to the person wronged; no, my Lord, the aggressor and the aggrieved are upon equal terms; and, as in your case, no less than in mine, the latter has often the most melancholy cause to be *dissatisfied*, where he is even *indulged* with the most *honourable* satisfaction. It is justly observed, by a very clever writer, that though men may live fools, they cannot die fools: Your Lordship and I have been both upon the verge of eternity, and therefore, with respect to the point of honour at least we may be supposed to possess a little share of understanding. Give me leave, therefore, to ask you seriously, whether any thing can be so absurd as the fashionable practice of duelling? We receive an affront, and we endanger our lives; we expose the long list of our friends to distress; we hazard all the glowing expectations of our tenderest social ties, all our dearest prospects in this world, and all our greatest in the next, to—to do what? I blush, my Lord, at my own question, punish some act of incivility that should excite our contempt, or some disrespect which is wholly below our indignation. The man who is not ready to apologize for any offence he offers another does not deserve to be considered as a gentleman; yet, supposing the case otherwise, the offence ought indeed to be deadly which induces us to take away a life. If it is of such magnitude as to require a bloody expiation, it should be left to the laws; and if it is not, we surely rebel against the majesty of our own hearts where we endeavor to wipe it away with blood.

In whatever light we look upon duelling, my Lord, I am persuaded you will concur with me in thinking that it is founded no less in folly than in barbarity. Where we are even the victors, what is our triumph? A triumph over humanity, a triumph over justice, a triumph over our families, our country, and our God. If our reason, therefore, is not alarmed at the very dangers attending this horribly custom, our pride should be roused at the charge of weakness, to which it exposes our characters. Few who go into the field have any wish to destroy the life of an adversary, yet all must unavoidably expose their own: Our universal study is to set a just value upon this blessing; yet our universal practice is to treat it as an object of the slightest consideration. A sour look, a haughty accent, or an abrupt reply, are with us motives enough to take a life at any time; in fact the life of an English gentleman is the only thing in which he seems to have the least property; make an attempt on his estate, and he seeks a judicial remedy; set fire to his house, and he seeks a judicial remedy also; but if you tread upon his toe, or doubt his veracity, no law can give him redress; his life must be instantly hazarded to procure satisfaction, and the moment another becomes rude, he is obliged to be desperate. Thus situated, he meets his adversary (as every feeling man must be an adversary) with an infinitely greater share of apprehension for consequences than of a person for revenge: Though he wants fortitude to do what he *wishes*, yet he musters up courage to do what he *abhors*, and is brave enough to kill perhaps his dearest friend, because his cowardice is too excessive to oppose the ridiculous tyranny of a despicable custom.

Seriously, my Lord, is the good opinion of the world worth enjoying upon conditions like these? In my opinion, it is not; and if, honour is something that must be gratified at the expence either of justice or humanity, I am convinced that it is not very honourable. We all acknowledge the propriety of this reasoning, yet we all continue the abject slaves of a custom we detest. What a glory would it, therefore, be to your Lordship, whose character for personal bravery is so thoroughly established, if you associated with a few sensible young men of quality, to rescue us from a tyranny so barbarous! You owe your country much for risking so valuable a life as your own, and this would be an exalted method of discharging the obligation.

I know, my Lord, that many elegant writers are apprehensive that if duelling was once abolished, a custom additionally dangerous would be immediately adopted in its room. The judicious author, particularly, who has obliged the world with the principles of penal law, asks in his chapter upon duelling, "Whether it is not "to be feared that the propensity of our natures to revenge would "substitute the more fatal, and the more odious practice of assassi-"nation?" For my part, I think not; and for the very reason which he himself assigns to show the inefficacy of declaiming against duelling. "Of little avail (says he) it is to object that true honour "depends not on the prejudices of the people, but hath its source "in the heart; that it is more courageous to resist the absurd "tyranny of custom than to submit to it; that the defence of honour "is not placed in occasional appeals to the sword and the pistol, but "in a life of integrity and virtue; that when a fencing school is "made the court of justice, there is no law but violence, no argu-"ment but murder. All these assertions (concludes our author) "may be true, but the most solid reasoning is received as mere "declamation, when opposed to the impetuosity of passion, or the "*fear of shame.* "When *shame* (says he in another place) is the "consequence of obedience to law, the sword of justice loses its "terrors. Hence the duellist kills his friend whom he loves, and "the judge condemns the duellist, while he scarcely knows how in "his own heart to disapprove his behaviour." Surely, my Lord, if *shame* is so very irresistible as to *force* us into *duelling*, it would be equally powerful to keep us from *assassination*; if *shame* is necessary to *make* us seek for *honourable* reparation, it would certainly be sufficient to save us from the infamy of a *dastardly* revenge. It would unquestionably be as efficacious on the side of law, prudence, humanity, as upon the side of injustice, absurdity and blood; nothing, therefore, my Lord, is wanting but a generous association among a few young men of rank, to root out the custom of duelling.—If such an association was once established, and if the members only made it publicly known that they would never admit a man into their company who either refused to apologize for an offence he had given, or required the life of a fellow creature as an atonement for an affront, the most salutary consequences would speedily result to society. It is better, my Lord, that there should be no redress *at all* for insults than to adopt a mode of redress, if *redress* it may be called, which accumulates the injuries of the party insulted. Many are the associations to improve the opera, to encourage race horses, and to preserve the game: For the love of Heaven, my Lord, let there be one association as

Opposite Page Left:
William Goddard came to Baltimore from Philadelphia in 1773 and published the town's first newspaper, the Maryland Journal and Baltimore Advertiser

Opposite Page Right:
Mary Katherine Goddard, William's sister and frequent editor of the newspaper, later served as Postmistress of Baltimore

Above:
The first issue of the Maryland Journal and Baltimore Advertiser, *Baltimore's first newspaper, appeared on Friday, August 20, 1773*

kettles, pots and pans imported from England.

Although all these goods were available, they were fairly expensive, compared to the wages of a working man. At this time, a day laborer during the harvest earned 1 to 2 shillings a day. A regular farmhand earned 8 to 10 pounds a year. A teacher earned 15 to 30 pounds a year. (Twelve shillings equals one pound). Clearly only the elite could afford more than the necessities.

Many problems still plagued the young city. The streets remained unpaved and rather dirty. Fire continued as a major hazard although the Mechanical Company and its "Dutchman" offered more effective relief than had been available previously. The approximately ten doctors and Henry Stevenson's innoculating hospital couldn't remove the threat of fevers and epidemics which periodically swept through all cities, leaving many dead in their wake.

Crime troubled city residents even then. A September 1773 issue of Goddard's paper included this account of the robbery of a prominent Baltimore physician and druggist: "On Saturday night last, the house of Dr. John Boyd, of the Town, was broke open, and sundry goods taken away. The Thief or Thieves appear to have forced their Way through a Window, by first boring a Shutter with a Gimlet, and then introducing a small saw, with which an Hole was made large enough for the Admission of a Finger, by which the Key that secured the Window, was pushed out, and entrance obtained."

The list of stolen goods included clothing, surgical instruments and a pair of pistols. These apparently were sold around town as the article summarized: "Many of the Goods have not yet been recovered, but the Persons with whom they are lodged will, no Doubt, think it prudent, after this Notification, to return them to their Owner, without further inquiry, as they *now know them to be stolen goods.*" Not only would the holder of the goods know them to be stolen, but so would most of their neighbors who had read the article.

In 1773, Baltimore combined the characteristics of a colonial city and a small town. With a population of just under 6000, it was small enough that most people could still know each other. Certainly all the leading citizens and merchants and their families knew each other and probably most of the other residents as well. Although much smaller than the older cities like Philadelphia with 40,000 people and New York with 25,000, Baltimore offered a wide variety of goods and services to its inhabitants and was receiving widespread attention for its remarkable growth rate.

The town's population was quite cosmopolitan, including an increasing number of children and grandchildren of Baltimoreans, natives and immigrants with backgrounds in England, Scotland, Ireland, the west coast of Africa, Germany, and France. People spoke English or German, and a few spoke both. A wide variety of religious groups including Anglicans, Quakers, German Lutherans, followers of the German Reformed tradition, Roman Catholics, Presbyterians, Methodists, and Baptists, were represented. In 1773, Baltimore's first permanent Jewish residents settled. Benjamin Levy, the shopkeeper, and his wife Rachel and their son, Robert Morris Levy, who had been named for their good friend and future financeer of the Revolution, came from Philadelphia.

The war soon to come, with all its factionalization, would serve to lessen divisiveness based on religion and ethnicity. Baltimore would go into the Revolution with a cosmopolitan population typical of America's leading cities and a thriving economy based primarily on the success of the port. When the trauma of war ended, the city was ready to continue the pattern begun during its first forty-four years.

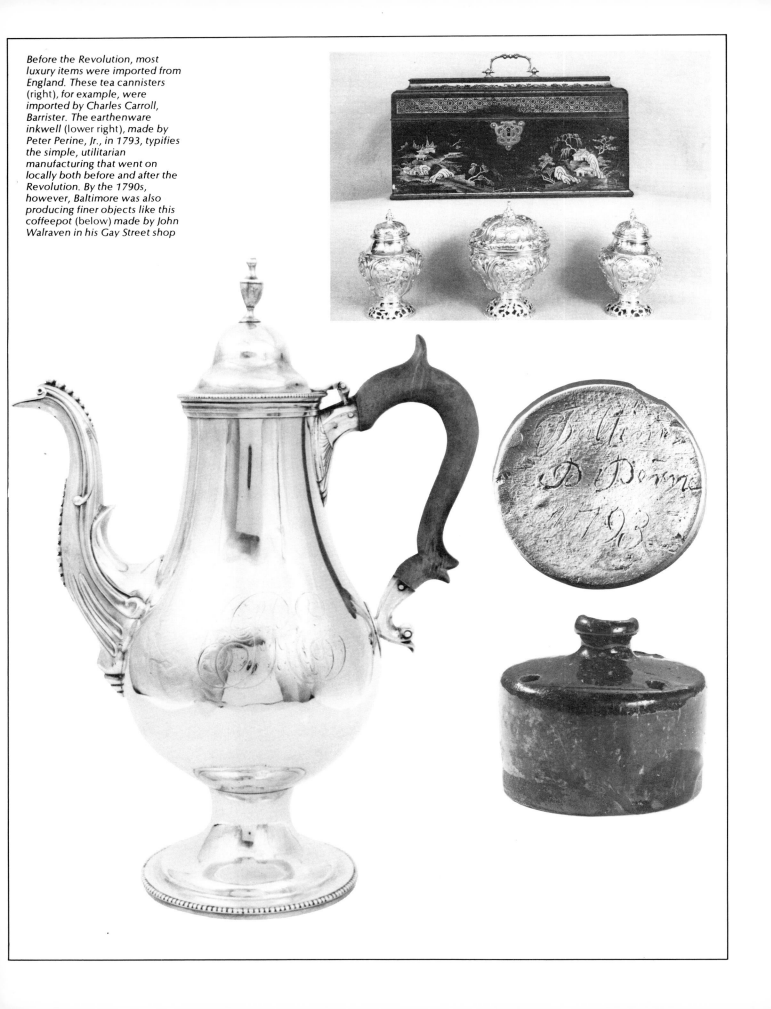

Before the Revolution, most luxury items were imported from England. These tea cannisters (right), for example, were imported by Charles Carroll, Barrister. The earthenware inkwell (lower right), made by Peter Perine, Jr., in 1793, typifies the simple, utilitarian manufacturing that went on locally both before and after the Revolution. By the 1790s, however, Baltimore was also producing finer objects like this coffeepot (below) made by John Walraven in his Gay Street shop

TO ALL BRAVE, HEALTHY, ABLE BODIED, AND WELL DISPOSED YOUNG MEN,

IN THIS NEIGHBOURHOOD, WHO HAVE ANY INCLINATION TO JOIN THE TROOPS, NOW RAISING UNDER

GENERAL WASHINGTON,

FOR THE DEFENCE OF THE

LIBERTIES AND INDEPENDENCE OF THE UNITED STATES,

Againſt the hoſtile deſigns of foreign enemies,

TAKE NOTICE,

THAT *tuesday, wednsday, thursday, friday and saturday at Spotswood in Middlesex* county, attendance will be given by *Lieutenant Reading* with his muſic and recruiting party of [illegible] company in *Major Sh.* [illegible] *Battalion*, of the 11th regiment of infantry, commanded by Lieutenant Colonel Aaron Ogden, for the purpoſe of receiving the enrollment of ſuch youth of SPIRIT, as may be willing to enter into this HONOURABLE ſervice.

The ENCOURAGEMENT at this time, to enliſt, is truly liberal and generous, namely, a bounty of TWELVE dollars, an annual and fully ſufficient ſupply of good and handſome cloathing, a daily allowance of a large and ample ration of proviſions, together with SIXTY dollars a year in GOLD and SILVER money on account of pay, the whole of which the ſoldier may lay up for himſelf and friends; as all articles proper for his ſubſiſtance and comfort are provided by law, without any expence to him.

Thoſe who may favour this recruiting party with their attendance as above, will have an opportunity of hearing and ſeeing in a more particular manner, the great advantages which theſe brave men will have, who ſhall embrace this opportunity of ſpending a few happy years in viewing the different parts of this beautiful continent, in the honourable and truly reſpectable character of a ſoldier, after which, he may, if he pleaſes return home to his friends, with his pockets FULL of money and his head COVERED with laurels.

GOD SAVE THE UNITED STATES.

War, Peace & War Again
1773-1814

II

The Revolutionary War resulted in independence from British rule and also a social and political transformation in the newly independent states. The conflict grew out of a combination of idealistic theories of the rights of the governed and specific interests of particular people living under British rule in North America. In Baltimore, as elsewhere, the decision to fight for independence rather than mere reform of the imperial system evolved through agonizing debate and the leadership of a fairly small group of men, many of whom had concrete stakes in the outcome.

In Baltimore, as in the colonies generally, the first widespread expression of discontent came in the wake of the French and Indian War which ended in 1763. The British chose the time when their troops were no longer needed for defense to commence programs of taxation to raise money to defray colonial expenses and regulation of trade and manufacturing to help bolster the troubled British economy. Colonists resented these intrusions, in part because of their effect on trade and manufacturing and in part because the regulations were new. Before Britain's warring with France and domestic economic and political problems prompted the interference, the colonies had been free, in reality if not in theory, to go their own way, largely unhampered by the mother country.

The post-1763 grievances generally exacerbated those already held by segments of the population of Baltimore and Maryland. A number of people were already dissatisfied with the enormous power held by the proprietor. The proprietors, Frederick Calvert, 1751-71, and his illegitimate son Henry Harford, 1771-76, and their governors, Horatio Sharpe, 1753-69, and Robert Eden, 1769-76, could exercise absolute veto power over the colonial assembly. This procedure was seldom necessary as the members of the Upper House of the legislature received their appointment by the governor on the advice of the proprietor. Generally, these representatives came from the great landholding families. The most lucrative appointive governmental offices went to these same men. By the 1760s, the governor could distribute over 12,000 pounds a year in patronage positions. Kickbacks from these salaries were customary. The proprietor himself received an income of over 13,000 pounds from quit-rents, land offices, and trade duties. Especially during down cycles of the economy, this situation was hard for the many Marylanders who were not part of the proprietor's inner circle to accept.

In addition to money paid to the proprietor and his colonial officials, funds raised by a general tax went to support the Church of England. While many of the large landowners did belong to the Anglican Church, some were Catholics, Quakers, or members of other non-established churches. Many of the prosperous merchants of Baltimore Town were Scotch-Irish Presbyterians or Germans who belonged to the Reformed Church or the Lutheran Church. Most non-Anglicans resented being forced to support a church to which they did not belong. Furthermore, many Anglican clergymen not only failed to perform their duties but were known to be corrupt. One particularly notorious priest absented himself frequently to run a bawdy house in Philadelphia.

Roman Catholics held the additional grievance of having been disenfranchised and barred from public office and the practice of law since 1718. During the French and Indian War, Catholics had to pay double taxes. For a while, they were forbidden to construct churches and could say masses only in private homes. Unlike the very small number of Jews who faced similar political restrictions and the large number of blacks who faced even harsher restraints, the Roman Catholics numbered among their leaders

some men of wealth and position, including Charles Carroll of Annapolis and, later, his son Charles Carroll of Carrollton.

To these and other existing grievances was added an economic crisis in the mid-1760s. This precipitated a dry run for the final battle which was joined a decade later. Economic events propelled Baltimore's merchants and those of other Maryland towns to undertake a protest, in which other troubled groups joined, against both proprietary rule and imperial regulation. By the 1760s, Baltimore's political leaders came predominantly from the merchant group. Even the owners of nearby large tracts of land were involved in commercial undertakings. Therefore, any events which affected mercantile interests in general had a particularly powerful impact on Baltimore Town.

A brief economic explanation must precede any comprehensible account of the political reaction. Maryland, like all the colonies, exported raw materials to England and imported manufactured goods and commodities, such as tea, not available locally. The most important cargoes loaded at the port of Baltimore and other Maryland docks included tobacco, grain, lumber and iron. Maryland currency and British pounds sterling were exchangeable at a rate that varied according to general economic stability and the import-export balance. When Maryland imported more than it exported, Maryland merchants owed British merchants and bankers the difference between the value of the imports and that of the exports. When Marylanders owed a lot of money to their British creditors and those creditors demanded payment, the exchange rate went against the Maryland currency and more Maryland money was required to satisfy the debt in pounds sterling. In 1764-65 tobacco prices sank. This meant that Americans received less money with which they could buy British manufactured goods. Many merchants owed money on manufactured goods already received. British creditors demanded payments which American merchants could not meet. Britishers then withdrew credit or raised the interest rates charged to Americans. Baltimore merchant William Lux had his credit cut off in 1765. Charles Ridgely became involved in a long dispute over the amount of interest he owed. Merchants whose credit was cut off or limited could not import the goods they wanted and thus could not sell them here. Both merchants and the growers of exportable agricultural staples felt the squeeze.

This troubled economic situation prevailed when the British Parliament passed the Stamp Act in March, 1765. The Stamp Act levied the first direct, internal tax ever imposed on the colonies by Parliament. And it was a heavy tax: 3 shillings on every kind of legal paper such as contracts or wills; 2 pounds on school or college diplomas; 1-4 pounds for a liquor license; 10 pounds for a license to practice law; $1/2$ pence a sheet on every copy (not issue) of a newspaper; 2 shillings an issue for each advertisement in a newspaper; 1 shilling per pack of playing cards; and so on. Furthermore, every document or sheet of paper subject to this duty had to bear a stamp sold by official distributors, whose jobs only added to the already high number of officials whose salaries colonists did not want to pay. Reaction in Baltimore, Annapolis and throughout the colonies came immediately. In Annapolis, a crowd chased the newly appointed stamp distributor, Zachariah Hood, from the colony and tore down his house. Maryland Attorney General Daniel Dulany wrote in the *Maryland Gazette* that Parliament should not tax Americans and suggested a peaceful boycott of English goods to remind England of the importance of the colonies to the imperial economy.

Baltimore merchants, like others through-

As a Catholic, Charles Carroll of Carrollton was barred from holding public office in colonial Maryland. He was a member of the local committees of Correspondence and Safety, a delegate to the Continental Congress, and a signer of the Declaration of Independence

A typical day of business in a Baltimore mercantile establishment of the eighteenth century. Many of the city's Revolutionary leaders came from the merchant class

War, Peace & War Again
1773-1814

out the colonies, met to protest and in November 1765, implemented a program of non-importation of British goods. It must be noted that the poor exchange rate and the cutting off of credit had already reduced imports to the town. In February 1766, Baltimore merchants William Lux and Robert Adair organized the first Maryland chapter of the Sons of Liberty by converting the Mechanical Company, which since 1763 had been responsible not only for fire protection but also for policing, drilling, and mustering in Baltimore. Mechanical Company members came from the merchant and tradesman classes in Baltimore. This group provided the core of resistance both at this time and later. Lux and Annapolis radical leader Samuel Chase formed an alliance which proved powerful in the years to come. Sons of Liberty delegates from all counties assembled in Annapolis in early March to try to get officials to agree to transact business without using stamped paper. Protests like these finally resulted in the official repeal of the Stamp Act on March 18, 1766.

With repeal, the outbursts quieted, but the leaders particularly did not forget their wider-ranging grievances and were unwilling to let others forget or to allow their organization's collapse. Governor Robert Eden, after he took office in 1769, called the Baltimore Sons of Liberty the most "pronounced rebellious and mischievious organization in the province of Maryland." Yet things did quiet down for a while. Both wheat and tobacco rose in price. Exports increased, and that meant that imports also could increase and credit was easier to obtain. In the fall of 1766 an emission of currency in Maryland further eased the monetary situation by putting more currency in circulation. Baltimore's merchants did not forget, but prosperity assuaged their immediate distress.

The contrast in the reaction to taxation by Britain can be seen in Baltimore's response to the Townshend Acts of 1767, which imposed a tax on popular imports such as paper, glass, tea, and paint. At the behest of Philadelphia's merchants, Baltimoreans finally met in March, 1769. Leaders of the Sons of Liberty like William Lux, John Moale and Alexander Lawson won another non-importation agreement. This time, however, such a long list of exceptions were attached to the agreement that its impact was slight. In Baltimore, most merchants considered business too good to ruin for the sake of political protest. Because of the strength of protests elsewhere, Britain repealed all the duties except that on tea in April, 1770.

Another economic crisis preceded the final phase of the colonial rebellion which resulted in the outbreak of war and the declaration of independence. In 1771 and 1772 prices paid for American wheat, tobacco and corn began to decline. A general European depression in 1773 led English creditors to try to collect on all their American debts, just when the Americans did not have currency with which to pay. Economic chaos resulted. This led to the emergence in Maryland of a new political coalition whose quest for local economic stability resulted in their support for independence several years later. Leaders among the Baltimore merchants included William Lux, Charles Ridgely, and a newcomer to town, Samuel Purviance. Samuel Chase resurrected the Baltimore-Annapolis coalition around the leadership of Charles Carroll of Carrollton.

Several general points are crucial to understanding what went on in Baltimore in the 1770s. One is that by that decade the protest movement and the issues that moved its leaders had to be viewed as American, not local. Grievances about economic instability, the established church, and the corruption and wealth of colonial officials existed throughout

Samuel Chase, son of the Reverend Thomas Chase, rector of Old St. Paul's, practiced law in Annapolis during the years immediately preceding the war. In 1786 he returned to Baltimore and ten years later was appointed to the Supreme Court by President George Washington

the colonies. Certain groups in all the colonies sought a change in government in order to democratize political power, to bring the franchise or governmental control to groups who had been excluded because of property requirements or religious faith. Furthermore, throughout the years of conflict, an ideology had been put together which would find its ultimate expression in 1776 in the Declaration of Independence. Colonists from Massachusetts to Georgia read and talked about ideas of natural rights of all men, ideas that certain privileges and inequalities were wrong, theories of government that declared that all individuals had the right to choose their governors, the idea that people could be taxed only by representatives whom they had chosen. These theories went beyond specific complaints about taxes or the state of the economy and invoked a higher morality on the side of the rebellion. This mixture of economic strife and ideological protest took place throughout the colonies. The leaders, the decisions, the conflicts and the activities in Baltimore all formed a part of this national pattern.

Communication among the colonies played a vital role in forming the unity that was necessary for the ultimate victory. Baltimorean William Goddard, editor of the *Maryland Journal and Baltimore Advertiser,* made a major contribution to this communication when in 1774 he undertook the organization of a colonial postal system which would be free of the espionage practiced by royal postal officials. In Baltimore, the mails were collected and distributed at the *Journal* office by Postmistress Mary Katherine Goddard, William's sister. Communication among the revolutionary leaders meant that Baltimoreans could know and object to British policies not only in Maryland but throughout the colonies.

After Boston radicals dumped a boatload of taxed tea in their harbor in December 1773, the British closed the port of Boston until such time as the tea was paid for. Bostonians met and agreed to forego trade with Britain and passed a resolution urging other colonies to do the same. Sam Adams wrote to sympathizers throughout the colonies requesting support and aid. He wrote to William Lux in Baltimore, "As the very being of every colony, considered as a free people, depends upon the event, a thought so dishonorable to our brethren cannot be entertained as that this town will now be left to struggle alone. The town of Boston is now suffering the stroke of vengeance, in the common cause of America. I hope they will sustain the blow with a becoming fortitude, and that the efforts of this cruel act, intended to intimidate and subdue the spirits of all America, will by the joint efforts of all, be frustrated."

Baltimoreans met at the courthouse on May 25, 1774 and appointed a Committee of Correspondence to be in charge of intercolonial communication. A second meeting held on May 31 resulted in a resolution to end trade with Britain and the West Indies. The group also called for a meeting in Annapolis of delegates from all Maryland and for a meeting of delegates from all the colonies in a general assembly. An enlarged Committee of Correspondence was appointed with Samuel Purviance as chairman. In June and July of 1774, Baltimoreans collected funds for the relief of Boston and Charlestown, Massachusetts and sent several vessels with gifts and provisions.

In June 1774 each county chose delegates to attend the general convention in Annapolis. Seven men represented Baltimore Town and County: Captain Charles Ridgely, Thomas Cockey Deye, Walter Tolley, Jr., Robert Alexander, William Lux, Samuel Purviance, and George Risteau. This Maryland Convention entered into general non-importation

Above:
William Buchanan, Baltimore merchant, served as commissary general of the Continental Army

Left:
John Smith with his brother-in-law, William Buchanan, established a shipping firm in Fells Point. He served as a member of the Committee of Correspondence and later as a state senator. His oldest son, Samuel Smith, became a well-known merchant, soldier, and statesman

agreements, made further collections for the relief of Boston, and appointed delegates to the all-colony First Continental Congress which would meet in Philadelphia in September. The convention chose Matthew Tilghman, Samuel Chase, William Paca and Robert Goldsborough. Although none of these men came from Baltimore, they represented the faction led by Charles Carroll of Carrollton which worked closely with the town's mercantile revolutionary leadership.

The Continental Congress recommended the appointment of committees in towns and counties throughout the colonies to enforce the non-importation agreements on which that general congress had also resolved. Baltimoreans assembled at the courthouse once again. All freeholders and others eligible to vote elected twenty-nine members to the town's Committee of Observation. The Committee predictably included Samuel Purviance who became chairman, William Lux who became deputy chairman, Robert Alexander, John Moale, William Buchanan, and Jeremiah Townley Chase. James Calhoun, who would later serve as first mayor of Baltimore, Mordecai Gist, William Spear, Dr. John Boyd, John Merryman and many others were also elected. Two Germans, Barnet Eichelberger and George Lindenberger, joined the predominantly Scotch-Irish and English merchants on the Committee of Observation.

One major effect the Revolution had on Baltimore was the integration of the German population into the political life of the town. Until this time, except for several members of the Mechanical Company and the Sons of Liberty, the Germans had formed a community apart from the English-speaking elite, valued for their skills, but not included in the power establishment and, for the most part, without the franchise. The pre-war protest marked the beginning of change in their position.

By the fall of 1774, violent incidents began to erupt throughout the colonies. The perpetrators and the opponents of violence reflected the division between radicals and conservatives within the protest movement. Although Maryland's leaders were generally cautious, the violent incidents were beginning to polarize the various factions.

The Maryland incident which received the most attention was the burning of the ship *Peggy Stewart* in October, 1774. The *Peggy Stewart*, owned by James Dick and his son-in-law Anthony Stewart, arrived in Annapolis carrying seventeen chests of tea. In rampant violation of the anti-importation agreements (but well within the law), Stewart paid the duty on the tea, preparatory to unloading it. The local committee suggested a general meeting of the citizenry to determine what action should be taken. Baltimoreans Charles Ridgely, Mordecai Gist, and John Deaver attended. The group decided to burn the tea and the vessel. The more moderate Carroll-led group wanted to burn only the tea. In the end, Anthony Stewart set fire to his own vessel to assure the safety of his family. From this time on, open splits between the conservatives, moderates, and radicals continued, with individuals frequently shifting sides. The moderates generally held the greater power in Maryland throughout the Revolutionary period.

By the end of 1774, the Maryland Provincial Convention and local revolutionary groups clearly held control of the colony, despite the continuing nominal existence of the proprietary government. In December, the Convention undertook military preparations. All white males aged 15 to 60 were to be enrolled in companies, armed, equipped and drilled. A levy on the counties was to raise 10,000 pounds to furnish the militia with arms and ammunition. These were the first of numerous similar levies. In

anuary 1775 the Convention decreed that all vho refused to support the militia would be con-idered "an enemy to America" and their names ublished in the *Maryland Gazette*. The first ompany raised in Baltimore called itself the Baltimore Independent Cadets." Its captain was Aordecai Gist. By July 1775, three months af-er the fight at Lexington and Concord, seven ompanies were under arms in Baltimore. In the ollowing year, two all-German companies were ormed. At this time, slaves and free blacks were ot recruited for the militia. Slave owners, nowing the conditions under which slaves ived, were reluctant to arm men who might then ight for their own freedom. Later, when white nlistments declined, free blacks and some laves fought with the Maryland troops. hroughout the Revolution, black sailors atrolled the Chesapeake Bay.

Clearly, confusion was a predominant char-cteristic of this period. A Continental Congress f delegates chosen by various revolutionary roups met in Philadelphia. The proprietary olonial government continued to exist in Mary-and and to perform a host of routine functions, ut the real power lay in the hands of a revolu-onary convention and local committees of bservation whose vast numbers precluded any entralized decision-making. Committee mem-ership changed frequently. Militia companies pringing up throughout the colony elected their wn captains. On all levels, something had to e done.

During the spring of 1775, the Second ontinental Congress began to organize its owers and lines of authority. One major step ame in the appointment of George Washington s commander of the revolutionary forces. Vashington passed through Baltimore en route receive his command, spending the night at e Fountain Inn, Baltimore's most famous ostelry of the period. Even at that early date, an appearance by Washington drew out large cheering crowds.

During July 1775, the Maryland Provincial Convention began to bring some order locally. The Convention declared itself an official provisional government and adopted the "Articles of Association of the Freemen of Maryland" as its governing document. The Convention created a Committee of Safety to serve as its executive arm. This committee and its local branches were charged with the responsibility for military preparations and the administration of government. County Committees of Obser-vation were to be elected to see that the orders of the Convention were enforced. In September, Baltimore County chose 37 members of its Committee of Observation as well as five new delegates to serve a one-year term in the Provincial Convention.

By the middle of 1775, the revolutionary leaders in Baltimore had established their posi-tions. The men already mentioned as members of the various committees and as delegates to the Provincial Convention continued as political leaders for the duration of the war. Titles changed, the names of organizations changed, individuals differed on specific issues and on the extremity of measures to enforce loyalty, but the same men continued in power for the next decade.

From the middle of 1775 through 1776, several important developments took place. As fighting intensified, the army units became more tightly organized. In Maryland, during the summer of 1775, the Convention began to appoint battalion and field grade officers. At the session in December 1775-January 1776 the decision was made to appoint company officers as well. Many militiamen objected to the loss of the power to elect their captains. Service in the army already was a vehicle of upward mobility, politically if not economically. Because of their

pressure and the necessity for loyal troops, the Convention finally granted the franchise to all militiamen.

Local committees began enforcing loyalty among the civilian population. In Baltimore, the Committee of Observation began a series of actions against people suspected of pro-British leanings. When merchant James Christie wrote in a letter to his brother that British troops should be kept in the colonies to maintain order, a guard was stationed at his house. He was then taken before the Convention for discipline and finally he was banished from Maryland.

Samuel Purviance led in the formation of the Whig Club, the aim of which was the expulsion of anyone not favoring the "American cause." The Whig Club's activities were confined to the immediate area of Baltimore and did lead directly or indirectly to the departure not only of people loyal to England but also of those who took neither side in the war and those wrongly suspected of misdeeds. Dr. Henry Stevenson, founder of the inoculating hospital and brother of Dr. John Stevenson who sat on the Baltimore Committee of Observation, left Baltimore and joined the British Navy as a surgeon. He did not return until 1786, when passions had finally calmed. The Whig Club's most noted undertaking was the expulsion of editor William Goddard from the city for printing a controversial letter. It turned out later that Samuel Chase had planted the letter in order to publish a particularly strong rebuttal. The later safe return of Goddard could not undo the severe beating he received or the destruction of his offices and equipment. It is quite clear from this and other incidents that even the appearance of disloyalty to the patriot cause could be dangerous in Revolutionary Baltimore.

The Declaration of Independence was printed on page one of the *Maryland Journal and Baltimore Advertiser* of July 10, 1776. The official proclamation of independence took place at the courthouse on July 29. Baltimoreans illuminated the town that night and paraded through the streets bearing an effigy of King George III which they then burned.

Independence meant that all the states were obliged to write new constitutions. Maryland's Constitutional Convention met in August, 1776 and produced a rather interesting document. Each county sent four representatives to the Convention. Annapolis, as always, and Baltimore, in a tribute to its rising importance, were allowed to send two. Baltimore County sent radicals Charles Ridgely, Thomas Cockey Deye, John Stevenson and Peter Shepherd. Baltimore Town's delegates, Jeremiah Townley Chase and John Smith, as moderates were part of the political faction led by Charles Carroll of Carrollton. The moderates prevailed. The hottest issue was the franchise. Some radicals proposed universal manhood suffrage. The more conservative leaders of the state believed that only property owners had a stake in society sufficient to make likely their choice of capable rulers. The constitution of 1776 changed the property requirement for voting from 50 acres or 40 pounds sterling of visible property to 50 acres or 30 pounds current money or visible property. It established property requirements for officeholders: 500 pounds for members of the Lower House; 1000 pounds for members of the Upper House; and 5000 pounds for the governor. Of these, voters could elect directly only members of the Lower House. More than any other factor, this maintenance of control of the machinery of government by an economic elite rendered the Maryland Constitution a very conservative document.

Despite its conservatism, the Convention incorporated several democratic reforms into the document. It made the office of county sheriff elective, by a direct vote. It disestablished

John Merryman, whose ancestors had come to Baltimore County sometime before 1659, was a member of the Committee of Observation. He later served as President of the Second Branch of the City Council

Mordecai Gist, a merchant at the outbreak of the war, rose from captain of the Baltimore Independent Company to general in 1779. He was present at the surrender of British General Cornwallis at Yorktown

Fountain Inn, Baltimore's most famous hostelry during the Revolutionary period. George Washington and a great many other famous Baltimore visitors stayed here

the Church of England, which meant that no one church had greater privileges than all the others. It granted religious freedom to all Christians. (Jews remained disenfranchised, much as Catholics had been earlier.) It gave representation to Baltimore in allowing the town to join Annapolis in electing two delegates each to the Lower House. And, perhaps most surprisingly of all, the document placed no racial restrictions on the franchise with the result that free blacks who met the property requirements, and a few did, could vote in Maryland until 1810 when a law limited voting and office-holding to white persons. On November 3, 1776, a Bill of Rights was passed. On November 8 the Constitution was accepted. Elections took place. In March, the legislature elected Thomas Johnson Maryland's first governor and, the following day, the Committee of Safety officially surrendered its powers. Military victory was necessary to assure the permanence of the independent states, and that would follow after several years.

Articles in the *Maryland Journal and Baltimore Advertiser* reflect the wartime society in which Baltimoreans lived until British General Charles Cornwallis' surrender at Yorktown, Virginia in 1781. News from the battlefront and lists of the dead appeared prominently. When the state began confiscating Loyalists' property, advertisements for its sale appeared regularly. Pleas for enlistment, aid, provisions and equipment recurred frequently. Announcements of amusements such as fairs and theatrical performances disappeared during the Revolution. Such frivolities had been outlawed by the Congress so that energies and resources might be directed towards the war effort.

Maryland troops fought in New York, New Jersey, Pennsylvania, Virginia, the Carolinas and Georgia. The Maryland Line gained national fame as an effective fighting unit. Baltimore merchant and landowner John Eager Howard was one of the best known field commanders. Another Baltimorean, James McHenry, received an appointment to General Washington's staff and later served as adviser to the French General Lafayette. Local militia units played the largest role in the defense of Baltimore, which luckily saw very little military action.

The first war scare hit Baltimore in March 1776 when the British sloop "Otter" approached, bringing some captured American ships with her. Baltimoreans feared a bombardment of the town. Captain Samuel Smith's company boarded the Maryland ship "Defense" under the command of Captain James Nicholson. Their surprise attack succeeded in chasing the "Otter" and recapturing the prizes. The incident hastened the completion of the city's defenses. Two hundred and fifty blacks were employed to erect a boom between Whetstone Point and the Lazaretto and to build batteries and mount guns. Beacons and signal stations were constructed along the banks of the Patapsco River and the Chesapeake Bay. Colonel Mordecai Gist took command of Fort Whetstone (later renamed Fort McHenry.)

The closest the fighting came to Baltimore occurred in August 1777, when the British fleet sailed up the Bay and anchored in the Elk River. Baltimore and Harford Counties summoned over 1000 militiamen. The British landed and began to march toward Joppa, but their goal was Philadelphia, not Baltimore.

The last scare took place in May 1779, when the British squadron entered the Chesapeake Bay and took possession of Portsmouth, Virginia. Baltimoreans, on full alert, removed records and portable valuables from town and waited. The British did not come, but sailed towards New York instead.

In the Revolution, as in most American wars, the army took in all able-bodied men and tended to level out some of the differences

Top left:
Washington, Lafayette, and Charles Carroll, Barrister, in front of Mt. Clare. As General Lafayette's forces moved toward Virginia for the final battles of 1781, he asked for loans of money, which were proffered by men bearing such names as Rogers, Purviance, Carroll, Calhoun and McHenry

Center left:
John Eager Howard, whose grandfather Joshua Howard took out a patent in Baltimore County in 1685, was appointed captain in the Maryland militia in 1776 at the age of 24. He rose to the rank of colonel and is credited with the victory at the battle of Cowpens. He later served as Governor of Maryland and United States Senator

Bottom left:
James McHenry, a merchant before the Revolution, served as an officer in the Continental Army. Later he was a delegate at the convention which framed the United States Constitution and served as President Washington's Secretary of War. Fort McHenry is named for him

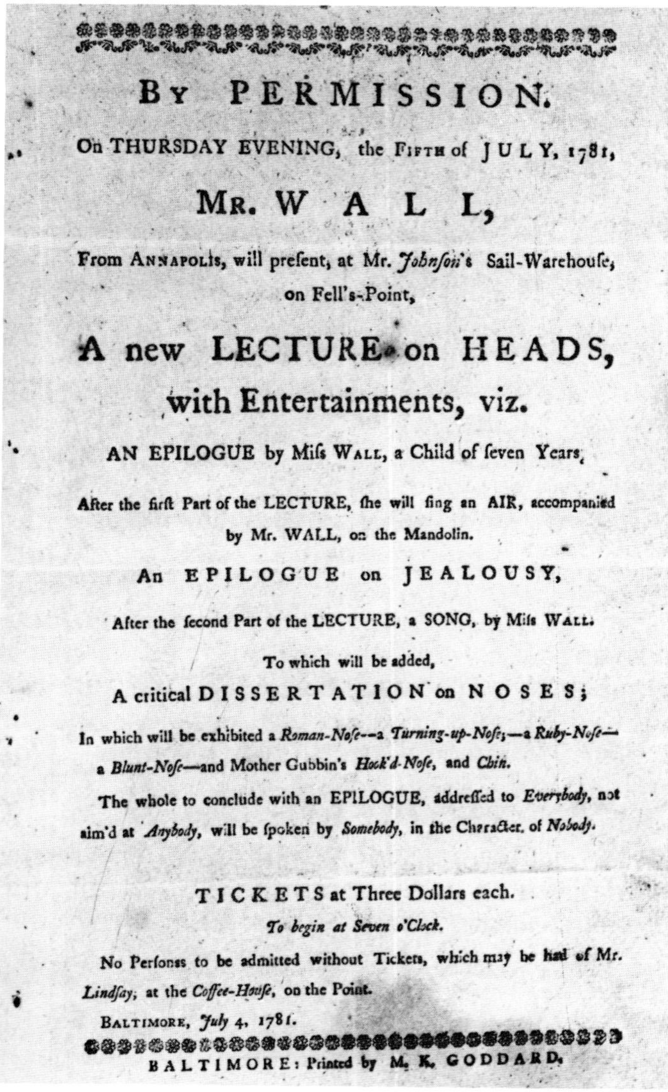

BY PERMISSION.

On THURSDAY EVENING, the FIFTH of JULY, 1781,

MR. WALL,

From ANNAPOLIS, will preſent, at Mr. *Johnſon's* Sail-Warehouſe, on Fell's-Point,

A new LECTURE on HEADS, with Entertainments, viz.

AN EPILOGUE by Miſs WALL, a Child of ſeven Years,

After the firſt Part of the LECTURE, ſhe will ſing an AIR, accompanied by Mr. WALL, on the Mandolin.

An EPILOGUE on JEALOUSY,

After the ſecond Part of the LECTURE, a SONG, by Miſs WALL.

To which will be added,

A critical DISSERTATION on NOSES;

In which will be exhibited a *Roman-Noſe*—a *Turning-up-Noſe*;—a *Ruby-Noſe*—a *Blunt-Noſe*—and Mother Gubbin's *Hook'd-Noſe*, and *Chin*.

The whole to conclude with an EPILOGUE, addreſſed to *Everybody*, not aim'd at *Anybody*, will be ſpoken by *Somebody*, in the Character of *Nobody*.

TICKETS at Three Dollars each.

To begin at Seven o'Clock.

No Perſons to be admitted without Tickets, which may be had of Mr. *Lindſay*, at the *Coffee-Houſe*, on the Point.

BALTIMORE, *July* 4, 1781.

BALTIMORE: Printed by M. K. GODDARD.

Above right:
With the theatres closed, lectures like this one provided rare public entertainment during the war

between them. The need for brawn overpowered considerations of race, religion and class, at least to some extent. Baltimore's German companies have already been mentioned. Germans also served in English-speaking units. Nathaniel Levy, son of Baltimore's first Jewish residents, Benjamin and Rachel Levy, enlisted in the Baltimore cavalry and served under Lafayette. As enlistments slackened off around 1780, Maryland became the only southern state to recruit black soldiers. Black pilots sailed ships on the Chesapeake Bay and Maryland's rivers, where their work served the patriot cause well. It should be noted that many Maryland blacks supported the Loyalists because of Britain's promise of freedom to all slaves who served. Although some states further north matched this offer, Maryland never did. Financial encouragement was held out in a law of 1780 to lure all freemen, white and black, to enlist. Men who volunteered for three years service were to receive $200, fifty acres of land, and exemption from paying taxes while in uniform and for four years afterwards. A law of 1781 required the drafting of all able-bodied vagrants.

The army needed supplies and provisions almost as badly as it needed troops. Baltimore merchants sold grain and other necessities to the army and eventually made a good profit from those sales. Urgent situations called forth contributions without pay. Probably the greatest single outpouring of donations went to General Lafayette's forces as they moved towards Virginia for the final battles of 1781. In February, the army commandeered all wagons, carriages, teams of horses, drivers and vessels available in the Baltimore area to transport Lafayette's troops southward. Major James McHenry suggested that the French general seek the aid of local merchants. They established a procurement committee. Lafayette asked for loans of money and backed his request with a pledge of his personal fortune. Newcomers like Irish immigrant William Patterson and Jewish merchant Jacob Hart joined with merchants bearing such names as Rogers, Purviance, Carroll, Calhoun and McHenry in proffering money.

Before Lafayette's departure, Baltimoreans gave a grand ball in his honor. He took advantage of the occasion to extract one further contribution from the town's residents. An early historian wrote that when one elegantly attired lady observed that he looked sad, Lafayette replied that "I cannot enjoy the gayety of the scene while so many of the poor soldiers are in want of clothes." He gained his objective when, the next morning, the very ballroom became a clothing factory where many of Baltimore's most prominent women sewed uniforms for the French general who had charmed them all.

The Continental Congress met in Baltimore from December 1776 through February 1777. When Washington retreated across the Delaware River to Trenton, he left Philadelphia without defenses. The Congress, fearing an attack, moved to Baltimore and set up headquarters in a large inn built by a recent German immigrant, Jacob Fite, at the corner of Baltimore and Sharp Streets. The Congress elected two local ministers, Rev. Patrick Allison of the Presbyterian Church and Rev. William West of St. Paul's, to serve as chaplains. It appointed numerous Baltimoreans to perform functional and administrative jobs for the duration of the sojourn here. Many of the Congressmen objected to Baltimore's lack of paved streets and other amenities to which they had become accustomed in the well established city of Philadelphia. John Adams, however, wrote that he liked the town's spirited inhabitants. After two months, the Congressmen's own longing for Philadelphia and their hope to boost public morale led them to return

Baltimore, *Dec.* 31, 1776.

This Morning Congreſs received the following Letter from General Washington.

Head-Quarters, Newtown, 27th Dec. 1776.

SIR,

I HAVE the Pleaſure of congratulating you upon the Succeſs of an Enterprize, which I had formed againſt a Detachment of the Enemy lying in Trenton, and which was executed Yeſterday Morning.

The Evening of the 25th, I ordered the Troops intended for this Service, to parade back of M'Kenky's Ferry, that they might begin to paſs as ſoon as it grew dark, imagining we ſhould be able to throw them all over, with the neceſſary Artillery, by 12 o'Clock, and that we might eaſily arrive at Trenton by five in the Morning, the Diſtance being about nine Miles. But the Quantity of Ice, made that Night, impeded the Paſſage of the Boats ſo much, that it was three o'Clock before the Artillery could all be got over, and near four before the Troops took up their Line of March.

I formed my Detachment into two Diviſions, one to march up the lower or River Road, the other by the upper or Pennington Road. As the Diviſions had nearly the ſame Diſtance to march, I ordered each of them immediately upon forcing the out Guards, to puſh directly into the Town, that they might charge the Enemy before they had Time to form. The upper Diviſion arrived at the Enemy's advanced Poſt exactly at 8 o'Clock, and in three Minutes after, I found, from the Fire on the lower Road, that that Diviſion had alſo got up. The out Guards made but a ſmall Oppoſition, though, for their Numbers, they behaved very well, keeping up a conſtant retreating Fire from behind Houſes.

We preſently ſaw their main Body formed, but, from their Motions, they ſeemed undetermined how to act. Being hard preſſed by our Troops, who had already got Poſſeſſion of Part of their Artillery, they attempted to file off by a Road, on their Right, leading to Princeton; but perceiving their Intention, I threw a Body of Troops in their Way, which immediately checked them. Finding, from our Diſpoſition, that they were ſurrounded, and they muſt inevitably be cut to Pieces, if they made any further Reſiſtance, they agreed to lay down their Arms. The Number that ſubmitted, in this Manner, was 23 Officers, and 886 Men. Col. Rohl, the commanding Officer, and ſeven others, were found wounded in the Town. I do not exactly know how many they had killed; but I fancy not above twenty or thirty, as they never made any regular Stand. Our Loſs is very trifling indeed; only two Officers and one or two Privates wounded.

I find that the Detachment of the Enemy conſiſted of the three Heſſian Regiments of Landſpatch, Kniphauſen, and Rohl, amounting to about 1500 Men, and a Troop of Britiſh Light Horſe; but immediately upon the Beginning of the Attack, all thoſe who were not killed or taken, puſhed directly down the Road towards Borden-Town. Theſe would likewiſe have fallen into our Hands, could my Plan have been completely carried into Execution. Gen. Ewing was to have croſſed before Day at Trenton Ferry, and taken Poſſeſſion of the Bridge leading out of Town; but the Quantity of Ice was ſo great, that though he did every Thing in his Power to effect it, he could not get over. This Difficulty alſo hindered Gen. Cadwallader from croſſing, with the Pennſylvania Militia, from Briſtol; he got Part of his Foot over, but finding it impoſſible to embark his Artillery, he was obliged to deſiſt. I am fully confident, that could the Troops under Generals Ewing and Cadwallader have paſſed the River, I ſhould have been able, with their Aſſiſtance, to have driven the Enemy from all their Poſts below Trenton; but the Numbers I had with me being inferior to theirs below me, and a ſtrong Battalion of Light Infantry being at Princeton, above me, I thought it moſt prudent to return the ſame Evening with the Priſoners, and the Artillery we had taken. We found no Stores of any Conſequence in the Town.

In Juſtice to the Officers and Men I muſt add, that their Behaviour upon this Occaſion reflects the higheſt Honour upon them. The Difficulty of paſſing the River, in a very ſevere Night, and their March through a violent Storm of Snow and Hail, did not in the leaſt abate their Ardour; but when they came to the Charge, each ſeemed to vie with the other in preſſing forward, and were I to give a Preference to any particular Corps, I ſhould do great Injuſtice to the others.

Colonel Baylor, my Firſt Aid de Camp, will have the Honour of delivering this to you, and from him you may be made acquainted with many other Particulars; his ſpirited Behaviour, upon every Occaſion, requires me to recommend him to your particular Notice.

I have the Honour to be,
with great Reſpect, Sir,
your moſt humble Servant,

G. Waſhington.

Incloſed I have ſent you a particular Liſt of the Priſoners, Artillery, and other Stores.

RETURN of Priſoners taken at Trenton, the 26th December, 1776, by the Army under the Command of his Excellency General Washington.

Regiment of LANDSPATCH.

1 Lieutenant Colonel, 1 Major, 1 Captain, 3 Lieutenants, 4 Enſigns, 38 Serjeants, 6 Drummers, 5 Muſicians, 9 Officers Servants, 206 Rank and File.

Regiment of KNIPHAUSEN.

1 Major, 2 Captains, 2 Lieutenants, 3 Enſigns, 25 Serjeants, 6 Drummers, 6 Officers Servants, 258 Rank and File.

Regiment of ROHL.

1 Colonel, 1 Lieut. Colonel, 1 Major, 1 Captain, 2 Lieutenants, 5 Enſigns, 2 Surgeons Mates 25 Serjeants, 8 Drummers, 4 Muſicians, 9 Officers Servants, 244 Rank and File.

Regiment of ARTILLERY.

1 Lieutenant, 4 Serjeants, 1 Officer's Servant, 32 Rank and File.

TOTAL——1 Colonel, 2 Lieutenant Colonels, 3 Majors, 4 Captains, 8 Lieutenants, 12 Enſigns, 2 Surgeons, 92 Serjeants, 20 Drummers, 9 Muſicians, 25 Officers Servants, 740 Rank and File. 918 Priſoners.

6 double-fortified Braſs Three Pounders, with Carriages complete.
3 Ammunition Waggons.
As many Muſkets, Bayonets, Cartouch-Boxes, and Swords, as there are Priſoners.
12 Drums. 4 Colours.

Publiſhed by Order of Congreſs,

Charles Thomſon, Sec.

General George Washington reported his first victory to the Continental Congress when it was meeting in Baltimore. Mary Katherine Goddard reprinted his letter in this broadside

William Patterson, who arrived in Baltimore during the Revolution, lent his support to the war effort and soon became one of the town's leading merchants

Congress Hall where the Continental Congress met when the delegates fled from Philadelphia to Baltimore in December, 1776. Recently built by German immigrant, Jacob Fite, the inn stood at the corner of Baltimore and Sharp Streets

to that city.

The visiting Congressmen had noted the lack of amenities in Baltimore. Not all of them had been as perceptive as John Adams, who understood that the town's development had been cut off abruptly by the outbreak of the Revolution. The war effort precluded the large-scale use of money or manpower for local building. Once peace came, Baltimoreans could turn their attention to their unpaved streets, the housing shortage caused by the town's rapid wartime growth, and the massive financial and social disarrangements that had developed over the preceding decade.

Seeming contradictions appear in reports on Baltimore in the early 1780s. The local economy was confused at best. Wartime inflation had resulted in a distrust of paper money. The state of Maryland was bankrupt and could not pay its soldiers nor pay for internal improvements (public works). Individuals, who had not received their salaries as soldiers nor been paid for goods they sold to the army, could not pay their taxes. The sale of confiscated property, which was supposed to put cash into the state treasury, led primarily to lists of buyers owing Maryland for their new possessions. Debtors had no money to pay old or new debts. British ports remained closed to American traders. The severe winter of 1784-85 left the port of Baltimore iced in until March.

Despite all the confusion, Baltimore prospered. In 1782 its population had grown to approximately 8000. Grain exports had made Baltimore a boom town. In October 1783, American Revolutionary hero, General Nathaniel Greene wrote in his diary during a visit to the town: "Baltimore is a most thriving place. Trade flourishes and the spirit of building exceeds belief. Not less than three hundred houses are put up in a year. Ground rents is [sic] little short of what they are in London . . ."

The building boom extended to more than houses. Baltimore's first brick theater was erected on East Market Street, and that street was laid with cobblestones. A board of special commissioners was appointed by the legislature to oversee the paving of streets and the construction and repairing of bridges. The commission assessed landowners to pay the bill. The town commissioners put up street lights and established a permanent police force of three constables on duty during the day and fourteen watchmen at night. They levied a property tax to support them. The legislature appointed a board of port wardens to oversee harbor operations and the construction of new piers.

By 1784, the city had grown so large that Calvert Street had to be extended northward. The townsfolk saved their handsome courthouse, which stood at the top of Calvert Street, by taking up a subscription to pay for the underpinning of the building. The courthouse then stood twenty feet in the air and Calvert Street ran underneath. In that same year, the town built three new markets: Center Market, known as Marsh Market because it stood on the site of Harrison's Marsh; the Hanover Market at Hanover and Camden Streets for the convenience of the residents of Howard's Hill in the western part of town; and the original Broadway Market for the people of Fells Point.

The national government during the years 1781 to 1789 bore the title of the Confederation. The states were joined together only loosely and had no chief executive. Fear of creating a tyrannical government like the one they had just revolted against held Americans back from vesting any great power in a central government. This lack of any central authority made post-war reconstruction difficult. The economic problems that existed in Maryland plagued the other states as well. Both the Confederation and the state governments were bankrupt and in

Money for local improvements, like paving streets, was often raised by a lottery. This ticket was sold to raise funds for the paving of Howard Street in 1790

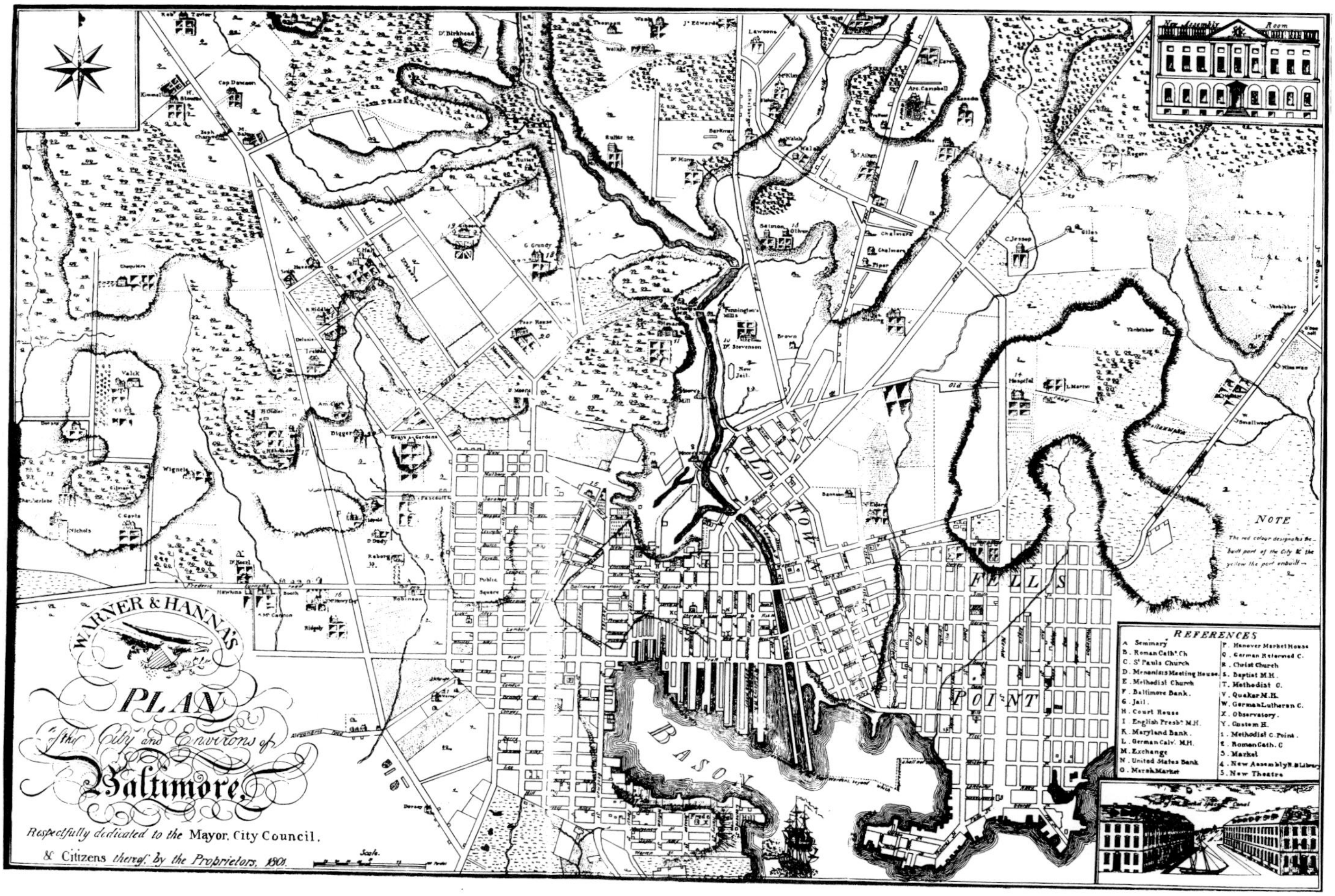

Warner and Hanna's map of Baltimore in 1801 shows the growth of the city in the two decades following the Revolution. The outline of the original town is visible in the center, just north of the basin

debt to foreigners and American citizens alike. The states tried to collect taxes from citizens who had no money. Many soldiers still had not been paid or had been paid in worthless paper money. Many had had to borrow to get started again after the war. Since more money in circulation would make debts easier to pay off, debtors agitated for relief in the form of the issuance of paper money and also laws to stay foreclosures on mortgages. These same debtors were outraged that a few people were in a position to accumulate fortunes during this period. Men lucky enough to have hard cash speculated by buying up both the paper money "Continentals" in which soldiers had been paid and land confiscated from Loyalists at reduced prices. Local speculators included Jeremiah Townley Chase and Charles Ridgely. Creditors wanted debts paid off at full value. The financial conservatives feared the power of the masses. Even more importantly, they believed that economic stability was necessary if the new country was to succeed. Therefore, throughout the 1780s, a group of people who came to be called Federalists pressed for a stronger central government with a stringent sense of financial responsibility. Their opponents, who feared that a strong central government would become a dictatorship or a monarchy and who wanted economic relief for the ordinary people, soon were called anti-Federalists.

In Baltimore County, the demand for paper money led to control by anti-Federalists. Charles Ridgely, espousing the paper money position, became the political leader of the county. Thomas Cockey Deye, elected as an anti-Federalist legislator from Baltimore County, became Speaker of the House of Delegates for a brief time. The leaders of the radical Revolutionary faction tended to fall into the anti-Federalist camp. The moderate forces tended to lean towards the stability of a stronger government. Most of the merchants of Baltimore Town hoped for a stronger government which would foster trade and manufacturing as well as control the potential for violence that all recognized was possible because of the financial plight of many veterans and other debtors.

In 1787 a group of delegates from all the states met in Philadelphia to consider ways to revise and strengthen the Articles of Confederation. They ended by writing a new Federal Constitution which provided for a much stronger central government. The document, as it still stands, but without the amendments, was signed on September 17, 1787 and submitted to the states for ratification. The text appeared eight days later in the *Maryland Journal and Baltimore Advertiser* and touched off widespread local debate. Baltimore Town, Annapolis, and all the Maryland counties witnessed campaigns by candidates who wanted to be delegates to the state convention which would ratify or reject the new constitution. Baltimore Town sent two Federalists who favored the Constitution, James McHenry and Dr. John Coulter, to the convention. The election was marred by frauds and violence on both sides. In Baltimore, where only 1,047 people were eligible to vote, 671 of those did not vote, and yet 1,050 votes were recorded. The Federalists won both in Baltimore Town as well as state-wide. The convention ratified the new Constitution, as did those of the other states, and the document stood as the basis for a new and stronger federal government. Baltimore celebrated ratification with a parade of some 3000 people. The procession terminated at Federal Hill, specially named for the occasion, where the marchers held a feast.

Federalist policies prevailed in the national government as it began to function under the presidency of George Washington. Secretary of

Baltimore about 1800, with the courthouse and the First Presbyterian Church in the foreground

The main city spring, located on Calvert Street near Saratoga Street. In the early 1800s the city landscaped the grounds and built the dome and a gatekeeper's house

The old city watch located at the corner of Belvidere (now Guilford Avenue) and Orange Alley

the Treasury, Alexander Hamilton, successfully undertook a program to stabilize the economy and foster trade and industry. Baltimore benefitted from the national policies and Federalism received strong support. Baltimorean John Eager Howard, a Federalist, became governor of Maryland from 1788 to 1791. Federalist policies dominated the city and state.

Peace, stability, and prosperity brought a resumption of growth in the cultural life of Baltimore. Schools, libraries, and theaters sprang up during the post-Revolutionary years. The cultural expansion was not particularly systematic and was, for the most part, the result of the work of individuals and private institutions, not of the town's government.

Various religious groups and leaders worked at improving the town's educational offerings and made the most effective contributions. The Quaker Yearly Meeting voted in 1784 to support a school. In 1786 three local clergymen, Rev. John Carroll who would soon become America's first Roman Catholic bishop, Rev. William West of St. Paul's Episcopal Church, and Rev. Patrick Allison of the First Presbyterian Church, joined forces to establish a school to teach natural philosophy and classics and other higher level subjects. But by the end of 1787 the effort was abandoned. More successful schools were opened by the Zion Lutheran Church and the German Reformed Congregation. These taught German-speaking students in their own language.

By the first decade of the nineteenth century, several churches had organized schools which children could attend without paying the customary tuition. The Methodists began the Male Free School in the parsonage of a church on Light Street. St. Peter's Episcopal Church also operated a free school. The women of St. Paul's parish formed the "Benevolent Society of the City and County of Baltimore" to provide a free school for girls, especially orphans. Subjects included reading, writing, "cyphering," and needlework. The Society for the Abolition of Slavery and Protection of Free People of Color sponsored a school for black students. After the formation of the Sharp Street congregation of Negro Methodists, that church ran the school supported by a combination of tuition monies, donations from all the black churches, and gifts from Quakers and other abolitionists.

Several institutions of higher learning originated during the post-Revolutionary period. In 1791, Baltimore Roman Catholics established St. Mary's Seminary on Paca Street. In 1807 the College of Medicine of Maryland was opened, the first medical school in the state. From this partial listing, it is clear that a wide variety of individuals and institutions offered instruction in basic education and some fields of higher learning. Despite this, until the city's public school system was established in 1829 schooling was not available to more than a small percentage of students who could not pay their way.

The availability of books increased at about the same rate as that of schooling. While wealthy men had private libraries, circulating libraries to which readers subscribed made books available to far larger numbers of readers. Before the Revolution, Baltimoreans had to borrow books from a library in Annapolis. Then in December 1780, William Prichard advertised in the *Maryland Journal* that he was opening a bookstore and a circulating library of 1000 volumes. Four years later, William Murphy established a circulating library located on Market Street. The biggest library venture was another joint enterprise undertaken by three clergymen: Rev. John Carroll, Rev. Patrick Allison, and the new rector of St. Paul's, Rev. Joseph Bend, along with Dr. George Brown and several other wealthy citizens. In 1796 they

The Sharp Street Church, a congregation of African American Methodists, ran one of the early schools for black students.

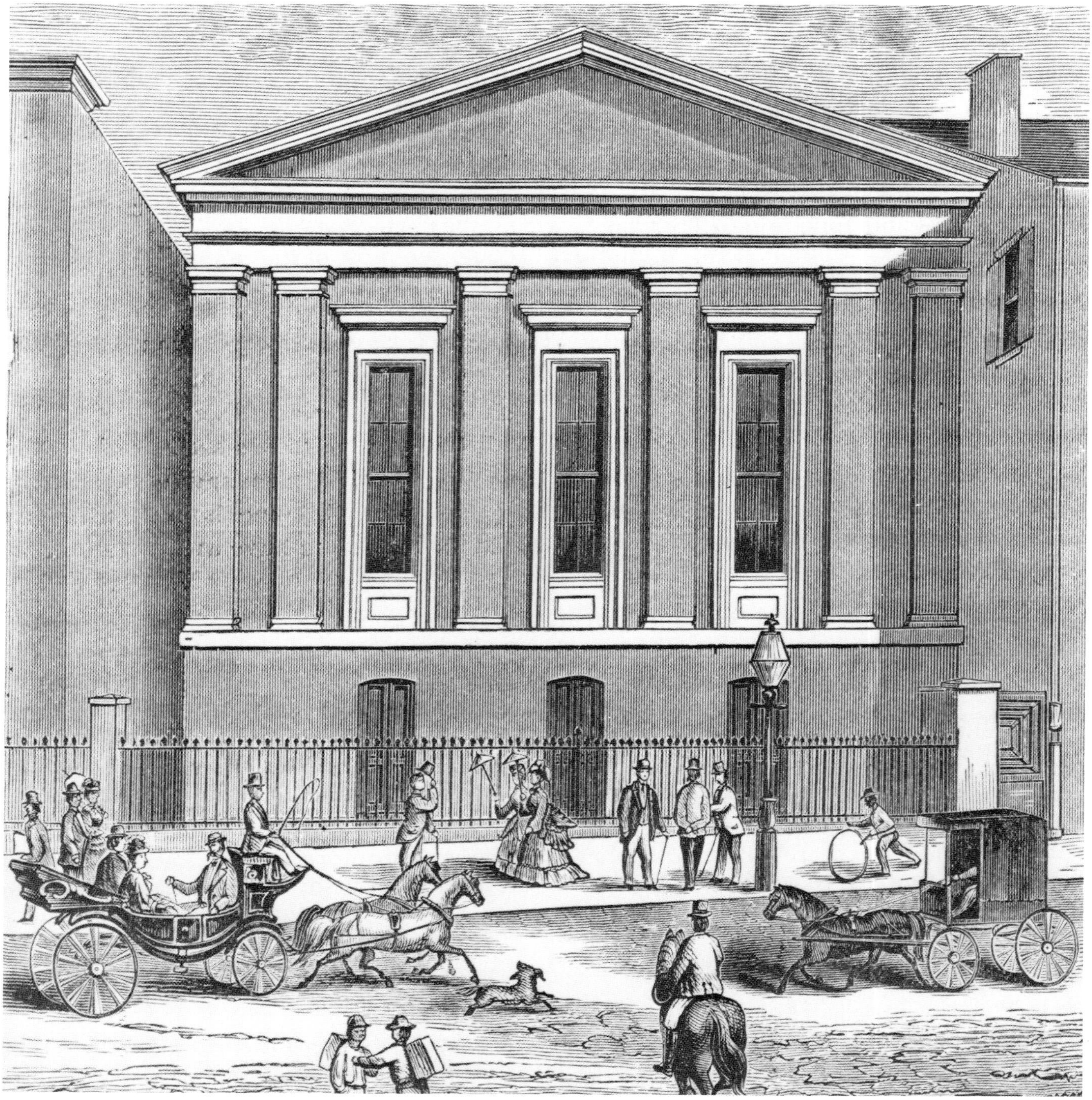

incorporated the Baltimore Library Company. Members bought a share of stock in the library for $20 and thereafter paid $4 a year. The membership grew from 60 original subscribers to 300 by 1798. By 1809 the library had over 400 members and 7000 volumes. In 1799 the Society of Friends established a library by appropriating $100 for books and appointing a librarian.

Newspapers also increased in number. Baltimore's first daily newspaper, *The Baltimore Daily Repository,* appeared in 1791. Publisher Alexander Martin brought out the first issue of the *Baltimore American and Daily Advertiser* in 1799 from his shop in Fells Point. Unlike most early nineteenth century newspapers, the *Baltimore American* merged with other newspapers and survived until the late 20th century. Most of the local papers that people read between the Revolution and the War of 1812 were short-lived. Most took clearly partisan political positions and were known to be strongly Federalist or strongly anti-Federalist. Their editors campaigned actively during elections and presented blunt opinions on major controversies. Objectivity was not even a goal for most editors.

Theaters, popular places of amusement in Baltimore before the Revolution, resumed operations as soon as peace permitted. In January 1782, the first brick theater in town opened on East Baltimore Street with a production of Shakespeare's *Richard III.* As was customary, a short farce, entitled *Miss In Her Teens,* preceded the program attraction. Box seat tickets sold for $1, seats in the pit (now orchestra) for 5 shillings and gallery seats for 9 pence.

In 1786, Lewis Hallam built the New Theater where his company performed. Seven years later, in 1793, William Godwin and Christopher Charles McGrath, managers of the Maryland Company, took over the building. Their opening year program included *She Stoops to Conque* *The Beaux Stratagem, School for Scanda* *Romeo and Juliet,* and at least three America plays: *The Contrast* by Royall Tyler, *The Fathe* by William Dunlap, and *A School for Soldiers* b John Henry. Wignell and Reinagle, well-know producers, opened the Holliday Street Theate in 1794. Throughout this period, Baltimorean could see most of the popular British plays an some American ones as well. Baltimore was good "theater town."

Another art form that enjoyed widesprea popular patronage was portraiture. Families c moderate means often commissioned minia tures, which were far less costly than the fu sized portraits painted of wealthier subject Several Baltimore portrait painters achieve renown during the post-Revolutionary perioc Joshua Johnson, a black artist, produced po traits of many Baltimore merchants and the families, including the John Moales. Anothe portrait painter, Rembrandt Peale, achieved hi greatest fame through the museum he opene on Holliday Street. In it he exhibited portraits o Revolutionary heroes and all sorts of artifacts preserved birds, beasts, fish, Indian dresses an ornaments and, most notably, one of th mastadon skeletons that his father, Charle Willson Peale, had excavated near Newburg New York in 1801. The famous architect Rober Carey Long designed the museum on Hollida Street, Baltimore's first. Lectures and th ever-popular flashy scientific experiments wer presented several times a week. Band concert and other performances were given on th intervening nights to draw an audience that paic an admission of 25 cents per adult and 12 1/ cents per child.

The years after the Revolution saw a rebirt of a bright and widely varied social life ir Baltimore. Horse-racing drew crowds of al classes. More elite patrons attended the meet

BALTIMORE THEATRE.
On MONDAY EVENING, April 13, 1812,
WILL BE PRESENTED THE COMEDY OF THE

Wheel of Fortune.

WRITTEN BY RICHARD CUMBERLAND, Esq.

Sir David Daw,	Mr. FRANCIS.
Governor Tempest,	Mr. WARREN.
Penruddock,	Mr. WOOD.
Woodville,	Mr. DOWNIE.
Sydenham,	Mr. CONE.
Henry Woodville	Mr. BARRETT.
Weazle,	Mr. BLISSETT.
Woodville's Servant,	Mr. HARRIS.
Officer,	Mr. LUCAS.
Jenkins,	Mr. DURANG.
Richard,	Mr. BRIERS.
Harry,	Mr. F. DURANG.
Mrs Woodville	Mrs. BARRETT.
Emily Tempest	Mrs. MASON.
Dame Duckley,	Mrs. SIMPSON,
Maid,	Miss PETIT.

After which will be presented
(FOR THE THIRD AND LAST TIME) A CELEBRATED DRAMATIC ROMANCE, IN THREE ACTS, CALLED THE

LADY OF THE LAKE.

WRITTEN BY JOHN EDMUND EYRE.
(From the much admired Poem of that name, by Walter Scott, Esq.)
Performed at the Theatre Royal, Edinburgh, and the Philadelphia and Charleston Theatres, with the most distinguished success, with entire

NEW SCENERY, DRESSES AND DECORATIONS.

The Scenery designed (exactly after the poem) by Mr. Robbins, and executed by him, assisted by H. Warren and T. Remagle.
The Dances and Processions by Mr. Francis, assisted by Mr. Harris. The Dresses by Shrœder and assistants.
The Music by the celebrated Sanderson and Dr. Clarke, of Cambridge, and M. Pellesierre, the accompaniments by the latter.

SCENE FIRST DISCOVERS

LOCH KATRINE,

Several islands in perspective, scattered on the Lake, with a distant view of BEN VENUE and BEN-AN. A boat appears in the distance, which approaches swiftly, and *Ellen lands from it.*

Ellen, Lady of the Lake, - Mrs. TWAITS.

INTERVIEW BETWEEN ELLEN AND FITZJAMES

Fitzjames, the Knight of Snoudoun - Mr. WOOD.

SCENE SECOND.

THE BOWER.

Around the walls of this picturesque scene are hung *Battle-Axes, Targets, Broad words, Bows and Arrows*; several trophies of the fight and chase. *Invisible Chorus;* "Huntsman rest, thy chace is done." The door is thrown open and Fitzjames enters conducted by Ellen. Chorus repeated, while the knight is regaled by Ellen and maids. The sounds of the *PIEBRACH* (or gathering) are heard, which warn him to be gone. He views the approach of the clan of Roderick with concern from the window, takes his leave of Lady Margaret and the Minstrel, and presents Ellen with a ring.

Lady Margaret, Mother of Roderick, Mrs. BARRETT.
Allan Bane, - the Minstrel, - Mr HARDINGE.

Baltimore's theatres drew large crowds to see popular British and American plays. Lady of the Lake, as noted here, was based on a poem by Sir Walter Scott, who took both Britain and America by storm

NEW THEATRE.

On Saturday, September 5, 1795.
Will be prefented a COMEDY, (never performed here,) called,

THE

CLANDESTINE MARRIAGE

Lord Ogleby,	Mr. *Bates.*
Sir John Melvil,	Mr. *Green.*
Sterling,	Mr. *Morris.* X
Lovewell,	Mr. *Marfhall.* X
Canton,	Mr. *Harwood.*
Brufh,	Mr. *Moreton.*
Serjeant Flower,	Mr. *Francis*
Traverfe,	Mr. *Bliffet,*
Trueman,	Mr. *Warrell,*
Servant,	Mr. *Darley* junr.
Mrs. Heidelberg,	Mrs. *Shaw.*
Mifs Sterling,	Mrs. *Morris.* X X X
Fanny,	Mrs. *Marfhall*
Betty,	Mrs. *Harvey.*
Chambermaid,	Mrs. *Francis.*
Trufty,	Mrs. *Bates.*

To which will be added, a FARCE in two Acts, called,

THE SULTAN;

Or, A Peep into the Seraglio.

Soliman,	Mr. *Moreton.*
Ofmyn,	Mr. *Harwood.*
Elmira,	Mifs *Oldfield.*
Ifmene, (with fongs,)	Mifs *Broadhurft.*
Roxalana,	Mrs. *Oldmixon.*

††† BOX, One Dollar—PIT, three fourths of a Dollar.
The Public *are requefted to take notice the doors of the Theatre, will open at a quarter before Six and Curtain rife at a quarter before Seven o'Clock precifely.*

Places for the Boxes to be taken at the Office in the front of the Theatre, on the days of performance from ten in the morning till three in the afternoon.

No admiffion without Tickets, which are to be had at the Office of the BALTIMORE TELEGRAPHE, at JAMES RICE's Book-Store, the corner of South and Market-ftreets, and at the OFFICE adjoining the THEATRE.

Ladies and Gentlemen are requefted to fend their fervants to keep places at a quarter before 6 o'Clock and direct them to withdraw, as foon as the company are feated, as they cannot on any account be permitted to remain.

No Tickets to be returned, nor any perfon admitted behind the fcenes, on any account whatever.

Vivat Respublica!

[BALTIMORE: PRINTED BY CLAYLAND, DOBBIN AND CO. MARKET-STREET.]

This program from a performance at the New Theatre in 1795 suggests the nature of some of the racier plays popular among Baltimore audiences

of the Hunt Club. The Baltimore Dancing Assembly attracted most of the town's upper class residents to its balls held at the Fountain Inn. Probably the most sensational social event of the entire period was the 1803 Christmas Eve marriage of Betsy Patterson to Jerome Bonaparte. Although Napoleon found the belle of Baltimore an unsuitable wife for his brother, annulled the marriage and summoned Jerome home to Europe, Betsy and her son, Jerome, stayed in town and Baltimoreans talked and wrote about the marriage for a long time afterwards.

Epidemics and fevers played havoc with life during this period, killing off large numbers of people with each recurrence. Many people moved to the country during the summer months in the belief that they could escape contagious diseases like yellow fever and influenza in the less densely populated areas.

Another preventive measure, generally unsuccessful, was the imposition of a quarantine against infected areas. A yellow fever epidemic in Philadelphia in 1793 evoked a quarantine on all vessels entering the port of Baltimore from that city. Any intercourse with Philadelphia was forbidden. Companies of the Maryland militia were stationed along the northern boundary of the state and at the major intersections of roads leading from Philadelphia. The militiamen turned away at gun point any traveller who might be carrying yellow fever. Despite the precautions the disease spread to Baltimore and recurred for a number of years. A hospital was opened on the site where the Johns Hopkins Hospital now stands to treat fever victims. The newspaper *The Federal Gazette* reported on one case where the doctor in treating a fever patient took 130 ounces of blood, gave 35 grains of mercury and rubbed in 12 ounces of mercurial ointment. In 1800, a Dr. J. J. Gireaud published his formula for the prevention and cure of yellow fever: ipecac, rhubarb, columba, magnesia, kermes mineral, camphor, and nitre.

Despite the rather peculiar variety of treatments for yellow fever and other diseases as well, Baltimore's physicians undertook several projects that pointed the way towards the city's future leadership in medicine. In 1788, Dr. Charles Wiesenthal issued an appeal to the doctors of Maryland to put together a plan for the regulation of medical practices, to suppress quackery and restrict the profession to those who were qualified. As a result, a city Medical Society was organized and Wiesenthal elected president. Shortly thereafter, Maryland's doctors organized a State Medical Society. Local physicians conducted classes in their own homes and offices. Lectures predominated. In 1790, for example, the Medical Faculty announced the following lecture program: Andrew Wiesenthal (son of Charles) on Anatomy, George Brown on the Practice of Medicine, Lyde Goodwin on Surgery, S. S. Coale on Chemistry and Materia Medica, and George Buchanan on Midwifery. An attempt to teach anatomy by dissecting a cadaver failed. In 1788, when the city donated for research the body of Patrick Cassidy, an executed murderer, a mob snatched it away.

Permanent institutions began to appear in 1799 with the organization of the Medical and Chirurgical Faculty of the State of Maryland. Then in 1807 the College of Medicine of Maryland was incorporated. The college hired a faculty. Dr. John Beale Davidge erected an Anatomical Hall at Liberty and Saratoga Streets as a lecture and dissecting room. Once again the populace objected and showed it by tearing down the hall.

Along with their interest in teaching and regulating the practice of medicine, the town's doctors showed concern that medical care be available to the poor as well as the rich. Early in 1798, with the support of Baltimore's doctors,

The Maryland Hospital opened on the site now occupied by the Johns Hopkins Hospital to treat victims of yellow fever, a disease which plagued the city for many years

Dr. John Davidge first erected an Anatomical Hall at Liberty and Saratoga Streets in 1800 and offered courses in midwifery, surgery, and anatomy. The original hall was demolished by rioting citizens who objected to the dissection of corpses. Until a new medical school was built, lectures were held at the county alms house

Betsy Patterson and Jerome Bonaparte at Grundy House, before Napoleon summoned his brother home to Europe

the state legislature appropriated $8000 and later another $3000 for the construction of a City Hospital for the "sick and lunatics." A city council committee chose a site at Broadway and Monument Streets and the Baltimore General Dispensary opened there. The city and state augmented their responsibility for the poor in other ways. The poor laws became more specific. A law of 1793 allowed children of vagrants, of destitute persons and of convicted criminals to be apprenticed within Maryland. A law of 1799 provided for a payment of pensions to a limited number of persons in each county whose situation made the almshouse particularly unsuitable. Between the Revolution and the years of the War of 1812, the almshouse provided shelter to an average of 230 people a year.

In 1793 a group of refugees who required an especially large amount of assistance arrived from Santo Domingo. Approximately fifteen hundred people who had opposed Toussaint L'Ouverture's rebellion against both slavery and French rule left when he won. One thousand whites and 500 blacks landed in 53 vessels, many of the refugees penniless. A benefit theater performance was given to raise money for their relief. A general subscription yielded $12,000 to help the destitute.

Churches grew along with the population of the city. Most denominations built either larger or additional churches during the years following the Revolution. In 1791 the Presbyterians erected a new larger church with two steeples on the lot of their old church on Fayette Street. When they installed an organ in 1811, a few families left the congregation in protest against the playing of music. The Baptists opened a second church in 1797, on Broadway near Pratt Street. In 1808 the Zion Lutheran congregation moved to its current location on North Gay Street.

The German Reformed Church experienced several crises during the 1770s and 1780s. The first resulted in a split in the congregation when one group tried to replace the original pastor, the Rev. John Christian Faber, with a new minister, Benedict Swope. The followers of Swope finally withdrew and built a Second Reformed Church on Conway Street at Sharp. In 1774, Mr. Swope was succeeded by the Rev. Philip Otterbein, a German who came to Baltimore from Lancaster, Pennsylvania. Otterbein's congregation in 1785 constructed the church which now bears his name and is the oldest in Baltimore. They built the two-foot thick walls with bricks discarded by ships which had used them for ballast. Otterbein led his congregation into the new Church of the United Brethren of which he was a founder. This denomination later merged with the Methodists.

The first German Reformed Church began a new building at Baltimore and Front Streets in 1785 with contributions collected from the membership. The following year, a flood of the Jones Falls swept away the walls before the new church was finished. In an early display of ecumenism, Mr. West of St. Paul's, Mr. Allison of the Presbyterian Church, and Mr. Kurtz of Zion Lutheran Church, all took up collections to aid in rebuilding the destroyed edifice. The church later rebuilt on a new site on Holliday Street further away from dangers of the Jones Falls.

Baltimore was the scene of major developments in both the Catholic and Methodist churches. Several events of national importance took place here shortly after the Revolution.

When the Revolution began, Maryland Catholics were still disenfranchised. The Constitution of 1776 removed the restrictions on their voting and holding office. For many years they had not been allowed to build public

Above:
Looking east across the Jones Falls in 1800. The wooden bridge along Baltimore Street was built in 1775. The large building is the First German Reformed Church which was bought by Christ Church (Episcopal) in 1796. The first Baptist Meeting House of 1773 is on the left

Far Left:
The new two-steeple First Presbyterian Church, on the northwest corner of the present Fayette Street and Guilford Avenue, was erected in 1791. When an organ was installed twenty years later, some families left the congregation in protest against the playing of music during worship

Left:
The first town clock was in the steeple of the new German Reformed Church

houses of worship. In the early 1770s Baltimore Catholics began construction of their first church, St. Peter's, and worshipped there before the building was finished. When the builder, John McNabb, went bankrupt, the principal creditor locked up the church. It was reopened during the war by a company of soldiers and remained in use. In 1784, the Rev. Charles Sewell became the first resident pastor. He was joined several years later by the Rev. John Carroll, cousin of Charles Carroll of Carrollton. John Carroll held an almost unique position in the combination of his elite family background and his priesthood. When the American Roman Catholic clergy met in 1789 and decided to request the establishment of an Episcopal see in this country, they also asked that John Carroll be bishop. He did become the first American Roman Catholic bishop, was consecrated in London in 1790, and returned to Baltimore where he served not only as head of the nation's Catholic hierarchy but as a local civic leader as well. St. Mary's Seminary opened in 1791. Fells Point Catholics formed a second congregation in 1792 and worshipped in private homes until St. Patrick's Church on Apple Alley was completed in 1796. In 1806 the cornerstone of the new cathedral was laid on land that had belonged to John Eager Howard, now the corner of Cathedral and Mulberry Streets. Two years later, John Carroll became the first American archbishop. It was appropriate and logical that the foremost city of Maryland, the only one of the original colonies granted to a Catholic proprietor should be the home of the first Catholic bishop and archbishop in the United States. Maryland's Catholics had been leaders in the revolutionary movement and now John Carroll from Baltimore led in the integration of Catholicism into the American religious mainstream.

Whereas Maryland's Catholics gained because of their association with the cause of independence, local Methodists frequently suffered because Methodism was often associated with the Tories. Although Francis Asbury favored the Americans, John Wesley spoke out against the Revolution. In addition, the known Methodist opposition to slavery led people to connect the denomination with the slave uprisings that took place during the Revolution. Despite all this, Baltimore, along with Philadelphia, was an acknowledged center of Methodism. After Baltimore Methodists built their second meeting house on Lovely Lane just south of Baltimore Street in 1774, Methodist preachers held several conferences in Baltimore culminating in the Christmas conference of 1784. At this meeting the American preachers voted to separate themselves from the Church of England and establish the Methodist Episcopal Church in America. This decision removed the taint of Toryism and also formally removed them from the jurisdiction of the new American Episcopal hierarchy. The Methodists chose Francis Asbury as their first American bishop at this same landmark conference.

The history of Methodists, Quakers, and American blacks is inextricably combined during this period. Methodists and Quakers had opposed slavery since before the Revolution. In Baltimore, both groups encouraged their members to free their slaves before and after the War for Independence. Quakers always stood in the vanguard of abolitionist activists, not only encouraging manumissions but donating substantial monies to schools for black students such as the African School opened on Sharp Street in 1793. The Baltimore Yearly Meeting several times enjoined individual members to educate blacks.

Methodists, at a conference held in Baltimore in 1780, instructed their preachers to free their slaves and declared that Methodists should educate blacks and exert pressure for

Top left:
Archbishop John Carroll, cousin of Charles Carroll of Carrollton, was both America's first Roman Catholic bishop and an important civic leader in Baltimore

Left:
The Old Lovely Lane Methodist Church, where American preachers voted in 1784 to separate themselves from the Church of England and to establish the Methodist Episcopal Church in America

Top right:
The ordination of Francis Asbury as the first bishop of the Methodist Episcopal Church in America at the Lovely Lane Church, December 27, 1784. Asbury, who is kneeling, is surrounded by Thomas Koch, Thomas Vasey, Richard Whatcoat, and William Otterbein

Above:
St. Mary's Seminary, the Sulpician School founded in 1791, occupied the building on the right. When the college was established in 1805, the building on the left was constructed. The chapel, designed by Maximilian Godefroy, was dedicated in 1808. The tower, designed by Robert Cary Long, Jr., was not added until 1839

emancipation. Francis Asbury supported this. Methodists went a step further in establishing mixed congregations which sometimes heard black preachers. At the Christmas Conference of 1784, delegates passed a resolution declaring that slavery was "contrary to the Golden Law of God . . . as well as every principle of the Revolution." They declared that all Methodists should free their slaves. This proviso met strong opposition and was later revoked. Many manumissions did result, however.

Nationally as well as locally, the ideals proclaimed in the Declaration of Independence led many Americans to recognize the paradox of talking about the rights of all men, for which they claimed to have fought, and the continuation of the institution of slavery. In the northern states, the acknowledgement of the disparity was a major factor in the passage of laws abolishing slavery shortly after the Revolution. Although a number of Marylanders desired to do the same, the state legislature voted against abolition. It did, however, enact legislation making it easier for individuals to free their slaves.

In Baltimore in 1789 a group whose members included Samuel Chase, Luther Martin and Gerard Hopkins founded the Society for Promoting the Abolition of Slavery and the Relief of Poor Negroes unlawfully held in Bondage. Its several hundred members assisted runaways and free blacks and helped support the school on Sharp Street. Opposition eventually led to the disbanding of this group, but other societies followed. The combined activities of abolitionist societies and the legislation which eased the manumission process led to a significant growth in Baltimore's free black population. In 1800, 2,771 free blacks and 2,843 slaves lived in the city. By 1810, free blacks outnumbered slaves 3,973 to 3,713.

A large number of free blacks belonged to the Methodist Church. Methodist support for abolition and the presence of black preachers in the integrated churches encouraged this membership. However, although many Methodist preachers supported abolitionism and integrated worship, many individual Methodists did not. As early as the 1780s, some white Methodists began segregating black worshippers in galleries so white members did not have to sit next to them. As the discrimination became overt, blacks began withdrawing from the mixed congregations. Baltimore with its growing free black population played a major role in the development of independent black churches and the leadership they required.

As early as the mid 1780s, blacks began withdrawing from the Strawberry Lane and Lovely Lane Methodist meeting houses. One group organized themselves into a prayer group and gave themselves the name of Bethel. Jacob Fortie, Caleb Hyland, Stephen Hill and other leaders helped build the group until it was large enough in 1797 to purchase an old building on Fish Street (now Saratoga) for use as a church. In that same year they drew up a formal letter of separation and soon joined with a group in Philadelphia to form the African Methodist Episcopal Church. While these developments were taking place, a Methodist church with a black congregation and a white pastor was formed and stayed within the Methodist Conference. The Sharp Street Methodist Church took over operation of the African School. Church and school prospered together. An outstanding black preacher from Sharp Street, Daniel Coker, moved to the Bethel A. M. E. Church and became its first ordained preacher in 1811. Coker had been born in Maryland to an English indentured serving woman and a black slave. He himself escaped slavery by running away to New York, where he met Francis Asbury and converted to Methodism. He returned to Maryland where he

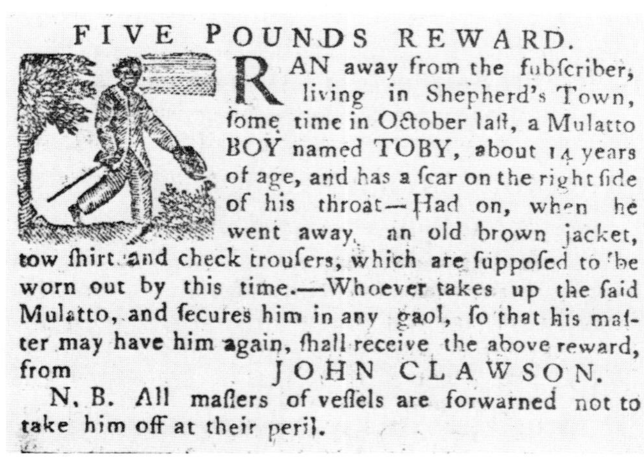

FIVE POUNDS REWARD.

RAN away from the fubfcriber, living in Shepherd's Town, fome time in October laft, a Mulatto BOY named TOBY, about 14 years of age, and has a fcar on the right fide of his throat—Had on, when he went away, an old brown jacket, tow fhirt and check troufers, which are fuppofed to be worn out by this time.—Whoever takes up the faid Mulatto, and fecures him in any gaol, fo that his mafter may have him again, fhall receive the above reward, from JOHN CLAWSON.

N. B. All mafters of veffels are forwarned not to take him off at their peril.

Top left:
The Bethel African Methodist Episcopal Church was formed by the first A.M.E. congregation in Baltimore

Top right:
Although increasing numbers of Baltimore's blacks became free each decade, slavery continued in the city and state until 1864. People were sometimes imprisoned in pens such as this one before a slave auction

Bottom right:
Many slaves ran away. Advertisements such as this one appeared frequently in the Baltimore Journal and Daily Advertiser *and other local newspapers*

remained hidden until he could raise the money to purchase his freedom. After rising to a position of prominence in Baltimore, he played a major role in the formal organization of the African Methodist Episcopal Church in 1816. The founding conference named Coker as first choice for bishop, but he declined and Richard Allen of Philadelphia was elected. The A. M. E. Church, which Baltimoreans had helped organize, has remained a major institution of the black community down to the present day.

Baltimore's Jewish community was by far the smallest minority group in town. The first United States census, in 1790, reported only six Jewish families, thirty-three individuals, living in Baltimore. By 1820 there were twenty-one Jewish families. One leader among these was Solomon Etting, who had opened a hardware store here in the early 1790s. In 1797 he and others petitioned the Maryland legislature for the right to vote and hold public office. Although Jews had participated in the patriot cause, the Maryland constitution of 1776 had limited suffrage to Christians and that restriction remained in force until 1826. Despite the limitation, Solomon Etting and his brother Reuben both were active Jeffersonians. In 1798 Reuben became captain of the Baltimore militia unit, the Independent Blues, and in 1801 President Thomas Jefferson appointed him federal marshal of Maryland, although he still could not vote. From the Ettings and others, it is clear that individual Jews were active in political and civic affairs. During this early period their numbers remained so small, however, that they had neither political clout nor enough men to form a synagogue or any other unifying institutions for the community.

During the post-Revolutionary period Baltimore's population remained heterogeneous. Residents spoke English, German, and some French. Several groups had become more fully integrated into politics and society because of the Revolution. Germans regularly were included in the economic and political power structure. Some Germans like Dr. Charles Wiesenthal began to move into positions of prominence based on their own individual skill and achievements. Catholics had gained full political rights. Bishop John Carroll, as a religious and civic leader, fostered Americanization of the Catholic church, cooperation with other local churches, and integration of individual Catholics into all phases of life in Baltimore. Other ethnic and religious groups did not gain such full inclusion after the Revolution. Jews, who joined in the economic and social life of Baltimore, were forbidden to vote or hold public office by the constitution of the state of Maryland. Baltimore's black population faced even greater hardships. Roughly half were slaves. Free blacks, although not entirely disenfranchised on the basis of race until 1810, faced growing discrimination by the white majority and were beginning to establish separate institutions to avoid that discrimination and to put some of the rights of leadership in their own hands.

Besides ethnic and religious groupings, Baltimore's population could be divided into two other major categories. Economically, a small group of wealthy men, many of whom by now could trace their families back several generations in Baltimore or the area nearby, stood above the ever growing numbers of craftsmen, mechanics, and shopkeepers who in turn outranked ordinary laborers. The Maryland constitution required the possession of a certain amount of property to enable a man to vote and an even larger amount of land or visible assets for a man to hold public office. This inequity and the problems of the economy in the immediate post-war period began to divide Baltimoreans into two political parties: the Federalists and the anti-Federalists who soon took on the name of

Above:
A formal presentation by Baltimore's black community to the city occasioned this sketch of the interior and congregation of Bethel

Left:
The Reverend Daniel Coker was the first ordained preacher at Bethel African Methodist Episcopal Church. Born in Maryland, he escaped slavery by running away to New York, where he met Francis Asbury and converted to Methodism. He was one of the leaders in the formation of the A.M.E. Church

War, Peace, & War Again
1773-1814

their national leader and were called Jeffersonians and later Republicans. Any account of Baltimore during the years between the Revolution and the War of 1812 must include consideration of these divisions. They were of central concern in the process of establishing an incorporated city government. The eventual reconciliation of the factions allowed the efficient functioning of the city that helped make possible the military victory during the War of 1812.

During the period of the Confederation, it will be recalled that most of Baltimore's leading merchants joined in the Federalist thrust for the new and stronger central government that they hoped would foster trade and manufacturing and sort out the financial chaos that had grown during the Revolution. In supporting the constitution, the Baltimoreans joined with the large land owners from the Eastern Shore and the area along the Potomac region who advocated Federalism as a bulwark against economic and social change. Once the economy had grown stable and Baltimore began to boom, it is not surprising that the alliance between the urban and rural politicians began to collapse. In fact, the two groups soon came into direct conflict.

The first big dispute centered on the location of the national capital. Baltimore, like many American cities, put in a bid to be chosen as the seat of the federal government. Merchants subscribed over 20,000 pounds in two weeks for public buildings. Baltimore's congressmen pushed their city. The Eastern Shore and Potomac leaders favored the site where Washington, D. C. is now located. After this time, Baltimore began to vie with the rural landed gentry for control of the state and to move out of the Federalist Party into the Jeffersonian camp.

The growth of Jeffersonianism took place throughout the nation, partly because Alexander Hamilton's economic policies had brought stability and partly because the anti-democratic excesses of the Federalists elicited immediate opposition. People feared the elitism of the Federalists and believed that it might lead to a monarchical government. Furthermore, many Americans believed that Federalist policies would lead us into another war. By the end of the eighteenth century, when fighting broke out between England and France following the French Revolution, the Federalists openly favored the British, because the United States had reopened trade with that country. Jeffersonians favored neutrality or took the side of our recent French allies. The fear of war led to the passage of the Alien and Sedition Acts. These controversial laws worked primarily against Jeffersonians. They extended from 5 to 14 years the time that aliens had to live in this country to be eligible for citizenship at a time when immigrants tended to vote for the Jeffersonian party. They outlawed all writing and speaking against the government or any of its policies. The first man convicted under this Sedition Act was a Jeffersonian newspaper editor from Vermont. Many similar arrests followed. The atmosphere became ever more repressive as the national elections of 1800 approached.

Baltimoreans clearly noticed the connection between strong centralization of the federal government and loss of individual liberty. As early as the celebrations of President George Washington's birthday in 1795, even before the passage of the Alien and Sedition Acts, public speakers proclaimed different points of view. Everyone celebrated Washington's birthday with partying and drinking toasts. At the elegant Fountain Inn one patron offered a toast to "George Washington, the early, the uniform, the unshaken friend of his country." More typical

was the toast offered at Winant's Tavern, where an obvious Jeffersonian volunteered, "The Congress of the United States. May they never be influenced by Despotic Council." At Evans' Tavern one man said, "George Washington. May he retain the Applause of a Free People." In the 1800 presidential election, Baltimore voted overwhelmingly for the victor Thomas Jefferson over Federalist John Adams.

Despite the widespread support of the national Jeffersonian party, Baltimoreans split on local issues, and the divisions tended to reflect people's economic status. The wealthy merchants fought to retain control against the opposition of those who wanted the power spread out among a wider range of citizens. The first big battle was fought over the issue of a charter of incorporation for Baltimore City.

Since the colonial period, Baltimore had been administered by commissioners appointed by the legislature. Residents could not elect local officials and had no legal control over them. During Baltimore's astonishingly rapid growth after the Revolution, when the town commissioners could not handle all the city's problems, special commissions and jobs proliferated. A commission on streets and bridges, a board of port wardens, and others shared the responsibility for running Baltimore. There was no central authority. Even such obvious undertakings as the building of a new market required a special act of the legislature. This system resulted in great inefficiencies.

In 1793, Baltimore's merchants began to work for a charter of incorporation which would allow the city to choose its own officials and set its own policies. The specific provisions would have consolidated power in the hands of the wealthy merchants. Under the proposed charter, citizens would vote only for a lower house of the city council. That group in turn would vote for an upper house, and the whole council would vote for mayor. This system of indirect elections was opposed by the artisans and shopkeepers who formed the majority in the Republican (Jeffersonian) Society, and by the Mechanics and Carpenters' Societies. Most of the working class residents of Fells Point also opposed the charter. They had the additional worry that one of the primary programs of the Baltimore merchants was the deepening of the harbor basin to allow big ships to dock there. Fells Point, with its deep harbor, had profited from the shallowness of the basin. Fells Point residents certainly did not want to be taxed to pay for the dredging of a competitive anchorage. All this opposition combined led the legislature to abandon the plan for several years.

The charter that was finally passed in 1796 was once again a product of the merchant aristocracy and served to centralize power in the hands of that group. Under the charter, Baltimore City was to be governed by a mayor and a two-house city council. The charter divided Baltimore into eight wards. Voters from each ward would vote annually for two members of the First Branch of the City Council. Every two years they would choose an elector. The board of eight electors would vote for mayor and the Second Branch of the City Council. (Direct election of the Second Branch began in 1808 and of the mayor in 1833.) Members of the First Branch had to be rated on the assessor's books at $1000 and members of the Second Branch at $2000. This system clearly concentrated power in the hands of the men of means.

Despite its undemocratic features, the charter increased enormously the efficiency in governing Baltimore by placing in local hands the authority over police powers, levying of taxes, surveying the city, locating and bounding streets, the preservation and deepening of the harbor (Fells Point residents were exempted from taxation for this purpose), and establishing

markets and fire companies. For the first time in Baltimore, a locally chosen central government would be able to control and coordinate all these municipal functions.

The city was divided into wards which gave the advantage to the neighborhoods around the basin where the wealthier men lived. The outlying wards took in both a larger area and more people. The results of the first elections held in 1797 gave the overwhelming majority of offices to merchants and upper class gentlemen. Baltimore's first mayor, James Calhoun, was president of the Chesapeake Insurance Company, an elder of the First Presbyterian Church, and son-in-law of William Gist. Most of the councilmen were men of means. Revolutionary War leaders were elected to other major offices as well. Colonel John Eager Howard and Charles Ridgely of Hampton were chosen to be state senators. Since Howard was appointed to the U. S. Senate, David McMechan succeeded him in Annapolis.

As this elite group solidified its power, the opposition in Baltimore joined with allies throughout the state and began to press for universal suffrage, by which they meant giving the vote to all white men, 21 years or older, regardless of the amount of property they owned. This continued struggle did not affect the Jeffersonian alliance of either group within the city. In fact, the Federalists' national policies served only to strengthen Republicanism in Baltimore. An unsatisfactory treaty with England negotiated by John Jay drew opposition from residents of all ports. The Alien and Sedition Acts evoked a strong negative reaction from Baltimore's large numbers of emigrants from Germany, France and the French West Indies. Baltimoreans of Irish and Scottish backgrounds disliked the strong pro-British position of the Federalists. So, despite the feuding, Baltimore remained Republican.

One key factor in the endurance of the Republican sway in Baltimore was the enormous personal popularity of some of the men who became the city's political leaders. Men acceptable to both factions moved into positions of power and maintained party unity. Foremost among these stood General Samuel Smith. A wealthy merchant who cultivated and won over artisans and workers, he also maintained a staunch following among members of the militia. A significant lieutenant of Smith's was Edward Johnson, son of a Baltimore physician, and owner of a brewery in Old Town. Although his assessed value was $2,088 in 1798, he lived near his brewery and enjoyed close relations with many people in Old Town and Fells Point. Other Jeffersonian party leaders resembled Johnson in that their financial worth was considerable but they came from outside the old merchant elite. Among these were: Robert Steuart, a stonecutter; Adam Fonerden, a manufacturer of wool and cotton and president of the Mechanical Company; Joseph Biays, a shipjoiner; and Cumberland Dugan, a ropemaker and tanner. The political coalition oversaw the continuing growth of Baltimore that took place during the late eighteenth and early nineteenth centuries. It also successfully led the defense of the city the only time it ever faced foreign attack, during the War of 1812.

The causes of the War of 1812 have been debated since it was fought. Opponents said that a war fever had caught hold of a group of young Congressmen who used the war as an excuse for territorial aggrandizement and their own political advancement. Supporters of the war claimed that we had to fight England in order to reaffirm our rights as a truly independent nation. Certainly, most of the conflict that led up to the fighting took place because of the British failure to recognize American rights as neutrals while they were engaged in warfare against Napoleon.

Far Left:
Edward Johnson, a close political ally of Samuel Smith and mayor during the War of 1812, held office when the city began to illuminate the streets by gas. During his administration the city acquired the fire plugs of the Baltimore Water Company

Left:
General Samuel Smith, a military leader in the Revolution, was responsible for the defense of Baltimore during the War of 1812. A leading Jacksonian, Smith combined his martial skills, his political powers, and his personal popularity in this successful effort

Above:
Water piped through fire plugs greatly increased the efficiency of fire fighters such as these. The volunteer companies did continue to operate independently and often in competition with one another

Right:
James Calhoun, a native of Carlyle, Pennsylvania, was one of Baltimore's leading merchants at the time of the Revolution. His wife, Ann Gist, came from an old Baltimore family. He was a member of the Sons of Liberty and the Committee of Observation and later a Deputy to the Commissary General of the Continental Army. When Calhoun first became mayor, funds to run the city had to be raised by lottery until taxes were due

Because of their war with France, the British tried to stop American ships and to impress into service in their navy sailors whom they claimed to be British subjects. More importantly, British and French efforts combined resulted in practical strangulation of American trade. American ships were seized by England if they sailed to the Continent without stopping in England first for inspection. They were seized by the French if they had any dealings with England, including stopping for inspection.

Discontent rose to war fever in June 1807, when the British ship, the *H. M. S. Leopard,* fired on the Baltimore-built sloop, the *Chesapeake,* whose captain had refused the British permission to board. The British, having gained entry by force, proceeded to impress four sailors. In Baltimore, local leaders formed a Committee of Correspondence headed by General Samuel Smith. War did not come then, however. President Thomas Jefferson, believing that the young nation was not strong enough to wage war against Britain, persuaded Congress in December 1807 to invoke an embargo on all trade. This had the effect of removing American ships from places where they could be shot at or boarded.

The Jeffersonian Embargo also inflicted huge damage on the American economy. Baltimore's exports sank from $7,601,300 in 1805 to $1,904,700 in 1808. Merchants tended to support the Embargo in hopes of gaining a permanent solution. Harder hit than the merchants, many of whom had substantial assets on which to fall back, were the farmers who had no market for their wheat. Even after the Embargo's repeal early in 1809, trade did not pick up to its former level.

The continuing conflict finally led to an American declaration of war against England on June 18, 1812. Ironically, the British government had repealed its orders in council on restrictions on neutral shipping two days before, but word of this had not yet reached the United States. By the time it did, the war had already begun. The war split the nation. Many Federalists continued to speak against the war down through its end in 1814.

In Baltimore, on June 20, 1812, Alexander Contee Hanson, editor of the Federalist newspaper, the *Federal Republican,* wrote a scathing article against the war: "Thou hast done a deed whereat valour will weep. Without funds, without taxes, without an army, navy or adequate fortifications — with one hundred and fifty millions of our property in the hands of the declared enemy, without any of his in our power, and with a vast commerce afloat, our rulers have promulgated a war against the clear and decided sentiment of a vast majority of the nation."

Two days later, a mob of 300 to 400 people armed with axes, hooks, ropes and other makeshift weapons gathered in front of the newspaper's offices at Gay and Second Streets. They threw the presses, type, and paper into the street and levelled the building. Hanson took refuge in the house of his partner, Jacob Wagner, on South Charles Street. On June 27 the *Federal Republican* reappeared with a lead editorial that condemned the police, the town, and the mayor, Republican Edward Johnson, for conspiring to destroy Federalism with means as violent as those of the French Revolution. The mob verified his charges by attacking the house on South Charles Street. The following morning, Mayor Johnson and General John Stricker prevailed upon Hanson and the other Federalists inside the house to accept safe conduct to the jail where they could be protected. That night, the mob attacked the jail, killed Revolutionary General James Lignan, set one man on fire, and cut in two the nose of another. This series of events earned for Baltimore the nickname of

Alexander Contee Hanson, editor of the Federal Republican, *whose offices were attacked by a mob because of his opposition to the War of 1812. After the incident, local fear of crowd violence was so great that the city elected this Federalist to Congress later that year*

Mobtown. Local reaction was so extreme that Federalist candidates won the elections in the fall of 1812, among them Alexander Contee Hanson who was sent to Congress. After this unhappy episode, Baltimore settled down to conduct its own wartime effort with great success and unanimity.

When war broke out, Baltimoreans were convinced that the city would be subject to British attack. Naval and commercial vessels as well as government stores and local warehouses all offered tempting prizes. Furthermore, Baltimore was a center of privateering. Before the war ended, Baltimore sent out over sixty privateers that captured over 475 prizes. Privateers were commissioned by the government to sail the seas and seize the property of the enemy. They were unpaid, but kept the valuable prizes they captured and thus aided the war effort and their own fortunes at the same time. Captains like Thomas Boyle, who commanded the "Comet" and then the "Chasseur," and Joshua Barney, who commanded the "Rossie," struck fear in the hearts of the Englishmen they encountered.

Baltimoreans knew their city would not be easy to defend. The unfortified shores of the Chesapeake Bay allowed attack from almost every direction. Fort McHenry lay in a state of severe decay, without sufficient manpower or weapons. The federal government, with its very limited resources, could not spare much aid for the Chesapeake region while the main battles were being fought along the northern frontier. Baltimore's fate thus rested in the hands of its own citizens.

The military commander put in charge of the forces around Baltimore was General Samuel Smith. A fortunate choice, Smith had good contacts in Washington and the loyal support of both the Maryland militia and Baltimore's citizenry. The General began by rebuilding Fort McHenry, placing it under the command of Major George Armistead, and installing sixty large cannon. He set up a system of lookouts near the tip of North Point and a string of guard boats between North Point and the city. He put the militiamen from Baltimore City and County through rigorous training that made the citizen-soldiers ready for battle.

All these achievements were possible only because Baltimore gave Smith strong and unified support. A Committee of Public Safety appointed by Smith's old political ally Mayor Edward Johnson included Smith's business partner James A. Buchanan, and merchants William Patterson and Samuel Sterett. This committee provided the financial support which allowed the arming of all the local troops.

As the Napoleonic wars ended in Europe, large numbers of British troops were sent to the United States and the pace of the fighting increased. In August 1814 Vice-Admiral Sir Alexander Cochrane trapped Commodore Joshua Barney's flotilla in the Chesapeake and forced him to burn his gunboats to prevent their capture. Major General Robert Ross smashed the American militia at Bladensburg and moved on to Washington where he proceeded to burn most of the public buildings and the naval yard.

At this same time in Baltimore, an elective Committee of Vigilance and Safety took over the operations of the Committee of Public Safety. Although its members still came from the merchant class, it enjoyed a broad popular constituency and loyally supported General Smith.

While the British paused in the Patuxent River, Smith secured the harbor and then turned his energies to land defenses. The General requested the Committee of Vigilance and Safety to mobilize work brigades. On August 27 all free blacks and whites exempt from military service were ordered to report to Hampstead

Left:
Francis Scott Key wrote the words to "The Star Spangled Banner," while aboard a British ship where he and Lieutenant Frederick Skinner had been sent to arrange the release of Dr. William Beanes, a prisoner. During the first day they could observe the battle, but when night fell they could only hope the Americans were holding out. As dawn came, they saw the flag still flying over the fort
Below:
This 1821 version of the sheet music was one of many of the popular "Star Spangled Banner."

Hill (now the site of Patterson Park). Slaves also helped build the defenses. Smith asked the Committee of Vigilance and Safety to borrow $100,000 from the city's banks to buy arms and supplies. The money, raised from banks and private lenders as well, was collected within two days.

By September 10, the defenses stretched from Fells Point across to the flat lands north of the city's eastern hills. Troops numbering 15,000 waited for the attack. General Smith ordered General John Stricker and his crack third brigade to the western end of Patapsco Neck. Early on Monday, September 12, when Stricker learned that British troops were landing, he placed his troops on the narrow strip of land between Back River and Bear Creek and sent riflemen ahead to harass the British. Two of these men, generally acknowledged to be Daniel Wells and Henry McComas, shot and killed the British General Ross. That evening, after holding the British back for many hours, Stricker led his men back to Hampstead Hill.

On Tuesday morning, September 13, the British began their bombardment of Fort McHenry, and the troops that had come ashore at North Point began to march towards the fortifications on Hampstead Hill. They tried to go around the American left flank, but the defense there held. Smith then ordered a rearrangement of the American troops that would enable them to stop any direct attack on Hampstead Hill with a cross fire. The British saw this maneuver and retreated when night provided a cover. While the British troops were withdrawing from North Point, the American soldiers at Fort McHenry and other locations in the harbor repulsed the British effort there. Before British General Cochrane left the area, he released some American civilians, among them Francis Scott Key who had watched the battle at Fort McHenry and written the words to "The Star-Spangled Banner."

Shortly after the Battle of Baltimore and another American victory at Plattsburg, the British gave up demands for territorial concessions from the United States. Finally, both sides perceived that the underlying cause of the war, the war between Britain and France, had disappeared with the defeat of Napoleon, and a peace treaty was signed.

Baltimore from the end of the Revolution through 1814 experienced two major victories. One was its military triumph at the end of the War of 1812. The other was its ascendancy as a major port. The town's population and economy boomed during the turn of the century decades, placing Baltimore in the ranks of the largest and most prosperous of American cities.

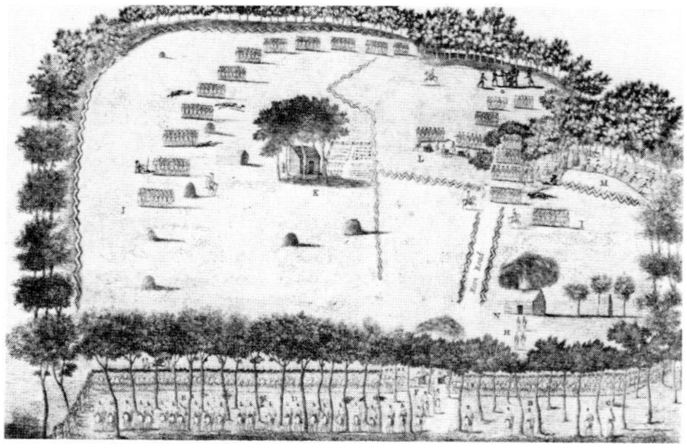

Left:
On September 12, General Samuel Smith ordered General John Stricker and his crack third brigade to the narrow western end of Patapsco Neck, where the Americans held the British back for many hours. The action is capsuled in this picture. Note the portrayal of the death of General Ross in the upper right corner

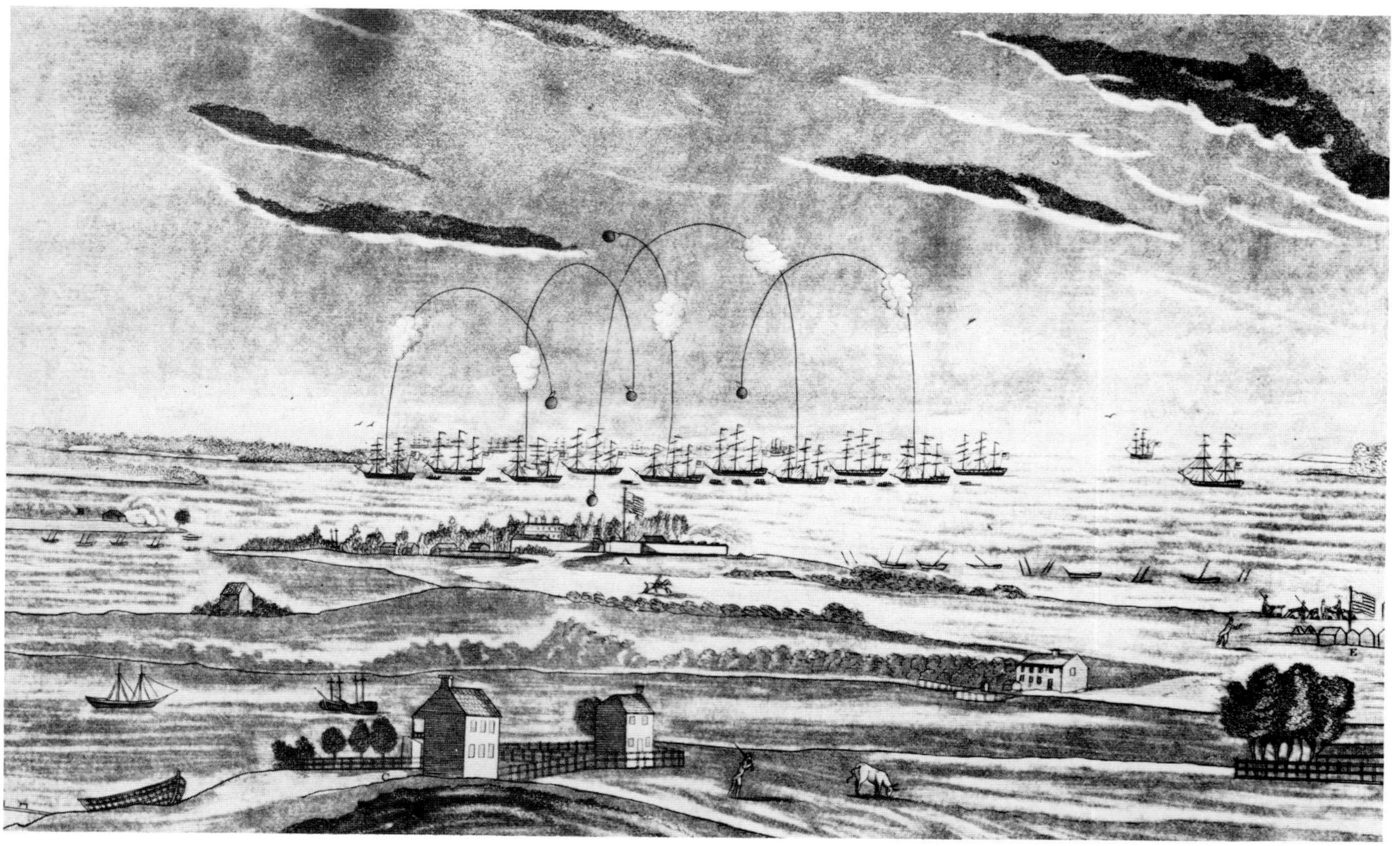

Above:
This view from the observatory on Federal Hill, September 13, 1814, shows the British fleet bombarding Fort McHenry during that morning

Left:
The death on September 12, 1814 of British General Robert Ross at the hands of Baltimore soldiers, generally acknowledged to be Henry McComas and Daniel Wells, was a severe blow to the British troops who had landed at North Point

The battle monument, designed by Maximilian Godefroy, was erected in 1814-1815 to commemorate the defense of Baltimore. It was unusual in that it honored all who gave their lives, regardless of rank. This drawing was made by William Goodacre, Jr., around 1825, when Monument Square was already a prestigious residential area

A City Divided

1814-1865

III

In Baltimore, a brief but marvelous boom followed the conclusion of the War of 1812. Peace brought prosperity and growth to the port city on the Chesapeake. The fast clipper ships returned to peacetime trade. Steam-powered industries, which had begun to develop before the war, expanded swiftly. Demand for labor drew immigrants from other American cities and from Europe. New buildings rose up. Streets were extended into former countryside. Soon the city added thirteen square miles of territory from surrounding county lands. Institutional growth accompanied the enormous population increase, although not always rapidly enough to meet the needs of all Baltimore's citizens.

Then in 1819, boom gave way to bust. Economic uncertainty hastened a transformation that was already underway locally and throughout the United States. New groups began to demand power in an increasingly factionalized society. The growth and change occurred so rapidly and the dislocations were so pronounced that confusion and conflict often resulted. All this was evident in the life of the city during the decades that followed the War of 1812.

The single fact that stands out above all others is population growth. In 1810, 35,583 people lived in Baltimore. By 1820, newcomers from other cities and from Europe made that number grow to 62,738, by 1840 to 102,054 and by 1860 to 212,418. They met the labor need of the new industries.

People immigrated from American cities further north and from Europe. Increasing numbers of free blacks became industrial workers. Roads, canals and railroads connecting Baltimore with points west, south and north employed thousands of other workers. And all of these people provided an additional market for goods and services. New housing was constructed. Roads were extended into new areas. Master craftsmen and their journeymen produced consumer goods in such volume that they soon hired more helpers and began to call themselves manufacturers.

Baltimore's population quickly spilled over the city limits and by 1818 approximately twelve thousand people lived in the precincts of Baltimore County contiguous to the city. These "precincters" enjoyed the benefits of proximity to the city and its facilities without having to pay the considerably higher urban taxes. City officials wanted to bring these people and their tax resources under Baltimore's jurisdiction. Discussions of the question centered around coordinated planning as well as tax revenues. Many of the precincters preferred the low level of services in the county to the higher taxes of the city.

Although the precincters' protests stalled the process for several years, the state legislature in 1818 passed an annexation bill, adding thirteen square miles of county land to Baltimore City. The final decision was a political one. A Federalist-controlled legislature took the Republican precincters out of the county in the hope that Federalists would then dominate there and added them to the already heavily Republican city without changing its representation in Annapolis. The city sent two delegates and each county sent four to the state legislature. There city Republicans attempted to gain two additional delegates, but that amendment failed to pass the Federalist legislature. So, in 1818, the city gained thirteen square miles, twelve thousand people and the benefit of their taxes, but had proportionally lower representation in the House of Delegates.

Many newcomers worked in manufacturing establishments that proliferated with the introduction of steam power for production and processing. Textile manufacturers pioneered

the use of steam power before the War of 1812. Many of the textile factories were located outside the city. The owners generally provided living accommodations and sometimes garden plots for their workers. Early operations remained relatively small. In 1814, for example, Robert and Alexander McKim opened the Baltimore Steam Works Factory within the city limits. By 1820 they employed seven men, twelve women, and fifty girls aged eight to thirteen. In 1829 Charles Crook, Jr. opened the Baltimore City Cotton Factory with 200 employees. A few master weavers organized a cottage industry that employed men and women working at home. By 1829, over 100 master weavers engaged in this hiring procedure.

Other industries also converted to steam. Charles Gwinn opened the first steam powered flour mill directly on the wharves in 1813. Flour milling expanded rapidly after that. Baltimore exported wheat and flour in increasing quantities to South America and elsewhere. Coffee, sugar and copper came into the port. Several Baltimoreans opened sugar and copper refineries. Industrialization increased the demand for iron ore and coal. Baltimore imported these from western Maryland and the Susquehanna Valley.

Population growth necessitated the increase of various services of the city. In the early 19th century, many services and utilities represented a cooperative effort between private individuals and the city government. For example, fire protection was provided by the volunteer companies until the 1850s, but they were regulated by city ordinance. The Baltimore Water Company, incorporated in 1805 to increase the supply of water in the city, was formed by a group of investors including James Buchanan, Jonathan Ellicott, Solomon Etting, John Hollings, John McKim, and James Mosher. Although it was a private enterprise, the company was granted free use of Baltimore's streets and city protection for its property and facilities.

Baltimore pioneered in the field of street lighting when the City Council in 1816 authorized the establishment of the Baltimore Gas Light Company and contracted with its board of directors to install and maintain a system of street lights throughout the city. Although the network was not completed for many decades, Baltimore was the first American city to illuminate its streets with hydrogen gas instead of oil. Rembrandt Peale had introduced gas lighting to the city when he installed a system in his museum earlier in 1816. It created a sensation at the time. An account in the *Federal Gazette and Daily Advertiser* written by its editor William Gwynn publicized the experiment: "Yesterday evening, for the first time, the citizens who attended at Baltimore Museum were gratified by seeing one of the Rooms lighted by means of Carburetted Hydrogen Gas. The effect produced by the beautiful and most brilliant light far exceeds the most sanguine expectations of those who had not before witnessed an illumination by similar means." Soon Gwynn joined with Peale to persuade merchant William Lorman, who served as the company's first president, architect Robert Cary Long, and banker James Mosher to form the Baltimore Gas Light Company. On February 7, 1817, the first street lamp was lighted at the corner of Baltimore and Holliday Streets.

Other municipal services besides utilities expanded as the population did. One of the most difficult tasks facing the city was poor relief. The rapid economic changes and large numbers of newcomers strained an already difficult situation to the point where, in 1818, Baltimore created a poor relief board known as the Managers of the Poor. The mayor appointed one board member from each ward. These members

This view of Baltimore from Federal Hill, painted in 1831 by William J. Bennett, shows the active port that was crucial for the city's existence, and the rural rolling hills that surrounded the central business and residential area

had the authority to determine who needed aid from their own ward and to commit the indigent sick and crippled to the almshouse. The almshouse was administered by another group of appointees called the Trustees of the Poor. Public help never sufficed, and much of the burden fell on private charities, religious institutions, ethnic organizations, and individuals. The depression which began in 1819 worsened the situation even further.

In 1819 the nation's economy lurched into a decline that startled many because it followed what had seemed like strong prosperity. Actually, over-expansion, speculation, and mismanagement of funds by officials of the Second Bank of the United States were the roots of the disaster. In those days of convertible paper money, the U. S. Bank tried to improve its own condition by calling in gold and silver specie from state banks. This led to a severe shortage of specie in Baltimore as well as throughout the nation. The local situation was complicated by the fact that many bank officials had used the institution's funds for private speculative ventures. When the crash came, many businessmen faced financial hardship or failure. They included many of the city's leading merchants like politician and general Samuel Smith, former mayor James Calhoun, and James A. Buchanan who was president of the Baltimore branch of the national bank. Because many of these same businessmen were implicated in the scandals they faced both bankruptcy and the loss of the dominant position in politics that they had enjoyed for so long.

Baltimore also suffered stagnation in its maritime trade. Investment capital, always comparatively scarce in Baltimore, was even harder to come by during the depressed 1820s. Furthermore, men who possessed cash turned to industrial investments. These included former merchants as well as those with new fortunes made during the War of 1812. Buyers in the back country, who were also hit by the depression, began buying in New York City which could sell imported goods at lower prices because it lay closer to the British port of Liverpool. The port of New York grew at the expense of Baltimore. The worst blow came in 1825 when the opening of the Erie Canal gave New York City direct access to an enormous hinterland. After that, New York's volume of trade increased to a point where neither Baltimore nor Philadelphia could ever catch up again.

Such economic reverses meant hard times for Baltimore's workers. The lot of the nineteenth century laboring man was not a particularly enviable one. He commonly worked six days a week, fourteen hours a day during the summer and sixteen during the winter. Wages ranged between $1 and $2 a day. An unskilled laborer did well to bring home $1 per day.

Desperate for work, new immigrants often accepted even less. Construction and some other jobs were seasonal, with the result that the majority of unskilled workers could not earn more than $200 in a year. November through February marked the low point in employment and the peak of reliance on charity for food, clothing and wood. This scarcity of jobs and low wage scale sometimes led to bitter competition among native whites, the growing number of free black workers and immigrants. Everyone felt the tensions.

These strains were visibly reflected in politics, where change and redefinition marked the decades of the 1820s and 1830s. In Baltimore and the nation new leaders pushed innovations. Andrew Jackson's election to the presidency in 1828 was hailed by his supporters as a victory for the common man. Actually, the election signaled changes that had already begun throughout the country. More democratic suffrage requirements, officeholding by men

Left:
The only surviving volunteer company firehouse, that of the Independent Fire Company built in 1819, stands at the corner of Gay and Ensor Streets in Old Town. The Venetian-Gothic bell tower was added in 1853.

Below:
Volunteer companies provided the city's fire protection until 1858, when the municipal fire department was organized. Here a company is shown fighting the burning of the Front Street Theatre in 1838

Left:
After the depression of 1819, the city, needing a larger almshouse, purchased "Calverton," which was located on Franklintown Road near Edmondson Avenue. The two wings were added before this engraving was made in 1824 by Joseph Cone

from groups other than the old elite, and the growth of institutional services that benefitted ordinary people were taking place in Baltimore and elsewhere as part of a gradual change rather than a sudden revolution.

In Baltimore, the old political elite group dominated by General Samuel Smith had drawn its leadership largely from the mercantile class. The mayors who held office from 1808 to 1820, Edward Johnson and George Stiles, came from this faction. In 1818 a new suffrage law increased the eligible voters from all property-holding white males to all taxpaying white males. In 1819 the financial panic and the closing of many Baltimore banks resulted in a decline in popularity of many of the politically active men who were thought to be involved in irresponsible financial dealings. In 1820 John Montgomery, leader of a new rival faction, defeated Edward Johnson's try for reelection.

Montgomery had come to Baltimore by way of Pennsylvania and Harford County, from which he had served as a Republican Congressman from 1807 to 1811. His subsequent tenure as Attorney General of Maryland and Delegate from Baltimore City gave him broad publicity. The appeal of his statewide connections, which led voters to hope he could effect economic improvement, and the disrepute of the old political leadership contributed to his victory. Much of his support came from Ward 4 where many of the textile workers lived and from the rapidly growing southern and western sides of the city where trade provided new jobs and led to the growth of new industries using raw materials from the hinterland.

In 1822, Edward Johnson recaptured the mayoralty. The bulk of his support came from the older established business area just north of the harbor basin and from the part of the city east of the Jones Falls which drew much of its income from maritime trade. But his return was brief.

John Montgomery recaptured the mayor's office in 1824. In this same year John Quincy Adams, representing the National Republican faction, defeated Democratic-Republican Andrew Jackson's first try for the presidency. Despite Sam Smith's alliance with Jackson on a national level, many of the new voters in Baltimore gave their support to Montgomery or to a third candidate for mayor, Jacob Small. The latter was a carpenter and building contractor who opposed the property taxes which were particularly hard on small property owners like tradesmen, craftmen and journeymen. Although the small property owners supported Jacob Small, the victory went to Montgomery.

Recognizing the growing need for urban services and the increasing voting power of the mass of ordinary people, Montgomery inaugurated a program of deficit spending to pay for all the new undertakings. Montgomery's administration pushed authorization of a new public school system for the City of Baltimore by the state legislature in 1826.

One of the major reforms of the Jacksonian era, public education was developed in many cities during this period. Democrats believed that all people should have access to an education. Elitists believed that public school systems should be established to teach the proper values to pupils who might otherwise fall prey to demogogic rhetoric. In 1827 the City Council approved Baltimore's public school system. Two years later, four small elementary schools began holding classes in houses rented by the city for use until proper schools could be constructed. The eastern and western sections of town each received one male school and one female school. Only white children could attend. In 1830, 3 percent of all white school-aged children took advantage of the new system. By 1840 a high school, the original

Above Left:
John Montgomery, a Jeffersonian Republican first elected mayor in 1820, won support from the city's new industrial neighborhoods. During his tenure, legislation to establish the public school system was initiated

Left:
Isaac McKim, son of "Quaker John" McKim, who endowed the free school for poor children, was a successful shipping merchant and aide-de-camp to General Samuel Smith during the War of 1812. He was active in the Protective Society of Maryland, a merchant group organized to aid free blacks

Above Right:
Jacob Small, a carpenter and builder, gained the support of the city's mechanics and small property owners with his opposition to property taxes and became mayor in 1826. Under his administration, Peale's Museum was acquired and used as the City Hall

A City Divided
1814-1865

Baltimore City College, had extended the education available. In that year, 7 percent of all eligible children attended. High schools for female students opened in the eastern and western section of the city in 1844 and 1845. A "Floating School" on a large sailing ship was added to the public school system in 1857.

Schools, students and teachers in the system increased gradually until 1860 when 23 percent of those eligible (over 14,000) were taught by more than 300 teachers. Education was available but not compulsory. Children whose families needed income from their work generally could not take advantage of the new public schools. Most students came from middle-class families.

Democratic forces in Baltimore made themselves felt not only in programs like the school system but increasingly at the ballot box as well. In the mayoralty elections held in October 1826, the Smith group joined with the middle class property owners and mechanics in support of their candidate, Jacob Small. The combination succeeded and the electors, chosen for that purpose, made Small mayor of Baltimore.

In 1827, Samuel Smith organized a group of Baltimoreans to work in Andrew Jackson's 1828 presidential campaign. The Smith Jacksonians and Small's faction split before the Baltimore mayoral election of 1828. For that campaign, Jacob Small realigned himself with Montgomery's faction and gained much of the Irish Catholic and German vote which he used against the Scotch-Irish Presbyterian and Quaker supporters of the Smith faction. Small won reelection in 1830.

By 1831 taxes had risen so high that a group of 85 large property owners persuaded the legislature to limit Baltimore's taxing power. Small resigned and was succeeded by William Steuart, a stone cutter and builder.

Samuel Smith, throughout this period, had retained his seat in the United States Senate and his powerful position as chairman of the Senate Finance Committee. Chief dispenser of federal patronage in Maryland, Smith arranged the appointment of James H. McCulloh as Collector of the Port of Baltimore, the most remunerative federal office in Maryland, and multitudes of lesser officials. Locally, the Smith faction gained by shifting its emphasis away from the ethnic considerations that Small and Steuart had been stressing. In 1832 Jesse Hunt, the Smith candidate for mayor, successfully used economic issues and identified himself with the city's working men. By that time, Smith had introduced the Jacksonian style political machine which required party fidelity in both national and local elections in exchange for patronage and other benefits of power. The tactics succeeded and Jesse Hunt became mayor. The Jacksonian party reigned in Baltimore.

Despite the political confusion, the final years of the 1820s saw the success of several major pioneering economic ventures in Baltimore. The Canton Company, probably the first planned industrial and residential community in the nation, was chartered in 1828. Columbus O'Donnell, son of the sea captain who had brought the first cargo from China and owner of three miles of waterfront land directly east of Fells Point, joined with William Patterson, William Gwynn and other local investors to develop the new community. The charter gave the corporation the right to improve land belonging to the company "by laying out streets, etc., in the vicinity of Baltimore, on or near navigable water, and erecting and constructing wharves, slips, workshops, factories, stores, dwellings, and such other buildings and improvements as may be deemed necessary, ornamental and convenient." O'Donnell and Patterson were instrumental in bringing Peter

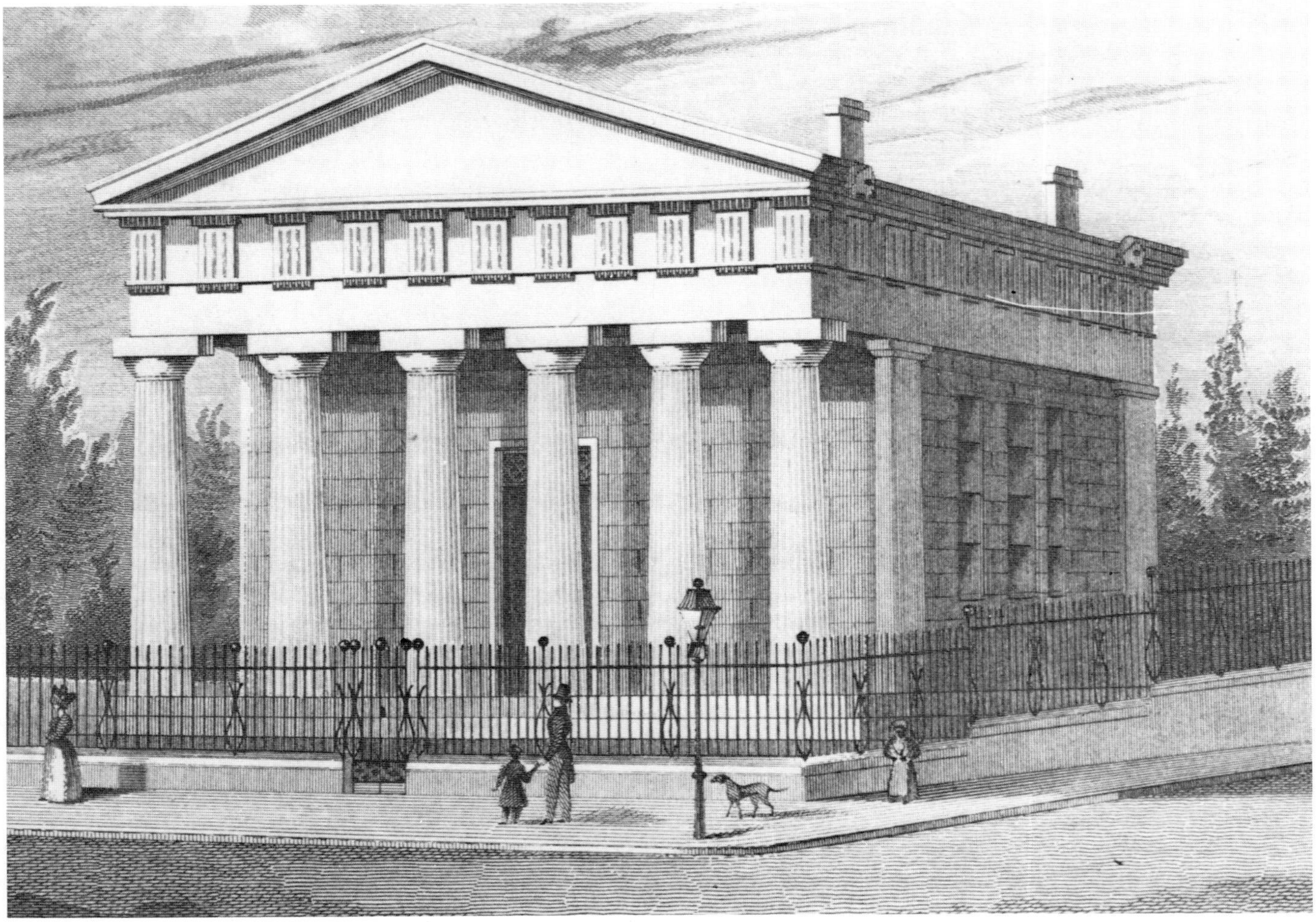

To help make up for the city's lack of a public school system before 1829, Isaac McKim donated funds from his father's estate for a free school that was built in 1822. The building is still standing at Baltimore and Aisquith Streets

Cooper from New York to Baltimore to invest in this endeavor. He established an ironworks at the foot of Clinton Street.

An even more important event of 1828 was the laying of the first stone of the Baltimore and Ohio Railroad. Baltimore businessmen viewed with alarm the advantage that the Erie Canal gave New York. Instead of trying to duplicate that, the Baltimoreans were willing to risk building the first commercial railroad and hope for its success. In February 1827 a group of twenty-five merchants and other civic leaders met at George Brown's house and determined to build a two-track railroad from Baltimore all the way to the Ohio River. This would yield large amounts of trade between Baltimore and points west.

The planners agreed to raise money by the sale of stock. Although the city bought some stock, control of the B&O remained in private hands. Directors included: Philip Evans Thomas, president; George Brown, treasurer; his father, investment banker Alexander Brown; Charles Carroll of Carrollton; William Patterson; Robert Oliver; future Jacksonian Congressman Isaac McKim; William Lorman; Solomon Etting; and future mayor William Steuart.

On July 4, 1828, Charles Carroll of Carrollton, by then a national hero as the last surviving signer of the Declaration of Independence, turned over the first spadeful of earth for the laying of the first stone. On May 24, 1830 the B&O began regular service between Baltimore City and Ellicott's Mills, 26 miles away. Passenger fare was $.75 per ride.

Peter Cooper believed that the success of the Canton Company depended on the B&O Railroad. When the B&O directors said that they thought a steam engine could not manage the curves on the tracks, Cooper set out to disprove them. Working with scrap iron and borrowed wheels, and using gun barrels as boiler tubes, he built the *Tom Thumb,* the first successful steam locomotive. During the summer of 1830, Cooper took the directors of the B&O on a 13 mile run in the unbelievably fast time of 57 minutes. Shortly thereafter, the famous grey horse beat the *Tom Thumb* in a race of one or two miles along tracks just west of Baltimore, but only because the engine's fan belt slipped. Convinced by the *Tom Thumb's* performance, the B&O directors announced in January 1831 a contest offering $4,000 for the best engine. The *York,* built by Davis and Gartner, won. It burned anthracite coal and carried 15 tons at 15 miles per hour.

The steam engine succeeded and the B&O boosted Baltimore's economy and prestige. Tracks reached Frederick by 1831, Harper's Ferry by 1834, Cumberland by 1842, and finally Wheeling on the Ohio River in 1853. Benjamin Latrobe, chief engineer of the B&O, personally explored the route through the Appalachian Mountains. He built the Thomas Viaduct at Relay which still supports trains.

But even the success of the B&O could not solve Baltimore's economic problems. The cycles of apparent prosperity were actually inflation, and financial panics and depression continued. National banking policy still produced local havoc. President Andrew Jackson believed that the Bank of the United States had too much power and he was determined to destroy it. In 1833 he withdrew the government's deposits from that bank and put them in favored state banks around the country. The fallout from the destruction of the national bank included many local bank failures, a scarcity of money and widespread unemployment.

The Bank of Maryland collapsed in March 1834, and failures of numerous smaller banks and savings institutions followed. In April, Baltimore lawyer and former Jackson supporter Reverdy Johnson became chairman of the Whig Party,

Many of Baltimore's leading merchants and bankers participated in the founding of the B&O. (From left to right) Alexander Brown, his son George Brown, Solomon Etting, and Philip E. Thomas, the railroad's first president, were among them

Baltimoreans pioneered in the building of the first major American railroad, the Baltimore and Ohio. In 1827 a group of local merchants and civic leaders met at George Brown's house and made the decision to build the two-track railroad from Baltimore to the Ohio River

newly organized in Maryland to protect Jackson's economic policies. Johnson served on the board of directors of the Bank of Maryland.

Another group protested economic losses in a somewhat different fashion. Many small depositors found that their savings had disappeared during the bank failures. By February 1835, their protests had become violent. Fires were set at the Athenaeum and the Maryland Academy of Fine Arts. In April, mobs attacked the houses of trustees in whose hands the affairs of the Bank of Maryland had been placed. Reverdy Johnson's house on Monument Square was a primary target of the mob. On the first night, a small group broke a few windows. On the second night, a larger crowd came but dispersed after a speech by Mayor Jesse Hunt. The following night the crowd attacked with bats and stones the armed guards stationed around the house. Then they moved on to John Glenn's house, where they gained access, and proceeded to break up all the furniture and woodwork. The next night, they succeeded in bypassing the guards at Reverdy Johnson's house. They made a bonfire in the street of his furniture and his extensive law library. They raided the wine cellars of Johnson, Glenn, and others, and hawked fine wines at low prices to all takers. Eighty-three year old General Samuel Smith was asked to take charge and called for an assemblage of armed citizens. The fire companies joined the effort. Mayor Jesse Hunt resigned. Guards took up stations throughout the city and finally order was restored. In a special election, Samuel Smith became mayor, a post to which he was reelected in 1836. The voters turned once again to the hero of the Battle of Baltimore of 1814 because they could find no one else to bring peace.

Violence was not limited to isolated riots. Turbulence frequently accompanied labor protests that punctuated the 1830s. Many of the worst incidents occurred during protests by railroad workers. In 1829, riots among B&O workers left one man dead and several wounded. Two years later, a contractor building one section of the B&O absconded, leaving his workers unpaid. Two or three hundred workers attacked the rails and other company property with pick-axes, hammers, and sledges. Instead of winning their wages, many were arrested. In 1834 a group of B&O railroad workers attacked a contractor and several of his assistants. After they killed three of them, the militia moved in and arrested 300 workers. Frequently the workers involved in incidents like these were immigrants whom employers paid the lowest possible wages. They were so desperate for work and for income that they were forced to accept pay far below what native Americans considered enough to live on. Any delay in wages generally meant no food for the workers' families.

Low pay and the insecurity of the job market led to bitter competition among individual workers and between native white Americans, immigrants and black workers, both slave and free. Employers often replaced native workers with the more easily exploitable immigrants. Resentments grew stronger when employment was scarce. Some white workers, both native and foreign-born, wanted the best positions reserved for them with black labor excluded.

Frederick Douglass, later a leading abolitionist, worked as a ship's carpenter in Baltimore. A slave, he was hired out to the owner of the shipyard, a Mr. Gardner. In his autobiography, he described an incident that happened to him as labor competition grew bitter:

> Until a very little while after I went there, white and black ship-carpenters worked side by side and no one seemed to see any impropriety in it. All hands seemed to be very well satisfied. Many of the black carpenters were freemen.

Many industries, like the Avalon Nail and Iron Works shown here, were built along the Baltimore and Ohio tracks west of Baltimore. Homes along the road on the right housed two families

> Things seemed to be going on very well. All at once, the white carpenters knocked off, and said they would not work with free colored workmen. Their reason for this, as alleged, was, that if free colored carpenters were encouraged, they would soon take the trade into their own hands, and poor white men would be thrown out of employment . . . My fellow-apprentices soon began to feel it degrading to them to work with me . . . They commenced making my condition as hard as they could . . . They at length combined, and came upon me, armed with sticks, stones, and heavy handspikes . . . the one behind ran up with the handspike, and struck me a heavy blow upon the head. It stunned me. I fell, and with this they all fell to beating me.

After receiving more blows, Frederick Douglass managed to escape to his home. His master took him to see a lawyer to inquire what could be done about the incident. The lawyer replied that no recourse could be had unless a white man would testify. No black man's testimony was acceptable in court. No white man would dare testify against another white on behalf of a black man. So the case was dropped.

In light of the riots, labor violence, and individual attacks, Hezekiah Niles' comment in his nationally famous *Register* of September 5, 1835 is not surprising: "*Society seems everywhere unhinged,* and the demon of blood and slaughter has been let loose upon us!" All the conflict and danger led many to seek safety and protection within a limited, identifiable community.

Factionalization of society as a whole led to a greater cohesion within various groups themselves. Ethnic communities particularly developed a wide range of supportive and social organizations. The city's largest pre-Civil War ethnic groups, the German (including German Jews), the Irish, and blacks (both free and slave), all experienced a growth of institutions within their own community and a consciousness of group identity.

Germans had been coming into Baltimore since long before the Revolution. The descendants of some of those early immigrants held positions of political, social and economic leadership after the War of 1812. Mayor Jacob Small and a Jacksonian leader of the 1830s, William Frick, were of German descent as was a hero of 1814, General John Stricker. Their identity as individuals and as Baltimoreans far outweighed their German background in people's minds. The old German community had integrated into the mainstream of the city's life. But the arrival of many new immigrants, especially during the 1840s and 1850s, revitalized a sense of community among the Germans. Churches served as focal points for the city's ethnic communities. The German churches reflected the Americanization process in their addition of the English language. At the Reformed Church, in the midst of a public controversy, Dr. Michael Diffenderffer and thirty-five other members petitioned to have the sermon preached in English every Sunday afternoon. The Rev. Lewis Mayer delivered the first English sermon in September, 1818. The system of dual services continued until 1827 when the congregation dropped German altogether. Not until 1845 was another German Reformed church founded because a new wave of immigrants preferred services in their native tongue. The Zion Lutheran Church, which held German services, remained the only church of that denomination until the first English-speaking Lutheran congregation was formed in 1823. They worshipped in a schoolhouse on south Howard Street until 1826 when their

Above:
Frederick Douglass, an editor of the abolitionist newspaper North Star, *lived seven years of his childhood, from 1825-1832, on Aliceanna Street in Fells Point. He returned later, still a slave, to work in a local shipyard, but in 1838 escaped, riding the train north to find freedom in New York. After the Civil War, Douglass worked for civil rights and for women's rights and held several important federal and diplomatic posts.*

Right:
Reverdy Johnson, a lawyer and former supporter of Andrew Jackson, organized the Whig Party in Maryland to protest the president's economic policies

church was built.

Four additional English Lutheran congregations were formed in Baltimore before the Civil War. Non-Germans began joining these very Americanized churches. The Roman Catholic Church had always resisted attempts to establish a separate German-speaking congregation. The large immigration of the mid-nineteenth century included Redemptorist priests who worked in the German Catholic community. With some help from missionary societies in Germany, Austria, and France (King Ludwig I of Bavaria is said to have contributed $4000), the congregation built St. Alphonsus Church at Park Avenue and Saratoga Street. St. James at Aisquith and Eager Streets, formerly an Irish parish, became German. Before the Civil War, two more churches were opened to serve Baltimore's six thousand German Catholics.

All the German churches had schools. In the Catholic schools, many of the teachers were members of religious orders: Redemptorists, Christian Brothers, or Sisters of Notre Dame. The Zion Lutheran Church school, in existence since 1769, experienced a major revival from the efforts of liberal Pastor Heinrich Scheib. When Scheib came to Zion in 1835, he found the school in such a state of deterioration that determined to establish a new German-English school. It opened in 1836 with 71 pupils. A secular school, only loosely affiliated with the church, the Scheib School attracted students of varied backgrounds. Just before the Civil War, over 400 pupils attended grades kindergarten through seven. The school lasted for sixty years. The St. Johannes German Reformed congregation brought several famous teachers to its school, among them Valentin Scheer and Friedrich Knapp.

Friedrich Knapp, one of the participants in the liberal revolution which failed in 1848 in Germany, arrived in Baltimore in 1850 and found employment as a tutor and bookkeeper in the house of William A. Marburg. In 1851 he became principal of the school at St. Johannes Church. Then in 1853 he opened his own school, known as Knapp's Institute, which grew in reputation so much that by the time of the Civil War over 700 pupils were enrolled. Knapp's Institute survived long enough for H. L. Mencken to attend during the 1880s. Mencken's description of Knapp survives in an essay entitled "Caves of Learning." Mencken wrote of his principal:

> He was a Suabian who had come to Baltimore in 1850, and he still wore, nearly forty years afterward, the classical uniform of a German schoolmaster — a long-tailed coat of black alpaca, a boiled shirt with somewhat fringey cuffs, and a white lawn necktie. The front of his coat was dusty with chalk, and his hands were so caked with it that he had to blow it off every time he took snuff. He was of small stature but large diameter, and wore closely-clipped mutton-chop whiskers. His hands had the curious softness so often observed in pedagogues, barbers, and Y.M.C.A. secretaries. This impressed itself on me the first time he noticed me wiggling a loose milk-tooth with my tongue, and called me up to have it out. He watched for such manifestations sharply, and pulled, I should say, an average of six teeth a week. It was etiquette in the school for boys to bear this barbarity in silence. The girls could yell, but not the boys. Both, however, were free to howl under the bastinado, which was naturally applied to the girls much more lightly and less often than to the boys.

Gradually the German church and private schools died out, but not until the end of the 19th century when they lost a large share of their

Pastor Heinrich Scheib of the Zion Lutheran Church founded a school that lasted for sixty years

pupils to the German-English public schools that opened in 1879.

The immigration of the first half of the 19th century enlarged the German population so greatly that by 1860 roughly one-fourth of Baltimore's population claimed German descent. Although a clear differentiation between the old wealthy merchants and the new immigrants existed, the older group banded together to aid the newcomers, especially those in greatest need. The German Society, founded in 1783, was reorganized in 1817 in response to the terrible conditions aboard the ship *Juffrow Johanna* which carried 300 immigrant redemptionists. The latter were people whose labor for a specified number of years would be sold by the agent in exchange for their passage. The cold and hunger that the group suffered were so severe that General John Stricker led a movement to find a means to regulate the redemption system. Lawyers William Frick, David Hoffman and Charles Mayer joined him as did many merchants including Lewis Brantz, Benjamin Cohen, Jacob Cohen, Michael Diffenderffer, Jesse Eichelberger, Samuel Etting, Philip Sadtler and Lawrence Thomson. They chose Christian Mayer president of the German Society, which was now reconstituted specifically for the purpose of "the protection and assistance of poor emigrants from Germany and Switzerland and of their descendents."

Led by such prosperous and influential men, the German Society secured rapid gains. In 1818 they won legislation regulating the redemption system for German and Swiss workers. Under the new law, no immigrant was to serve longer than four years; those under 21 had to attend school at least two months a year; and no one could be held on board ship longer than 30 days. The German Society took cases of mistreatment of redemptioners to court. Their charitable work was so extensive that an 1832 law granted a portion of the $1.50 head tax collected for each immigrant to the Society for such purposes.

A law of 1841 required that a German interpreter be available in all Baltimore courts. In 1845 the German Society established the so-called "Intelligence Bureau," really a free employment agency for German immigrants. In 1846 the bureau located positions for 3500 applicants.

The huge immigration of the 1840s led to the establishment of a wide variety of clubs. The Germania Club, a literary and social club, had the most elite membership. Another club, the Concordia, became famous for its musical and dramatic presentations as well as its lectures and social gatherings. Singing clubs included Liederkranz, Harmonie, Arion, and the Germania Mannerchor. In 1849 a *Sozialdemokratische Turnverein* opened in Baltimore. It combined gymnastic activities with lectures on political and literary topics. The membership tended to be working-class and freethinkers. They frequently met opposition from the German clergy, except for the liberal Pastor Scheib of the Zion Church.

The German community supported numerous newspapers, including several that survived into the Twentieth century. *Der Deutsche Correspondent* founded in 1841 by Friedrich Raine, when he was 19 years of age, became a daily in 1848. It supported the Democratic Party from its early years until World War I. The *Baltimore Wecker,* founded by writer and poet Carl Heinrich Schnauffer in 1851, was the voice of the liberal refugees from the 1848 revolution. The *Wecker* was the only Republican Party newspaper in Baltimore during the Civil War.

The German Jews formed a very special but integral part of the pre-Civil War German community. Like the Protestant and Catholic Germans, Jews in Baltimore counted merchants and political activists among their number. The

census of 1820 listed only 21 Jewish families in Baltimore. Although they had been participants in both the Revolution and the War of 1812, Jews could not vote or hold public office under Maryland law, which required a profession of Christian faith, even for jurors. In 1818 a legislator from Washington County, Thomas Kennedy, introduced a bill, finally passed in 1826, which changed that situation. Popularly called the "Jew Bill," the legislation stated that

> ". . . every citizen . . . professing the Jewish Religion and . . . hereafter appointed to any office of public trust under the State of Maryland shall in addition to the oath required by the Constitution and laws of the State or of the United States, make and subscribe a declaration of his belief in the future state of rewards and punishments, in the stead of the declaration now required by the Consitution and form of government of this State."

Shortly after the passage of the new law, Baltimore businessmen Jacob Cohen and Solomon Etting were elected to the First Branch of the City Council.

Most Jews who immigrated to Baltimore before the Civil War came from Bavaria, where many German Jews lived and where they faced the greatest discrimination. Most of the Jews, like other Germans, arrived on the ships that carried Maryland tobacco to Germany on the return trip. By 1840 about 500 Jews had settled in Baltimore, many in the vicinity of Lombard Street between Lloyd Street in the west and the Jones Falls in the east. A number of Jews worked as peddlers when they first arrived. One of them was Moses Hutzler who emigrated from Bavaria in 1836. His three sons founded the department store which still exists.

Not until after the passage of the Jew Bill did members of the community establish a formal religious organization. The Baltimore Hebrew Congregation was incorporated in 1830. At first members worshipped in a rented room above a grocery store at Bond and Fleet Streets. Their first rabbi, Abraham Rice, came to Baltimore from Bavaria in 1840. Five years later the congregation built the first synagogue in Maryland, the Lloyd Street Synagogue. Designed by Robert Cary Long, Jr., this building is the third oldest surviving synagogue in the United States.

Several thousand German Jews came in the 1840s and early 1850s, and the community added three more synagogues before the Civil War: the Eden Street Synagogue, Har Sinai and Oheb Shalom. The congregations held the same sorts of debates that their Christian counterparts did over Anglicization of language and Americanization of practices.

Synagogues conducted schools. The first regular Hebrew school opened at the Lloyd

The Baltimore Hebrew Congregation invited Rabbi Abraham Rice from Bavaria to serve as the Jewish community's first rabbi

Friedrich Raine founded the Deutsche Correspondent, *one of many newspapers which served Baltimore's German community*

Thomas Kennedy introduced the legislation which finally granted the franchise for Jews in 1826

The Schutzen (shooting club) located on West Baltimore Street was a popular recreational spot for many of Baltimore's Germans

Street Synagogue in 1848. Joseph Sachs, a native of Bavaria, taught the classes. At the same time, Samuel Gump conducted a school at the Eden Street Synagogue. When Jonas Goldsmith, a graduate of the University of Wurzburg, replaced Gump, so many students attended that the school had to hire five teachers. In the 1850s, Mrs. Solomon Carvalho organized the first free school, a Sunday school which offered instruction in Hebrew, German and English.

While Jews participated in the numerous German charitable groups, they also organized some of their own, among them the Society for Educating Poor and Orphan Hebrew Children, and the Hebrew Ladies Sewing Society which made clothes for the poor. Social groups included the Young Men's Literary Society, the Mendelsohn Literary Society, the Y.M.H.A., and the Harmony Circle which held balls.

Thousands of people came from Ireland to Baltimore during the first half of the nineteenth century. By the Civil War, over 15,000 people born in Ireland lived in the city, as did innumerable children and grandchildren of earlier immigrants. The potato famine of the 1840s forced a massive emigration by a people facing death by starvation and disease. The desperate situation in Ireland drove thousands of people onto the ships headed for America. Most were rural people who arrived with little or no money and without urban skills. Many had to take the lowest paying unskilled jobs, especially the seasonal construction work. Some had contracted to work for years in exchange for their passage and could not accept higher paying jobs until the specified years had passed.

Of all the pre-Civil War immigrant groups, the Irish bore the harshest fate. A Baltimorean recorded in a journal the arrival of the immigrant ship *Hampden* in the spring of 1847: "The ship *Hampden* had just arrived, freighted with human misery and death. Six of her passengers died at sea, and there are about 60 more on board, languishing with fever and destitution." Those that did survive the trip often faced prejudice because of their poverty, their lack of education, and sometimes because of their Catholic religion.

An older Irish community in Baltimore joined together to help the newcomers. Even before the potato famine the Irish had faced the difficulties experienced by most immigrants. In 1803 Baltimoreans of Irish ancestry organized the Hibernian Society to provide financial, social, medical and moral assistance to newcomers. The society chose Dr. John Campbell White its first president and Thomas McElderry vice-president. In 1815 John O'Donnell, the sea captain who had participated in building Canton, assumed the presidency. In 1818, John Oliver was elected head of the group. The Hibernian Society counted some of Baltimore's most prestigious business and civic leaders among its membership: John McKim, Robert Oliver, William Patterson, John Pendleton Kennedy, and J. H. B. Latrobe who was general counsel of the B&O and founder of the Maryland Institute. Though most of these early leaders were Scotch-Irish Protestants, their Hibernian Society continued to provide aid as the immigrants became predominantly Catholic.

The Hibernian Society offered assistance in various forms. Sometimes it made cash payments to families in need. In 1838, for example, the society donated between $.50 and $20 to 105 families. In 1852 it gave money to 700 families. The funds came from membership dues and from the head tax paid by steamship companies. A portion of that tax was divided between the Hibernian Society and the German Society for their charitable work. For several years after 1852 the Hibernian Society operated an employment agency that placed at least 25 men and women a month.

Right:
Hebrew Hospital was one of many institutions established by Jewish immigrants to serve their community

Below:
Lloyd Street Synagogue, designed by Robert Cary Long, Jr., and built in 1845, was the first synagogue in Baltimore and is the third oldest surviving in the nation

The Irish immigrants coming to Baltimore arrived in a city with a long Catholic tradition. The first two archbishops, the Rev. John Carroll and the Rev. Leonard Neale, came from old Maryland Irish Catholic families. The parish churches played an especially important role in the lives of people uprooted from their familiar villages and thrust into an unfamiliar and impersonal city. Many of the newcomers settled around St. Patrick's Church on Broadway and St. John's Church at Valley and Eager Streets. So many of Baltimore's Irish lived in the vicinity of the present City Jail that the area was known for a while as "Old Limerick." It should be noted that Baltimore was not a ghettoized city. Irish and German immigrants and blacks lived in all wards of the city. Often the Irish and the blacks shared alley housing behind the homes of the more prosperous residents.

Although extensive poverty meant that many Irish children had to go to work, several schools served the community. St. Patrick's School, the oldest parochial school in Baltimore, opened in 1815. In 1824, John Oliver bequeathed $20,000 to the Hibernian Society for the establishment of a free school for the poor children of Baltimore. He specified in his will that preference be given to those with at least one Irish parent and that no distinction be made because of sex or religion. It is estimated that before it closed its doors in 1891 the teachers of the Oliver Hibernian Free School educated 12,000 pupils. The Christian Brothers opened a free school at the St. Vincent de Paul Church and also ran the St. Peter the Apostle School and the Cathedral School for boys at Calvert Hall.

One unique fact about Baltimore's ethnic history is that the city was home to the nation's largest free black community of the antebellum period. Baltimore combined the population characteristics of a typical northern city and a typical southern city in its large numbers of both European immigrants and Afro-Americans.

The widely diverse black community in Baltimore was a mixture of slaves and free men and women. Urban slavery differed from plantation slavery in that cities offered a measure of freedom unknown in rural areas where slaves generally could not leave the property of their owner. In the cities, most slaves worked either as house servants or in some industrial or skilled trade. Some slaves hired themselves out, that is found a job, received wages, and paid part of their wages to their master. With the remaining income, they provided for their own lodging, sustenance and amusement. The line between slavery and freedom blurred under such conditions.

An increasing percentage of Baltimore's black population became free from 1800 until 1864, when slavery ended in Maryland. In 1810, the census registered 3,713 slaves and 3,973 free blacks. By 1860, over 90 percent of the total 27,898 were free. Men and women worked in a wide range of occupations and received commensurately varying incomes.

The majority of blacks held unskilled jobs in homes, restaurants, and factories and on the docks and railroads. A substantial number of black men worked as draymen and wagoners and women as washers and ironers. A significant proportion of blacks worked in the skilled trades as blacksmiths, butchers, carpenters, cigar-makers, coopers, milliners, shoemakers, tailors, and so on. Until the middle of the nineteenth century, blacks dominated the barbering and caulking trades and also the catering business in town. A few blacks owned small commercial establishments such as confectioneries, drug stores, groceries and tobacco shops. One black doctor, Lewis Wells, reportedly worked in Baltimore before the Civil War. Blacks as well as whites taught in schools for both children and adults. Black clergymen were prominent as

Benjamin Henry Latrobe, who designed the new cathedral, also served as architect of the United States Capitol

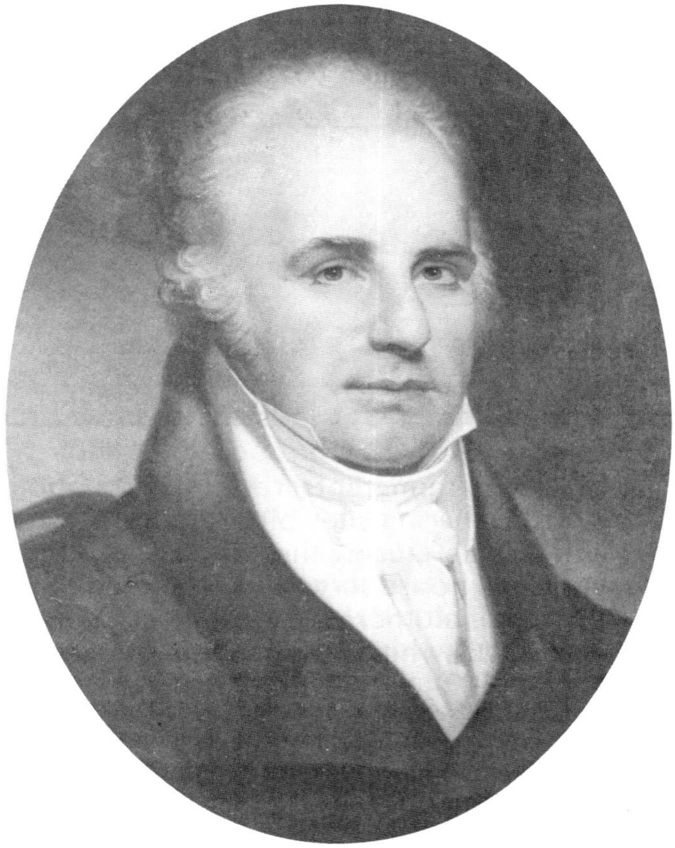

John Oliver, a local merchant, bequeathed $20,000 to the Baltimore Hibernian Society for the establishment of a free school for poor students

The sale of lottery tickets like this one helped pay for the new cathedral, seat of the first American Roman Catholic bishop

the land for the park, laid out in the shape of a Greek cross, in 1831. The surrounding space was divided into lots and sold. By the 1850s, Mt. Vernon Place and Washington Place, the squares to the north and south of the monument, became the social center of Baltimore.

The rapid population growth spurred concern for planning the physical development of the city. During the decades preceding the Civil War, the government and several individual Baltimoreans made provision for maintaining open spaces within the ever more crowded city. Only a few houses had been built near the Washington Monument in 1839 when two builders, James and Samuel Canby, proposed a large-scale development of middle-class housing on the western outskirts of the city. They bought a 30-acre tract and offered a square of ground in the middle to the city as a public park. Franklin Square became the first of many similar small squares, followed by Lafayette, Harlem Park, Perkins Spring, Johnson, Madison and Collington. Landscaped boulevards such as Eutaw Place, Park Avenue and North Broadway were planned to serve the same purpose. The row houses for which Baltimore has become so famous soon lined the squares and boulevards where they offered an attractive alternative to downtown living.

The early suburbs were made viable by the beginning of an omnibus service in 1844. Within the first decade, Washington Square, Fells Point, Canton, Towsontown, Ashland Square, and Franklin Square all could be reached by omnibus. Their popularity increased after 1859 when the horsedrawn trolleys of the Baltimore City Passenger Railway Company began to link the new residential neighborhoods to the central business district. These nineteenth century suburbanites became Baltimore's first regular commuters.

Awareness of creating a pleasant environment also led to the establishment in 1860 of a Public Park Commission. Using tax money paid on the gross receipts of the street railway company, the Park Commission purchased the 500-acre estate Druid Hill from Lloyd Nicholas Rogers and began landscaping according to the plan of Howard Daniels, a landscape gardener and engineer. Daniels planned the park to provide picturesque views, wooded pathways and formal promenades, lakes for swans and boats, and a grand formal entrance at the gate at Madison Avenue. The official opening of Druid Hill Park took place on October 19, 1860. Several thousand of Baltimore's public school children marched in the parade. A military display, band music, a dedication address by Mayor Thomas Swann, the firing of a gun for each state and territory and a final salvo for the park all marked the occasion.

When Druid Hill Park was planned in the western section of town, the city purchased 29 acres in East Baltimore to add to Patterson Park. Most of the planned improvements had to be put off until after the Civil War when a lake, music pavillion, and 19 more acres of land were added.

Parks built for the use of all the citizens were symbolic of a broadening of life in Baltimore. During the antebellum period the government and individuals both established many institutions with the wide variety of membership and purposes possible only in a large city with its diverse population. Facilities for education and entertainment received widespread support for all segments of the population.

In addition to the schools already discussed, numerous institutions and societies came into existence. In 1822 the Apprentice's Library was formed with the purpose of making books available to young people wanting to better themselves. In 1823 a number of Baltimoreans joined together to sponsor the construction of

Below:
In 1848 the land adjacent to the monument was still countryside, as shown by August Köllner in this lithograph. The wide street on the right is Pennsylvania Avenue

Bottom:
Lotteries were a popular way of raising money for all sorts of civic and charitable projects. Here the blindfolded boy on the platform is drawing a winning number

an Athenaeum, whose rooms would be used for meetings and lectures for many years to come. The cornerstone was laid in 1824 at the site at the corner of St. Paul and Lexington Streets. In 1825 two other important and enduring institutions were incorporated: The Maryland Academy of Science and the Maryland Institute for the Promotion of the Mechanical Arts, now known simply as the Maryland Institute.

In 1829, the "New Theatre and Circus" opened on Front Street with a performance of a musical farce, "The Spoiled Child." Announcements advertised the price of seats: boxes 50¢, pit 25¢, colored gallery 25¢. Three thousand spectators attended the first night. During that same year, a group of Baltimoreans formed a temperance society to combat the evil influence of liquor on the town's citizens.

In 1839, a new subscription library appeared: the Mercantile Library Company. Initiation cost only $2, a sum much more readily payable than the old Baltimore Library Company's $50 fee. Several facilities came together nine years later in 1848 when the new Baltimore Athenaeum opened. Built with $40,000 raised by contributions, the building housed the merged Baltimore and Mercantile Library Companies and the Maryland Historical Society which a group of local citizens had organized in 1844. John Spear Smith, son of General Samuel Smith, served as the latter's first president.

One notable fact about the institutions established during this period is that many have survived to the present day. The educational and cultural institutions especially received sufficient support from the expanding city's private sector to allow them to prosper. Several important educational institutions opened their doors during this period. In 1846, Professor Evert Marsh Topping, whose unorthodox methods of teaching Latin had created great controversy at Princeton, opened a school on Garden Street and began teaching Latin to sixth grade students. After Topping's death, George Gibson Carey took over what became known as the Carey School and later as the Boys' Latin School.

In 1848 the School Sisters of Notre Dame began their work in Baltimore when they established a school for boarding and day students. In 1873 the academy purchased 64 acres from David Perine and Joseph Reynolds and began construction of the campus on North Charles Street. The college of Notre Dame of Maryland graduated its first class with an A.B. degree in 1899.

Loyola College opened in September, 1852 with 58 young men enrolled. The president, the Rev. John Early, S.J., and eight Jesuits comprised the faculty. After two and a half years of holding classes in two rented houses on Holliday Street, the college moved to its new home on Calvert at Madison, the current location of Center Stage, where the college remained until 1922 when it moved to Charles Street and Cold Spring Lane while the high school remained downtown. In the year 1857, George Peabody donated $300,000 to the city to establish an institute. His philanthropy and the Peabody Institute will be discussed later.

No account of the antebellum period would be complete without some mention of the "great happenings" of those years. From time to time a famous visitor or a major event drew enormous crowds. Rich and poor, members of all ethnic groups, turned out to mark certain grand occasions.

In late summer, 1824, the Revolutionary War hero, French General Lafayette, made a return visit to Baltimore. A delegation met his ship at the Delaware line and sailed with him to Fort McHenry where the formal welcome took place. Four ships fully dressed with flags and streamers sailed into the harbor to greet the

Baltimore's Washington Monument, the first in the nation, was paid for by funds raised by a lottery conducted in 1816. When it was first built the monument stood in the country and was a popular spot for picnickers. By the middle of the century, the squares surrounding the monument had become the city's most fashionable residential area

This view of the Washington Monument in 1850 shows the fashionable houses that had been built on Mt. Vernon Place and Washington Place

Omnibuses, like the one in the foreground, began service in Baltimore in 1844. This 1859 view of Baltimore Street looking east from Calvert Street shows the wide variety of people and vehicles along the city's main business thoroughfare

Horse-drawn trolleys such as this one shown in front of the Holliday Street Theatre began to link new suburban neighborhoods to the central business district after 1859

General and his son Washington Lafayette and Secretary of State John Quincy Adams. The crowd of dignitaries included Samuel Smith, John Eager Howard, Charles Carroll, and Maryland Governor Samuel Stevens. A later chronicler described the reunion with Revolutionary War comrades: "The scene was one of the most impressive and heart-touching that was ever witnessed. All were convulsed into tears, but they were tears of joy and gratulation." The welcome in town was even more elaborate. Special arches, paintings and crowds lined the route. After the mayor welcomed him, Lafayette reminisced: "It is under the auspices of Baltimore patriotism, by the generosity of the merchants, by the zeal of the ladies of this city, at a critical period when not a day was to be lost, that I have been enabled in 1781 to begin a campaign, the fortunate issue of which has still enhanced the value of the service then rendered to our cause." All this endeared him even more to the city whose parades and celebrations continued for several days until Lafayette's departure.

Several years later, a crowd of 20,000 turned out to mourn John Adams and Thomas Jefferson who died on the same day, July 4, 1826, exactly fifty years after the signing of the Declaration of Independence. On the morning of July 20, the tolling of bells announced the commencement of ceremonies. Businesses closed. The Battle Monument was draped with black shrouds. A funeral procession marched northward through the city to Howard's Park, turned through the Belvedere gate at the north and into the woods to a natural amphitheater where 20,000 people heard Methodist Bishop Joshua Soule deliver the eulogy.

The newer generation of politicians drew smaller crowds than did the Revolutionary heroes. Baltimoreans welcomed Andrew Jackson in March, 1825 with a ball at Barnum's Hotel, a military presentation of colors, an open public reception and an evening at the theater. When Henry Clay came to town in May, 1828 the ship *Patuxent* carried a crowd down the river to greet him. Like Jackson, he held hours of open reception for all who chose to visit him. Clay, however, declined formal festivities like dinners and theater parties so commonly arranged for visiting dignitaries.

Henry Clay and Andrew Jackson both came to Baltimore in 1833. Clay typically received citizens individually but declined the invitation to a public dinner. On the other hand, Jackson's visit this time drew enormous crowds. Most people turned out not so much to see President Jackson as to catch a glimpse of the man with whom he met: Chief Black Hawk. The year before, Black Hawk had led the Sauk and Fox tribes in rebellion against Jackson's policy of removing all Indians from land east of the Mississippi River. Even in defeat, the chief defied Jackson magnificently at the conclusion of the hostilities, "I am a man and you are nothing more." The government imprisoned Black Hawk for several weeks and then took him on tour of the eastern cities to impress him with their strength. Two of his sons and several other prisoners accompanied him. Crowds expected to see a savage but discovered instead a patriarch, standing tall in a red-collared blue coat, wearing bright ear decorations and carrying the "medicine" skin of a sparrow hawk at his side. The press of people was so great that Jackson and Black Hawk had to move to Fort McHenry to carry on their discussions.

A less happy but very enthusiastic crowd assembled in Monument Square on May 23, 1846 to support the American annexation of Texas and the war that followed. Reverdy Johnson, General Sam Houston, and William Yancey, a member of Congress from Alabama, all addressed the Baltimore audience. The city

contributed a unit of soldiers known as "Baltimore's Own" and three other companies which left the city on June 4 under the command of Col. William H. Watson. They fought at the battle of Monterrey and in other engagements until their term of service expired in May, 1847. Other Maryland companies fought throughout the war. The, Baltimore *Sun,* founded by Arunah S. Abell in 1837, did some extraordinary reporting of the Mexican War. Using relays of horses and riders the newspaper often brought stories before the official messengers did. In the spring of 1847 the *Sun* telegraphed to President James K. Polk word of the fall of Vera Cruz. Samuel F. B. Morse's first telegraph message had been sent from Washington to Baltimore only three years earlier.

A different sort of crowd assembled to welcome the Swedish singer, Jenny Lind, on December 8, 1850. Several thousand people waited at the depot and at Barnum's Hotel to catch a glimpse of the young woman who was taking America by storm. The great demand for tickets for her performances at the Front Street Theater led to an auction. Although the price had originally been set at $3, the first choice ticket sold for $100, and the sales finally averaged out at $7 a seat. Spectators were allowed to sit on the stage. On the night of the last concert, theater officials charged $12\frac{1}{2}$¢ for the right even to bid in the ticket auction. Even this financial chicanery did not deter people's quest to hear the famous "Swedish Nightingale."

In 1851, a foreign political leader, the exiled Hungarian patriot Louis Kossuth, drew cheering crowds who identified his struggle for national liberty with America's own. Kossuth had led the Magyars in 1848 and 1849 in their losing struggle against Austrian domination. Ice and snow notwithstanding, Baltimoreans paraded in his honor.

An assemblage of a rather macabre nature occurred in April, 1859 when 30,000 spectators turned out to witness the execution of four convicted murderers. The event marked the culmination of a legal drama. Three of the four convicted were young men of respectable parentage. Influential friends had tried to convince Governor Thomas Hicks to intervene. Twice he delayed the execution but finally he declined to lessen the sentence. Some called the execution a tragedy, others a victory for the impartiality of the law.

One uniquely American festivity is the political nominating convention. Baltimore was a popular convention city from the 1830s through 1860. Good transportation facilities made the city easily accessible. Baltimore lay close to Washington, D. C., the practical residence of many of the leading delegates. Furthermore, in this border city neither the worst aspects of slavery nor too many abolitionists were visible. For all these reasons, Baltimore frequently witnessed parades of the politically famous and nominations of winners and losers throughout the antebellum period.

In 1831, in September, the Anti-Masonic Party met at the Athenaeum and nominated Baltimore lawyer, William Wirt, for president. The Anti-Masons, the first party to hold a nominating convention, made the secrecy of Masonry its primary concern, but were drawn into the anti-Jacksonian camp because Andrew Jackson was himself a Mason. The other anti-Jackson group, the National Republicans, also met in the Baltimore Athenaeum in December and chose Henry Clay to oppose Jackson's bid for reelection. The following May, the Democrats gave Baltimore a clean sweep of the convention trade when they assembled in the city to confirm Jackson's renomination and chose Martin Van Buren as his running mate. This group spilled over into the Universalist

Church which seated 1600 people.

The Democratic delegates returned to Baltimore in 1835, met in the First Presbyterian Church and nominated Martin Van Buren, who followed Jackson into the presidency. In 1840, the party returned to nominate Van Buren for a second term. While the Democrats held their sessions in the Music Hall, the Whig Party rented the Canton Race Track, offered free hard cider, and invited Baltimore citizens to hear Henry Clay, Daniel Webster and others praise their candidate, William Henry Harrison, who won the election the following November.

In 1844 both the Whigs and the Democrats met in Baltimore. The Whigs assembled at the Universalist Church and chose Henry Clay to carry their party banner. When the Democrats met at the Odd Fellows Hall, the contest was between John Tyler who had proposed that the United States annex Texas and Van Buren who opposed the acquisition. A deadlock between the two finally resulted in the nomination of a dark horse, James K. Polk, who became president.

Only the Democrats came to Baltimore in 1848 when they met in the Universalist Church and nominated Lewis Cass of Michigan. This convention established the first national committee, which consisted of one member from each state and was charged with the job of running the campaign. Their techniques must not have been perfected as the Whig candidate, General Zachary Taylor, took the victory.

The Democrats returned to Baltimore in 1852 when five thousand assembled at the Maryland Institute and labored through 49 ballots. The result was a rather obscure figure, Franklin Pierce of New Hampshire. Later the Whigs also came to the Maryland Institute, and in 53 ballots, chose Mexican War hero General Winfield Scott, whom Pierce defeated.

In 1856, only the nativist third party, the American Party, convened in Baltimore where they nominated Millard Fillmore. The local strength of the Know-Nothings, the name generally used by the nativists, may have been responsible for the major parties' choices of other locations for their conventions.

In 1860 Baltimore more than made up for its lack of conventions in 1856. The year before the Civil War broke out, the Constitutional Union Party and two groups of Democrats brought their troubles to the city. By 1860 slavery was the dominant question in the country. Passions ran high, and many already believed that civil war was unavoidable. A group of men, mainly from border states, formed a Constitutional Union Party whose primary purpose was to remove the slavery question from national politics. Sam Houston, headquartered at Eutaw House, and John Bell of Tennessee, working from Barnum's Hotel, vied for the nomination. The party delegates, meeting in the First Presbyterian Church, chose Bell. Baltimorean John Pendleton Kennedy was a leading local supporter of this party that hoped for compromise but lost.

The Democratic Party divided so severely that its first convention, held in Charleston, adjourned without agreement on a candidate. The delegates reconvened in Baltimore's Front Street Theater on June 18, 1860. Unionists and secessionists faced each other for a second time. Sen. Stephen Douglas of Illinois, who proposed "popular sovereignty," whereby each state and territory would be allowed to decide for itself whether or not to have slavery, ran his campaign from Reverdy Johnson's house. The secessionists, who wanted the Democratic Party to endorse slavery without reservation, operated out of Robert Gilmor's house. Because both men resided on Courthouse Square, the area became the scene of rival speeches and bands, and crowds alternately cheering and booing. When the pro-Southern delegates found that they

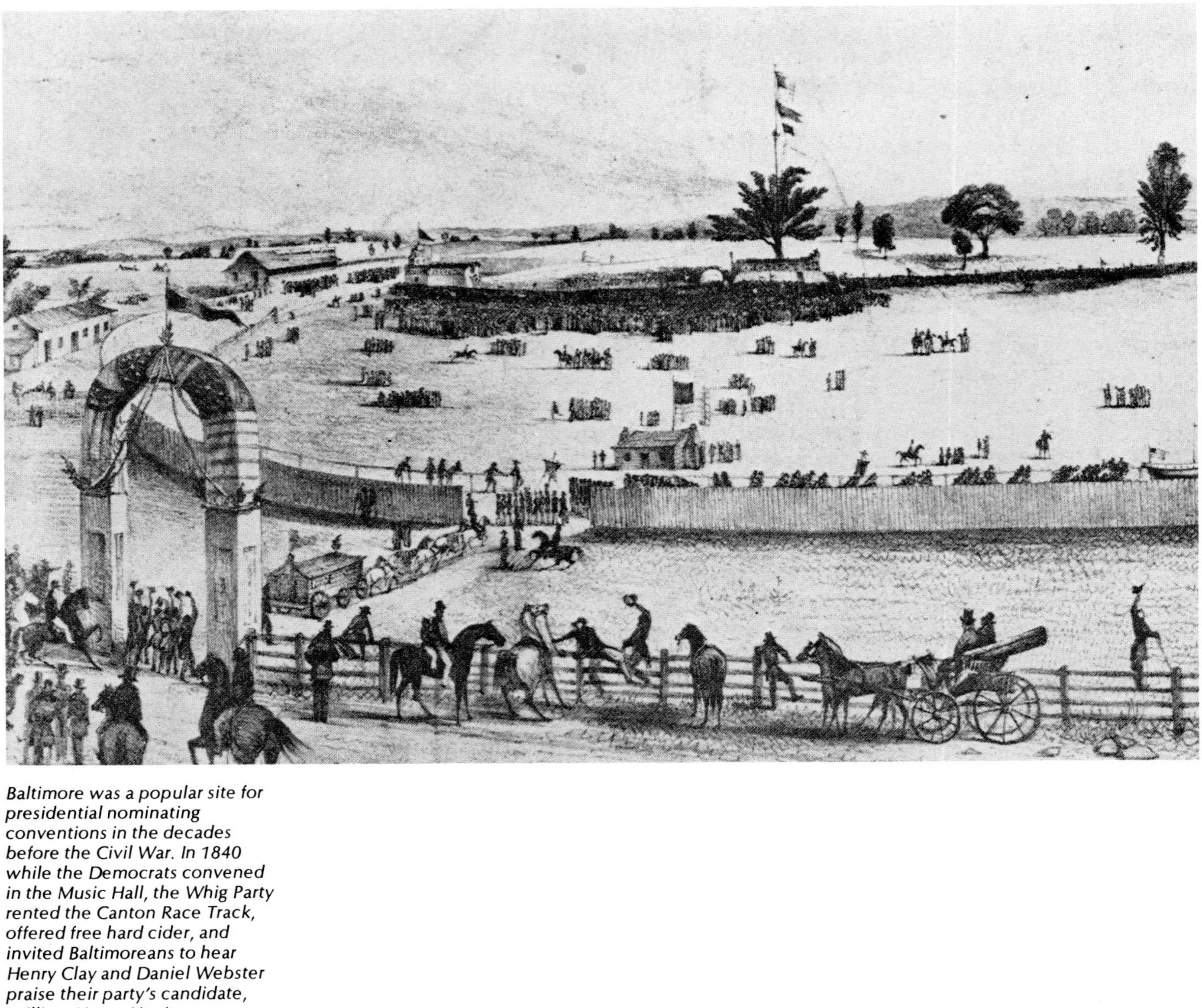

Baltimore was a popular site for presidential nominating conventions in the decades before the Civil War. In 1840 while the Democrats convened in the Music Hall, the Whig Party rented the Canton Race Track, offered free hard cider, and invited Baltimoreans to hear Henry Clay and Daniel Webster praise their party's candidate, William Henry Harrison

could not carry the convention, they withdrew, reconvened at the Maryland Institute Hall and nominated John C. Breckinridge of Kentucky. This left the regular Democrats free to nominate Stephen Douglas. The only candidate not nominated in Baltimore in 1860 was Abraham Lincoln. Changing their name to the Union Party, the Republicans did come to this border state city in 1864 when Lincoln was renominated at the site of the 1860 Democratic cleavage, the Front Street Theater.

Baltimore's local politics was as confused as national politics was during the decades that preceded the Civil War. Confusion, disorder, and violence characterized the last antebellum generation. But through it all, there was a beneficial trend towards greater centralization of city services, facilities, and powers. This movement continued in the hands of whichever party or faction held power. Democrats, Whigs, and, later, Know-Nothings vied for control. Regardless of which group was in power, they presided over the construction of new public buildings, the extension of city streets, increasing governmental control of services and utilities, and a continuing drive for greater municipal authority and autonomy.

After the termination of Samuel Smith's mayoralty in 1838, a succession of Whigs and Democrats held the office, none for very many years. From 1838 to 1854, Baltimore had eight different mayors. In chronological order these were: Sheppard C. Leakin, Samuel Brady, Solomon Hillen, Jr., James O. Law, Jacob G. Davies, Elijah Stansbury, John Hanson Thomas Jerome, and John Smith Hollins.

Following the riots of 1835 and the panic of 1837, the city faced huge administrative problems. For one thing, its tax collection procedures were unreliable. In its most prosperous year, 1836, Baltimore collected just over half of the total $295,000 levied. To remedy this situation the state legislature authorized the city to confiscate the property of delinquent taxpayers in 1841. For another example, before 1834, street repairs could be made only when *every* resident in the affected area agreed and paid two-thirds of the cost in advance. In 1834 the requirement was changed to approval by only two-thirds of the residents. And in 1836 the power of street extensions within the city was transferred from the state to the city. Only under Mayor Samuel Brady, in 1841, did Baltimore begin appointing street commissioners with the power to initiate both construction and repairs.

Other municipal services, especially police and fire protection, were equally far from the professional calibre modern urbanites expect. In Baltimore, the daytime police remained separate from the night watch. Politicians appointed the policemen, only one-third of whom earned salaries. The other two-thirds' income came from fines collected for violations of city ordinances. Fire protection continued in the hands of the volunteer companies that were also undisguised political organizations. In order to stop the fights over which company would put out a given fire, the City Council in 1842 divided Baltimore into three fire districts and appointed over each a Chief Marshal with absolute authority in his area.

In politics, the transformation to Jacksonian style machines took place in all groups. Politics became fun. Political parties offered steamboat rides, picnics, dances, free food and free liquor to their followers. One of the more gala events occurred in 1844 when the Democrats invited thirty thousand Baltimoreans to a picnic in Gibson's Woods and distributed free hard cider to all. On election days, the party faithful distributed circulars, transported voters to the polls, and sometimes even provided lodging for potential voters. They also fought for their

Some Baltimoreans considered visiting conventioneers from the West a bit rowdy

candidates, and election days were marked by much violence.

A common practice was "cooping," the rounding up of drunks, strangers, and anyone else who looked like an easy victim for the purpose of marching them from precinct to precinct to vote as ordered. The writer Edgar Allan Poe, who lived in Baltimore during part of this period, was probably the most famous person cooped during the city's electoral contests. Poe, who was the grandson of Baltimore's Revolutionary Deputy Commissary General, David Poe, died here in the Washington College Hospital in 1849, shortly after being cooped during the October elections.

One major cleavage was at least partially resolved before the end of the 1830s. The Democrats had remained split between the old Jacksonians like General Samuel Smith and his son John Spear Smith, longtime Baltimore merchants whose family connections played a role in their political ascendancy, and newer leaders like William Frick whose position was based on service to the party. By the mid-1830s, leading Democrats like Benjamin Chew Howard, John Eager Howard's son, were beginning to recognize the need for cohesion within the party. The appointment of Frick to the lucrative position as Collector of the Port of Baltimore symbolized the rise of the new faction. Frick reigned as the Democratic boss in Baltimore in the late 1830s.

A big gain for Baltimore City came in the Reform Act passed by the legislature in 1837. This gave Baltimore representation in the State Senate equal to that of each county and representation in the House of Delegates equal to that of the largest county. Continuing efforts by reformers to reduce the state budget and to modernize Maryland's constitution finally succeeded in 1851. The new order shifted apportionment in such a way that Baltimore and the populous counties of Western Maryland held the power. It also separated Baltimore City and County, making each an independent political unit. This constitution remained in effect until 1864.

By 1850 the Whigs were a dying party. Their last national effort came in the unsuccessful presidential bid of General Winfield Scott against Franklin Pierce in 1852. Their demise and the corruption within the ranks of the local Democrats led one former Jacksonian, later converted to the Whigs, to withdraw from politics. John Pendleton Kennedy declared, "Nothing can be more contemptible than the state of politics and management in Maryland. We have not a man in public office above mediocrity, and the whole machinery of our politics is moved by the smallest, narrowest, most ignorant and corrupt men in the State." Many men apparently agreed with Kennedy. The state was ripe for a new party. The first was a short-lived Temperance Party that swept Baltimore in 1853 and sent ten delegates to Annapolis. These men and their colleagues failed to gain prohibition of alcoholic beverages, and the party quickly declined in favor of a second new party, one promulgating a platform that more completely aroused people's ardor and loyalty.

The Know-Nothing Party began as a secret society whose members received instructions to say that they "knew nothing" if asked about the organization. Strongly nativist, the Know-Nothings served as a focal point for all the confusion and discontent resulting from the rapid industrialization, low salaries and poor working conditions, the massive immigration of the 1840s and 1850s, and the increasing violence and crime, all of which frightened people and seemed uncontrollable.

One group of victims were native American workers, whose wages and standard of living

Local politics had declined to such a low level in the 1850s that John Pendleton Kennedy declared that "We have not a man in public office above mediocrity"

ment. In 1854, after the Baltimore Water Company refused to extend its services into areas with new housing, Samuel Hinks directed the purchase of the facility and organized the municipal Water Department.

Over the years from 1853 to 1857, the city government consolidated the day police and the night watch and organized four police districts under one city marshal. Policemen, about 350 of them, received their appointments from the mayor, often as a reward for political service.

In 1857, Mayor Thomas Swann created the office of city comptroller. One result was increased efficiency in the collection of taxes. In 1858, Swann replaced the volunteers with a salaried municipal Fire Department, administered by a Fire Board appointed by the mayor. In 1859 the Swann administration granted the franchise for the Baltimore City Passenger Railway Company. Within a few months, Baltimore had 22 miles of tracks and 65 passenger cars. All these measures, and many similar ones, aided in the ongoing expansion of Baltimore.

Despite the effective measures of Hinks and Swann, the bigotry, corruption and violence of the Know-Nothings soon led to organized opposition. In August 1857 the *Baltimore American* called for a town meeting to discuss the problems of corruption and disorder. This meeting and the Know-Nothing victory in 1858 resulted in the creation of the City Reform Association by old elite Baltimoreans, often Democrats. Statewide, the Know-Nothings were declining. In October 1859, Democrats regained control of the Senate and House of Delegates. This legislature, responding to a request by the Baltimore reformers, took control of the city police away from the mayor and put it in the hands of the state government. They also voided the results of the 1859 election on grounds of fraud and unseated Baltimore's Know-Nothing delegates.

In the mayoral election of October 1860, reform candidate George William Brown, a member of the Baltimore banking family, defeated Know-Nothing Samuel Hindes in a landslide. Reformers also gained control of the City Council. Sadly, the reformers had little opportunity for real reform as the Civil War broke out a few months later. As war approached, many former Know-Nothing leaders moved into the Unionist camp to try to deal with the crisis.

On the eve of the Civil War, Baltimore was truly a city divided. Half northern, half southern, Baltimore's heritage included abolitionism and slavery, old southern families and recent immigrants, industries and remnants of a landed aristocracy. About sixty percent of Baltimore's trade was with the north. At the same time Baltimore was considered the southern city with the most manufacturing. In 1860, roughly one-fourth of Baltimore's population had been born in Europe, a bit less than in many northern cities, a bit more than in most southern cities.

Twelve percent of all Baltimoreans were black, most of them free. Northern cities had only small black populations. Southern cities repressed free blacks, fearing the growing number of uprisings and escapes. As 1861 began, some Baltimoreans supported Lincoln while others talked of secession. Most stood in between those extremes. When war broke out, Baltimoreans fought for both North and South. Families, friends and business partners split. Baltimore was a city divided during the Civil War.

The conflict had been a long time coming. Post-Revolutionary abolitionism resulted in free states in the North and slave states in the South. In Baltimore, slave owners and abolitionists lived side by side. Late in the eighteenth century, a Baltimore chapter of the Maryland Society for Promoting the Abolition of Slavery was

Thomas Swann became Baltimore's second Know-Nothing mayor in 1856. He later served as Maryland's Unionist governor during the Civil War

This rare photograph of Baltimore Street taken in the 1850s shows the urban congestion that had grown in Baltimore during the antebellum years

established. The membership, although heavily Quaker, included many prominent Baltimoreans like Philip Rogers, Dr. George Buchanan, Samuel Sterett, and Alexander McKim.

During the 1820s, an abolitionist of national renown, Benjamin Lundy, lived in Baltimore and published the nation's only exclusively anti-slavery newspaper, *The Genius of Universal Emancipation.* His printer, Daniel Raymond, ran for the City Council in 1826 but was defeated. In 1829 and 1830, William Lloyd Garrison came to Baltimore to work as Lundy's co-editor. Garrison, for the first time, lived where slavery existed and the experience led him to take a more extreme anti-slavery position. An article Garrison wrote against Francis Todd, the owner of a slave ship, resulted in a libel suit. Garrison was convicted, was unable or unwilling to pay the $5000 fine and instead spent several months in the Baltimore jail. After his release, Garrison moved to Boston and on January 1, 1831 issued the first edition of his own famous anti-slavery newspaper, *The Liberator.* Although Lundy remained a gradualist, even that position was becoming unpopular in Baltimore and he moved the *Genius* to Washington, D. C.

After 1830, the few abolitionists left in town were shunned by much of the community. A small abolitionist paper, The *Saturday Visitor,* was viewed as an outrage by most citizens. Baltimore's most vocal abolitionist of the 1840s and 1850s, William Gunnison, had to close his mercantile establishment in 1851 because the local bankers refused to do business with him. Undeterred, he campaigned for the Republican Party in 1860, when only 1087 Baltimoreans voted for Lincoln. During that election, the few Republicans that dared campaign had eggs and bricks thrown at them. The one Republican newspaper in town, the *Baltimore Wecker,* voice of the German liberals, was the target of mob attack a few months later.

As abolitionism became suspect and as popular fear of the increasing number of free blacks grew, more and more Baltimoreans became involved in the movement to "colonize" free blacks in Africa. The American Colonization Society began in 1816. In 1831 a group of Baltimore businessmen founded the Maryland State Colonization Society "to promote and execute a plan to colonize *(with their own consent)* the free people of color in our country, either in Africa or such other place as Congress shall deem most expedient . . ." Many prominent Baltimoreans, including Solomon Etting, John Eager Howard, John B. Latrobe, and Luke Tiernan, actively supported the effort to send people to the Society's colony at Cape Palmas, known as Maryland in Liberia. Benjamin Lundy and other former abolitionist leaders became active once abolitionism was impossible in Baltimore. Despite heavy propaganda and expenditures, no more than 1,250 people were convinced to make the move. Most free blacks agreed with the resolution passed at a meeting of black Baltimoreans in 1831: "that we consider the land in which we were born and in which we have been bred our only true and appropriate home . . ."

By 1860, most Baltimoreans were less interested either in destroying or in maintaining slavery than they were in the question of whether there would be war. Republicans were feared, because they were considered radicals. In the election, John C. Breckinridge of Kentucky, the nominee of the southern Democrats, carried Baltimore, as did the reform Democratic candidate for mayor, George W. Brown. The year 1860 saw a realignment in Maryland politics because of the desire to avoid war, the fear of Republicans and also free blacks and the collapse of the Know-Nothing Party. Many former Know-Nothings, consistent with their earlier position, became Unionists. Th

Right:
Reform candidate George William Brown won the mayoralty in 1860 as the public showed its increasing dissatisfaction with continuing political corruption and violence

Below:
This view of the harbor, c. 1850, shows different vessels engaged in Baltimore's already established shipping trade

Democratic Party revived its strength in Baltimore and throughout the state. Democrats tended to favor states' rights, including the South's right to secede. Unionists, including the slaveholders among them, opposed secession and also, before the fighting broke out, generally opposed war.

The year 1861 was destined to be an agonizing one for Baltimore. The city was suspect in the North because of the pro-Southern leanings of some of its residents. As the year progressed, Baltimore fell into increasingly greater disrepute in the North. The first blot on Baltimore's reputation came from what was probably a non-event. When Abraham Lincoln left Springfield, Illinois early in February to go to Washington for his inauguration, the detective Allan Pinkerton warned him that there was a plot to kill him when he passed through Baltimore. Lincoln was due to pass through the Monumental City around noon on February 23. Because an ordinance forbade railroad engines from traversing the city, Lincoln was to ride from the Calvert Street Station of the North Central Railroad to the Camden Street Station of the B&O in a horse-drawn carriage. Pinkerton asserted that a group of assassins would approach the carriage and kill the president-elect. This would then be the signal for Southern sympathizers to seize Washington, D. C.

Lincoln resisted cancelling engagements at Philadelphia and Harrisburg but was finally convinced to leave Harrisburg early in order to traverse Baltimore under cover of darkness. Taking a Philadelphia, Wilmington and Baltimore train, he arrived at the President Street Station at 3:30 A.M. A team of horses pulled his sleeping car silently through the streets of Baltimore. The group departed from Camden Station at 4:15 A.M. The next day, when crowds lined the streets to see the new president, he was already in Washington. Baltimoreans generally were offended. Later, Pinkerton was accused of inventing the plot to gain publicity for his detective agency. No proof has ever been found that the plot really existed.

April 1861 was marked by violence in Baltimore. One week after the first shots of the Civil War were fired at Fort Sumter on April 12 the first deaths of the war occurred in Baltimore On April 19, the Massachusetts Sixth Regimen

Opposite:
John Work Garrett, president of the B&O during the Civil War, was a staunch supporter of the Union and offered the government the services of his railroad

Above:
En route to his inauguration, Abraham Lincoln traversed Baltimore in the middle of the night and arrived in Washington just after dawn the following morning. He had been warned of possible danger from the city's Southern sympathizers

arrived in Baltimore on its way to Washington, D. C. Many residents objected to their transit and barricaded the streets between the President Street Station and the Camden Station where they were expected to march. Although Mayor George Brown walked at the head of the line of soldiers and Police Marshal Kane at the rear, bystanders began throwing rocks. Soon somebody fired a shot. The riot was on and, before it ended, four soldiers and twelve Marylanders lay dead, the first casualties of the war.

On the following day, a mob attacked the *Wecker* office, because of the newspaper's Republican stance, and destroyed the press o *Sinai,* a German-Jewish monthly edited by Dr David Einhorn, an abolitionist. When word came that additional troops might be headed fo Baltimore some of the authorities, fearing further violence, burned all the railroad bridges north of the city. Mayor Brown and Maryland Governor Thomas Hicks met with Lincoln and requested that no further troops be sent through Baltimore. Lincoln agreed, and temporarily troops going south bypassed the riot-torn city. Calm returned slowly and pro-Union sentiment began to reassert itself.

Then on May 13, Union General Benjamin Butler and one thousand troops arrived in the city. When Baltimoreans awoke the following morning, they found the unit encamped on Federal Hill, setting up weapons designed to ensure Baltimore's loyalty to the Union. Genera Butler issued a series of proclamations, among them that his troops would enforce the law, tha armed men were not to assemble, that arms and ammunition headed south to aid the Confede rates would be seized, and that no one was to display Confederate flags or banners. After thi time, federal troops began to pass through Baltimore again.

Once it was clear that there was to be war pro-Union sentiment began to assert itself more strongly. By the spring of 1861, the Know-Nothing and Constitutional Union parties had collapsed and the Democrats were split between unionists and secessionists. On May 23, 1861 a convention met in Baltimore to organize the Union Party. Brant Mayer became chairman. The new Maryland party opposed secession endorsed the federal government's right to use force to preserve the Union, and supported Lincoln's war policies. At a special election held in June, Marylanders chose members of the

Opposite:
Police Marshal George P. Kane joined Mayor George Brown in escorting the Massachusetts regiment. Despite their escort, bystanders began the attack

Below:
Rifles like this, with bayonets attached, were carried by the Massachusetts soldiers

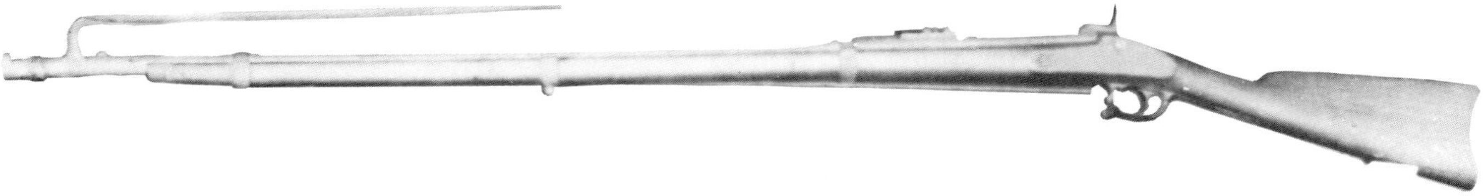

Left:
Baltimoreans awoke the morning of May 14, 1861, to find Northern General Benjamin Butler and 1500 troops encamped on Federal Hill to assure the city's loyalty to the Union

Above:
The first deaths of the Civil War occurred in Baltimore on April 19, 1861, when local citizens rioted against the Massachusetts Sixth Regiment which was passing through the city on its way to Washington, D.C.

Unionist Party to fill all six of the state's Congressional seats. In August, the party convened in Baltimore and nominated Augustus W. Bradford to oppose the States Rights Party candidate, Benjamin C. Howard, for governor.

Before the November victory of Bradford and the Unionist candidates for the State Senate and House of Delegates, there was some fear that pro-Southern forces in Annapolis would try to get Maryland to secede and join the Confederacy. The Union would not tolerate a Confederate state between the northern states and its capitol. Operating under Lincoln's suspension of the writ of *habeas corpus,* federal forces took into custody a large number of Marylanders who were merely suspected of harboring pro-Southern sentiments. The most important case was the arrest of John Merryman of Cockeysville, who was imprisoned in Fort McHenry for seven weeks before his release was secured, probably with the help of Chief Justice Roger B. Taney. The inventor and builder of railroad cars, Ross Winans, who was a member of the House of Delegates and favored secession also served time in Fort McHenry. Police Marshal George P. Kane was imprisoned there too and the federal government took over the city's police force. Many other Baltimore officials, including Mayor George Brown, and Delegates Severn Teackle Wallis and Henry M. Warfield spent time in prison. Once the elections of November 1861 put Unionists in power in the state government, Northern fears that Maryland would fall into the hands of secessionists subsided and the repression grew less harsh. Gradually the federal authorities released the civilians and Fort McHenry housed predominantly military prisoners through most of the war.

The Union Army maintained an active presence in Baltimore throughout the war. Well-equipped military establishments stood on Federal Hill, which by the end of 1861 held fifty heavy cannon, and at Fort Marshall just east of Patterson Park. Army encampments appeared in Druid Hill and Carroll Parks, in Lafayette Square near the McKim mansion, and on the grounds of the Maryland Agricultural Society around the present corner of Charles and 27th Streets. The Army brought Confederate prisoners taken at Antietam and Gettysburg to Baltimore. By 1863 Fort McHenry housed 680 southern prisoners and the Baltimore City Jail an additional 700. Pro-Confederate Baltimoreans sent clothing, food, blankets, and money to the prisoners.

The federal government confiscated the estate of General George H. Steuart, Confederate States Army, and turned it into Jarvis Hospital. Located near Mt. Clare Station, the hospital was protected by a nearby ridge. Other large hospitals were located in Patterson Park, in the National Hotel near Camden Station, and in the Union Dock on Pratt Street.

Although the situation eased somewhat after 1861, pro-Confederate Baltimoreans felt repressed by the federal occupation. Display of Confederate banners was forbidden. The most famous pro-Confederate newspaper, *The South,* and eight others were suppressed. Organizations and clubs run by Southern sympathizers were closed. The occupying army wanted to ensure that northern soldiers' lives were not endangered because of pro-Confederate activity in Baltimore.

Baltimore men joined the armies of both the North and the South. No exact figures are available. One estimate is that thirty thousand people left Baltimore during the Civil War, some to fight, some to live where there was less danger of war. From Maryland as a whole, roughly sixty-three thousand men, including nine thousand blacks, served in the Union forces and twenty thousand fought for the Confederacy.

Very little military action took place in the

Far Left:
John Merryman's detention at Fort McHenry became a cause célèbre. Many of the area's leading citizens were arrested because of their suspected or certain confederate sympathies

Left:
Severn Teackle Wallis, a Baltimore member of the House of Delegates, spent time in prison

Major General Benjamin Butler commanded Union troops stationed at Fort Federal Hill

Sergeant Major Christian Fleetwood, from Baltimore, was awarded the Congressional Medal of Honor for bravery in battle.

vicinity of Baltimore. Fighting near Frederick in July 1864 and the Union defeat at Monocacy made Baltimore fear that the Confederates would next attack Baltimore. Women and children fled the city. Businesses loaded their money and valuables onto ships in the harbor. The attack did not come, however, because the Southern troops headed towards Washington.

Military action took place within the current city limits only during the raids of Confederate General Bradley T. Johnson and Major Harry Gilmor. Just before the Battle of Monocacy, General Johnson's cavalry brigade and the Baltimore Light Artillery received orders to cut off Baltimore and Washington from the north and then release over fifteen thousand southern prisoners detained at Point Lookout, Maryland. Johnson's men rode from Frederick through Westminster and on to Randallstown, Reisterstown and Cockeysville. Following the Northern Central Railroad tracks, they destroyed bridges, ripped out track, and pulled down telegraph wires. Then they rode into Towson and south along Charles Street to burn the summer home of Maryland Governor Augustus Bradford, located where the Elkridge Club now stands. Next they rode west to the Northern Central Relay House by Lake Roland, destroyed more railroad equipment, and pushed on through Owings Mills towards Washington, destroying B&O property along the way.

The arrival of northern reinforcements forced abandonment of plans to free the Point Lookout prisoners and to attack Washington. Before the Confederates turned south from Cockeysville, Johnson ordered Major Harry Gilmor of Baltimore County to take the 135 men of the First and Second Maryland Cavalry to raid the Philadelphia, Wilmington and Baltimore Railroad. They rode through Texas and Timonium and on along the Dulany Valley. In Kingsville they burned the farmhouse of Ishmae Day who refused to lower the United States flag at their command. Then, at Magnolia, the captured and destroyed two trains and took five Union officers prisoner. They returned sout along the Philadelphia Pike. At Towson, the encountered a group of Union cavalrymen whom they chased down York Road as far a Govans. Then they rode west through Riderwood and the Green Spring Valley, turned south down Reisterstown Road, cut across to Randallstown and rejoined General Johnson a Poolesville.

The major political development of 1864 was the passage of a new constitution for the state of Maryland. More than a year afte Lincoln's Emancipation Proclamation went into effect in rebellion areas, Marylanders voted to hold a convention to write a new constitution. The document, which passed by a narrow margin in October, ended slavery in Maryland set up a system of test oaths and voter registration, and reapportioned the state in such a way that Baltimore increased its representation in the legislature. Democrats opposed the constitution and argued against Unionists using dire predictions about the future of blacks without slavery as a means of control. The constitution went into effect on November 1 1864, and the war continued.

On April 9, 1865, General Robert E. Lee surrendered the Army of Northern Virginia to General Ulysses S. Grant at Appomattox Cour House in Virginia. The remaining Confederate forces surrendered within a few days. Finally, the war had ended. On the night of April 14, John Wilkes Booth assassinated Abraham Lincoln as he watched a performance at Ford's Theater in Washington. Most Baltimoreans mourned their dead president. Then, like the nation as a whole they began the long, slow, and painful process o reunification.

This early photograph shows troops marching through the city

Camp Carroll was one of the many installations that the Union Army maintained throughout the Civil War

This lithograph portrays Baltimore's celebration of the passage of the Fifteenth Amendment, which enfranchised the nation's slaves, and depicts scenes from black history and heroes of the struggle for emancipation as well as the local festivities

Reconciliation & Growth

1865-1917

IV

The tragic Civil War left a nation and a city divided. On June 6, 1865, Baltimore soldiers who had served in the Union Army paraded through town, then marched to the new Druid Hill Park where they stacked their weapons and heard Governor Augustus Bradford thank them and welcome them home. A month and a half earlier, in the wake of Lincoln's assassination, the City Council had passed a resolution against allowing ex-Confederates to return to the city. Despite the resolution, Confederate veterans slowly came home, too, and soon violent clashes broke out between the two groups of former soldiers. Some Baltimoreans formed societies to aid the devastated South, among them the Baltimore Agricultural Aid Society, the Southern Relief Association and the Ladies' Depository.

Ultra-Unionist John Lee Chapman was mayor and was reelected in 1866. Thomas Swann, the former mayor of Baltimore and also a Unionist, was governor. A required oath of past loyalty limited the franchise to Marylanders who had remained loyal to the Union. But change was brewing. The conservative Unionists were moving closer to a coalition with the Democrats, many of whom had been pro-Southern. This new coalition opposed the voter registry law and its required oath, African American suffrage, and the Radical Republicans in Congress. The Democrats accused the Unionists of supporting black equality. The Unionists countered by calling the Democrats traitors.

In 1866 Baltimore, along with Southern Maryland and the Eastern Shore, returned the Democratic Party to power in Annapolis. In April, 1867 the Unionists became Republican Unionists, and in May they held the first racially integrated political convention in Maryland. They adopted a position in favor of universal manhood suffrage, which meant enfranchising black men. The Democrats' popularity had returned so quickly that the Republicans needed all the votes they could get. Also in May, 1867 a convention controlled by Democrats produced a new state constitution to replace that of 1864. When it was adopted in September, the test oaths disappeared and control of the state returned completely into the hands of the Democratic Party. Reconstruction had ended in Maryland. In October 1867 Democrat Robert T. Banks was elected Mayor of Baltimore. In November Democrat Oden Bowie replaced Thomas Swann as governor. Swann and Montgomery Blair, both former Unionist leaders, joined the Democratic Party. The Democratic Party acknowledged Maryland's return to the fold when it held the 1872 convention here. Horace Greeley won the nomination but lost the general election to Ulysses S. Grant.

The one irony of Maryland's Reconstruction is that, although it ended a decade before Northern troops withdrew from the last Southern states, African Americans began to vote three years after the Democrats regained power and, unlike what happened further South, they never lost that right. The Democratic Maryland legislature itself revised the registration laws after it became obvious that the 15th Amendment which enfranchised black men, would pass. On April 8, 1870, Elijah Quigley of Towson voted in an election for county commissioners. Blacks in Baltimore City voted in the municipal elections in October. Reconstruction had ended quickly, but not as finally as it did in the former Confederacy.

All the accommodations to political realities did not mean that the wartime bitterness had passed. Indeed, as long as the men who fought in the armies and their contemporaries remained politically active they were always associated with the side they had served. The

Baltimoreans lay the cornerstone for the new City Hall in 1867. In the aftermath of the war, the city began to look to its future

immediate hostilities did disappear though, and reminiscences of local writers who grew up in Baltimore in the 1880s and 90s show a very different city than the suspicious, war-torn, town of the 1860s.

Henry L. Mencken spent his childhood, as well as most of his adult years, in a house on Hollins Street, one of the newer squares that had been built following the success of Mt. Vernon Square. Looking back many years later, he wrote:

> The city into which I was born in 1880 had a reputation all over for what the English, in their real-estate advertising, are fond of calling the amenities. So far as I have been able to discover by a labored search of contemporary travel-books, no literary tourist, however waspish he may have been about Washington, Niagara Falls, the prairies of the West, or even Boston and New York, ever gave Baltimore a bad notice. They all agreed, often with lubricious gloats and gurgles, *(a)* that its indigenous victualry was unsurpassed in the Republic, *(b)* that its native . . . females of all ages up to thirty-five were of incomparable pulchritude, and as amiable as they were lovely, and *(c)* that its home-life was spacious, charming, full of creature comforts, and highly conducive to the facile and orderly propagation of the species.
>
> There was some truth in all these articles, but not, I regret to have to add, too much. Perhaps the one that came closest to meeting scientific tests was the first. Baltimore lay very near the immense protein factory of Chesapeake Bay, and out of the bay it ate divinely.

Mencken proceeds to wax eloquent on the subject of crabs, terrapin, and luncheons at the Rennert Hotel. Truthful to the core, he also

Above:
In the Baltimore of Mencken's childhood, wagons still banged over cobblestone streets. Here Franklin Street has been torn up and the cobblestones have been laid along the sidewalks

Left:
This circus parade was clearly a grand event, drawing a large and varied crowd

Public parks enjoyed great popularity and wide use in the nineteenth and early twentieth centuries. The boat lake in Druid Hill Park was a Sunday afternoon favorite

described the summertime stench around Back Basin and the Inner Harbor where the sewage drained, the noisy streets where delivery wagons still banged over cobblestones, and the epidemics of typhoid, malaria and smallpox which killed many, especially children living in overcrowded slum neighborhoods.

On the lighter side, he wrote of grass growing to such heights in the cobblestone streets that carters allowed their horses to graze there. He also recorded that:

> On the steep hill making eastward from the Washington Monument, in the very heart of Baltimore, some comedian once sowed wheat, and it kept on coming up for years thereafter. Every spring the Baltimore newspapers would report on the prospects of the crop, and visitors to the city were taken to see it.

Another local newspaperman, Meredith Janvier, wrote of attending Barnum's *Greatest Show on Earth* in the mid-1880s when circuses showed out on Belair Road, of riding for three cents the horse-drawn phaetons in Druid Hill Park, and of minstrel shows that played at the Academy of Music and at Ford's, Holliday Street and Front Street theaters. Janvier remembered seeing Blind Tom, a black musician, at Ford's Theater, and the composer and performer James Bland at the Holliday Street Theater. He remembered the opening in 1890 of the New Lyceum Theater where Edwin Booth, Otis Skinner and William S. Hart all performed. Helena Modjeska played Camille and Lady MacBeth there. Janvier saw Buffalo Bill's *Wild West Show* at the baseball park in the middle 1880s. Annie Oakley, who lived for a while in Cambridge, Maryland, was travelling with the show. When the show arrived, Druid Hill Park had recently acquired its first sea lion. The seal conveniently escaped just in time to be

Above:
Sheep grazed in Druid Hill Park until the mid-twentieth century

Left:
Spectators in their own carriages lined the edge of the Pimlico Race Track where the first running of the Preakness took place in 1873

Bicycles built for one and for two gained wide popularity at the end of the nineteenth century

recaptured by cowboy Buck Taylor and his lasso. Janvier, like Mencken, wrote about what he ate and drank:

> On the corner of Charles and Mulberry Streets, opposite Reese's grocery, was the apothecary shop of Dr. Adam Gosman, a fine old character with a long grey beard. He invented a gingerale and manufactured it for years in a small way in the rear of his store. His men could be seen at work through a doorway in the wall. Just here on Mulberry Street was Carrington's Dairy, where milk and ice-cream were sold. Delicious claret and port ices I got here on hot summer days. Dr. Gosman also had a small "single-cylinder" soda fountain, where the knowing one could get a glass of his famous "tonic" flavor. It must have consisted for the most part of a fine old rum and the uninitiated fellow who drank it on an empty stomach walked off sideways. This "tonic," I understand, was always a great favorite with the clergy and the few drys who existed in those days.

A wide variety of sporting activities gained in popularity in the latter days of the nineteenth century. Pimlico Race Course opened in 1870 and drew large crowds from Baltimore and out of town. The first running of the Preakness took place during the spring meeting of 1873. The new sport of lacrosse was acquiring fans, and in 1879 the first interclub lacrosse game was played in Baltimore. New York's Ravenswood Lacrosse Club defeated the Baltimore Athletic Club 3 to 1. By the 1890s, the newest craze was cycling, and several thousand cyclists belonged to at least eight bicycling clubs in town.

Major league baseball came to Baltimore in 1872 when the billboard firm A. T. Houck and Brother bought a franchise in the National Association and built a new club, the Lord Baltimores (known simply as the Lords), and a new stadium, Newington Park. Both the team and the league disappeared in 1875. A variety of Baltimore teams played non-league games until 1883, when the American Association Brooklyn Athletics moved here and became the Baltimore Orioles. Since that time a team called the Orioles has almost always played ball in this city. They belonged to the American Association, the Eastern League, the International League and finally the American League. In the days of segregated sports, Baltimore fielded teams in a Negro league beginning in 1887, when a new Lord Baltimores team began to play in Oriole Park. After 1920 the famous Black Sox played for a decade followed by the Elites just before World War II.

One grand event of the period signaled a new civic spirit and enthusiasm which had been lacking for many years before the Civil War. Baltimore's Sesquicentennial celebration in 1880 evoked sentiment and enthusiasm of an enormous magnitude and served as a focal point around which the city's diverse population could unite. Two thousand vehicles and thirty thousand persons marched in the parade. The city raised ten elaborately decorated arches. Virtually all public and private buildings were decorated. By the year of this sesquicentennial outburst the scars of division and warfare were healing and Baltimore began to prepare to enter the twentieth century.

Turn of the century Baltimore was a city of contrasts. While wealthy merchants donated fortunes to build civic and cultural institutions, many people lived in filthy, over-crowded, disease-ridden slums and worked twelve or fourteen hours a day. Political machines organized the city's voters and drew wide support. Reformers fought them for control of both offices and policy-making. The happy memories of Mencken and Janvier show only

Baltimore
BALTIMORE ELITE GIANTS 1949 NEGRO NATIONAL
LEAGUE CHAMPIONS.
TOP ROW: JOE BLACK, LEROY FARRELL, DAVIDSON, MONTE PEARSON, BILL BYRD,
AL. WILMORE, BOB ROMBY, JOHNNY HAYES, JUNIOR GILLIAM, HOSS
WALKER, Mgr.,
BOTTOM ROW: BUTCH DAVIS, LESTER LOCKETT, SYLVESTER RODGERS, HENRY
KIMBRO, VIC HARRIS, Coach., HENRY BAYLIS, FRAZIER ROB-
INSON. FRANK RUSSELL, PEEWEE BUTTS, LEON DAY.

The Baltimore Elite Giants, like many of the Negro League teams, produced top baseball players. Included here are Joe Black (top row, left), Junior Gillian (2nd from right, top row), Henry Kimbro (front row, 4th from left) and Leon Day (front row, far right). The Elites won the Negro National League championship in 1949.

Reconciliation & Growth 1865-1917

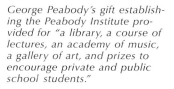

George Peabody's gift establishing the Peabody Institute provided for "a library, a course of lectures, an academy of music, a gallery of art, and prizes to encourage private and public school students."

one part of the very complex new urban world that grew at the end of the nineteenth century.

One very important facet of late nineteenth century urban life was the establishment of many major cultural, educational, and civic institutions that have benefitted the city ever since. Throughout the nation, before and primarily after the Civil War, men who had accumulated fortunes in business and industry gave large portions of their wealth, not to charity, but rather to create schools, museums, libraries and hospitals which would serve all who came to them. The creations of these philanthropists still provide the cultural base in many American cities. Baltimore's philanthropists included George Peabody, William Walters and his son Henry, Enoch Pratt, and Johns Hopkins.

George Peabody, whose gift of $1,240,000 established the Peabody Institute, was born in Danvers, Massachusetts in 1795. Because his parents were poor, he was apprenticed to a storekeeper at age eleven. In his middle teens, he journeyed to Georgetown to work with a merchant uncle there. At nineteen, Peabody formed a partnership with Elisha Riggs in a wholesale dry-goods business which they moved to Baltimore in 1815. The firm occupied "Old Congress Hall" at Baltimore and Liberty Streets. By 1830, when Peabody became the senior partner, it was one of the largest mercantile establishments in the nation. Peabody, like so many nineteenth century magnates, maintained a frugal existence. He lived in rented quarters, would not hire a cab, and carried a lunch of bread and cheese in his briefcase. Although several stories of shattered romances are told, Peabody never married.

While living in Baltimore, he mastered the principles of banking, and later he formed George Peabody and Company in London. In 1836 he moved to England. By 1850 he was beginning to distribute his fortune. Peabody sponsored a pioneering slum clearance projec in London and later an educational func designed to help rebuild the shattered Sout and extend educational opportunities tc ex-slaves and their children.

To Baltimore, Peabody gave the Institute providing for "a library, a course of lectures, ar academy of music, a gallery of art, and prizes tc encourage private and public school pupils." Although the cornerstone was laid in 1859 anc the original white marble wing completed ir 1861, the dedication had to wait until 1866 wher Peabody returned to attend the ceremonies in a city once again at peace.

William Thompson Walters was born in 182 in Pottsville, Pennsylvania, studied civil anc mining engineering in Philadelphia, and came tc Baltimore in 1841. He entered the produc commission business and became a controllin director of the Baltimore and Susquehann Railroad. In partnership with Charles Harvey h sold foreign and domestic liquors. As hi business shifted southward to Virginia and th Carolinas, Walters discovered the need for a fas freight line to carry perishable souther produce to the northern urban markets. H began consolidating small railroad lines, process which led eventually to the building c the Atlantic Coast Line Railroad and Walter fortune.

Because he sympathized with the Sout Walters chose to leave occupied Baltimore i 1861. For the duration of the war he lived in Par where he got to know contemporary Frenc artists like Corot, Millet, Delacroix, Daumie and the sculptor Antoine Louis Barye. H purchased many of their works as well as collection of Oriental ceramics. On returnin home, he displayed his collection in a gallery i his house on Mt. Vernon Place. Walters opene it to the public on selected days.

Henry Walters, William's son, shared h

Far Left:
William Walters began collecting paintings and sculpture when he was living in exile in Paris during the Civil War

Left:
William Walters' son, Henry, added to the painting and sculpture collection, built the original museum, and bequeathed both to the city of Baltimore

For the city's sesquicentennial celebration in 1880 Baltimore raised ten of these elaborate arches, decorated virtually all the buildings, and held a parade in which 30,000 persons marched

1730
1880
"INDUSTRY THE MEANS- PLENTY THE RESULT"
LORD BALTIMORE'S MOTTO.
"THE BEST OF PROPHETS FOR THE FUTURE IS THE PAST"
GEORGE PEABODY,
JOHNS HOPKINS.
TOYS

father's business acumen and his love of art. He doubled the fortune he inherited and was reputed to have been the wealthiest man south of the Mason-Dixon line. He is said to have spent $1,000,000 a year on art works from 1891, when William Walters died, until his own death forty years later. He built the original museum which still stands at the corner of Mt. Vernon Place and Center Street. Henry bequeathed his entire collection, the gallery, and a maintenance fund of $2,000,000 to the city of Baltimore.

Enoch Pratt was born in North Middeborough, Massachusetts in 1808. His father, Isaac Pratt, originally a farmer, moved into the wholesale hardware business. Enoch attended the local academy and then worked as a clerk in a wholesale hardware store in Boston. In 1831, at 22 years of age, Pratt arrived in Baltimore and organized a company which sold nails, horse shoes and mule shoes. Pratt abandoned the Puritanism of his ancestors and joined the Unitarian Church which some New Englanders living in Baltimore had built. For many years he served as treasurer of that church, often paying its debts out of his own pocket. In 1848 he erected his home at Park Avenue and Monument Street, the building which is now owned by the Maryland Historical Society. Pratt supported the Union cause in the Civil War and rejoiced publicly when General Butler occupied Federal Hill.

As Pratt's profits from the hardware business grew, he diversified, gained control of the Maryland Steamship Company, became a vice-president of the Philadelphia, Wilmington and Baltimore Railroad, and invested in banking and fire insurance. Pratt, like Peabody, was reputed to be something of a miser. Baltimoreans jested about his habit of picking up nails from the street. One legend has it that a tramp, seeing the poorly dressed Pratt walking towards his own house, called out, "There's no use going in there, Brother. You'll not get a damned crust."

Pratt's good works around Baltimore belie his reputation. He provided financial support fo the Maryland School for the Deaf and Dumb in Frederick and for Cheltenham, a reform schoo for young black boys. He bestowed $2,000,00 on his friend Dr. Moses Sheppard for a hospita for the mentally handicapped. Pratt kept his bes known gift, the Free Library, a secret unti excavation for the main building had alread begun. Then he offered the city the library plu $833,333 provided the city give $50,000 annuall to support and maintain the library. Pratt himsel selected the nine original trustees and stated in a letter to them that the books were "for all, rich and poor, without distinction of race or color who, when properly accredited, can take out the books, if they will handle them carefully and return them." On January 5, 1886 the centra library opened its doors and 28,000 books to the public. Four branches opened the same year.

The founder of Baltimore's internationall best known institution, Johns Hopkins, was the only native Marylander of the four majo philanthropists. Born in 1795, Johns Hopkin grew up on a large farm in Anne Arundel Count where the family performed all their own labo after his Quaker father freed their slaves. It is said that Hopkins always valued education especiall highly, since he had had so little time for it. A age 18, he came to Baltimore to work with hi Uncle Gerard, a commission merchant and grocer. Johns Hopkins got in trouble with both his uncle and the Quaker community during the 1819 depression when he began allowing customers to pay their bills in whiskey. He left hi uncle, opened his own wholesale provisior company, and bottled whiskey sold under the label "Hopkins Best."

Hopkins later invested in the developmen of the port and the B&O Railroad, of which he was the largest single stockholder at the time o

Opposite Page:
Enoch Pratt kept his library gift a secret until the excavation for the main building began

Left:
The original main building of the Enoch Pratt Free Library opened at the corner of Cathedral and Mulberry Streets in 1886

Johns Hopkins made detailed plans before his death for the hospital and university which he endowed

Below:
Johns Hopkins left his estate Clifton to be the site of the university he endowed. The trustees chose to build downtown, and Clifton later became a park

Reconciliation & Growth
1865-1917

his death. Hopkins supported B&O president John Garrett during the Civil War and even contributed $50,000 to furnish transportation facilities to the Union. As Hopkins accumulated his fortune, he moved into banking and became the leading financier in town.

Johns Hopkins, like his friend George Peabody, never married. The traditional explanation is that he was in love with his cousin Elizabeth and that his Uncle Gerard forbade the marriage. When Hopkins made his will he left one million dollars to various relatives and local charities. He divided the rest of his eight million dollar estate to provide for the founding of the hospital and university which bear his name. Before his death, he made detailed plans and chose his trustees. He bequeathed his Clifton estate to the university. He purchased the grounds of the Old Maryland Hospital on Broadway and oversaw the early planning of the hospital. His will specified that the hospital should constitute part of the university's medical school and that there should be full cooperation between the two institutions. The will also specified that only the interest should be used to pay for the buildings. The capital itself was not to be touched.

Hopkins died in his sleep on December 24, 1873. The university trustees convened. After consulting the presidents of Harvard, Yale, Michigan and Cornell, they invited Daniel Coit Gilman to become president. Gilman accepted and began to recruit a faculty. Proven scholars such as English mathematician James Joseph Sylvester and classicist Basil L. Gildersleeve committed themselves to teach at the new university, where studies were to follow the German practice.

Johns Hopkins became the first American institution to grant a Ph.D. for accomplishment in research work. The university, situated near Mt. Vernon Square, not at Clifton, grew by 1900 to nine buildings. By 1901 when Gilman retired 143 faculty members and 651 student constituted the community. In that same yea William H. Buckler, Francis M. Jencks, R. Bren Keyser, Samuel Keyser, J. LeRoy White an William Wyman gave to the university the 17 acres of land on Charles Street wher "Homewood", built by Charles Carroll, stood Clifton was sold to the city and the money from the sale used to erect the new buildings. Dr. Ir Remsen, the university's first professor o chemistry and known for his work on saccharin succeeded Gilman and presided over the mov to Homewood.

The hospital opened in 1889 in fourtee buildings on the East Baltimore site that John Hopkins had selected. As the hospital neare completion, financial difficulties of the B&C Railroad led to a shrinkage in the university' income from that stock. The university ha already attracted prominent professors for th future medical school with promises that i would be modelled after the best Europea ones. By 1890, other institutions were beginnin to try to lure these professors elsewhere.

A group of local women came to the rescue Mary Garrett, who had inherited a large fortun from her father John, the president of the B&O joined Martha Carey Thomas, who had earned Ph.D. at the University of Zurich, and severa other girlhood friends, and women's activist Mary Gwinn and Elizabeth King. In 1890 the established the Women's Fund Committee an by 1892 had raised the necessary $500,000, muc of it coming from the gifts of Mary Garrett. The offered the money to the university on th conditions that women be admitted to th medical school on the same terms as men, tha it be a graduate school, and that prospectiv students be required to have a knowledge o physics, chemistry, biology, French and German

The medical school finally opened in 1893

In 1885, future president Woodrow Wilson sang in the Hopkins Glee Club pictured here. Wilson is second from the left in the back row

The original biological laboratory of Hopkins' downtown campus stood at Eutaw and Little Ross Streets

In Hopkins Hall on Little Ross Street, the seminary of History and Politics looked like this around the year 1890

Its high standards and stringent admission criteria made it a model for the nation. Dr. William Osler, the hospital's first Physician-in-Chief, is reported to have joked to Dr. William Welch, first dean of the medical school, "Welch, we were lucky to get in as professors, for I am sure that neither you nor I could ever get in as students."

The magnitude of the growth of educational institutions at the turn-of-the-century period is quite remarkable. Not only did the four philanthropists give to Baltimore the nationally renowned facilities of the Peabody Institute, the Walters Gallery, the Pratt Library and the Johns Hopkins University and Hospital, but many other colleges and schools first opened their doors in these decades. In fact, most of the city's centers of higher learning originated late in the 19th century.

In 1865 when the General Assembly in Annapolis authorized a statewide public school system, it also established the Maryland State Normal School. At the time of its formal opening in the old Red Man's Hall on North Paca Street in January 1866, eleven women students had enrolled. H. A. Newell was principal. By the end of the first year 48 students attended. In 1872 the Normal School moved to larger quarters at Charles and Franklin Streets. By 1876 when the school moved to its third location at Carrollton and Lafayette Streets, the student body had grown to 206. In 1915 the State Normal School moved to its current location on York Road north of the city where it now exists as Towson University.

The first normal school to train black teachers formally opened in December 1867 in a renovated Friends' Meeting House at Saratoga and Courtland Streets. Privately supported, this school received added funds in 1871 when the trustees of Nelson Wells' estate contributed the entire remaining capital to the school after the opening of the black public schools.

The normal school eventually evolved int the present-day Bowie State College located i Anne Arundel County. It was not until 1900 tha the Baltimore Board of School Commissioner established a Colored Training School t prepare black teachers. This public institutio was renamed the Fannie Jackson Coppi Normal School in 1926 in honor of a forme slave who bought her freedom and became th first American black woman to earn a colleg degree. The institution became the Coppin Stat Teachers' College in 1950 and, when it broad-ened its curriculum, the Coppin State Colleg in 1963.

In 1867 a second African American colleg was chartered: the Centenary Biblical Institute which is now Morgan State University. Centenar was established by the Methodist Conference of Baltimore, Washington, Wilmington an Delaware. The school held classes at the Shar Street Church until the building on East Saratog Street was completed in 1872. The Rev. J. Emor Round served as first president of the school whose primary function was to train young me as Methodist ministers.

By 1880, the student body of 125 ha outgrown the Saratoga Street building. Whe this was discussed at the Methodist Conferenc Dr. and Mrs. John F. Goucher offered to donat a lot at Fulton and Edmondson Avenues alon with $5000 towards a building on the condi-tion that black Methodists raise the additiona money needed. In this way the building woul open free of any mortgage. Hundreds of smal donations from the black Methodist churche poured in, and in 1881 an $18,000 building wa dedicated.

In 1890, Dr. Lyttleton F. Morgan, forme chairman of the Board of Trustees, donated a large sum of money which enabled the schoo to offer general collegiate courses, and the

Opposite Page:
In the 1880s, Dr. John F. Goucher, shown here, and his wife Mary donated land and funds to Methodist Colleges that were established in Baltimore for both black and female students

Left:
A group of local women founded a college preparatory school, Bryn Mawr, for girls in 1885. The same group raised money for the Hopkins Medical School and donated it on the condition that women students be admitted on the same terms as men. This group included (left to right) Martha Carey Thomas, Mary Mackall Gwinn, Mary Elizabeth Garrett (seated), Julia Rebecca Rogers (on floor), and Elizabeth Tabor King

Nurses working at the Johns Hopkins Hospital in the late eighteen hundreds practiced one of the few respectable women's occupations of the day

The first campus of Goucher College on St. Paul Street remained in use until the move to Towson was completed in the 1950s

institution became Morgan College. At the end of World War I, Morgan purchased its current property on Hillen Road. In 1939 the school affiliated with the state college system.

The Methodist Conference of Baltimore sponsored another local college, one for female students. The Women's College of Baltimore, incorporated in 1885, opened three years later under the leadership of its first president, William H. Hopkins. In 1890, the Rev. John F. Goucher, donor for a second time of a site and main building for a Baltimore college, became president. In a period when women were forbidden admission to most major men's universities, including Johns Hopkins' undergraduate school, Goucher College, as the school became known in 1910, offered an academic program in an urban location to young women from Baltimore and out of town. Goucher was one of a number of women's colleges established throughout the country which played an enormously important role in offering professional and academic training and creating a large and significant group of educated women.

A Roman Catholic college for women, Mount Saint Agnes, increased the availability of education for women in Baltimore. It opened in 1890 in conjunction with St. Mary's School, which had been established in 1867 by the Sisters of Mercy. The Mount Washington Seminary, later the Mount Washington Country School for Boys, opened on the same campus in 1899. A different sort of school, St. Mary's Industrial School, was established in 1866 by Archbishop Martin John Spalding for boys without homes and boys who were sent there by the courts. Babe Ruth was surely the most famous alumnus of that Catholic institution which served the community until 1950.

Most of Baltimore's leading private schools also opened during this period. They met a variety of needs not served by the city's public school system which, following the Civil War, provided a less than excellent education. The schools were overcrowded and understaffed. Teachers got jobs because of political connections, not ability or training. All the private schools benefitted from the philanthropy typical of the era.

McDonogh School, originally a "farm school for worthy boys" which was to provide sound academic offerings as well, opened in 1873, the gift of John McDonogh. In 1884 the group of women who later raised the money for the Hopkins Medical School pushed for the establishment of an institution to prepare girls to attend good universities. Bryn Mawr School was the result. Previously, only the Quakers offered high level academic subjects to girls in Baltimore. Now, Martha Carey Thomas, who served as the first dean of Bryn Mawr College outside Philadelphia, Mary Garrett and the others led the way and the new school opened in 1885. Less than a decade later, in 1894, another girls' institution, the Roland Park Country School, began offering instruction. Until 1908, it benefitted from the sponsorship of the Roland Park Company, then in the process of developing the new suburb.

Another Baltimore woman activist, Mrs. Francis Carey King, led in the founding of the Country School for Boys of Baltimore City in 1897. It was located at Homewood until it moved to Roland Park in 1911. The purpose of the school, which received strong support from Daniel Coit Gilman, for whom the school was renamed in 1910, was to provide the educational offerings and activities of boarding schools which most of Baltimore's upper class boys had attended previously. In the same year that Gilman opened, a small school, later called the Calvert School, began teaching fifteen pupils in a room over a drugstore at Madison Street and

Opposite Page:
This picture of Morgan's fourth year class in 1923 shows a formality characteristic in all schools during the pre-World War II period

In the late nineteenth century, only a small percentage of the students in the city's public school system managed to graduate from the elite high schools such as Baltimore City College .

Right:
Prior to World War I, Morgan College was located downtown. Since its founding in 1867, Morgan has educated generations of African American leaders

Park Avenue. Its goal was to provide excellence in primary education. The school, now located on Tuscany Road, pioneered in developing home instruction courses. The Park School, opened in 1912 in a house near Druid Hill Park. At a time when most private schools admitted very few Jewish students, Park welcomed them and children of all faiths. Like the other schools, Park moved from the center city, first to Liberty Heights Avenue and then in 1959 to its current location on Old Court Road.

The establishment of the new schools, although some offered a free education to a small number of select students, benefited primarily the well-to-do residents of Baltimore. In this period of great contrasts, people of fairly substantial means were not only acquiring wide opportunities for entertainment and education but were engaged in the process of moving into newly burgeoning suburbs with their open spaces and new homes.

First horse car lines and then electrified trolleys allowed people to commute downtown from even more distant locations. Fashionable town houses were built north of the business district along streets like Madison Avenue and McCulloch Street, on Eutaw Place, in Bolton Hill. East, south and west of town, smaller row houses soon lined the streets and boulevards. The development of these moderately priced homes and the growth of neighborhood building and loan associations allowed many middle and working class residents to become home owners. Baltimore consistently enjoyed one of the highest rates of home ownership among major American cities.

More rapid public transportation led to the development of suburbs as urban residents sought to combine the benefits of spaciousness with the conveniences of city living. During the 1870s and 1880s such diverse areas as Arlington, Catonsville, Highlandtown, Huntingdon, Mt. Washington, Peabody Heights, and Pimlico began to grow. Old mill towns like Hampden and Woodberry along the Jones Falls were connected to central Baltimore by the street railway lines.

The suburban belt, located in the county, grew rapidly during the latter part of the nineteenth century. As more and more belt residents became commuters, annexation once again became an issue. Under Maryland's constitution of 1867, residents of the area to be annexed had to vote their approval. Several times the belt's populace chose to remain in the county with its inferior services and lower taxes. The eastern segment of the belt, Canton and Highlandtown, strongly opposed the city's regulations of slaughterhouses, many of which were located there, and also the blue laws which would close the beer gardens and other drinking establishments on Sundays.

By 1888, however, the belt's problems were becoming unmanageable. The population was increasing rapidly. The county failed to provide adequate water and sewer facilities and this lack threatened the public health. Police and fire protection were meager. The county government reaped large revenues from the suburbanites of the belt but favored the rural areas when money had to be spent. When the annexation question was put on the ballot in 1888, the western, northern, and eastern districts of the belt voted separately. The northern and western districts chose to join with the city, while Highlandtown and Canton opted for continued freedom from urban restrictions. Baltimore City thus gained about 23 square miles of land and 38,000 people.

The acquisition of so much new land apparently inspired schemes both for development and for protection of open spaces. The city purchased additional land for public parks. In the southwest, Baltimore bought the land of a

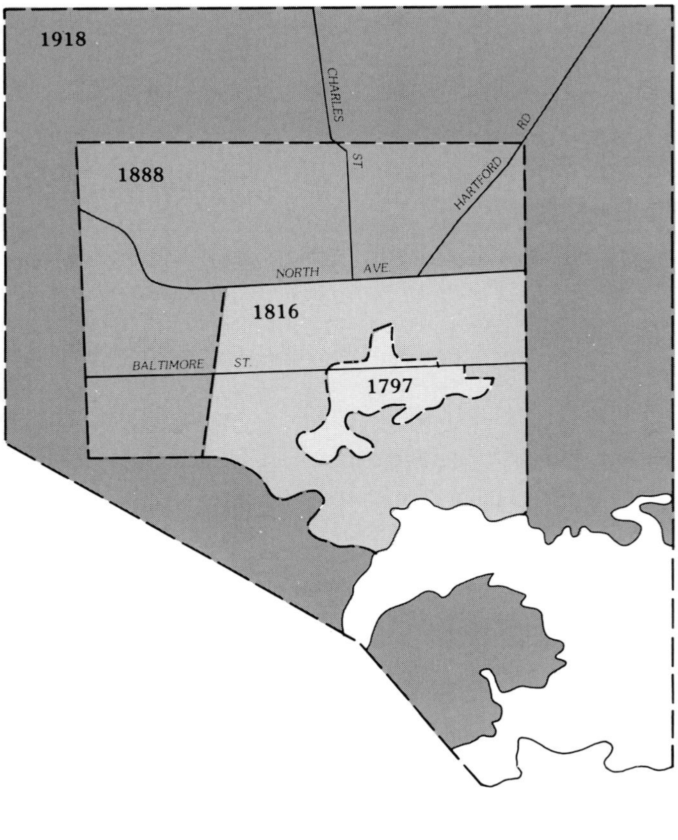

Above:
The construction of moderately priced row houses and the growth of neighborhood building and loan associations created a high rate of home ownership among Baltimoreans

Left:
Baltimore gained twenty-three square miles of land in 1888 and more than fifty additional square miles in 1918

German Schuetzen (shooting) park and landscaped Carroll Park there. Mount Clare, the home of Charles Carroll, the Barrister, which was located in the new park, was renovated. At the same time, the city purchased Johns Hopkins' estate, Clifton, to be converted into a park for residents of the northeast.

A major suburban innovation came in the 1890s in the form of Roland Park, which was privately developed and planned first by George E. Kessler and then Frederick Law Olmsted, Jr. and John C. Olmsted. One goal of the planners was to preserve the natural beauty of the landscape. The streets curved with the contours of the land. Large and comfortable family houses were built and a trolley car line opened. Restrictive covenants designed to preserve the residential nature of the area prohibited stables and other unhealthy use of the land. Business development was limited. The restrictions went much further, however, and effectively prevented both Jews and blacks from buying property in Roland Park for many years.

Once Roland Park was completed, Frederick Law Olmsted, Jr., whose father had planned Central Park in New York, formulated a plan for a system of parks throughout the city. At the behest of reformers like Theodore Marburg of the Municipal Art Society, whose primary interest lay in beautifying the city and making it a healthful place to live, Olmsted introduced a scheme for maintaining as green areas all the valleys along Jones Falls, Herring Run, Gwynn's Falls, and parts of the shoreline of the Patapsco.

Parks and suburbs were only part of the expansion that permeated Baltimore's life during the end of the nineteenth century. The real basis of the prosperity that allowed beautification and pleasant living was the income produced by commerce and industry.

Baltimore's commerce had been hurt when the Civil War ended much of the trade between the city and the South. Once peace returned, however, Baltimore investors began to pour capital into the rebuilding of the devastated region. By 1900 an estimated $100,000,000 had been invested by Baltimoreans in southern railroads, street cars, cotton mills, coal, iron and phosphate mines, lumber tracts and municipalities. Prominent firms like Alex Brown and Company, Wilson, Colston and Company, and Middendorf, Oliver and Company profited in these undertakings. While bringing raw materials out of the South, Baltimore gained further by selling many manufactured goods there, among them dry goods, notions, provisions and groceries, liquors, clothing, boots and shoes, hats, toys, and articles of the jobbing trade. The city was frequently called the "gateway to the South."

Baltimore was also nicknamed "The Liverpool of America," reflecting the size of its foreign trade. In 1870, Baltimore's $33,000,000 worth of foreign trade ranked fifth in the nation. By 1900, the city ranked third nationally with $130,000,000 in foreign trade. Baltimore was one of the chief outlets for raw materials: grain and grain products, cotton, and leaf tobacco. Imports from Latin America were especially important and included coffee, sugar, tropical fruits, copper and other metals, and Peruvian guano. The inauguration of direct steamship service between Baltimore and Bremen in 1868 augmented the already strong connections between the two cities.

Baltimore possessed all the prerequisites for the large-scale industrial development that had begun before the Civil War. The city was served by excellent rail and shipping facilities, had a supply of raw materials available at a low cost, potential markets, a supply of capital, and a ready labor force. Furthermore, the city's government actively supported industrialization. For example, in 1877 the City Council appointed a

Top Left:
Baltimore's industries expanded rapidly at the end of the nineteenth century. Hats, clothing, boots, and shoes were among the city's major exports. Shown here is an advertisement of Armstrong, Cator and Company

Top Right:
Bromo Seltzer had its home office and laboratories in Baltimore

Above:
The port was a major factor in the city's economic success. In 1870, the approximate date of this picture, Baltimore's foreign trade ranked fifth in the nation. By 1900 the city ranked third

commission to consider ways and means to encourage industrial development. Ferdinand C. Latrobe, who was mayor at that time, gave enthusiastic support.

Between 1870 and 1900, the number of industries established in Baltimore trebled and the capital invested increased six-fold. This was typical of the national pattern. Locally, growth came in widely diversified areas such as men's clothing, foundries and machine shops, straw hats, copper, and steel, especially steel rails made at Sparrows Point by the Maryland Steel Company. Boot and shoe making were important as was the manufacture of fertilizers. Slaughtering and meatpacking increased on the outskirts of town. Canning of fruits and vegetables and especially oysters benefitted from new techniques. By 1870 over one hundred packing houses were located in Baltimore. Cotton mills along the Jones Falls in towns like Woodberry became part of the city in 1888. Nationally-known rye whiskey was distilled here.

Baltimore's industries expanded to the south and east, along the waterfront and the tracks of the B&O and what was to become the Pennsylvania Railroad. The industrial center shifted from the Jones Falls Valley to new areas like Canton, Highlandtown, Locust Point and Curtis Bay. A subsidiary of the Maryland Steel Company built Sparrows Point, complete with housing for everyone from executives to unskilled workers, with a separate village for black workers on the other side of Humphrey's Creek.

Near the end of the nineteenth century, industries began to consolidate, both to acquire capital for mechanization and to end the competitive price wars that bankrupted many firms. In some cases the consolidation was a local affair as it was when sixteen breweries formed the Maryland Brewing Company and the street car lines joined in the United Railways and Electric Company. In other cases, local companies were absorbed by national conglomerates, as were many local canneries by the American Can Company and the Maryland Steel Company by Bethlehem Steel.

The increased use of ever more highly sophisticated machinery led to the replacement of skilled by unskilled workers. While mechanization meant lower prices for consumers, it also meant lower wages for workers. Many of the unskilled positions were held by women and children who might earn as little as $.40 a day. In 1885 the average male unskilled worker earned $1.25 a day, and skilled workers $1.75 to $3.00 a day. An average-sized row house rented for about $78 a year. The average work day lasted 10 to 12 hours. Many women and children worked in East Baltimore's sweatshops which produced over half the men's clothing manufactured here. The canneries also employed large numbers of women and children. Workers employed in hazardous jobs often were fired if faulty machinery injured them severely enough to prevent them from doing their work.

Various labor unions organized to press for better wages and hours, an end to blacklisting union members, abolition of child labor, and laws requiring compulsory education and workmen's compensation. The Knights of Labor formed their first local assembly in Baltimore in 1878. Eight years later, 16 local assemblies claimed twenty-five thousand members. On Labor Day, 1886, seventeen thousand marched in the parade. Locally and throughout the nation, the Knights of Labor was superseded by the craft-oriented unions that formed the American Federation of Labor. Members tended to be in the skilled trades. Because their skills were not easily replaced and because their relatively high wages allowed the accumulation of a strike fund, the strike became an important

Labor unions worked hard to improve wages and working conditions. But in 1890, the year of the Labor Day parade, their impact remained limited

Top:
Better lit than many, this garment factory shows the crowded conditions in which the women worked, often earning less than a dollar a day

Above:
Children often worked at hazardous jobs such as this one in a local cannery

Top:
This postcard picture of a parade in 1914, reviewed by Mayor James Preston, shows the growth in the influence of organized labor. Note the popularity of straw hats worn by almost all the spectators in the foreground

Above:
It was not until the turn of the century that laws were established to ban children from working in food processing establishments such as this one and requiring them to attend school

weapon in the hands of these craft unions. The Baltimore Federation of Labor, which affiliated with the AFL in 1889, consisted of a wide variety of craft unions. Despite a setback during the depression years 1893 to 1897 when almost half the industrial workers in the city were unemployed, approximately twenty thousand members belonged to 65 or 70 different trade unions in Baltimore in 1900.

Nearly two hundred strikes involving thirty thousand workers occurred between 1881 and 1900. Many were violent affairs. Sometimes workers lost their jobs. Other times they achieved limited gains. Before World War I, the few concrete gains were limited to strong unions or to measures supported by middle-class Progressive reformers. For example, the Federation of Labor won for municipal employees a 9-hour work day in 1892 and an 8-hour day six years later. But this was rare. In 1886, the building trades union achieved a reduction of their working hours from 10 to 9 per day. In 1892, clothing workers won a 10-hour day, reduced from 15 or more, but did not succeed in improving conditions in the overcrowded, unsafe sweatshops. The first law requiring city inspection and licensing of sweatshops was passed in 1902 and strengthened in 1914. The first workmen's compensation law was passed in 1902. By 1914, only a third of the labor force worked more than 60 hours a week.

An interesting sidelight on local labor developments were the policies developed by John Garrett of the B&O. After defeating the worst strike in the railroad's history in 1877, he offered several benefits to his workers: pension plan, a burial society, accident insurance paid for by the employees, and payments to widows. The company established savings accounts and a system of home loans for its workers. The whole plan served as a model for companies trying to rationalize some progressive scheme of

The children who attended school, black and white, were luckier than the children working in factories. Here students from the Schwarz Avenue School pose for a school photo.

Baltimore and Ohio workers benefitted from welfare policies developed by railroad president John Garrett after a strike in 1877

management-labor relations.

Child labor laws were supported strongly by many segments of society not involved in the labor movement as a whole. A series of laws culminated in the 1902 enactment of a compulsory education law for children 8 to 12 and a 1906 law which forbade children under 12 from being employed in any gainful occupation. Ten years later, children under 16 were prohibited from working except in the canning industry and domestic service.

World War I strengthened the status of labor organizations when the government agreed to grant unions the right to organize and bargain collectively in exchange for a promise not to strike. Wartime demands led to higher wages. Many of the gains were not permanent, however. Peacetime brought renewed resistance to labor organization that was halted only by the Wagner Act of 1935.

In Baltimore, industrial development, working conditions and labor organization followed the national pattern. The depression of 1893, however, ended the boom in Baltimore. At the time many local companies were bought up by larger corporations headquartered elsewhere, many of the new owners began to purchase in other cities things once supplied by local manufacturers. Consequently Baltimore industrial position relative to other citie declined. Baltimore ranked 8th nationally i total manufacturing in 1880 and 11th in 191 Despite this decline, however, the city absolute production grew as did its income an its population.

Immigration into Baltimore after the Civ War brought a wide variety of newcomers to liv and work in the city. Ex-Confederates fror Virginia arrived, as did farmers from Lancaste County. Black farm workers from Souther Maryland came seeking better opportunities i the urban economy. Europeans came from a increasing number of countries.

In 1860 and 1870, most of the immigrant still came from Germany or Ireland. Diversifica tion began slowly as Bohemians, Scandinavian Italians and Poles began to arrive. By 1880 mor than one thousand Bohemians lived i Baltimore. Ten years later, more than fou thousand Russians, mostly Jews, had settled o the eastern side of the city. By 1900, over te thousand Russians outnumbered the more tha two thousand people born in Poland and Ital and the country now called Czechoslovakia. I the early part of the twentieth century Lithuanians, Greeks, and smaller numbers fron other countries moved to Baltimore. From 192 until 1960 foreign immigrants came only in smal numbers. Changes in the immigration law resulted in the increases seen in the censu reports of 1960 and 1970.

Until 1920 Germans continued to be th largest foreign-born group in Baltimore. Ove thirty thousand German-born residents wer counted in each census from 1860 through 191 They maintained and augmented the wide rang of institutions they had established earlier German-English public schools, the Turnverein social and musical clubs, and churches al flourished. As many Germans began to mov

Above:
Delivering newspapers was popular work for children because they could earn money and attend school at the same time. This substation stood on Bank Street around the year 1910

Despite the gains by organized labor and reformers, enormous gaps in life-style remained between the upper class and the working class. Evergreen House (opposite page) on North Charles Street, was purchased by the Garrett family in 1878. Alley houses such as these (left) provided homes for a large segment of Baltimore workers

Mt. Vernon Place and Charles Street, one of Baltimore's elite neighborhoods, shown here during the blizzard of 1899

outward from the center city, their institutions followed them. A Schuetzen park was opened on Harford Road. The Redemptorists built churches on Belair and Hillen Roads. German Jews tended to move westward across town in the 1880s to the area west of Greene Street around Lexington and Lombard Streets, and then after 1895 turned northward. By 1910, all the German-Jewish synagogues were located in an area bounded by North Avenue, Bolton, Lanvale and McCulloch Streets. Many Germans, both Christians and Jews, participated in early labor organizations and often transmitted ideas on reform and class struggle from Europe. More and more Germans moved into political offices and professional and management jobs throughout the city.

Like the Germans, the Irish continued to solidify their position. They had a strong ally in James Cardinal Gibbons, who had been born in 1834 of Irish parents living on Gay Street in the heart of Old Town. Ordained in 1861, made bishop of Baltimore in 1877, and invested as cardinal in 1886, he rose to a position of eminence in Baltimore and played an active role in civic and social reform throughout his career. Other members of the Irish community rose to power through the political machines that characterized municipal politics in the latter part of the nineteenth century. The Irish population had increasingly dispersed throughout the city as large numbers of second and third generation Irish-Americans moved into better jobs and middle class status.

The newcomers who arrived in the late nineteenth and early twentieth centuries faced many of the same problems that had greeted the Germans and Irish of the previous generation. Most landed with little or no money and without the ability to read, write or speak English. Most had no jobs or could obtain only menial ones. They generally received the lowest pay and lived in the worst housing. They faced prejudice and discrimination from both native Americans and earlier immigrant groups.

Bohemians began arriving in Baltimore at the end of the Civil War and settled first in Fells Point, then further uptown along Barnes and

Most immigrant ships docked at Piers 8 and 9 at Locust Point

Abbott Streets near Broadway, then still further north along Collington Avenue near the Northeast Market. Many Bohemians migrated to escape the exploitation of the Austrian Empire, of which they were a subject people, and especially to avoid service in the Austrian army. By 1870, over 700 Bohemians had settled in Baltimore. They appealed to the Redemptorist priests at St. Michael's, a German church, to help them establish their own parish. St. Wenceslaus Parish was formed in 1872 and placed under the charge of the Rev. Valentine Vacula, the first Bohemian priest to come to Baltimore.

St. Wenceslaus parochial school opened in 1880 and offered morning sessions in Czech and afternoon sessions in English. Not until 1910 did English become the primary language in both sessions. The parish grew, and in 1914 Cardinal Gibbons was present at the laying of the cornerstone for the present Romanesque church on Ashland Avenue. Two additional churches served the Czech community: the Mount Tabor Bohemian Methodist Church and the Moravian Presbyterian Church whose pastor, the Rev. Frank Novak, played a leading role in sectarian activities as well as church affairs.

Many early Bohemian settlers worked as tailors. Others did piecework at home. Although most Czechs did not earn high wages, they tended to be thrifty and rapidly adopted the Baltimore practice of buying their own homes. In 1900, twenty men met at Joseph Klecka's Tavern on Ashland Avenue and formed the Slavic Savings and Loan Association, the first of many similar institutions that made it possible for a high percentage of Bohemians to buy homes. August Klecka, one of Joseph's sons, in 1915 was the first Bohemian elected to the City Council.

Another community leader, Col. Wenceslaus Shimek, had arrived in Baltimore at the age of 15, just after the end of the Civil War. Seven years later he opened a barrel-organ factory on President Street. Shimek served as president of the Bohemian Building Association. He started a Czech-language newspaper, the *Telegraf* which, after 1929, was edited by the Rev. Frank Novak and published by August Klecka. Shimek was a politician, too. He often went to meet the boats and greet newcomers, helping them find a place to stay and a job.

The Sokol was almost as important as the church in the Bohemian community. The Sokol, which means falcon, served originally as an organization to train members to fight for Czechoslovakian independence. In this country the Sokols resembled the German Turnverein, which emphasized athletics and physical conditioning and fostered an interest in major issues of the day. Baltimore's Sokol was formed in 1872. Members met on Frederick Street near Fells Point until 1902 when the group accepted an offer to use Shimek's Hall on North Broadway.

When an independent Czechoslovak state was created after World War I, local Bohemians and Slovaks joined in the celebrations and for years afterwards held parades and festivities on October 28, the Czechoslovak independence day. Before and during World War II, the community strongly opposed Hitler and his takeover of Czechoslovakia. After the war, many residents began to move away from the neighborhood around Collington Avenue, and people of Czechoslovak descent are now widely dispersed throughout the city.

Early Polish immigrants in Baltimore settled in Fells Point where about ten families lived in 1870. From then until 1920, Poles came in large numbers to escape the economic hardship that resulted from the partitioning of Poland by Germany, Austria and Russia. Many were peasants driven from their small farms by hunger and desperation. Although a lucky 25 percent knew German, most spoke no English. The new

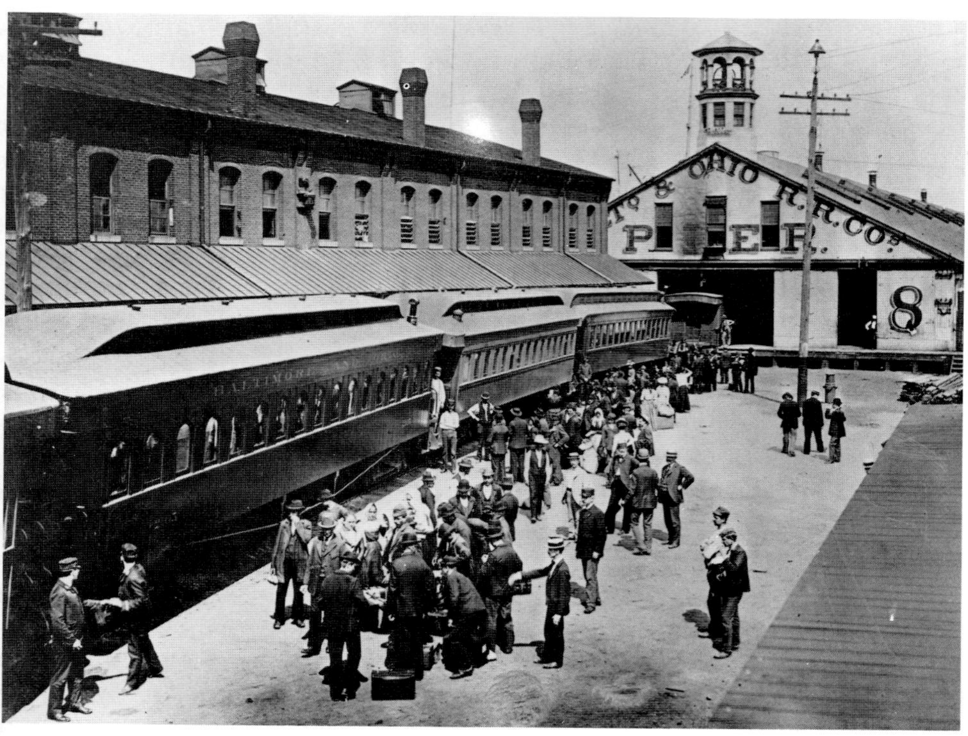

Above:
On arrival, newcomers had to wait to be processed by immigration and health officials. This photograph of an immigrant pen at Locust Point was taken early in the twentieth century

Left:
B&O trains came directly onto the piers to meet immigrants leaving Baltimore for points west

arrivals often worked on the railroads and in the shipyards, for construction companies and clothing manufacturers and in the steel mills.

The first Polish Catholic church, St. Stanislaus, was organized in 1880 when members of the community invited Father Peter Koncz to come to Baltimore. The church now stands at Ann and Aliceanna Streets in Fells Point. As the community continued to grow and move northward towards Eastern Avenue, a second church, Holy Rosary, was built on South Chester Street in 1886. In the early 1900s, the Polish community spread eastward towards Canton where St. Casimir's Church was built. Significant numbers of Poles settled in Locust Point and Curtis Bay, where St. Aloysius Church was founded. All the parish churches conducted schools.

Because the immigrants were extremely poor, the home buying process was often stretched out over several generations. Immigrants frequently lived in crowded conditions where both sanitation and health were poor. Families were large, and many women went to work, often in canneries, to make ends meet. Like the Germans and the Bohemians, Poles began to found building and loan societies, twenty of them by 1914, and to buy homes.

Numerous other institutions were created by the Polish community. The Polish Home has provided facilities for various social, educational, and recreational groups. The Polish National Alliance opened Baltimore's first library of books and other materials in Polish. The Polish Falcons began as a gymnastic club similar to the Turnverein and the Sokols, but the organization never played the major role in the Polish community that the others did among Germans and Bohemians. A newspaper, the *Jednosc-Polonia,* was published for many years. It had been preceded by other newspapers dating from 1891.

Perhaps because of their harsher economic struggles, Baltimore's Poles were comparatively slow in gaining political representation. The first Polish city councilman, a grocer named Edward Novak, won election in 1923 when roughly 11,000 Poles lived within Baltimore.

Polish people maintained an interest in the land of their birth, or their parents' birth. Before America's entry into World War I, several hundred men from Baltimore joined a Polish legion attached to the British army. Poles celebrated their nation's unification after World War I, and later opposed Hitler's invasion. Since the easing of immigration restrictions, Poles have once again begun to arrive in Baltimore. Although many people of Polish descent have spread throughout the city and county, especially to the east and northeast out Belair Road, centers of Polish settlement are still visible in East Baltimore and Locust Point, especially near the churches.

The most enduring ethnic community in a physical sense is Little Italy. In the 1870s and 1880s, Italians began to settle in this area around the President Street Station, often renting rooms from earlier German, Irish and Jewish immigrants. Driven from Italy by droughts and pervasive poverty, few spoke any English. Italian men worked on the railroad and as vendors of fruits and vegetables. Some were skilled barbers, masons, and tailors. Italian women tried to remain in the home instead of working in nearby industries. As families were able to buy their own homes, women often supplemented the family's income by taking in boarders.

The most pressing desire of the new community was to build a church in its midst. Archbishop Gibbons in 1880 appointed Father Joseph Andrei, a native of Turin, to build St. Leo's Church. Religious festivals became major events. The two largest were celebrated to

Left:
Immigrants often held festivals where they wore traditional clothes and enjoyed food, music, and dancing. This picture shows a Czech folk festival held in 1938

Above:
James Cardinal Gibbons, shown here at Mt. Royal Station later in his life, grew up in Baltimore's Irish community. He provided support for the many successive groups of newcomers as they arrived in the city

honor St. Anthony and St. Gabriel. St. Anthony's fete on June 13 began in 1904. When the great Baltimore fire had threatened Little Italy earlier that year, a group of residents had prayed to St. Anthony. The flames stopped at the Jones Falls and Little Italy was saved. The St. Gabriel's procession began soon after the canonization of the saint from Abruzzi in 1920. The festival bore special meaning because many Baltimore Italian families had their roots in the vicinity of Abruzzi. The church provided an institutional center for the community. As the Germans, Irish and Jews began to move away from the area around Exeter and Stiles Streets, Italians remained. By 1920 the neighborhood was almost exclusively Italian, a characteristic it has maintained to the present day.

As the Italian community became better established and people had time to save some money, prosperity increased. Men who had worked for Irish contractors began their own companies. Many worked in politically connected jobs in departments like public works and sanitation. Others opened the now famous restaurants. Others stayed in school and became professionals. As community resources im proved, a lodge of the Order of the Sons of Italy was founded in 1913 to aid new arrivals.

Italians gained political power relatively early compared to many immigrant groups. The community's first political leader, Vincent Palmisano, was elected to the Maryland House of Delegates in 1914, to the Baltimore City Council the following year, and to the United States Congress in 1926. A second powerful man succeeded Palmisano as Little Italy's best known Baltimorean. Thomas D'Alesandro, Jr., son of an immigrant, was elected as a Delegate in 1926, then went to Congress in 1938 when he defeated Palmisano, and was elected Mayor of Baltimore in 1947. His son, Thomas D'Alesandro III, was elected mayor in 1967. Since 1960, Italian immigration has increased again, and in 1970 more people born in Italy, almost 13,000, lived in Baltimore than in any previous census year.

Lithuanians came to Baltimore in smaller, yet significant numbers, beginning in the 1880s. Many left their homeland because of the efforts of the Russian government to force assimilation of Lithuanians by forbidding the teaching of the Lithuanian language in the schools and forcing Lithuanian men into service in the Russian army.

Early immigrants settled in East Baltimore, where many worked in the garment industry. They organized the St. John the Baptist Church whose congregation worshipped in the old Lloyd Street Synagogue building from 1889 until 1905, when they moved to a new church at Paca and Saratoga Streets. The Lithuanians gradually moved westward across the city until the center of the community was located around South Paca, South Greene, West Lombard and Hollins Streets. Around 1900, fraternal organizations and beneficial societies joined in purchasing a hall on West Barre Street to use for community functions. The new Lithuanian Hall was built in 1921 at Hollins and Parkin Streets. St. Alphonsus Church on West Saratoga Street now serves part of the Lithuanian community. Over two thousand persons born in Lithuania have lived in Baltimore every census year since 1920, when they were first counted separately from Russians. Like other groups, the total has increased since 1960.

Most of Baltimore's Greeks arrived after the turn of the century. They settled along Eastern Avenue, in an area which still remains the center of the Greek community with its shops, restaurants, coffee houses and one of the churches, St. Nicholas, located on South Ponca Street. The first Greek Orthodox church in Baltimore, "Evangelismos," the Annunciation, began in 1908 when the congregation purchased a building at Homewood Avenue and Chase

The Italian community produced prominent political leaders who won local and later national offices

Vincent Palmisano (above) *won the nomination and the subsequent election to the city council. Eleven years later he was elected to the United States Congress. Thomas D'Alesandro, Jr.* (left) *defeated Palmisano in the Congressional election of 1938. He became mayor of Baltimore in 1947*

Street. In 1936 the congregation bought and renovated the current building at Maryland Avenue and Preston Street. As Greeks followed East Baltimore's other immigrants in their northeastward path out from the city, they built a third church, St. Demetrios, on Cub Hill Road. As early as 1912 a school to teach the Greek language and religion opened. Children attended three times a week after their regular classes.

The Greek community has never been large enough to be a major force in urban politics. Political leaders like Peter Angelos and Paul Sarbanes have risen to prominence by appealing to the broader community. Although they are the last large group to immigrate to Baltimore, Greeks live in widely dispersed neighborhoods. They are joined more by a common heritage and church than by geographic unity.

By far the largest group of newcomers, other than Germans who outnumbered all other immigrant peoples before and after the Civil War, were the Russian Jews who began arriving in Baltimore during the 1880s. By 1900, over ten thousand Russians lived in the city and by 1910 almost twenty-five thousand. Most fled from persecution in Russia and nearby countries like Poland and Lithuania which were subject to Russian domination.

As the German Jews moved westward towards Eutaw Place, Eastern Europeans began to move into East Baltimore. Most were Orthodox and established their own synagogues, often using the buildings vacated by the German congregations. The vast majority of Eastern European Jews worked in the sweatshops, later garment factories of East Baltimore. Many of the owners were German Jews. The workers tended to be active in labor organizations. The largest, the International Ladies Garment Workers Union, formed a local chapter in 1909, the fourth in the nation. But despite their union activity, poverty pervaded the community.

At first, tensions grew between the older, Americanized German Jews, who had fought difficult battles to overcome prejudice and discrimination, and the new immigrants who spoke Yiddish, insisted on Orthodox observances, and frequently preferred to remain within their own closed community. Slowly, however, people began to bridge the gap. Henrietta Szold, the daughter of Rabbi Benjamin Szold, in 1889 organized the Russian Night School to teach English and American history to people who worked all day. Several thousand studied here. The Szold School, as it was known, became a model for night schools in many other cities.

A wide variety of charitable work among the new immigrants was supported by the more established segment of the community. In the first decade of the twentieth century, the German-Jewish charities united to form the Federated Jewish Charities. Jacob Hollander served as the first president. The Russian organizations joined in the United Hebrew Charities. Finally in 1921 these two merged into the Associated Jewish Charities. Jewish philanthropy was a well-established tradition and benefitted the immigrant community as well as the city as a whole. Over the years, settlement houses, like the Maccabean House, free schools, an orphanage, Sinai Hospital which was founded in 1866, and other institutions received strong support.

Time worked to overcome some of the differences. As years passed the newcomers moved into positions of political and economic power. In 1903, two Eastern Europeans, William Weissager, a Latvian, and Joseph Seidenman, a Russian, won election to the City Council. A Lithuanian immigrant of 1882, Jacob Epstein, began as a peddler and then opened a store which developed a large mail order business. By

Immigrant children often worked as vendors, sometimes in lieu of going to school

1910 he employed over 1000 workers and did over a million dollars worth of business a month. Epstein shared his good fortune with the Jewish community and with Baltimore as a whole. When the Museum of Art was first incorporated in 1914, he was among the original trustees.

At the end of World War I, the Eastern European Jews were beginning their move out of East Baltimore, first to Park Heights Avenue and then further north to Forest Park. New institutions which served the entire Jewish community came into existence. Baltimore Hebrew College opened in 1919. The *Jewish Times,* the newest of several papers, began publication. Recently, a new group of Eastern European Jews have been arriving in Baltimore, where the larger community is now in a position to provide significant aid for the resettlement process.

Certain settlement patterns characterized all of the various immigrant groups that came to Baltimore during the nineteenth and the early twentieth century. Most individuals arrived poor and without a skilled trade or knowledge of the English language. The majority began their new life in communities where they could use their own language. As soon as possible, they built a church or synagogue where services were conducted in their native tongue. Then each group established institutions to meet the needs of the newcomers: aid societies, schools, fraternal organizations, newspapers, building and loan associations, and so on. Such similar responses stemmed from similar needs and conditions. Moreover, the government did not yet operate in that sphere to any significant degree.

Over time, each generation of newcomers and their children learned English and began to ascend the socio-economic ladder. Participation in the city's political system generally accompanied this success. Gradually, people moved away from their original communities into new neighborhoods further from the central city. Often they built new houses of worship. Eventually the need for immigrant aid societies declined, and those that survived either changed their programs or became primarily fraternal organizations. Today, most foreign-language newspapers have disappeared.

These cycles of immigrant experience typify those of the nation. But Baltimore is somewhat unique in the nation in the combination of these sizeable immigrant groups with a large antebellum black population which post-war migration increased. Before the Civil War, the city's blacks created community institutions much like those of the German and Irish immigrants. After the war, however, the black community had not become as fully integrated into the life of the city as the pre-war immigrants had. Therefore, although they were one of the earliest minority groups, blacks continued to face the same deprivations and prejudices experienced by the newer immigrant groups and some additional disabilities imposed on them because of their race by both law and custom. In 1870, the year that they began to vote again, almost forty thousand blacks lived in Baltimore and represented 15 percent of the total population.

After the Civil War ended, large numbers of blacks from rural areas, especially southern Maryland, moved to Baltimore seeking work and better lives than they had known as slaves. Like immigrants, most were uneducated and had little or no money. Most worked at menial jobs. "Pigtown" in southwest Baltimore, where many rural migrants settled first, became a slum, at least as dirty and unhealthy as any immigrant settlement. Blacks, however, because of racial discrimination and the heritage of the disabilities of slavery, were less able to combat their problems than were many immigrant groups,

Henrietta Szold, daughter of Rabbi Benjamin Szold, organized a night school to teach the English language and American history to immigrants who worked all day. Her school became a model that was copied in cities throughout the country

A Lithuanian Jewish immigrant who began as a peddler, Jacob Epstein later opened a store and developed a very successful mail order business. As he shared his good fortune with his adopted city, he became one of Baltimore's most prominent philanthropists

whose members were less recognizable visually. Despite their numbers, blacks held very little economic or political power. Every gain came slowly and with great effort.

The public school system provides an example of the difficulties the black community faced. Before 1867, blacks had to pay public school taxes but could not attend. When the City Council voted to open public schools for Negro students, the city took over the 16 schools run by the Baltimore Association for the Moral and Educational Advancement of Colored People. Within a year, all the black teachers were fired and whites hired in their place. Only money collected from black taxpayers was assigned to these schools. After several years, the city began to contribute additional funds to the black schools, which were frequently in buildings abandoned when new schools for white students were constructed. When continuing efforts to convince the city to rehire black teachers failed, the Rev. Harvey Johnson of the Union Baptist Church led a group of Baptist ministers in forming the Brotherhood of Liberty in 1885. One major concern was education. They succeeded in winning an ordinance in 1887 allowing the hiring of black teachers in new colored schools, and two years later Colored Primary School #9 opened with twelve black teachers.

In 1896, Dr. John Marcus Cargill, a Negro physician and member of the City Council, introduced an ordinance calling for the gradual replacement of white teachers by blacks in all the colored schools. The process was not completed until 1907. In all areas, the black schools lagged behind the white schools. No colored high school was opened until 1882 when the future Douglass High School first opened, housed with the Colored Grammar School in the old City Hall on Holliday Street. The first teachers' training school for blacks did not open until 1900.

Black churchmen continued to play a major role in community affairs. The history of the *Afro-American* newspaper illustrates this. In 1892, three small newspapers were in circulation in Baltimore's black community. The Rev William Alexander, pastor of the Sharon Baptist Church, had organized a provision store and started printing a newspaper called the *Afro-American* to advertise his business. John H. Murphy was publishing the *Sunday School Helper.* The Rev. George F. Bragg, rector of St. James Episcopal Church from 1891 to 1940, published the church-related *Ledger.* Murphy bought Alexander's paper. Then in 1907, Murphy and Bragg merged their papers and called their publication the *Afro-American Ledger.* As the enterprise grew, editions for other cities were published.

Another important institution of the black community, Provident Hospital, originated in 1894 in a small building on Orchard Street. Because white hospitals often gave different treatment to African American patients, Dr. John Marcus Cargill and Dr. William T. Carr, with their own money established a hospital to be run by black physicians, primarily for patients of their own race, although patients of other races were never excluded.

The single most difficult problem faced by blacks was unemployment. Often fired in favor of white workers, almost always paid less, most black workers were unable to build the financial base that the immigrants gradually did. One black Baltimorean pioneered in this area. Isaac Myers, born in Baltimore in 1835, stands out as an entrepreneur and labor leader. When Civil War veterans returned and immigrants arrived after 1865, many blacks were driven out of skilled jobs they had held for years. In view of this, Myers, who had been apprenticed as a ship caulker at

Above:
Booker T. Washington, shown here addressing a Baltimore audience, encouraged the development of black-owned businesses to provide a stable economic base for the community

Opposite Page:
The Reverend George Bragg, rector of St. James Episcopal Church from 1891 to 1940, provided religious, intellectual, and social leadership within Baltimore's black community

This group of ministers and lawyers worked for the improvement of education for Negro children and for the hiring of black teachers. Included in this group are: Harry S. Cummings (front row center), W. Ashby Hawkins (second row center), Warner T. McGuinn (third row, third from left), and the Reverend Harvey Johnson (back row center). The picture was taken in front of Johnson's house on Druid Hill Avenue

Tom Smith, the Democratic leader, held a prominent position in the predominantly Republican black community because of his power to distribute patronage jobs and procure political favors

the age of 16, decided to found a black-owned shipyard which would employ black workers. He solicited funds from merchants and the black churches and sold shares of stock for $5. The Chesapeake Marine Railway and Dry Dock Company opened in 1868.

Myers also organized a Colored Caulkers Trade Union Society, one of the first black labor organizations. The shipyard operated until 1879 when it went out of business primarily because the wooden clippers were being replaced by steelhulled ships. Another problem, ironically, was that other shipyard owners were paying lower wages to their white workers. By the time Myers' company went out of existence, the union had forced the white caulkers' union to accept blacks into their ranks.

African Americans in Baltimore had one advantage not possessed by most black residents in cities of former slave states. They voted. In northern cities, where blacks also had the franchise, their numbers were so small that they wielded little power. In Baltimore, blacks had both numbers and the franchise. Most blacks voted for the Republican Party until the time of the New Deal. This was true in Baltimore and throughout the country. Several early 20th century attempts by the Democratic party to disenfranchise blacks in Maryland failed when reform Democrats, white Republicans, and many immigrants joined blacks in their opposition to measures like grandfather clauses and literacy tests.

Beginning in 1890, black Republicans won seats on the City Council almost every election until 1931. Harry S. Cummings represented a predominantly black ward for fifteen years between 1890 and 1917 when he died. When first elected, Cummings, who grew up in Baltimore and was one of the first two blacks to graduate from the University of Maryland Law School, received favorable newspaper comments because of his educational and professional background. Dr. John Marcus Cargill and Hirar Watty, a teamster and party regular, were th other black councilmen before World War I. A one of many councilmen, none possessed muc power. Their greatest achievements lay i improving the colored schools and funnelin some jobs into the black community. A fev black Democrats also distributed patronag jobs. Most prominent among them was Tor Smith who, although he never held publi office, wielded considerable power.

In the early 20th century, a system of rigi racial segregation grew up in the deep South In Baltimore, some facilities and institution were segregated while others were not. Schools railroad cars, hotels, restaurants, and man stores were segregated. Streetcars were not. Cit Council ordinances of 1910, 1911 and 191 requiring segregated housing were defeate when local black lawyers like W. Ashb Hawkins and Warner T. McGuinn along wit others tested their constitutionality in court.

By the outbreak of World War I, a smal black middle class had moved into houses alon Eutaw Place, Druid Hill Avenue, Madison Av enue and Mosher Street, formerly occupied b German Jews who by then were moving furthe out from the city. That relatively small group o lawyers, doctors, ministers, and teachers al worked to provide the best services and institu tions possible in the society. The vast majorit of blacks lived in poor conditions, received lov wages, and had little or no opportunity to gai a good education. While the immigrants becam more thoroughly assimilated, most Africa Americans were forced to remain in a segregate world with limited opportunities.

Late nineteenth century politics was marke by the growth of political machines that domi nated most of the nation's cities. Generally, the based their strength on the voting power o immigrants and their descendants to whos

Below Left:
Harry Sythe Cummings, a Republican, was the first black man elected to the Baltimore City Council in 1890

Center:
Hiram Watty, a Republican, served several terms on the city council before World War I

Below Right:
Isaac Myers, an entrepreneur and labor leader, organized one of the nation's first Negro unions

Bottom:
Myers founded the Chesapeake Marine Railway and Dry Dock Company in 1868. He employed black workers who were faced with an increasing discrimination in employment when the abolition of slavery put them in competition with free white workers

needs the leaders catered. Members of the machine hierarchy, often immigrants or first generation Americans, generally met new arrivals at the docks. They helped the newcomers find lodging and a job. The machine often provided emergency food, coal, and even medical care. In exchange, the beneficiaries of these services voted their friends into office.

Baltimore had a machine, but with a difference. Its first boss, Isaac Freeman Rasin, grew up on Maryland's Eastern Shore, the son of an old Maryland, Protestant family that was listed in the Social Register. Local supporters of his Democratic machine reflected Baltimore's unique political situation as a city whose heritage was half northern and half southern.

Baltimore's foreign born population was proportionately smaller than that of most northern, industrial cities. Alone, the foreign born and their children could not have dominated the city's politics. Baltimore had, however, a strong source of Democratic party strength in its southern sympathizers and others who considered the Republican party of the 1870s to be the party of Reconstruction and black equality. When these two Democratic groups joined forces, they made their party dominant in Baltimore.

Rasin worked his way up through the Democratic party hierarchy, representing the 7th ward on the city's executive committee and later becoming Clerk of the Court of Common Pleas, a lucrative job which he held from 1867 to 1884. In 1870, Rasin met Arthur Pue Gorman, Maryland's future United States Senator, and the two formed an alliance between city and county political groups which lasted until Gorman's death in 1906 and Rasin's in 1907. When the system was perfected, Rasin controlled the city and Gorman the state, and they cooperated with each other.

Rasin consolidated his power in the city when his candidate for mayor, Joshua Vansant, won in 1871 as did his candidate for governor, William Pinkney Whyte. The double victory gave Rasin control over many patronage jobs, the essence of machine power. Like all bosses, he also distributed city contracts, received campaign contributions from contractors, and placed his people in jobs with their companies. Rasin's powers included choosing the Democratic nominee for mayor. In addition to Vansant, at various times he backed Mayors Ferdinand C. Latrobe, whom he also opposed on occasion; George P. Kane, the former Police Marshal; James Hodges; Robert Davidson; Thomas G. Hayes; and Robert McLane, the last Rasin mayor. He made his former ally, William Pinkney Whyte, mayor of Baltimore in 1881 in order to get him out of state politics.

Like most machines, Rasin's faced opposition from groups who called themselves reformers and who accused the politicos of all sorts of corrupt practices. As early as 1873 in Baltimore, Republicans and some independent Democrats founded a Citizen's Reform party which accused the organization Democrats of fraudulent voter registration, stuffing ballot boxes, and irregularities in the awarding of city contracts, which invariably went to friends of Rasin.

Rasin's most effective response to the reformers was the nomination of respectable individuals for mayor. Ferdinand C. Latrobe, for example, who held office for 13 years between 1875 and 1895, was the son of the general counsel for the B & O. He worked hard for the city and was not a spoilsman. Rasin gave his mayors a free hand to make policies for the city except where they affected the machine. The boss kept a check on the mayors by retaining control of the City Council.

A serious challenge to Rasin came in 1885 when Charles J. Bonaparte and John Cowan led

Isaac Freeman Rasin, Baltimore's most powerful Democratic boss, dominated the city's politics from the 1870s until his death in 1907

Rasin consolidated his power in 1871 when his candidate, Joshua Vansant, won the election for mayor

The choice of competent mayors like Ferdinand C. Latrobe helped Rasin maintain his influence

in the formation of the Reform League. Bonaparte, who was the grandson of Betsy Patterson and Jerome Bonaparte, at that time was a successful lawyer and well-known local reformer. After his friend and fellow reformer Theodore Roosevelt became president, Bonaparte served as his Secretary of the Navy and later Attorney General. John Cowan had already fought the machine for the principle of non-partisan judges. As president of the B & O, he naturally favored any opponent of Gorman's, because the Senator favored the Pennsylvania Railroad over his. These leaders were typical of Progressive reformers in cities throughout the United States. They came from prosperous families, were well educated, and sought to change the system by replacing men they considered crooked and poorly trained with ones they deemed honest and competent.

The reformers' first big victory, one of their few complete ones, came in 1895 when a Republican candidate for mayor, Alcaeus Hooper, won the election. Hooper was supported by Republicans, white and black, and reform Democrats. During the campaign, Hooper had attacked not only the corruption of the machine but also slum conditions in Baltimore, the lack of food inspectors, gross mismanagement of city departments, especially the school system, and the Policy, a lottery run by the machine.

The reformers were aided by Charles H. Grasty whose *Baltimore Evening News* had been exposing problems it attributed to the political leadership: the high prices and poor service of the Consolidated Gas Company; the telephone monopoly; the streetcars; the system of paving streets where contracts were awarded to machine supporters; slums, where there was inefficient garbage removal and building regulation; and the Policy, which lured precious nickels from people who earned few of them.

Once in office, Hooper began personal inspections of schools, streets, and sewers. One January night in 1896 he was on the streets after midnight checking on the cleaning crews. Hooper's major contribution was the replacement of some incompetent officials and the institution of more business-like administrative policies.

Hooper was followed in 1897 by a second Republican mayor, William T. Malster. The most important reform during his term was a new city charter. The new charter provided several major changes. School reform stood out, especially the provision requiring merit appointment for teachers, for whom the sole qualifications previously had been good political connections. A Board of Estimates, consisting of the mayor, comptroller, president of the Second Branch of the bicameral City Council, and two others, was created to draft the budget, set limits on expenditures, and grant franchises. A Board of Awards was established to award contracts, taking that power away from the City Council. With these boards that were limited in membership, responsibility for both good and bad deeds was easy to assign.

The success of the reformer-Republican alliance brought several responses from the organization Democrats. One was a series of attempts to disenfranchise blacks because their vote was so heavily Republican. Democratic campaigns became openly racist. In Annapolis, Democrats passed three separate constitutional amendments in 1904, 1908, and 1910 designed to disenfranchise blacks and thus make a Republican majority impossible. All failed because of strong opposition from all Republicans, reform Democrats, and many Baltimore machine Democrats, including Rasin, who feared that literacy tests, property requirements, and grandfather clauses might disenfranchise immigrants as well as blacks.

Charles J. Bonaparte, grandson of Betsy Patterson and Jerome Bonaparte, was one of the local reform leaders who challenged Rasin and his machine

Republican mayors Alcaeus Hooper (above) *and William Malster* (left) *defeated the machine in 1895 and 1897*

A second response by the Democrats was the nomination of a known reformer, Thomas G. Hayes, to run for mayor in 1899. He won and then appointed the president of the Reform League president of the Board of School Commissioners. He also chose able and trained men as city engineer, building inspector, water engineer and health commissioner. Several state laws passed during his administration effected major reform in Baltimore City. A building inspection act brought the beginning of the end of the sweatshops. A primary election law for the city removed the nomination machinery from the party caucus and gave it to the voting public.

Hayes accumulated enough personal power that Rasin dumped him in 1903 in favor of Robert McLane, who did, however, promise continued "good government." Both Hayes and McLane supported the undertaking of a project to build a sewage system for the city where raw waste still drained in open gutters. Both also supported the Olmsted plan for city beautification. On February 2, 1904 the Board of Estimates approved a loan for sewers, schools, street paving, fire houses, and parks. The commitment was made just in time, because on Sunday, February 7, a fire broke out in the Hurst Drygoods Company on Liberty Street.

Inside the warehouse, smoldering cotton exploded, spewing debris over the neighborhood. A half dozen buildings were soon blazing as a southwest wind spread the fire across German Street. Before the fire stopped, 140 acres in the heart of the downtown business district, the area of the original Baltimore Town, had been consumed. The fire did not cross the Jones Falls, thereby sparing the residents of Little Italy the destruction of their homes. Miraculously, no one was killed. Estimated damage from the great fire was set at $125,000,000 with approximately two thousand buildings destroyed.

Mayor McLane appointed an Emergency Committee headed by a Progressive, William Keyser, to advise him on the best plan to deal with the burned-out area and a subsequent Burnt District Commission which carried out the first group's recommendations. Keyser's committee, which included many members of the Municipal Art Society, determined to use the tragedy as an opportunity to institute improvements long needed. They suggested the widening of streets to accommodate increased traffic. Although the property owners, whose lots would be smaller, protested, all but Baltimore Street were rebuilt with extra footage and smooth paving.

Sewer connections were installed under the new streets in anticipation of a complete system which followed soon. Seven years and $20,000,000 later, the system described by a visiting engineer as "the most modern and progressive engineering feat in the world" was completed. In May, 1904 Baltimore's voters approved a $6,000,000 loan for modernization of the harbor. The reconstruction of buildings was managed on an individual basis with no attempt at coordination of design and style. Wide-scale planning of that sort lay two generations in the future.

Mayor Robert McLane's suicide in June, 1904 made E. Clay Timanus mayor. Timanus, a Republican businessman and president of the Second Branch of the City Council, chose prominent reformers George Gaither and William Cabell Bruce as advisors. The new mayor called a General Public Improvements Conference in December. Neighborhoods, business groups, charitable agencies and planners all sent delegates. The program the group produced had the support not only of reformers but also of Rasin and his rising lieutenant, John J. "Sonny" Mahon. Under Timanus and J. Barry Mahool, who was elected mayor in 1907, sewers, parks,

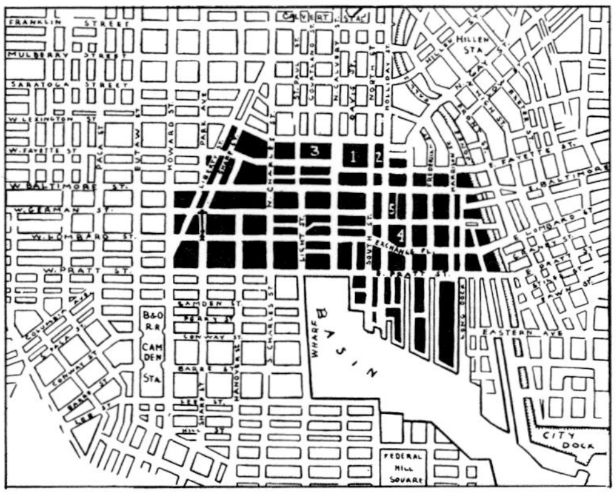

The Great Fire of 1904 demolished 140 acres in the heart of the downtown business district

Above:
Though the B&O building was gutted by the flames, the offices of Alexander Brown and Company survived

Left:
Guards patrolled the area to prevent looting

school facilities, paving, fire equipment and the city's water supply all improved. The changes meant better public health and safety and also the creation of jobs.

Two important political events occurred in 1907: the death of I. Freeman Rasin and the election of Mayor I. Freeman Rasin and the election of Mayor J. Barry Mahool. Rasin's demise left the way open for a new leader at the top of the machine. Mahool's victory was the last for Baltimore's Progressives.

Sonny Mahon, the only politician in the city with practical knowledge of each ward and a strong following in each, moved to the pinnacle of the political hierarchy. Born of Irish immigrant parents who ran a boarding house on South Frederick Street, Mahon as a boy had thrown bricks at the 6th Massachusetts Regiment as it marched through Baltimore in 1861. By 1870 he was the youngest of the Democratic ward helpers. His 9th ward waterfront gang helped him gain control. In 1878 he served his first of eleven terms on the city council.

Unlike Rasin, Mahon always had to share power with others. By 1911, *News* cartoonist McKee Barkley drew Mahon as king of a political "Royal Family" which included two street cleaning contractors, John S. "Frank" Kelly and Danny Loden, and Robert "Paving Bob" Padgett who owned a contracting business. Mahon, Kelly and Loden were all Irish. Padgett was of recent English stock. Irish-Americans dominated Baltimore's politics even though they were greatly outnumbered by Germans and native Americans. Mahon, like Rasin, worked closely with the business community and also adopted a conciliatory approach towards reformers. Even more than Rasin, he capitalized on the needs of the new immigrants, whose numbers were expanding rapidly at this time. Mahon maintained his power until his death in the late 1920s.

In the same year Rasin died, 1907, the last progressive mayor of Baltimore, J. Barry Mahool, took office. He believed in "good government" (by reformers), regulation of corporations, women's suffrage, and social reform. Mahool's government, like those of his recent predecessors, operated efficiently under the influence of a number of well-trained and responsible high officials. It compared favorably with those of many large cities. In 1910, the state legislature passed a bill creating a public service commission to regulate utilities. A pure food law was also passed in 1910 allowed regulation of slaughtering and food processing.

Women's suffrage had long been an issue in Baltimore. In 1894 Etta Maddox, the city's first female lawyer, and her sister, Emma Maddox Funck, led in the creation of the Baltimore Women's Suffrage Association. By 1905 the group had 160 members and in 1906 sponsored the annual convention of the National American Women's Suffrage Association. Susan B. Anthony, Jane Addams, Clara Barton and Carrie Chapman Catt all attended as did local activists Mary Garrett and Elizabeth King Ellicott. Sarah Collins Fernandis, Ida Cummings and other leaders formed suffrage organizations within the African American community.

All the suffragists were involved in the wider reform movement and worked for clean water and streets, pure food and milk, playgrounds, and better schools. Mrs. Benjamin Corkran formed the first Baltimore chapter of the National Consumers League. Elizabeth King organized the Maryland Federation of Women's Clubs. Sarah Collins Fernandis in 1913 founded the Cooperative Women's League, an interracial organization working for health and sanitation and promoting home economics and art education within the black community. Eliza Jane Davage Cummings, mother of Ida and Harry, founded the Colored Empty Stocking Club and Fresh Air Circle. Its members filled Christmas stockings and ran a summer camp for poor children. All these groups, along with the Arundell Good Government Club and many others, supported a wide range of progressive reforms and empowerment for women.

Social reform was a major component of

Opposite Page:
Mayors E. Clay Timanus (far left) *and J. Barry Mahool* (left) *oversaw construction of major improvements including sewers, parks, school facilities and roads*

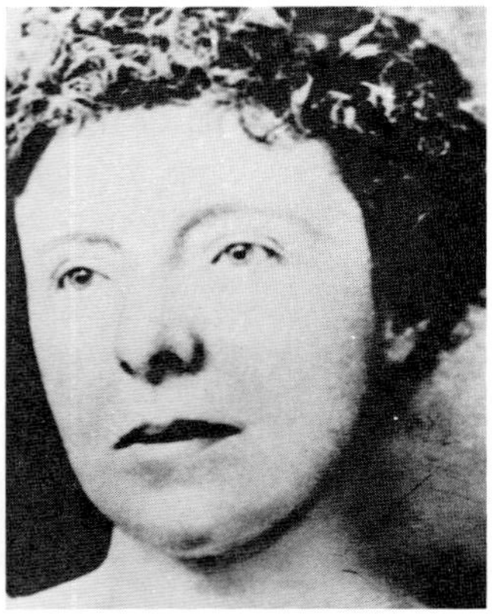

Top:Ida Cummings, sister of the first African American city councilman, was a leader in the causes of women's suffrage and social reform.

Left:Sonny Mahon (right) took over control of the Democratic machine in 1907. He is shown here with his lieutenant, Frank Kelly, apparently studying their racing forms.

Above:Etta Maddox, Baltimore's first female lawyer, was a leader in the formation of the Baltimore Women's Suffrage Association in 1894.

progressive programs in cities throughout the nation. In addition to achievements already mentioned in labor legislation, housing regulation, sanitation and health, several other notable programs were instituted before World War I. Under the leadership of Eliza Ridgely, a Children's Playground Association was established. Robert Garrett organized a Public Athletic League. Most reformers including Mayor Mahool supported their efforts and by 1908 the city had opened 28 park and school yard playgrounds with supervised programs.

Proponents of public health programs supported the establishment of public baths, where people whose houses had no running water could bathe and wash clothes. Henry Walters contributed the money for the city's first three public baths. These were followed by additional baths, portable showers, and swimming pools. In 1909, another public health proposal finally became a reality. A hospital for infectious diseases was opened on the grounds of Bay View, the city's poor house.

The progressives' efforts at reforming the process of government were all aimed at bringing about concrete reforms such as those achieved in Baltimore in the late nineteenth and early twentieth century. The last great effort of the local reformers before the outbreak of World War I was a new charter designed to increase still further the efficient operation of the city government. Although the charter was rejected in 1910 by the state legislature, its provisions all became law during the post-World War I years. In 1918 Baltimore won home rule and a merit system was instituted for civil service jobs. In 1922 the City Council was revamped. The unwieldy bicameral body was replaced in 1923 by a single chamber whose members were to be elected from six districts instead of 28 wards. Eventually the Boards of Estimates and Awards were combined.

As the election of 1911 approached, Mahon made it clear that he was not satisfied with the number of patronage positions that Mahool had allotted him. Sonny and all the ward bosses threw heavy support to the Democratic candidate, James H. Preston. Preston's victory and subsequent two-term administration, which lasted until 1919, gave more power to the machine than it had enjoyed since 1895. City contracting became political again, and a big campaign to pave cobblestone streets and cover open sewers resulted in lucrative contracts and lots of jobs.

The Jones Falls was covered over by the Fallsway, thus in one stroke ending the danger of flooding and creating a new expressway. The sanitary sewer system was completed. The Baltimore Symphony Orchestra and the Municipal Band were established, both supported by the city. Parks were improved and extended. The personnel had changed with the return to power of the machine, but most of the improvements instituted by the reformers remained and often were extended. Ironically, just after the city's political power reverted to the machine, the national Democratic Party convened here, in 1912, and nominated Woodrow Wilson, the last of the progressive presidents.

From 1914 to 1917 people's attention turned more and more to events in Europe. As the war there continued and the war at sea worsened, the American's position evolved from neutrality to involvement. Although it is too arbitrary a date, April 6, 1917, the day of our declaration of war on the Central Powers, is generally given as the end of the progressive period. Energies, both national and local, turned away from domestic reform to the pursuit of the war effort. When the war ended, life was different. Clearly, World War I marked the end of one era and the beginning of a new one.

Opposite Page:
Reformers like Eliza Ridgely pressed for the establishment of playgrounds and supervised recreational programs. This one on Calvert Street was one of twenty-eight opened by 1908

Left:
Reformers and public health workers supported the establishment of public baths, where people whose homes had no running water could bathe and wash clothes

Above:
The public baths enjoyed wide use for many years. These girls were photographed around 1920

Left:
The opening of public swimming pools followed the successful establishment of the public baths. The Gwynns Falls Swimming Pool was a popular place for outings such as this one

World War I aroused a fierce patriotism in many Americans. Baltimoreans turned out in large numbers to see this parade along Mt. Royal Avenue

National Crises & New Beginnings

1917-1970

On April 6, 1917, the United States declared war on Germany. President Woodrow Wilson, former student and lecturer at Johns Hopkins, had gone before Congress four days earlier and asked for the vote to "make the world safe for democracy." He plunged America into the conflict which he knew "would overturn the world we had known." He told Frank Cobb, editor of the New York *World,* that the end of our neutrality would mean: "that we should lose our heads with the rest and stop weighing right and wrong . . . that a majority of people in this hemisphere would go war-mad, quit thinking and devote their energies to destruction."

He predicted that later we would "attempt to reconstruct a peacetime civilization with war standards." In all his predictions, he was sadly correct. Our entry came at the crucial moment, however, for Great Britain had less than a two-month's supply of grain on hand and the German blockade at sea was succeeding in preventing new foodstuffs from reaching that island nation. American ships made the difference.

When war first broke out in Europe in 1914, most Americans believed that it would not affect their lives. But as time passed, more and more Americans, Baltimoreans among them, grew less and less neutral. Involvement came for a wide variety of reasons. All groups strongly asserted their American patriotism. Many individuals, like President Wilson, felt an affinity for the country whose language and culture formed the basis of our own. These people, many of whom traced one or another of their ancestors to England, believed that British civilization must be preserved.

Other people took sides with the Entente nations against the Central Powers for different reasons. American Jews observed anti-Semitism growing in Germany and Austria during the war and therefore opposed the governments guilty of it. Furthermore, if the British drove the Ottoman Turks out of the Holy Lands, there was the possibility of the establishment of a Jewish homeland in the Palestine, a hope the British government promised to support in the Balfour Declaration. Italian Americans supported Italy, which was allied with the British and French, and they knew that a German-Austrian victory might lead to their subjugation of Italy. And, finally, Americans with roots in central Europe, like Polish Americans and Bohemian Americans, sided with the British in the hope that their homelands would gain independence from imperial domination if Germany and Austria were defeated.

Other people in Baltimore and throughout the nation favored Germany or at least wanted to maintain neutrality during the early part of the war. German Americans, of course, did not want to wage war against the nation where many of their relatives and friends still lived and whose language many continued to speak. Many Irish Americans opposed helping England which was then engaged in trying to prevent Irish independence. And, of course, some people opposed war out of principle. Pacifists, especially Quakers, believed that all war was wrong. A significant number of progressives and some socialists believed that the war would take the national attention, energy, and resources away from reforms that were needed to better living conditions in American cities and asserted that the Europeans should be left to solve their problems without our intervention.

Intervene we did, however, and the effects of war were felt rapidly in Baltimore and throughout the nation. Baltimore's sixty-one thousand eligible men hastened to register for the draft. Many German Americans enlisted quickly to prove their loyalty before it could be questioned. City Councilman Harry Cummings

wrote to Governor Emerson C. Harrington on behalf of the states' African Americans: "...we are willing and ready to defend our State and Nation. We know but one country and one flag." Before the fighting ended, over sixteen thousand Baltimoreans served in the American armed forces. The 313th Infantry "Baltimore's Own" and the 115th Infantry commanded by Colonel Milton A. Reckord fought with General John J. Pershing's Expeditionary Force in France.

The war effort involved the community. Along with soldiers, the government needed money. Liberty Bonds were sold and Baltimore's quota was set at $25 million. Everyone bought them. School children collected pennies until they had enough. The *Sun* reported that by April 16, Baltimore's German American community had purchased bonds worth $500,000. Promotion gimmicks included a Liberty Bond Balloon in which rides were given to any purchaser of a $1000 bond.

Baltimoreans also feared sabotage and took various precautions. Guards were posted around munitions plants and by railroad bridges. Loch Raven Dam and the Montebello filtration plant were patrolled to prevent the enemy from poisoning the city's water supply.

Shortages occurred quickly. Sugar and cheese became scarce early, and a near panic developed when Baltimore ran out of potatoes. The cessation of trade with Germany cut off equipment for medical and scientific laboratories. Before long, most foodstuffs and consumer goods were in short supply and what was available rose in price. Wages increased, too, but prices went up faster. The disparity created hardship throughout much of Baltimore, particularly as coal and food prices accelerated abruptly. Children began to gather coal along the railroad tracks where it had fallen from trains. A child was killed while doing this.

Despite the hardships, Baltimoreans rallied to support the cause. Rallying was almost mandatory because those who did not were viewed with disdain or hatred by their neighbors who believed that nonconformity and treason were the same thing. The federal government's Committee on Public Information made visible patriotism seem obligatory. Most people, however, did their part with enthusiasm. Baltimoreans planted liberty gardens in window boxes, school playgrounds, city parks, and vacant lots as well as in their own backyards. Dr. John Goucher plowed up the front lawn of his estate, Altodale, and the college students helped plant and harvest 256 bushels of potatoes.

Women made bandages for the Red Cross as the wartime economy accelerated social change. Baltimore's industry boomed, supplying the necessities of war. While local industries expanded their output, some of their employees were leaving to join the army. Suddenly women were welcomed in jobs previously closed to them. They worked on assembly lines and drove streetcars. Women's working became an act of patriotism rather than one of economic necessity. Blacks, too, found jobs from which they had been excluded suddenly opening up to them. Industrial positions and wartime wages drew both blacks and whites from rural areas into the city. During the decade from 1910 to 1920, Baltimore's population increased by over 175,000. Public facilities were strained and housing was hard to find. All resources were directed towards the war effort, not civilian comfort.

The war touched everyone, but, as a group, Baltimore's German Americans were probably affected the most. In 1914 many German Americans throughout the country had sided with the Central Powers and had spoken out against Britain's propaganda here. They wanted the United States to remain neutral. German-language newspapers openly supported

Far Left:
The Baltimore American *promoted sugarless Tuesdays to help preserve the scarce commodity*

Left:
Goucher students joined the war effort by farming a large liberty garden on the front lawn of Altodale, home of Dr. John Goucher

After Baltimore's women said goodbye to the soldiers, a variety of jobs were left vacant and many women joined the work force

National Crises & New Beginnings 1917-1970

neutrality. German Americans sent aid to German civilians. Then the situation changed. When the war at sea, especially the attacks by German submarines, led to the breaking of diplomatic relations, the *Deutsch Correspondent* warned Baltimore's German Americans in February 1917 that: "It is not yet a crime to defend Germany's position, but it is unpatriotic and, above all, unwise." Several days later the newspaper cautioned readers: "Be calm! Keep your tongue! Keep wisely silent! Remember your oath of allegiance! Keep in mind that while Germany is the land of your fathers, this is the land of our children and children's children."

After war was declared, German Americans in Baltimore joined the war effort, enlisting for service in the army and buying war bonds as soon as they were sold. Many applied quickly for naturalization so they would not be classified as enemy aliens. Others went to court to have their names Americanized. Despite the clear pro-American stance of the vast majority of the German community, suspicions and hostile feelings grew. Although Mayor James Preston forestalled any massive detentions, a few people defended the United States by attacking individual Germans. Accusations and humiliations abounded. H. L. Mencken, whose anti-war writings led to suspicions that he was a spy, responded with verbal scorn and sent to the authorities long, elaborate, anonymous accusations against him.

The year 1918 marked the end of many German-American institutions, including the *Deutsch Correspondent.* Although groups like the singing clubs and the Turnverein reappeared in the mid-1920s, the strength of the community was never as great as it had been before the war. A new bi-weekly newspaper, the *Baltimore Correspondent,* came into circulation after peace returned, but the German-language schools were closed forever. In an early symbolic gesture, the City Council changed the name of German Street, where many German shopkeepers' businesses had once been located, to Redwood Street, in honor of George Buchanan Redwood, the first Maryland officer to die in France.

By October, 1918, when the Allied forces drove through the German lines, the German high command urged the chancellor to propose an armistice on the basis of Woodrow Wilson's Fourteen Points. On November 9 Kaiser Wilhelm abdicated, and two days later Americans received the happy news that an armistice had been arranged. The brutal war had finally come to an end.

Although the war had ended, it was several years before there was much peace at home. Severe post-war dislocations continued the hardships for many people. One immediate effect of the peace was economic confusion. Returning veterans found many industries laying off workers who had been hired to produce war material. White and black rural migrants were laid off. Sometimes veterans got their jobs back, but often there were no jobs.

Wartime had brought union recognition and gains in wages and working conditions for many workers. Peacetime brought strikes to maintain these gains. Workers struck the B & O and Western Maryland Railroads and the Maryland Drydock Company. Longshoremen struck; mill workers in Hampden and Woodberry struck; and some Baltimoreans, accustomed during the war to blaming all troubles on foreign espionage, held Russian Communism responsible. They feared a Bolshevik revolution would take place in the United States similar to the Russian Revolution of 1917.

Housing had become scarce during the war as thousands moved into Baltimore to work in the war industries. Returning veterans found

Colonel Milton Reckord leads the homecoming of the 115th Infantry in 1919

homes were even harder to locate. The scarcity of homes and the poverty that resulted from unemployment resulted in visible slums by 1920. Blacks, who were not allowed to live in many neighborhoods and who were often the last hired and first fired, suffered most. Fighting for democracy abroad had not brought full democracy at home.

Rivalries for jobs and housing intensified prejudices that had existed before the war. Wartime fears and experiences predisposed men to violent and summary actions. The time was ripe for the rise of groups like the Ku Klux Klan. The Klan was active in Baltimore in the early 1920s. All their enemies were here: Catholics, immigrants, Jews, blacks, and union members, whom the Klan viewed as Communists. Although Governor Ritchie denied them the use of the 5th Regiment Armory, masked Klansmen paraded in Baltimore in 1922. The *Catholic Review*, under the direction of Archbishop Michael Curley, led the opposition. The *Afro-American* stressed black wartime contributions. The *Jewish Times* stressed contributions to the city by Jewish families and patriotism during World War I. Eventually the city passed an antimasking ordinance. Revelations of scandals within the Klan contributed to its decline. The Klan never became as dominant a force in Baltimore as it did in other cities, and a gradual return of prosperity resulted in a distinct decline in the limited popularity that the group did enjoy here.

The housing shortage, deteriorating living conditions in the central city, and the rapid population increase stimulated the movement to the suburbs by white families already in progress before the war. As the peacetime economy picked up in the early 1920s, more people could afford the move. Baltimore's last major annexation of county land occurred in 1918 and brought large open tracts within the

city limits. By vote of the state legislature, 46.5 square miles of Baltimore County and 5.4 square miles of Anne Arundel County filled out the city. Further annexations were forbidden by a constitutional amendment passed after World War II.

Suburban communities developed rapidly in the annexed area and contiguous land beyond. Working-class commuter suburbs like Dundalk in the east and Brooklyn in the south opened up green spaces and the new life-style to blue-collar workers. Upper-class Baltimoreans continued to move northward. The Roland Park Company first offered lots in Guilford for sale in 1913. Guilford proved so popular that in 1924 the company bought Homeland, the estate of David Perine, which the city had considered purchasing for park land two years before.

Institutions follow people, but the intervention of the Depression and World War II slowed the process in this case. After the end of the Second World War, a number of the city's leading churches were built along North Charles Street.

Planning for the Episcopal Cathedral of the Incarnation took several decades. The structure as it now stands was finally completed in 1947. The Episcopal Church of the Redeemer, which began as a small country chapel used by the Perines and a few neighboring families, grew to be the largest parish in the state. Architect Pietro Belluschi of the Massachusetts Institute of Technology designed a new, larger church building in the 1950s to complement the older Gothic chapel. The Roman Catholic Cathedral of Mary Our Queen is located on Charles Street, two blocks south of the Church of the Redeemer. The Cathedral, also built in the 1950s in a neo-Gothic style, stands on land donated by the Baltimore dry-goods merchant, Thomas J. O'Neill. The legend is that he decided to make the gift when his store survived the great fire of 1904. The Grace Methodist congregation, a union of three older churches, began worshipping at Charles Street and Northern Parkway in 1951. The Brown Memorial Presbyterian Church of Bolton Hill did not move, but opened a second church on North Charles Street in 1961.

After World War I, German and Eastern European Jews moved to the northwest suburbs. Like blacks, Baltimore's Jews in the 1920s faced restrictive housing covenants which excluded them from many neighborhoods. The northwest was open, however. By the 1950s, the major religious congregations had begun building new synagogues. The Baltimore Hebrew Congregation, Har Sinai, Oheb Shalom and many others with histories going back to East Baltimore during the mid-1800s moved northwest to Park Heights Avenue, both inside and beyond the city limits.

As the immediate post-war dislocations subsided, the country slipped into the period historians have dubbed the "Roaring Twenties." Prosperity and rebellious assertion of new freedoms characterized the period. An economic boom supported the social and intellectual rebellion.

Baltimore's 1920s boom, like that of the rest of the nation, was based on demands for consumer products that had not been available during the war as well as new items like radios and automobiles. The construction industry boomed. Baltimore businessmen reflected the nation-wide mania of boosterism and promoted their city. Both of Baltimore's mayors during the period, Republican William F. Broening and Democrat Howard W. Jackson, joined with them. They attracted new industries to the city. Glenn L. Martin Aircraft came. American Sugar built a processing plant. Western Electric opened a plant for manufacturing telephone equipment. Bethlehem Steel added a $100,000,000 expansion at Sparrows Point. In the

Right:
The new Roman Catholic Cathedral of Mary Our Queen, built on North Charles Street in the 1950s, is two hundred and seventy feet long. Its stone towers stand one hundred and twenty-eight feet high

Center:
The Episcopal Church of the Redeemer, which began as a small country chapel (right), *added the new main church designed by Pietro Belluschi in the 1950s*

Above:
The Baltimore Hebrew Congregation, which first worshiped in the Lloyd Street Synagogue, moved to this new synagogue on Park Heights Avenue at the city line in the 1950s

six years following 1920, Baltimore's volume of foreign trade rose from seventh in the nation to third. The boosters were succeeding magnificently.

The city's building program reflected its prosperity. The Baltimore Museum of Art opened next to the Hopkins campus. A new municipal office building and fire and police department headquarters appeared around War Memorial Plaza. The city built a wading pool in Carroll Park, a swimming pool in Riverside Park, and two swimming pools in Druid Hill Park, one for whites and one for blacks. For all the new commuters, the city constructed new roads and extended existing ones like Charles Street Avenue, Walther Avenue, the Alameda, and Loch Raven Boulevard out into the developing suburbs. Automobile ownership caused a new problem for the city: traffic congestion. Everyone discussed it, but little was done.

Throughout the boom, politics continued as usual. Sonny Mahon and Frank "Slot Machine" Kelly, vied for power within the Democratic Party. In 1919, Kelly's candidate, George William Weems, defeated James Preston for the Democratic mayoral nomination. In the general election, Mahon's forces sat by and let the Republican candidate, William Broening, win. His party won nine City Council seats as well. Two of these men, Warner T. McGuinn and William L. Fitzgerald were black. Democrats resumed their use of Reconstruction politics and charged that Republican Mayor Broening was a threat to Baltimore's system of white supremacy, even though he had allowed the Ku Klux Klan to parade as evidence of his support for segregation.

Kelly and Mahon scrambled to register new Democratic voters to enlarge their own camps. They had a substantial pool of potential voters to fight over. Rural white migrants voted Democratic as did most foreign immigrants except for a large minority of Germans and some Jews who registered as Republicans. By 1923, about 75 percent of Baltimore's voters were Democrats.

The election of 1923 showed the results of a temporary truce between Mahon and Kelly that had been orchestrated by Governor Ritchie two years before. Kelly allowed Mahon's candidate, Howard Jackson, to run for mayor with the understanding that the other city offices and patronage jobs would be divided evenly. Jackson defeated the incumbent Broening in a landslide. For the first time the City Council was chosen in that year from six districts which elected three councilmen each. The Democrats had gerrymandered most of the Republicans into the 4th District, containing heavy proportions of blacks and Jews. Much to the surprise of everyone, only one Republican, Daniel Ellison, a Lithuanian Jewish immigrant, won a seat in the City Council. The two black candidates were defeated by white Democrats, although by the next election, those two seats reverted to black Republicans.

Clearly, neither Jackson, nor Mahon, nor Kelly possessed the kind of city-wide control that the pre-war Rasin machine had exercised. The mid-twenties saw even greater dispersion of power with the rise of William Curran, who in 1923 helped the Kelly faction gain control of the City Council. In 1927, the Democrats nominated Curran for mayor. William Broening, with Mahon's help, defeated Curran and carried nine city councilmen into office as well. Frank Kelly and Sonny Mahon both died in 1928 leaving control of the Democratic Party in the hands of Governor Albert Ritchie and William Curran. Curran, a criminal lawyer, was the last city-wide leader. He maintained his influence until he died in 1954. Under Curran, several district leaders acquired considerable influence, among them Richard Coggins and Patrick O'Malley in the

Left:
William Curran is generally considered to have been the last Democratic boss of Baltimore city. Since his death in 1954, political power has been divided among various district leaders

Below:
The United Railways buses parked by the Johns Hopkins campus ran along Charles Street carrying commuters from the popular new northern suburbs to the central business district

Left:
This filling station which opened in 1911 is said to have been the first in Baltimore. It was located on the corner of St. Paul and Lexington Streets

Above:
Automobile ownership caused a new problem for Baltimore: traffic congestion

third district and James H. (Jack) Pollack in the fourth district.

In 1931 Curran and Ritchie conceded to popular demand and allowed vote-getter Howard Jackson to run for mayor, provided he accept Curran men for City Council president and comptroller on his ticket. A group of reformers, working with some independent ward bosses, managed to elect their own candidate, E. Lester Muller, as City Council President. Jackson did win the mayoralty and became Baltimore's first four-term mayor, remaining in office until 1943.

One archenemy of Jackson's was Marie Bauernschmidt. A reform leader who campaigned for years to rid the city school system of graft and politics of corruption, she found Jackson particularly objectionable because of his periodic bouts with demon rum. She challenged him to "take the cure" or resign from office. Jackson's drinking helped him politically in some parts of town, especially during Prohibition.

The 18th Amendment, originally proposed as a wartime conservation measure, became effective in 1919 when the Volstead Act provided enforcement procedures and funding. Throughout the dry years, Baltimore was known as a "wet" town. Several breweries continued to produce the real thing under the guise of near-beer. Distilled liquor arrived regularly through the ports of both Baltimore and Annapolis and was manufactured locally as well. Speakeasies proliferated as the laxity of prosecution became apparent. The city government under Jackson and the state government under Ritchie, a national leader of the wets, never appropriated money for enforcement of Prohibition. In fact, Ritchie's attorney general ruled that the local police did not have the right to make arrests under the Volstead Act. Federal agents did occasionally conduct raids in Baltimore, but frequently they were met by hostile crowds and violent opposition against which local police officials declined to provide aid.

Drinking in spite of Prohibition was one of many forms of rebellion during the "Roaring Twenties." Although roots of the rebellion stretched back into the late nineteenth century, it was nurtured in the wartime spirit of "eat, drink, and be merry for tomorrow we may die." Many people, particularly members of the younger generation who had served overseas, began to question old values, to look for new meanings, and to experiment with new life-styles. This breaking out and innovation, often accompanied by a rejection of traditions was opposed particularly by those members of the older generation who felt that their whole way of life and moral system were being threatened. People who already felt threatened by immigrants, strikes and Communists, tended also to react with fear to cocktail parties, new fashions, new trends in music and theater, and the new life-style of women. Despite the opposition, rebellion flourished in the prosperity of the 1920s.

New forms of music, especially jazz, and theatrical presentations with themes of realism, rebellion, and explicit sex drew large crowds. Baltimore both before and after World War I was a good theater town. Leading actors and musicians performed before large audiences in the city's numerous theaters. A gradual transition from vaudeville and live theater to movies took place during the early decades of the twentieth century.

At the turn of the century, at least eight theaters were thriving in Baltimore. The two leading playhouses were the Holliday Street Theater, housed in the 1872 structure which survived until 1927 when it was razed to make way for War Memorial Plaza, and Ford's Grand Opera House, which opened in 1871 with a

It appears that Baltimoreans expected liquor to be available, but more expensive, after the Volstead Act went into effect

Marie Bauernschmidt, a reformer and an archenemy of Jackson's, was unfortunately noted for leading many unsuccessful campaigns against him

Howard Jackson, one of Baltimore's most popular mayors and the masterful leader during the depression of the 1930s, makes a speech at the laying of the cornerstone of the new Enoch Pratt Free Library central building which opened in 1933

performance of *As You Like It* and closed ninety-three years later with *A Funny Thing Happened on the Way to the Forum.* For many years a family business, Ford's Theater brought stars like George M. Cohan, Edwin Booth, Helen Hayes, Maurice Evans, and Tallulah Bankhead to Baltimore. When movies were new, Ford's screened big features like D. W. Griffith's *Birth of a Nation* in 1915 and Cecil B. DeMille's *Ten Commandments* in 1925. Under the ownership of Morris A. Mechanic, Ford's remained beyond World War II the only legitimate theater in town.

At the turn of the century, vaudeville reigned as the national entertainment. Admission usually ranged from 25 to 50 cents. Some shows were rough and ready; others were billed for the whole family. James Kernan, who donated the land for the hospital for crippled children, made his fortune from the Monumental Theater, where some of Baltimore's more daring acts were presented. Women dancers wore tightly laced corsets, but raw flesh was taboo. Hawaiian style hula dancers provided the most naked entertainment. With his profits from the Monumental, Kernan opened the Maryland Theater for "refined" vaudeville. He censored the acts himself to make sure nothing would offend the ladies and children in his audiences. Ethel Barrymore and Lillian Russell appeared, and Al Jolson debuted in Kernan's Theater. Variety shows included jugglers, bicyclists, acrobats and animals. In the winter, when cool temperature modified the odor, acts featuring horses and elephants were popular. The Maryland led the way in incorporating movies into its live shows, a practice the theater began in 1904. Finally, it became exclusively a movie theater before it was torn down in 1951. Most of the old vaudeville theaters became movie theaters and then either closed or burned down.

One rather unique theater, the Lyceum, shows the transition well. Built in the 1890s in the fashionable neighborhood of 1200 North Charles Street, the stage originally featured amateur performances. A little bar and smoking room were located beneath the lobby. The first few rows of spectators sat on comfortable sofas. John Albaugh, who operated a vaudeville syndicate, purchased the theater and brought in stars like George Arliss, Blanche Bates, and George Fawcett. During the Great War, the Lyceum offered a mixture of road shows, musicals, vaudeville, and films. In the early twenties, when legitimate theater drew smaller crowds, offerings like *White Cargo* and *Seduction* brought audiences seeking the sensational. The police gave the theater good publicity when they arrested some of the performers and charged them with indecent exposure. The next show, *Getting Gertie's Garter,* was a sellout. In 1925, the Lyceum burned down.

As filmmaking technology improved, movies proliferated and drew even larger crowds. By 1920, Baltimore's biggest movie houses, the New, the Hippodrome, and the Victoria, each averaged thirty thousand spectators weekly. The Hippodrome featured big band concerts as well. The Municipal Band and the Colored Municipal Band played summertime concerts in the city's parks. With all the merrymaking, many people forgot the fears that had characterized the immediate post-war period.

Baltimore's segregated society led to the growth of a widely celebrated black entertainment district. Pennsylvania Avenue emerged as the center of black culture in the 1920s. The spirit of the Harlem Renaissance came to Baltimore, and "the Avenue" flourished. The Douglass Theater, built by the black-owned Douglass Amusement Company, dominated the 1300 block of Pennsylvania Avenue. Later known as the Royal, the theater throughout the years between the

In the 1920s, elaborately decorated movie theatres like the New drew an average of 30,000 spectators weekly

wars featured the big-name musicians like Eubie Blake, Count Basie, Cab Calloway, and Duke Ellington. After World War II, Ella Fitzgerald, Nat "King" Cole, Dizzy Gillespie, and Billie Holiday all performed at the Royal, and later the Supremes, the Platters, and James Brown. Live performances lasted until 1965 at the Royal, when it went the way of the city's other old vaudeville theaters and became exclusively a movie house. Five years later it was bulldozed to make space for a new school.

During the heyday of the Royal Theater a cluster of clubs, where big name entertainers also appeared, opened along the Avenue. Gamby's, the Ritz, the Comedy Club, owned by Isaiah Dixon, and the Casino Club, where owner Willie Adams introduced Redd Foxx, all drew crowds. Some of the performers stayed at the Casino Club. Others made their quarters at the black-owned Penn Hotel, whose guests included Ethel Waters and Pearl Bailey as well as the band leaders.

Pennsylvania Avenue meant more than theaters. Movie houses were there. A YMCA was located nearby. Businesses that catered to blacks opened stores along the Avenue. As black customers found themselves unwelcome in many of the big downtown stores, they turned more and more to the Avenue shops. From the 1930s through the 1950s, the Pennsylvania Avenue Merchants Association sponsored an Easter Parade. While whites paraded their Easter finery around Mt. Vernon Square, Negroes showed theirs along the Avenue.

A major institution, Douglass High School, moved in 1925 to new quarters just west of Pennsylvania Avenue at Calhoun and Baker Streets. Almost all of Baltimore's middle class blacks sent their children to Douglass, which was noted for its high academic standards. In the 1920s fully one-third of its graduates went on to college or normal school. Douglass' more famous alumni include band leader Cab Calloway, civil rights activists Clarence Mitchell, Jr. and his wife, the former Juanita Jackson, and Supreme Court Justice Thurgood Marshall.

Although some black Baltimoreans clearly shared in the prosperity and revelry of the twenties, many did not. Discrimination in hiring and lack of educational background left many in poverty. Overcrowded and unhealthful living conditions were one result of that. Tuberculosis especially plagued Baltimore's Negro community. The city's health officials dubbed as "Lung Block" the square bounded by Pennsylvania Avenue, Druid Hill Avenue, Biddle and Preston Streets because so many cases of tuberculosis occurred there.

But progressivism was not completely dead. Medical officials and social workers still labored in black and white slums. City-wide charity organizations carried an increasing share of the burden previously borne by ethnic and religious societies. Reformers like Elisabeth Gilman, the daughter of Johns Hopkins' first president, a social worker who became a socialist, fought to keep people's consciences aroused. The reform impulse remained, but it was no longer as dominant as it had been before the war to save the world for democracy had been fought and won and left the world still unperfected. Social activists were no longer society's celebrities.

Popular heroes of the twenties and thirties tended to be either outstanding individual achievers or outspoken rebels. Baltimore provided its share of national heroes. H. L. Mencken, who never really left, and F. Scott Fitzgerald, who came to Baltimore during the 1920s, drew the attention of the nation's literati to the city on the Patapsco. Babe Ruth, even after he played for the Yankees, and Roy Campanella who played for the Baltimore Elites, gave the city fame among sports fans.

The joyous days of the twenties provided a

Left:
Supreme Court Justice Thurgood Marshall is one among many nationally famous alumni of Douglass High School

Below:
Big names like Al Jolson (left) *and Cab Calloway* (right) *performed on Pennsylvania Avenue in its heyday*

Left:
Douglass High School, noted for its high academic standards when Baltimore's public schools remained segregated, sent an unusually high number of graduates on to college or normal school

needed respite between World War I and the difficult years of the Depression and World War II which followed. Although the date of the great crash, October 24, 1929, generally marks the beginning of the crisis, in reality the transition from prosperity to depression was somewhat less abrupt. Throughout the nation, several sectors of the economy were in trouble before 1929. Housing construction fell off after the post-war shortage was satiated. Farmers faced the consequences of their wartime expansion once a recovered Europe no longer purchased so much American food. Such poor agricultural markets and also the devastations of the boll weevil drove many farmers and agricultural workers into cities like Baltimore in search of employment.

Just as some segments of the economy had wound down before the crash, others continued to operate at a fairly high level after 1929. All states and cities faced grave difficulties, but the specific problems varied somewhat from place to place. During the period immediately following the stock market crash, Baltimore fared better than some other cities.

Unemployment spread more slowly in Baltimore because of the city's diversified economy. The numbers of jobless people rose gradually here. Towns that were dependent on one major industry often felt a more sudden shock wave. Furthermore, only a few big banks in Baltimore failed. The Baltimore Trust Company was the first to close its doors in September, 1930. Most of the big banks in town did not fail. They were managed by conservative bankers not given to the speculative policies of their more adventuresome colleagues. Because of this, most Baltimore depositors did not see their lifetime savings wiped out. One other advantage Baltimore possessed was its large number of home owners. In an era when many mortgages were paid off in five years, a large number of people owned their homes clear of debt and therefore did not face losing them in foreclosure proceedings.

All these factors notwithstanding, Baltimore soon began to feel the effects of the national slowdown. Men and women began to face layoffs or salary cuts. Unemployment ran highest among the city's blacks, who were often the first

Opposite:
Novelist F. Scott Fitzgerald, pictured here in his World War I uniform, lived in Baltimore during the 1920s, for some time occupying an apartment overlooking the campus of the Johns Hopkins University on North Charles Street

Henry L. Mencken, who lived most of his life on Hollins Street, brought renown to the city of his birth as one of the leading pundits of his time

Roy Campanella, who played in the Negro League for the Baltimore Elites, was one of many players who moved into the major leagues when they desegregated after World War II

George Herman Ruth first played baseball at St. Mary's Industrial School. Jack Dunn, owner of the Orioles, gave the Babe his first major league job, and the Baltimore boy became a national hero

fired. Women workers faced layoffs from employers who felt they should not take jobs away from men. This was true sometimes even when the women were responsible for the support of their family. Blacks and women may have lost their jobs first, but everybody was threatened. By January 1931, roughly 42,000 Baltimoreans, or one-eighth of the total work force were unemployed. In September 1931, Baltimore's labor unions reported that 31 percent of their members were unemployed and 27 percent could find only part-time work. President Herbert Hoover's Commission for Unemployment set Baltimore's rate at 19.2 percent in 1931. People were suffering.

The men in charge in 1930, while this situation was developing, were known humanitarians. Maryland's Governor Albert C. Ritchie began his career as a progressive. A popular politician, he held his office from 1920 to 1935. Baltimore Mayor William Broening was known for siding with the "little guys" and working for safety rules in industry and other such protective measures. In particular, Ritchie was loathe to accept funds from the federal government. Maryland was one of only eight states that turned down the first federal monies offered.

In 1930 no state agency existed to handle unemployment or relief problems. The Board of State Aid and Charities served primarily to give advice to private charities and to make inspections. In May, 1930, Mayor Broening established a Commission on Employment Stabilization and in December a Municipal Free Employment Service. Neither agency could handle the large numbers of unemployed. There simply were not enough jobs to go around.

Private charities did their best to provide relief. In Baltimore, 80 percent of the relief cases were handled by the Family Welfare Association. Additional help came from the Bureau of Catholic Charities, the Jewish Social Service Bureau, the Salvation Army, and smaller groups. In 1930, the city reluctantly granted $8900 to the Family Welfare Association and $3900 to the Jewish Social Service Bureau when those organizations ran out of funds.

Police Commissioner Charles Gaither announced that the department would assume a role in providing relief and asked for donations of money and gifts in kind. By February, 1931, the Police Department had provided fuel and food for 7500 families and had fed 6600 persons at local station houses. That same month, the Baltimore Association of Commerce organized a Citizens' Emergency Relief Committee. W. Frank Roberts served as its chairman. Mayor Broening contributed $50,000 from the city's contingency fund. By April the businessmen had raised $350,000. The *Sunpapers* sponsored Self-Denial Day on March 27, 1931. Boxes appeared all over town. Baltimore's citizens were asked to deny themselves something they wanted and contribute the money for distribution among the needy. The 1931 Community Chest drive raised $2 million for relief in Baltimore. The Citizens' Emergency Relief Committee total rose to $650,000. Ritchie contributed $125,000, four days proceeds from the racetrack, for relief in Baltimore. But none of this was enough.

As the May, 1931 mayoral election approached, Howard Jackson campaigned promising that the municipal government would do all it could to bring relief and employment. He won. And the situation continued to get worse. In September, 3800 families in Baltimore received aid from the Citizens' Emergency Relief Committee. Five months later, 14,100 families requested relief. By March, 1932, the committee needed $50,000 a week. That month, Jackson contributed $100,000 from the city's contingency funds. Other money was raised by bonds which Ritchie had reluctantly agreed to issue. By January, 1933, 20 percent of all Baltimore's

By 1933 scenes like this showed the desperation of the city's unemployed. Over 20 percent of the population was unemployed during the worst days of the Depression

vorkers were unemployed. Over 20,000 families vere on relief. Finally, in March, Ritchie applied o the Reconstruction Finance Corporation for loan to bring some federal money into the tate.

Governor Ritchie's slowness, similar to 'resident Hoover's, to experiment with new nethods of government financing to meet the risis, contributed to his election defeat in 1934. ackson's people did not support Ritchie. The epublican candidate, Harry W. Nice, carried altimore and the state.

Howard Jackson soon realized that the ituation he found when he took office in 1931 eeded more than temporary relief. He led altimore into the New Deal, and he set out to un the city like a business. The logo he nprinted on his stationery bespoke his pproach to his office: "Be courteous, efficient, nd economical."

Jackson launched Baltimore on a plan of usiness-like management of municipal overnment, efficient relief projects, and useful ublic works. Accepting funds from Washington n one hand, he initiated a successful drive to ollect local taxes on the other. When other ities faced large defaults in 1933 and 1934, ackson collected 85 percent and 94 percent, espectively, of all monies owed. Such efficiency nabled him to reduce assessments and lower he tax rate from $2.54 to $2.34. Jackson did educe salaries paid to municipal workers: those vho earned more than $1000 received a five ercent cut, and those whose salaries were over 1200 lost 10 percent. He decreased his own alary by 20 percent. But unlike many other ities, Baltimore's employees received checks very payday and the city maintained a good redit rating. That proved beneficial in attracting ederal money, especially for programs that equired matching funds.

Jackson won national acclaim for his administration of Baltimore. His insistence on efficient management of all programs and appointment of competent people to run them were crucial to Baltimore's survival. Judge Thomas Waxter directed the Baltimore Welfare Department which handled all federal, state and municipal funds for general public assistance. Waxter was highly praised. Dr. Huntingdon Williams, who directed the city's Health Department, twice won awards for the most efficient health program in the nation.

Jackson insisted that all New Deal projects have long-term usefulness as well as providing employment for hungry people. City officials worked with representatives of the Civil Works Administration, the Works Progress Administration, the Public Works Administration and other agencies to plan the projects. The Maryland director of the Public Works Administration, Abel Wolman, a sanitary engineer from Johns Hopkins, was especially helpful. The list of projects is impressive. Jackson built a new wing for the Art Museum and the new Enoch Pratt Free Library. Collections at both places were catalogued. Additions were made to several city hospitals and to Morgan College.

New Deal funds constructed the Mount Pleasant Park and Golf Course, a second tunnel from Loch Raven Reservoir to Montebello, and the new Prettyboy Reservoir. New schools and playgrounds opened. Existing schools were repaired and beautified. Baltimore gained wider roads and the viaducts on Howard and Orleans Streets. Late in the New Deal the city's first public housing, the Edgar Allen Poe Homes, opened in East Baltimore.

With all these successes, it is not surprising that Howard Jackson won reelection in 1935 and 1939. In 1935 he defeated Willie Curran's man in the primary and in the general election won easily over both Republican Blanchard Randall, Jr. and Socialist Elisabeth Gilman. Jackson

entered the gubernatorial primaries in 1938 but lost the nomination to Herbert O'Conor, an ally of Curran's. O'Conor defeated Nice for the governorship. The following year, Jackson defeated the Curran-O'Conor candidate for the mayoral nomination and then went on to beat a popular new Republican, Theodore Roosevelt McKeldin, to win his fourth and last term as mayor.

Despite Mayor Jackson's efficiency, life remained exceedingly difficult for a great many people during the 1930s. Soup lines continued to feed many hungry people. Others scraped by without enough food, without decent homes, and without opportunities for education. Throughout the nation, different groups protested the system under which these conditions persisted through the decade. But although Socialists and other protest parties fielded candidates in many elections, most voters chose to work within the existing system. Somehow, President Franklin Roosevelt inspired confidence that everything would come out all right.

The New Deal marked a watershed in America's political history. Before Roosevelt was president, the usual national majority was Republican. After the New Deal, it became Democratic. Baltimore was already a heavily Democratic city, but national changes were reflected in local politics. The most dramatic change occurred as black voters switched their allegiance from the party of Lincoln to the party of the New Deal. Former Republican City Councilman William Fitzgerald's move to the Democratic Party and his work as a W.P.A. official typified the transformation. As in so many similar cases, Roosevelt's economic policies precipitated the move.

An interesting black protest group was formed in Baltimore in 1931, at a time when many civil rights organizations were stagnating. Their techniques and goals prefigured the broader civil rights movement of the 1960s. The Young People's Forum was organized by a group of well-educated, younger members of some of Baltimore's leading black families. Juanita Jackson served as president of the group. Her mother, Lillie Mae Carroll Jackson, an experienced civil rights activist, was an advisor. Members met at the Bethel A.M.E. Church and other churches. They invited speakers chosen "to promote youth consciousness," among them Walter White of the National Association for the Advancement of Colored People, athlete Jesse Owens, diplomat Ralph Bunche, birth control advocate Margaret Sanger, and

Opposite:
City Councilman William Fitzgerald moved into the Democratic Party to support the New Deal

Right:
As the depression made economic difficulties even harsher, black Baltimoreans protested discrimination in employment

Below:
Free entertainment like this baseball game in 1931 drew crowds during the depression years

newspaperman Gerald Johnson. In an effort to change policies that hurt the black community economically, the Young People's Forum sponsored "buy where you can work" drives. Their boycotts and picketing of Pennsylvania Avenue stores, including the A&P, resulted in the hiring of black clerks. The group also helped register blacks to vote.

All the protests and all the New Deal programs continued on through the 1930s, and none of them ended the Depression. British economist John Maynard Keynes had figured out the solution: spending. But no one, in or out of the New Deal, imagined the magnitude of spending that would be necessary to put America's millions back to work and start the economic cycle upward again. What really ended the Great Depression was World War II. Millions of men were taken out of the civilian work force and paid by the Army. Millions more were hired to produce war material which the soldiers of all nations destroyed almost as fast as it came out of the factories. Prosperity returned, but with it came the agonies of war.

Three days after the bombs fell on Pearl Harbor, Mayor Jackson organized a Civil Defense Committee, headquartered at City Hall and chaired by Baltimore's Highways Engineer, George A. Carter. A crash program to train instructors was put together. During the Christmas holidays 1,100 teachers qualified as civil defense instructors and then taught others. Within six months ten thousand persons had been trained. Before the war ended, over twenty-five thousand Baltimoreans participated in some form of civil defense activity. Air raid wardens, auxiliary police and firemen, a medical corps, messengers, demolition and clearance crews all received training. Over four hundred people were trained to work in decontamination squads in case of gas attacks. Warning centers staffed by volunteer women telephone operators were set up to operate 24 hours a day. The media ran a campaign to teach people how to react in case of a bombing. Practice blackouts allowed familiarization with some of the procedures.

As thousands of Baltimoreans left to join the Armed Forces, and student pilots practiced in the sky beyond Mt. Washington, Governor O'Conor authorized a state guard, known as the Minute Men, to give local protection in case of sabotage. Despite this precaution, fears of local enemies were not as great as they had been during World War I. Although a small percentage of Baltimore's German Americans had joined the pro-Nazi Bund during the thirties, many more had been outspoken in their condemnation of Hitler and their loyalty to the United States. East coast Germans faced little of the paranoia that sent west coast Japanese Americans to detention camps. Some German groups were placed under surveillance, and a number did not survive the war, but the irrational hatred of all things German that had characterized the First World War did not reappear.

Baltimore, as it had in so many wars, served as a major military supply center. Men, food, and supplies moved rapidly through the port. Two local industries, shipbuilding and aircraft, and their suppliers were especially important. As early as the fall of 1941 the Bethlehem-Fairchild Shipyards received contracts to build 62 ships. Before the war was over, the company had hired forty-seven thousand workers to construct 384 Liberty ships, 94 Victory ships, and 30 LSTs. The Maryland Drydock Company hired twelve thousand new employees to work on conversion and repair orders received before Pearl Harbor. At the same time, Glenn L. Martin Aircraft was backlogged with orders worth $743 million and hired six thousand people to work on them. This rate of production continued throughout the

Right:
The war abroad changed the appearance of the streets of Baltimore. Here several men inspect sandbags installed by local civil defense officials

Center:
Sailors with loaded duffel bags march past the Richmond Market

Above:
Air-raid sirens were installed throughout the city for use in blackout drills during the war

Left:
The Duke and Duchess of Windsor visited Baltimore in 1941. A large crowd, curiosity seekers among them, turned out to greet the former Wallis Warfield Simpson who once lived in the city

war.

Thousands of men, women and children poured into Baltimore from rural Maryland, Appalachia and points south to work in the war industries. Women and blacks were hired in jobs previously closed to them. The burgeoning population placed a burden on all city services: schools, health, sanitation, transportation. Ten thousand new housing units were needed. Military needs, of course, took priority.

Everyday life in Baltimore quickly reflected those military priorities. Sugar shortages hit early. Waitresses in restaurants asked "how many?" if a person ordered sugar with coffee and often refused to give more than two cubes. The *Sun* reported in April 1942 that tea was getting scarce and so were lawn mowers. Tires were rationed. Price ceilings were established for tires, retreads, sugar, electrical appliances and much more, so people had a fair chance at purchasing the limited supplies that were available. Favorite soft drinks were unobtainable at the end of each month as that month's quota ran out. Rubber heels were more expensive. Razor blade production was curtailed. People carried old tubes to the drugstore to get refills of toothpaste and shaving cream. Home heating oil deliveries were limited. The Baltimore Transit Company's ridership grew by leaps and bounds as more and more people saved their cars and gasoline for special uses.

Despite a great degree of unity in national politics and widespread support of the war effort, local political rivalries continued as usual. Baltimore elected a new mayor in 1943. Howard Jackson ran for an unprecedented fifth term. The Democratic Party alliances had fallen apart, however, and Curran's forces once again opposed Jackson. Curran and O'Conor had also split in a patronage dispute. The result of the Democratic disunity was a victory for Republican candidate Theodore Roosevelt McKeldin, who served as mayor through the final years of the war and the first years of the peace.

Baltimoreans followed the war in Europe and in the Pacific on the radio and in newspaper reports. They watched eagerly as the tide of battle turned slowly in 1943 and 1944. They cheered the June 6, 1944 landing in Normandy and the Allied arrival in Paris on August 25. They mourned the death of President Roosevelt on April 12, 1945, and less than a month later, on May 7, rejoiced at the unconditional surrender of Germany. They watched the new president, Harry Truman, and read of the results of his first major decision as the atomic bombs fell on Hiroshima and Nagasaki, and were glad and relieved when Japan also finally surrendered on September 2. The long war was over.

Once again Baltimore began the transition from a wartime to a peacetime society. Veterans returned, war industries ceased production, and some workers lost their jobs. By October, 1945 approximately thirty-nine thousand persons had been laid off; but several factors cushioned the shock. Industries quickly reconverted to meet the large demand for consumer goods. Government programs for veterans, especially the G. I. Bill, funneled many veterans out of the labor market. Returning soldiers hastened to take advantage of the opportunity for higher education. The Johns Hopkins freshman class in 1946 enrolled half teenagers and half veterans. By the academic year 1948-49, 70 percent of all Hopkins undergraduates were ex-servicemen. While these people studied, industry reconverted. The government supervised this and other processes more than it did after World War I. Consequently, socio-economic dislocations were fewer.

Almost immediately, however, a cold war replaced the past conflict as the absorbing international concern. One domestic result of the rivalry between the United States and Russia

Before the war's end, the workers at the Bethlehem-Fairchild Shipyards built over 500 ships. Here the Liberty Ship Patrick Henry *readies to set sail*

Below:
Rationing cards regulated the amount of many scarce commodities people could purchase. Here, precious sugar is being weighed carefully

was the rise of a strong anti-Communist movement in this country. Just as the threat of a Bolshevik revolution had been exaggerated after World War I, the fear of Communist infiltration mushroomed following World War II. Several Baltimoreans figured prominently in the tragic circumstances.

A graduate of Johns Hopkins and former editor of the student *Newsletter,* Alger Hiss received an honorary LL.D. from his alma mater in the university's Commemoration Day ceremonies in February, 1947. He was honored for distinguished service in international relations. Less than three years later, Hiss was convicted of perjury for lying about his affiliations with the Communist Party.

Owen Lattimore, director of the Walter Hines Page School of International Relations at Johns Hopkins and an expert on the Far East, was accused by Senator Joseph McCarthy of being the top Communist agent in the United States. The university resisted pressure to fire Lattimore, and faculty members, including George Boas and Clarence Long, rallied to his support. Finally, Maryland Senator Millard E. Tydings cleared his name before McCarthy's committee. McCarthy then undertook to remove Tydings from the Senate, which he did in the scandalous campaign of 1950 when McCarthy supporters juxtaposed photographs of Tydings and a former head of the American Communist Party, Earl Browder, to give the impression that they worked together. Ugly incidents like these occurred all too widely in Baltimore and elsewhere until the frenzy subsided in the mid-1950s.

Baltimore's post-war history includes great successes and serious problems. Like much of the rest of the nation, the city in 1945 faced major problems of readjustment and rehabilitation which had been accumulating through the crises of the Great Depression and World War II. One of Baltimore's solutions stirred enthusiasm throughout the nation. The involvement of many segments of the population and the broad co-operation between the public and private sectors in planning and executing rehabilitation projects have played a large part in the successful aspects of Baltimore's "renaissance."

The renewal program began under Mayor Thomas D'Alesandro, Jr. who was elected in 1947. He defeated Curran's candidate, Howard Crook, in the primary and Republican Deeley K. Nice in the general election. D'Alesandro had the support of a number of ward leaders including Ambrose Kennedy, Patrick O'Malley, Jack Pollack, and Joe Wyatt. D'Alesandro wanted to build, and he took office at the right time to do just that.

Blight had been spreading across downtown Baltimore through the poverty of the 1930s and the war years of the 1940s. A survey made in 1950 revealed the decay which was most extensive in a ring around the downtown area. Of Baltimore's two hundred fifty thousand homes, ninety-one thousand were in blighted areas. One-third of the city's people lived in those areas. Over forty-five thousand homes were classified as substandard and eighteen thousand as dilapidated. Between twenty thousand and thirty thousand homes lacked toilets, baths, hot water or all three. Most census tracts were either all black or all white.

Shortages of schools and recreation facilities had worsened during the war. Inner-city decay and post-war prosperity accelerated suburban growth. People who could afford to were abandoning the inner city to people whose needs for city services were greatest. The central business district suffered heavily as fewer people shopped downtown. Traffic congestion and lack of parking kept increasing numbers of Baltimoreans away. Its assessed value declined heavily.

Above:
V-J Day is hailed by this crowd at Baltimore and Charles Streets. Finally the long war had ended

Top:
News of the German surrender brought crowds to the streets

Above:
Peace brought happy reunions on Pier 11 at Canton

Several programs were initiated to ameliorate the decay. A comprehensive system of housing rehabilitation which became known as the Baltimore Plan resulted in the restoration of homes by the enforcement of sanitary and safety regulations. Despite a crash program, twenty-five thousand substandard homes still surrounded the downtown area in 1954. Mayor D'Alesandro's building program had given the city five hundred miles of new streets, 17 recreation centers and pools, 9 new schools, 7 off-street parking garages, 4 new hospital and health buildings, 4 new firehouses, a new expressway and the lower deck of the new Memorial Stadium.

Big league teams came to Baltimore to play in the new stadium. The National Football League Colts began to play here in the fall of 1953 after Carroll Rosenbloom and other local investors purchased the team. Their first win of an NFL championship in January, 1959 gave Baltimore a bigger boost than all the building projects combined. Major league baseball came to the city when the season opened in the spring of 1954, after Clarence Miles headed a group of Baltimoreans who purchased the St. Louis Browns. Joseph Iglehard and then Jerold C. Hoffberger served as chairman of the board. In 1966, the year after Hoffberger took over, the Orioles won the American League pennant and the World Series.

More innovations appeared. Baltimore became the first American city to add fluorine to its water supply. D'Alesandro hired the nation's foremost traffic engineer, Henry Barnes, to straighten out the city's horrendous traffic problems. The new Friendship Airport begun under Theodore McKeldin's administration opened. Mayor D'Alesandro, Governor William Preston Lane, and President Harry Truman dedicated the facility in 1950.

The years 1954 and 1955 saw several key events that set the future course of Baltimore's development. By the end of that time, a pattern of cooperation of the city's residents, business leaders, and government officials was beginning to evolve. Several processes occurred simultaneously. Blacks, the one major group which had been excluded from power, began to integrate more fully than ever before into the life of the city. At the same time, businessmen and politicians joined in a venture to promote the city and improve the environment for both business and living.

The events of 1954, the year of the Supreme Court school integration decision, signaled a new beginning for Baltimore's black community. Just under a third of the total population at one time, African Americans had been without elected political representation since 1931 when the last black Republicans served on the City Council. As blacks moved into the Democratic party in increasing numbers during the 1930s, a small number of patronage jobs were distributed among them, but the policy-making positions were retained by whites. Then in 1954, a group of blacks led by a Republican, Harry Cole, successfully challenged Jack Pollack's domination of the 4th District. Harry Cole won election to the State Senate. Emory Cole, also a Republican and no relation, and Truly Hatchett, a Democrat, gained seats in the House of Delegates.

The following year, Pollack included a black candidate, Walter Dixon, on his victorious City Council ticket. In 1958, Verda Welcome and Irma Dixon became the first black women ever elected to the Maryland General Assembly. Verda Welcome's supporters formed the nucleus of the Fourth District Democratic Organization. Dr. Carl Murphy and William "Little Willie" Adams were early contributors. Over the years, warring factions splintered off and formed new groups. As the black population in East

Right:
Pitcher Dave McNally and Brooks Robinson cheer the winning of the 1966 World Series

Below:
President Harry S. Truman joined Governor Preston Lane (left) and Mayor Thomas D'Alesandro (right) at the dedication of Friendship Airport in June 1950

Baltimore increased, they established a political power base there as well. By 1970, black political organizations were strong enough to elect Parren Mitchell to Congress.

As blacks were beginning to move into elective offices in Baltimore, where they would speak out in favor of rehabilitating the city's slum, some other people began to formulate a program to revitalize the downtown business district. They planned to rejuvenate the central area and make that a catalyst for future renewal programs throughout the city.

A group of businessmen formed the Greater Baltimore Committee in 1955. They chose Clarence Miles to be chairman, Thomas Butler vice-chairman, Jerold C. Hoffberger secretary, and Daniel Lindley, treasurer. James Rouse became chairman of the executive committee. William Boucher, III joined the group as executive director in 1956. Mayor D'Alesandro appointed municipal agencies to work with the G.B.C. Thus, from the start, the principle of partnership of public and private groups was established. They set out to define Baltimore's problems and then develop a concrete program to revive and promote the city.

The Greater Baltimore Committee, joined by the Committee for Downtown, presented the concept of the Charles Center to city government in 1958. The project was designed to halt the deterioration of the downtown business district and to rejuvenate the social, cultural and economic life of the city. The plan called for use of the resources at hand so development could take place in a relatively short time. Private business was to finance the major portion of the costs. The planners hoped that Charles Center would lead to improvements in the accessibility of downtown via mass transit. The city accepted the program and issued urban renewal bonds to help raise money. The Charles Center Management Office was opened under the direction of J. Jefferson Miller.

As the building began, a mayoral primary election replaced D'Alesandro with machine opponent J. Harold Grady as the Democratic nominee. Despite Pollack's "vote your conscience" support of Republican candidate Theodore McKeldin, Grady won and held the office during the initial construction stages. When he resigned to accept a judgeship in 1962, Philip Goodman, who was President of the City Council, filled the vacancy. The following year McKeldin defeated Goodman and became not only mayor, but the only Republican office-holder in the city. During this same period, the city benefitted from the recently created Maryland Port Authority which had been authorized by the state in 1956 when McKeldin was governor and Marvin Mandel the chairman of the city delegation in the House of Delegates.

Ground-breaking ceremonies for One Charles Center in 1961 marked the beginning of the renewal in new public and private investment in office buildings, apartments, a hotel, a theater, commercial and specialty space, parks, overhead walkways and underground garages. The Civic Center with its 10,000-seat sports arena and 100,000 square-foot exhibition hall opened nearby in 1962.

Before Charles Center was completed, part two of the dream started to materialize. Abel Wolman joined others who viewed the inner harbor as the perfect place to continue renewal. He urged McKeldin to set in motion plans for the neglected waterfront area. At the urging of William Boucher III, the mayor reassembled the winning partnership that had created Charles Center. David Wallace and Thomas Todd drew up the master plan in 1964. The following year, the city signed a contract to allow Charles Center Inner Harbor Management, Inc. to direct the planning and operation of both projects. By

Left:
James Rouse, who built Cross Keys, was chosen to develop a commercial complex at the Inner Harbor

Right:
Owner Jerry Hoffberger talks with three members of the winning team. Left to right: *Hank Bauer, Andy Etchebarren, and Boog Powell.*

Above:
Charles Center was the first stage in Baltimore's downtown renewal

Center Right:
Theodore McKeldin (center) *won the mayoralty in 1963 and became the city's only Republican official. With him here* (left to right) are: *John Marshall Butler, J. Glenn Beall, Samuel Culotta, and James Devereaux*

Right:
The Morris A. Mechanic Theatre in Charles Center began drawing crowds back to the downtown area in the evening hours

1967, with the full cooperation of the city's new mayor, Thomas D'Alesandro III, Project I which dealt with a one-block deep area along the harbor's edge was unveiled. With both public and private money, the actual development began in 1971.

During the planning years of the Inner Harbor, Baltimore saw racial tensions culminate in riots that followed the assassination of Dr. Marting Luther King in 1968. Those riots expressed in a vivid way the frustrations of blacks with the continuing poverty and discrimination that they faced. Although National Guard commander General George Gelston minimized personal confrontation by issuing orders against shooting, six people died and property damage was assessed at over $14 million. The city that the planners were trying to solidify split wider apart. More suburbanites than ever declined to come downtown for any reason at all. More middle-class families moved out. In fact, census figures of 1960 and 1970 revealed that Baltimore had lost residents in both preceding decades. And, despite all the planning, the city's public image remained poor.

The post-war decades marked the beginning of another problem that gained increasing recognition during the 1970s and afterwards. That problem was given the name "sprawl." The decline of the center city and the corresponding growth of the suburbs hurt both the old downtown and the surrounding areas. In the city, more and more buildings became vacant and then began to fall apart. The movement of people and businesses to the surrounding counties meant that farmland with its valuable topsoil was plowed under and then covered with concrete. The loss of local farmland meant that Baltimore would have to import more of its food from further away. Forests were cut down to make way for homes, malls, and businesses. The loss of both fields and woods brought increased water pollution as run-off from streets and parking lots went through storm sewers directly into streams, carrying with it all manner of harmful substances.

Federal, state, and local money went increasingly to road construction projects. The Baltimore Beltway, the Jones Falls Expressway, and other highways connected the city to the suburbs and the suburbs to each other. Often, no public transportation was available over the same territory. The increased reliance on automobiles resulted in increased air pollution and, at the same time, kept lower income city residents who did not own cars from venturing beyond the city's boundaries. At the time, few people noticed the double whammy. Most people who lived in suburban neighborhoods, both inside and beyond the city limits, enjoyed the lifestyle of single family homes with nice yards and the personal freedom of movement that automobiles allowed.

All the problems that began during the 1950s and 1960s would receive widespread attention in the years that followed. The situation worsened before it began to improve. While the problems were still growing, civic leaders and citizens alike realized what was happening and began to look for solutions. Baltimore's renaissance began, like most urban renewal projects, with businessmen planning buildings for the city's commercial district. Soon many segments of the population joined in the activism and began to work to revive the city. The fruits of this labor became apparent in the 1970s.

Left:
Joseph Meyerhoff presents a model of the new Maryland Concert Hall

Above:
The Inner Harbor, Baltimore's showplace, contains office and residential buildings, green space and promenades, museums, and a marina

Left:
Joining in the 1973 groundbreaking of the IBM Building on Pratt Street are (left to right) *Robert Hubner, Vice President of IBM, State Comptroller Louis Goldstein, Mayor William Donald Schaefer, and Baltimore Housing Commissioner, Robert Embry. Behind them, former mayors Theodore McKeldin and Thomas D'Alesandro, III look on*

The Surviving Past

VI

Baltimore is a kaleidoscope. It has been known variously as northern or southern, elegant or slum-ridden, metropolitan or provincial. Like many other cities, it has suffered and it has prospered. It spawned a lively mercantilism along with a wide assortment of industries. Mainly because its harbor has been, from the beginning, the primary attraction for most of those who settled here, the popular image that emerges is that of Baltimore: port city on the Patapsco.

The growth of Baltimore involved a colorful cast. There were sturdy seamen, rough-and-tumble railroad workers, canny merchants, tough military types, and other nameless categories of folk. Later, a great number of these were, of course, immigrants. The plurality of the latter added to the general social ferment, and antagonisms mushroomed at alarming rates. Quite naturally, war played its role in shaping the mind and spirit of this fledgling town. In 1776, when Congress authorized the fitting out of "private armed vessels," enthusiastic Baltimoreans seized the opportunity to aggrandize themselves while defending the port's commerce and protecting the citizens as well. Privateering, in the view of one cynical nineteenth-century observer, thus became not only an act of patriotism, but a lucrative business in the bargain. In the larger historical perspective, though, Baltimore's Revolutionaries, with their ideals and fervor, have lingered as gallant heroes in the minds of those generations which were to follow. But in spite of the numerous wartime adventures that have enriched Baltimore's past, there is little doubt that the inspiration of Francis Scott Key's "Star Spangled Banner," during the War of 1812, remains the cynosure of its military history.

Whether Baltimore is known as Monumental City, or Mobtown (as it was called after the riots of the mid-nineteenth century), or the City that Reads of today, it is indisputably a city whose past is more than prologue. What has gone before has a value of its own; preoccupations and focal points surface in the following color photographs, which are only a glimmering reflection of Baltimore's past and present.

Jean A. Wittich

Right:
Designed by Joseph Sperry in 1911, the Emerson Tower is one of the most well-known landmarks on Baltimore's skyline. The adjacent building, which has since been demolished, at one time housed the offices and factory of Captain Isaac Emerson, the developer of Bromo-Seltzer (the name by which it is most popularly known). The tower is modeled after the 13th century Palazzo Vecchio in Florence. A seventeen-ton reproduction of the Bromo-Seltzer bottle was removed in 1930 and battlements added to the top. Reportedly it contains the largest four-dial gravity clock in the world

An 1832 View of Baltimore

An 1840 lithograph of a Baltimore Clipper

Above:
Ladies at the Flower Mart

Left:
The many shops at Harborplace draw crowds year round.

Left:
The visit of Tall Ships in June 2000, dubbed OpSail 2000, was a celebration of the millennial year. Ships at the Inner Harbor, Fells Point, Canton and Locust Point were decked out at night with festive lights.

Left:
The Pride of Baltimore II *led the parade of Tall Ships.*

Top:
In a grand finale, the Tall Ships sailed out of the Inner Harbor, past Fort McHenry, and out into the Chesapeake Bay. The Danmark, a full-rigged ship, was built in 1932 to train young sailors. In 1983 the Danish government decided to accept female as well as male crew members.

Above:
The Esmeralda, *from Chile, a four-masted barquentine, was the largest of the Tall Ships that visited Baltimore in 2000.*

The Inner Harbor, vital and beautiful in its diversity, symbolizes the new Baltimore.

Baltimore Renaissance

1970-2000

VI

In 1971 a new mayor, William Donald Schaefer, proclaimed that "Baltimore Is Best" and made people here and elsewhere pay attention. Charles Center's tall towers and the new Civic Center did not do the trick. Mayor Schaefer's deliberate campaign began the turnaround. His enthusiasm for his native city quickly communicated itself to city and suburban dwellers alike. With his support, the City Fair, begun in 1970 by Robert C. Embry, Jr., director of the Baltimore Urban Renewal and Housing Authority, grew into the largest urban festival in the nation. The city added ethnic festivals and "Sunny Sundays." These brought people back to the downtown that many had come to fear in the 1960s. The real genius of these parties was their inclusiveness. Residents of all the city's neighborhoods planned and participated together.

The 1970s were not easy years across the country. Protests over racial and economic inequities and the war in Vietnam reached heights of violence that many people found deeply disturbing. Protestors thought that America had betrayed its basic ideology and that many people, including high government officials, were engaging in immoral and nationally destructive behavior. Men and women who served in the armed forces resented the protestors, especially in light of their personal sacrifices. They believed that many opponents of the war simply wanted to avoid military service. Meaningful communication between generations, racial and ethnic groups, pro-war and pro-peace factions declined as people accused each other of bad will. It seemed as if the melting pot had become a cauldron. Mistrust of anyone different was commonplace. These were difficult times in which to govern.

In Baltimore some changes from earlier decades were evident. The schools, department stores, and public facilities were legally desegregated, but desegregation did not always bring economic equality or social harmony. Most neighborhoods remained all black or all white. Local covenants, unspoken agreements, and the policies of lending institutions still prevented African Americans from buying homes in many neighborhoods. Volunteers from Baltimore Neighborhoods tested real estate and rental companies and found that properties shown to whites often were not shown to blacks. Nationally, there was increasing recognition that desegregation laws were just the beginning and that much more was needed, in enforcement and especially in the arena of economic reform, if all citizens were to have truly equal opportunities. An important change was the increasing numbers of African Americans elected to public office. In 1970, Milton B. Allen, elected Baltimore's state's attorney, became the first African American elected to a citywide office. Despite this progress, Baltimore was by no means an open city. Jews, like African Americans, were excluded from some neighborhoods and organizations. Many white people, of all income groups and religious affiliations, felt that Baltimore City was awful and abandoned it. The city declined physically, economically, and socially. The problems were complex and had no easy answers.

The high-profile job of governing a big East Coast city in the 1970s carried many political risks. Baltimore's city charter gives the mayor considerably more power than most mayors have, so the job also carries more responsibility. Schaefer's team of very committed women and men went to work right away. Businessmen like Walter Sondheim joined with civic leaders like Robert Embry, Sandra Hillman, Sally Michel and Hope Quackenbush to get things going. M.J. "Jay" Brodie joined the team when Embry went to Washington as Assistant Secretary of the Department of Housing and Urban Development during the Carter administration. In the mid-1960s, socially aware developer James Rouse had suggested doing something with the old harbor area which had fallen into disrepair as more modern port facilities

at Locust Point and the Dundalk Marine Terminal began to handle most of the shipping. After the old warehouses were torn down, Schaefer ordered that the area be planted, and it became the city's favorite park. The City Fair moved to the Inner Harbor, and in 1973, 2,000,000 people enjoyed the rides, food, and neighborhood booths. The Maryland Science Center opened on the southwest corner of the Inner Harbor in 1976 and the World Trade Center on the northeast corner in 1977. The Maryland General Assembly approved a bill to build a downtown Convention Center.

Schaefer worried correctly that people would like their attractive waterfront park too much. A referendum approved spending for the construction of Harborplace by a relatively narrow margin. Harborplace, a complex of shops and eateries designed by Jim Rouse, opened in 1980 with fireworks and a big party. The city sponsored free outdoor entertainment, and New Year's Eve fireworks and parties without alcohol at the harbor quickly became a Baltimore tradition. The National Aquarium in Baltimore, the city's largest single tourist attraction at the end of the 20th century, won a bond referendum. City Council President Walter Orlinsky called it "the mayor's fish tank" and it became just that on the day Schaefer donned an old-fashioned bathing suit and dunked in the seal pool when the Aquarium missed its original opening date. The Hyatt Regency Hotel opened just west of Harborplace in 1981 and the Gallery at Harborplace, a second successful Rouse commercial venture, in 1985. Scarlett Place offered pricey condominiums. Public-private partnerships were key to funding and operating the developments. *Esquire Magazine* named Schaefer the nation's best mayor. *Time* called Baltimore "Renaissance City."

Beneath the glitz and the real success of the Inner Harbor development lay serious problems recognized by all. As tourists flocked to Baltimore, industries left. From 1970 to 1995 the region lost 90,000 manufacturing jobs. Companies like Bethlehem Steel, General Motors, and W. R. Grace downsized their Baltimore operations. Recessions in 1973-75 and 1980-83 meant more job cuts. Many companies, all over the nation, moved manufacturing operations to the non-union southern states or overseas to developing nations where wages were extremely low. Major city retailers moved to the suburbs. Hutzler's, Hecht's, and Stewart's closed their big Howard Street department stores. Future generations of Baltimoreans would no longer enjoy the convenience of a central retail district. Suburbanites shopped at new, scattered malls that could be reached only by automobile, making it difficult for inner city residents, especially those who did not own a car, to shop or work there. With suburban sprawl, highway congestion and air pollution rose to new levels. As more people depended on the family car to get around, public transportation declined.

Baltimore had always suffered from being a branch town, and the pattern continued at the end of the 20th century. Of Baltimore's five largest banks in 1968, only one, the Mercantile Safe Deposit and Trust Company, remained in local hands in 2000. The brokerage firm of Alex. Brown was bought by Bankers Trust in New York which was in turn bought by Deutsche Banc. The *Baltimore Sunpapers* were sold to the Times-Mirror Company, publisher of the *Los Angeles Times*. Local companies and branch offices foresook their downtown offices to relocate in the suburbs where they replaced woods and farmlands with modern buildings and spacious parking lots. New city jobs in the service sector, tourism, entertainment, and sales tended to pay less than manufacturing and business employment. Women in service occupations received especially low salaries. There were some higher-paying new jobs in growth areas of the economy: banking, brokerage houses, insurance and real estate, but many of those were outside the city.

Above: Robert Embry played a major role in Baltimore's growth from 1970 on to the end of the 20th century. His creativity has impacted much of the city's life from the City Fair in the 1970s to innovative educational programs in the 1990s.

Above middle:
Parren B. Mitchell in 1970 was the first African American from Maryland elected to Congress. He represented a district in West Baltimore.

Above left:
William Donald Schaefer grew up in Old West Baltimore. A lifelong bachelor, his first loyalty was to his city. He won election to the City Council in 1955 from the 5th District as the candidate of political boss Irv Kovens. Schaefer was elected president of the City Council in 1967 and in 1971 became mayor of Baltimore, a job he loved for four terms.

The Port of Baltimore has been a mainstay of the city's economy since colonial days. Modern facilities such as the Seagirt Marine Terminal handles cargo from around the world. The Port of Baltimore supports over 100,000 jobs.

Baltimore Renaissance 1970-2000

All the losses, middle class homeowners, industries, retailers and businesses, meant that Baltimore's tax base was shrinking at the very time the city needed more money, not less, to deal with human needs and physical deterioration. In its attempt to bring in more funds, the city raised the property tax rate. Soon the city's rate was double that of the surrounding counties, and more people left to avoid the high taxes. In 1971, one fourth of all families living in Baltimore City had incomes below the federally established poverty line. Unemployment increased among inner city residents as did the number of "working poor," individuals whose salaries did not cover a decent place to live and healthy food for their families, who often could not afford medical care or a car that might give access to better jobs. Many American cities experienced similar problems.

At the same time, increasing drug use brought more problems for the city. Addiction brought human misery to thousands of users and their families and hundreds of millions of dollars in thefts each year as people stole to get the money to pay for drugs. Insufficient treatment facilities made it difficult for addicts who wanted to stop their drug dependency to do so. Increasingly, shared needles spread the human immunodeficiency virus, which became a major public health crisis. Teenage pregnancies meant more premature births, more babies with health problems, and more single mothers who often did not complete their high school education, could not earn a good income, and in turn sometimes were unable to provide for their children. At the same time, the city's population was aging. In 1966 retired people were 13 percent of Baltimore's population and by 1988 30 percent of the total. Retirees' incomes tended to be lower and their needs, especially medical needs, greater than those of working people. In 1985, the median income of city residents was just over one half that of residents in the surrounding counties.

From the early 1960s to the mid-1980s, Baltimore lost one fifth of its population. As the enforcement of open housing laws made the move possible, African American middle class families joined the exodus to the suburbs. In 1970, the census counted 905,787 Baltimore City residents. In 1980 the number had shrunk to 786,775 and by 1990 to 736,014. By the mid-1990s it was below 650,000. Baltimore's tax revenues decreased further. The city, in turn, spent less on education, social services, parks, playgrounds, and physical maintenance. Schaefer's administration turned to the state and federal governments for as much funding as possible. City officials and economic advisers deliberately concentrated the limited resources on downtown business district redevelopment as the basis of rebuilding the city's economy. As the Inner Harbor flourished, houses owned by absentee landlords were abandoned and boarded up. In this "city of neighborhoods" some neighborhoods became fearful places. Drug dealers and increasing numbers of homeless people used the vacant houses. Some people lived on the streets. Neighborhoods that had once been like a village, where all the adults watched out for all the children and neighbors knew each other, soon became empty as people hid inside their homes to avoid being the victims of violence. One proposed solution to the housing problem was the construction of public housing. Beginning in the 1950s, Baltimore and the federal government supported the construction of subsidized housing on both the east and west sides of the city. Projects such as Lafayette Courts and Lexington Terrace opened with great expectations that were quickly dashed. Public housing did not provide the relief it was designed to bring. Instead it concentrated poverty into poorly maintained and densely populated pockets. Crimes abounded in the high rise building elevators and long corridors.

The school system was especially hard hit by the decline in funding and the loss of middle class

The Maryland Science Center houses three floors of exhibits, the Davis Planetarium, and an IMAX Theater.

The glass, steel, concrete, and stone Baltimore Convention Center, built in 1979 and enlarged in 1996, attracts millions of dollars in convention business to the city every year

The National Aquarium in Baltimore is the city's largest tourist attraction. In 1994 the very popular Aquarium welcomed its 2 millionth visitor.

Mayor William Donald Schaefer (left) and Mayor Clarence "Du" Burns (middle) were political allies. Burns continued many policies begun during the Schaefer administration and retained many staff members.

students. School buildings deteriorated. Budgetary constraints meant fewer teachers were hired. Class sizes increased at the same time that more children came to school with learning disabilities and in need of special help. Teachers left for the suburban counties, where classes were smaller, students more prepared to learn, facilities newer and better equipped, and the pay scale higher. The city was forced to hire inexperienced teachers, pay them less, and provide them with less support when they really needed more. Test scores declined, with few schools even reaching the state or national median in reading and math. Many young people dropped out before graduating from high school. School violence increased. The widespread fallout worsened the process of decline as neither people nor businesses wanted to be in a city where the school system had so many problems.

By the mid-1980s, the wonderfully-successful Inner Harbor and the rows of boarded up houses stood in stark contrast to each other. While some neighborhoods continued to decline, others were experiencing a rebirth, and in some cases gentrification, as middle class people renovated and moved into areas such as Fells Point, Federal Hill, and Canton. Other contrasts were also evident. Most public schools suffered while independent schools grew stronger and more diverse. Urban public health programs fell short at the same time that wonderful medical advances were taking place at Johns Hopkins and the University of Maryland. Baltimore was by no means dead. It was just out of balance.

Race loomed large as a factor in discussions of Baltimore's conditions and policies. Between the 1970 and 1980 census counts, the majority population in Baltimore changed from white to black. Many Baltimore residents believed that African American leaders would be better able to solve Baltimore's problems. Some believed that the predominantly white leadership concentrated too much on business development that benefited the city's elite and that black leaders would be more interested in ordinary people. Some believed that black leadership would draw more community support while others said simply that it was time for the new majority to have its turn to run the city. That opportunity occurred when City Council president Clarence "Du" Burns, an African American from Baltimore's east side, became mayor after William Donald Schaefer was elected governor of Maryland in November 1986. A personable man and an experienced politician who had risen through the ranks of East Baltimore Democratic clubs, Burns enjoyed widespread popularity and support from many segments of the population.

When the Democratic mayoral primary took place in 1987, Kurt Schmoke, a young African American lawyer who had been serving as the Baltimore State's Attorney, challenged Burns and won. Schmoke grew up in Baltimore, was an academic leader and football star at City College, and graduated from Yale University and Harvard Law School. He won the prestigious Rhodes scholarship for graduate study at Oxford University in England. His wife Pat was a respected ophthalmologist. Their two children were still in school. Like every new official, Schmoke inherited both the good and the bad results of his predecessors' work. Clearly, there would be new directions. One early sign of a changing emphasis was the new slogan for the city. "Baltimore: The City that Reads" replaced "Baltimore is Best" on park benches and city vehicles. Schmoke, re-elected in 1991 and 1995, served three terms as mayor of Baltimore. These were tough years, despite growing national prosperity. The city, with its small tax base, could not meet all its own needs. Like Schaefer, Schmoke relied heavily on state and federal monies to help build Baltimore, but the early 1990s brought far less federal money than had been available in the early Schaefer years. Schmoke worked with re-

Harborplace quickly became Baltimore's playground. Recreational sailing is one of many activities that draw crowds here.

Restored homes in Federal Hill became popular during the 1980s. Houses that once sold for $10,000 brought over $100,000 in the 1990s.

Below:
In 1987 Kurt Schmoke became the first African American elected mayor of Baltimore. Black and white voters gave Schmoke the majority over the white Republican candidate.

Left:
Canton's location on the waterfront drew many residents to expensive new dwellings in this old blue collar neighborhood during the 1990s.

Right:
The implosion of the Murphy Homes took place in July 1999. The high rise buildings will be replaced with townhomes.

gional county executives and state legislators, and developed a good relationship with Democratic President of the United States, Bill Clinton. Maryland's United States senators, Paul Sarbanes and Barbara Mikulski, both from Baltimore, as well as many in the Congressional delegation helped bring federal monies to the city. Still, Baltimore and other cities around the nation suffered.

Schmoke made the schools a priority. He lobbied for state money, which sometimes carried strings such as the threat of state takeover for low-performing schools. He worked closely with Robert Embry, by then chair of the Abell Foundation, which paid for programs designed to find the best ways to improve Baltimore's schools. The determined efforts began to pay off and test scores edged upward at the end of Schmoke's administration. Three schools were, in fact, taken over by the state. Magnet schools, where certain fields are emphasized, succeeded. The most outstanding example is the Baltimore High School for the Arts where a multi-cultural student body concentrates on all forms of performing and studio arts. A successful partnership was formed between Dunbar High School and the nearby Johns Hopkins East Baltimore campus offering a health care professions program. In the 1990s, City College initiated the International Baccalaureate, a difficult degree program accepted around the world.

While the public schools were experiencing difficulties, private education in Baltimore changed significantly. Catholics, various Protestant groups, Jews, and Muslims opened new schools to meet the growing demand for stronger education and for the teaching of values. Baltimore's older independent schools, many with histories going back to the 19th century, maintained their tradition of academic excellence while welcoming a diverse student body. All the independent schools actively sought minority students and faculty members, and incorporated courses that include African American and Third World studies into their curricula. Baltimore's major institutions of higher education also grew increasingly diversified. Johns Hopkins, Goucher, and Loyola became co-educational. All have actively recruited a widely diverse student body. Decades of prosperity have supported expansion at all the local universities. Hopkins, Loyola, Morgan, Towson, and the University of Maryland both downtown and in Baltimore County have added all kinds of new facilities.

Housing problems continued to plague Baltimore during Schmoke's administration. Even as middle class people began to return downtown to live near where they worked, the number of vacant houses increased and public housing continued to deteriorate. A decision was made to get rid of the high-rise complexes was made. The first implosion took place at Lafayette Courts on Baltimore's west side in 1995. The public came to watch, much as people watched fireworks at the harbor, and the event was broadcast live on television.

Crime challenged the administration and everyone living in Baltimore during the 1980s and 1990s. Year after year, Baltimore's murder rate topped 300. While many of the perpetrators and victims were involved in the drug trade, some victims were innocent bystanders. Tauris Johnson, a 10-year old boy, just happened to be in the wrong place when he was shot and killed in 1993. Accustomed as Baltimore residents were to senseless crime, this murder was particularly shocking. Mayor Schmoke believed that decriminalization of drug use might help reduce crime and also make treatment a more viable option. Although he gained national attention, few people at any level of government were willing to give it a try. Dr. Peter Beilenson, the city's health commissioner, pleaded again and again for more drug treatment openings. Funds were not made available. That option, too, remained essentially untried.

Baltimore elected a new mayor in November 1999. Democrat Martin O'Malley, former member

Students at Friends School participate in the Lower School's annual Olympic Day.

Mary Pat Clarke won citywide election as the president of the Baltimore City Council in 1987. She was the first woman to hold that post.

Paul Sarbanes, the son of Greek immigrants and a Baltimore resident, has represented Maryland in the United States Senate since 1977.

Left:
Students at Friends School participate in the Lower School's annual Olympic Day

Bottom:
Pleasant View Gardens, a neighborhood of low and middle income townhouses, some for sale at market values, and a small commercial area replaced the old Lafayette Courts public housing project.

Senator Barbara Mikulski began her career in public office in the City Council where she represented an East Baltimore neighborhood.

City Council President Sheila Dixon is an important part of the city's new young leadership at the beginning of the 21st century. She taught in Baltimore's public schools before her election to the City Council.

of the City Council, brought youth and energy to the office. He vowed to do something about crime and education and to make the city more efficient. He will benefit from the educational programs already underway and from the movement of middle class people back to city neighborhoods such as Fells Point, Federal Hill, and Canton and Hampden-Woodberry. Poverty, crime, grime, and relations among the city's diverse racial and ethnic groups need careful attention and enormous energy. One over-arching problem is that long-term solutions are, in fact, just that. They take a long time to show results. The political reality is that people want short-term results. Politics makes a slow, methodical implementation of policies difficult. Partnerships have proven an effective approach to urban problem solving in part because the private sector has the freedom to set its own timetable and, for better or worse, to establish priorities that the public does not control through the electoral process.

By the end of the 20th century, several aspects of the city's economy were improving. With the active support of both the Schmoke and the O'Malley administrations, two new groups of employers began to set up operations in Baltimore. High-technology businesses and non-profit organizations added a new dimension to the life of the city. Both pay good wages. Both require an educated work force. Building on the existence of a high-tech corridor that stretches from Washington to Baltimore and Frederick, some companies have been putting operations in Baltimore City. Plans for a much larger "Digital Harbor" include the opening of the TidePoint Corporation, a provider of e-commerce services, in the old Proctor and Gamble facility at Locust Point and the conversion of the Montgomery Ward warehouse in southwest Baltimore into one of the region's largest office and high-tech employment centers. Developer Bill Struever, who has specialized in the conversion of old buildings into useful and visually pleasing locations, began work in Fells Point to establish a technology center there.

Several large non-profit organizations moved their headquarters to Baltimore in the late 20th century. Proximity to Washington, relatively low costs (as compared with New York and Washington) and the receptiveness of the city have encouraged this trend. The National Association for the Advancement of Colored People (NAACP) under the leadership of President and Chief Executive Officer Kweisi Mfume moved its headquarters to Baltimore during the Schmoke administration. Catholic Relief Services, engaged in worldwide relief programs, moved its headquarters to Baltimore as did the Annie E. Casey Foundation which works primarily with children and family programs.

Locally-based non-profit foundations not only employ Baltimore citizens but also provide generous funding for many projects in the city. The Abell Foundation, named for the founder of the *Sunpapers*, supports programs in education, the arts, and culture. The Enterprise Foundation, begun by James Rouse, states as its goal: provision of fit and affordable housing for everyone in the nation within one generation and help to move people from poverty to self-sufficiency. The foundation runs pilot programs in the West Baltimore neighborhood of Sandtown-Winchester. A number of successful area businessmen have established foundations that make donations to the community's local schools and universities, hospitals, and cultural institutions. Among the most generous are the Jacob and Hilda Blaustein Foundation, The France-Merrick Foundation, the Zanvyl and Isabelle Krieger Foundation, and the Harry and Jeanette Weinberg Foundation. The late 20th century philanthropists behind these and many other local foundations have added enormously to the quality of life in Baltimore.

Although politics is central to the democratic process, and programs to meet challenges in economic development, housing, public schools, and

Above left:
Mayor Martin O'Malley brought youth and enthusiasm to the difficult job of being mayor of a large Eastern city.

Above middle:
Kweisi Mfume represented a West Baltimore district in the United States Congress before he resigned to head the National Association for the Advancement of Colored People.

Above right:
Dr. Benjamin Quarles' book, The Negro in the Making of America, *provided first rate scholarship for newly popular classes in African American studies. Dr. Quarles taught at Morgan State University for many years.*

Right:
Fells Point businesses attract thousands of visitors each year. Refurbished brick houses in this oldest section of Baltimore began attracting young and middle aged families back to the city in the 1970s.

Below:
O'Malley, City Council President Sheila Dixon, and other officials turn out to clean graffiti from city walls. New energy and the hands-on approach to the city's problems won praise for the new administration.

crime are key parts of any administration's efforts, much of Baltimore's history lies beyond the realm of government and economics. Throughout the centuries, Baltimore has become home to people from faraway places. Men and women of English, Scotch-Irish, and African heritage built colonial Baltimore. Descendents of Irish and Germans, Italians, Poles, and Greeks have long been well-established members of the community. In the last few decades of the 20th century, immigrants from Asia, Latin America and the Caribbean brought a new diversity to the city. Baltimore is no longer just black and white; its people have roots all over the world.

Beginning in the 1950s and especially after the passage of the federal Immigration and Nationality Act amendments in 1965, the city's Asian American population began to grow. Chinese, Koreans, Japanese, Asian Indians, Vietnamese, and others have settled here. The Census Bureau estimated that over 60,000 Asian Americans lived in the Baltimore metropolitan area in 1997. They have added to the cultural diversity of the city in a variety of ways. Baltimore's small Chinese community began to grow during the 1950s and 1960s as people from the West Coast moved east and people from Taiwan came looking for professional opportunities. People from mainland China sought both economic opportunity and political freedom. Whereas the earlier Chinese immigrants usually spoke the Cantonese dialect, the newcomers often spoke Mandarin. Many were well-educated doctors, scientists and specialists in the high technology fields. They did not settle in one neighborhood but rather chose homes throughout the city and surrounding counties. One focal point for the community has been Grace and St. Peter's Episcopal Church where Lillian Lee Kim and others organized a Chinese language school offering both Cantonese and Mandarin, and a Chinese New Year's celebration, that has been popular among all segments of the city's population.

Koreans began to migrate to Baltimore in the 1950s, following the end of the Korean War. Some came because activities of a Korean student-protest movement in the 1960s led to retaliation by a totalitarian government in Korea. Many came for economic and educational opportunities. A look at the 1999-2000 Baltimore area telephone directory reveals 13 columns of listings under "Kim," a common Korean surname. Over 8,000 Koreans live in Baltimore City in the year 2000 (an increase from the approximately 2,000 in 1990) and many more in the metropolitan area. Like the Chinese, Korean families have settled in homes throughout the region. Korean Americans are known for the value they place on their families, the education of their children, and financial success. Some Koreans are Buddhists and are beginning to open temples where they can carry on religious traditions they learned as children. The many Christian Koreans have established churches, often sharing space with English-speaking congregations. Some of the churches offer classes in Korean for the English-speaking children of immigrants. A concentration of stores and Korean-owned businesses along Charles Street near North Avenue is known as Koreatown. Several weekly newspapers in Korean are published.

Many Koreans arrived with little, if any, savings. A frequent goal is to establish a small business. Once this is done, all members of the family work in the business. They save money to enlarge the business and to provide as good an education as possible for their children. There has been some conflict between Korean grocery storeowners and residents in African American neighborhoods who believe the prices are too high. Cultural differences have contributed to misunderstandings. For example, some African Americans felt insulted when Korean shop owners placed change on the counter rather than handing it directly to the customer. They said the Koreans did not want to touch them. Most Asians consider it rude to touch a

Baltimore's Hispanic community holds several festivals a year.

Right:
Korean Americans, like many immigrant groups, enjoy preserving their traditional culture including food and costumes.

Bottom:
Indian Americans in Baltimore hold an annual celebration of India Day. They share their foods and teach traditional dances to visitors.

stranger. Therefore, putting the change on the counter was the respectful thing to do. Misunderstandings come easily when people are unfamiliar with each other's customs. Recently, in a reflection of the size and importance of the population, both the mayor of Baltimore and the governor of Maryland have appointed liaisons from their office to the Asian American community.

Immigrants from India also came in significant numbers during the last few decades of the 20th century. Several thousand lived in Baltimore City and an additional several thousand in the surrounding counties at the end of the 20th cen-

Lillian Lee Kim and Paul Lee. Miss Kim is a leader in the Chinese American community

tury. Many are doctors, educators, technical workers, and financial experts while others have opened small businesses such as convenience stores and gas stations. Sometimes several families pool their resources to raise the capital needed for a small business. Like the Koreans, often the entire family works in the business. In India, the majority of people are Hindus. The immigrants have brought their religion with them, thus adding to the religious diversity in the area. Children of Indian Americans often speak only English and are fully integrated into American life and culture as is the case with many other second-generation Americans.

Latinos are another major new immigrant group in the Baltimore region. People have been speaking Spanish in North America since before the *Ark* and the *Dove* landed at St. Mary's City in 1634, but the Hispanic immigration to Maryland is a late 20th century phenomenon. In the 1970s, a few Mexicans, Puerto Ricans and other Spanish-speaking people lived in the area. Since 1980, increasing numbers of Latinos have settled here. The 1990 census counted over 28,000 in the metropolitan area, with 7,600 in the city. The Census Bureau estimated the 1997 figures to be over 40,000, with more than 8,400 in the city. The true numbers are almost surely higher because some are illegal immigrants who usually try to avoid being counted. Totals have grown dramatically during the 1990s. Many of the newcomers are from Mexico and Puerto Rico and also Colombia, Ecuador, El Salvador, and Guatemala. Civil wars in Central America rendered daily life treacherous and economic problems have made survival difficult. Latinos also have moved to Baltimore from California, Florida, New Jersey, and Texas, where the communities are much larger.

A large number of Latinos live in Upper Fells Point where they have opened businesses including grocery stores and restaurants. Many recent immigrants work in restaurant kitchens and in landscaping and construction jobs. The majority of the immigrants are Roman Catholic, but Protestant churches, including some Pentecostal congregations, also serve the community. In 1995, the Centro de la Communidad opened to provide a wide range of services. Haydee Rodriguez, director of the center, stated in an interview in the Baltimore *Sun* in 1998 that most of their clients had come to the United States within the last five years, came from Mexico or Central America, and averaged six to eight years of schooling. Most of the men, she said, were looking for jobs. Most of the women needed children's services. In 1997, the Centro offered space to La Familia Health Center, a bilingual clinic operated by the Greater Baltimore Medical Center. The Baltimore Latino Outreach (EBLO) is active in the community and runs a Latino festival every year. There is a Hispanic Business Association and several Spanish-language newspapers and newsletters, including *El Heraldo of Maryland* that began publication in 1993. Cable television provides Spanish-language programming. The mayor of Baltimore and the governor of Maryland both have a liaison officer for Hispanic Affairs.

In the 1980s and 1990s a large number of people began to emigrate from the former Soviet Union. Among them were Russian Jews who settled in northwest Baltimore. Other Russians live throughout the area. Many came looking for better economic opportunities and also for personal safety during a period when lawlessness increased as the Soviet government split up. Several organizations based in Baltimore's Jewish community provide services such as language classes and assistance in finding homes and jobs. Many of the immigrants are discovering, for the first time, the religious meaning of their Jewish heritage while Christian Russians often attend local Protestant and Orthodox churches. A Russian-language newspaper serves the Baltimore-Washington area. Local libraries stock Russian-language books, and satellite television offers a Russian-language station.

Significant immigration from the Caribbean took place in the late 20th century. The vast majority emigrated from islands where English is the language. Jamaica, Trinidad and Tobago, Barbados, and the U.S. Virgin Islands are among the places of origin. As with all the new immigrant groups, a Baltimore-Washington network developed as the basis of a larger community. People come together as West Indians and also in smaller groups based on their island of origin. Sports, such as soccer, popular in the West Indies and music, food, and a sense of community draw people together. Several Caribbean festivals take place annually. While a large number of newcomers from the Caribbean are working people, many others are professionals. Some came to study in the United States and then established their careers here. Doctors, professors, and others serve the wider Baltimore community. Many West Indians have started small businesses, often in the Pimlico/Park Heights community. West Baltimore is home to several organizations including the Baltimore Association of Caribbean Organizations and the Caribbean Business League. English-language newspapers carry news of the Caribbean.

Late 20th century immigration has continued the pattern established in early Baltimore. People from Korea, India, Russia and the Caribbean joined other newcomers speaking familiar languages such as Italian and Polish and also people speaking Arabic, Ibo, and Tagalog. The recent immigration has impacted education. Public schools, colleges, universities, and many organizations offer ESOL (English for Speakers of Other Languages) classes. Because Maryland's recent immigrants come from many lands, ESOL students speak many different languages and therefore have no option but to communicate in English. Religious diversity has increased as people from traditionally Buddhist, Hindu, and Muslim countries settled. Additionally, a significant number of African Americans espoused Islam during the last few decades. All

Artscape has replaced the City Fair as Baltimore's largest festival. Staged in the neighborhood of the Maryland Institute of Art and the Meyerhoff Symphony Hall, the July weekend featuring both visual and performing arts draws over a million people. Here local children's entertainer John Taylor "Kinderman" performs.

The city bought the houses in polluted Wagner's Point to allow the families to move to a safer area. Even children's playgrounds have been built near industrial sites where chemicals easily leak into the soil.

projections indicate that Baltimore will become a more diverse city in the 21st century than at any other time in its history.

On April 22, 1970 people in Baltimore celebrated the first Earth Day. It marked a turning point in the awareness of the environment in which we live. No matter what our ethnic background or religious beliefs, we all breathe the same air, drink the same water, and share the earth with all other living creatures. By 1970, growing numbers of people were aware that unhealthy air, polluted water, and dangerous chemicals in our environment that were causing serious illnesses in people and endangering the very survival of certain species. In the years that followed, people grew determined to attempt to undo the damage and to protect, as many say, the only earth we have.

Air pollution, caused in part by ozone from automobile emissions and various pollutants in industrial discharges, had been increasing unabated since the beginning of the industrial revolution with a resultant increase in lung diseases. By the late 20th century, asthma had become the number one cause of children's emergency room visits. "Red" and "orange" alerts became commonplace in Baltimore during the hot summer months. Although the federal Clean Air Act helped reduce the pollution, Baltimore's problems have remained among the nation's worst. Exposure to chemicals of all sorts in this old industrial city has jeopardized human health for decades. Industrial workers exposed to asbestos won a huge class action suit brought to court by the law firm of Peter Angelos. The disposal of industrial chemicals, unregulated for many years, left toxic sites in many parts of the city. For example, the old Allied Signal plant site near the Inner Harbor contains very toxic chromium. Federal Superfund legislation in 1973 marked the beginning of a clean-up process, but many Superfund sites and hundreds of less severely polluted "brownfields" remain. Some scholars and health care professionals blame Baltimore's high cancer rate on continuing exposure to the toxic chemical soup. In 1999, Baltimore bought the homes in Wagner's Point where chemicals were poisoning the residents so that the low income families there could move to healthier neighborhoods. The land will be used to expand a sewage treatment plant. Baltimore's children continue in the year 2000 to suffer from the ingestion of lead found in paint chips and dust in older houses. It is estimated that as many as 50,000 local children suffer from lead poisoning, and many go untreated. They are left with damage that can result in mental retardation, behavioral problems, poor performance in school, and the subsequent inability to hold a job. A new law requires testing of all children so that lead poisoning cases can be detected and treated before damage to the mind and body is irreversible.

The disposal of our waste has been a major problem since the early colonial days when Baltimoreans were fined for tossing trash into their neighbors' yards and pigs scavenged on the public streets. In the 20th century, city trucks collected trash and hauled it to landfills where it was out of the sight of most citizens. By recent decades, two things were clear. The dump sites were filling up very quickly and some of them were leaking dangerous substances. In 1988, Baltimore began a voluntary household recycling program with weekly pick-ups of cans, glass and plastic bottles, and paper. These are sold and the materials reused. Disposal of items we no longer want causes a problem that is greater than the lack of space. During the 19th century, human waste, slaughter house waste, and all forms of trash often wound up in rivers and ground water which people then drank. Epidemics resulted. Twentieth century industries also used the water to carry waste, including toxic chemicals, away from their properties, often into both surface and ground drinking water. This, joined with run-off of all substances

A study conducted jointly by the Baltimore Urban League and the Chesapeake Bay Foundation found that fish from the Baltimore harbor contained large quantities of mercury and other heavy metals, making them unhealthy to eat. Even today, some Baltimore residents take fish like these home to their families.

Above: Volunteers with the Aquarium's Marine Animal Rescue Program rescue and rehabilitate injured and stranded marine animals with the goal of returning them to the wild. This manatee, nicknamed "Chessie," had stayed in the Chesapeake Bay until the autumn water was too cold for him to survive. He was captured and returned to Florida.

Below: Volunteers from the National Aquarium in Baltimore's Aquarium Conservation Team restore wetlands at Fort McHenry. Wetlands help clean the water that flows through them. They also serve as a nursery for young crabs and fish

The Living Classrooms Foundation takes local students for educational trips on board several boats it owns. The organization works extensively with young people in job and character training programs.

from the streets including gasoline, lead from old batteries, and animal excrement has in turn polluted every stream and river and the Chesapeake Bay into which all Baltimore's rivers flow. By the late 20th century it had become clear that one of the major tasks facing government and private citizens alike is to make the environment safe.

This concern about the environment has been reflected in a number of programs and activities begun in Baltimore in the latter years of the 20th century. Almost all Maryland schools and universities now teach environmental studies classes. Many local organizations make environmental education a hands-on and fun experience. The Chesapeake Bay Foundation and Living Classrooms began conducting educational boat trips out of the Inner Harbor. The Irvine Natural Science Center pioneered a program called Natural Connections in which high school and college students are trained to lead groups of elementary school children to look at nature in their own city neighborhoods and see how they are connected to other forms of life. Popular Baltimore Orioles first baseman Eddie Murray endowed a nature center in West Baltimore in honor of his mother. The National Aquarium in Baltimore educates people about local and global environmental problems, particularly as they affect the water. Local organizations began working in all three major stream valleys in Baltimore City. The Gwynns Falls, the Herring Run, and the Jones Falls associations all sponsor clean-ups and festivals designed to make people more aware of Baltimore's urban waterways. Interesting new and diverse coalitions have formed across the city to work on environmental problems. One example is the alliance between the Baltimore Urban League and the Chesapeake Bay Foundation. They have sponsored Clean Block/ Clean Bay activities. Andrew Sawyers of the Urban League and Jay Sherman of CBF have led the effort. The very logical theory behind the alliance is that a clean city and a clean bay will benefit everyone.

Stream valleys, city parks, and even downtown buildings have attracted back some of the wildlife that was pushed from the city when people filled up so much of the space that had once been fields and woods. Residents of many areas now see foxes and even deer. Great blue herons and kingfishers frequent the stream valleys. These animals have adapted to the urban surroundings. The Baltimore Zoo has become a center for environmental education and conservation. Natural-style habitats for the animals and work with endangered species have resulted from the zoo's expanded mission. The new children's zoo and Maryland wilderness provide the opportunity for hands-on interactions.

Baltimore has long been a national leader in medicine and medical research and this pattern continued in the late 20th century. The Curtis National Hand Center at Union Memorial Hospital in North Baltimore developed successful restorative surgical techniques that have saved the use of many people's hands. The Shock Trauma Center at the University of Maryland Hospital, founded by Dr. R. Adams Cowley, expanded in 1989 with the opening of a new eight-story building. Hospitals around the world embraced Cowley's emphasis on treatment within the "golden hour" following an accident or injury to save the lives of those who would otherwise die. The Johns Hopkins Hospital and University are known around the world for medical treatment and research. Hopkins faculty members Dr. Daniel Nathans and Dr. Hamilton O. Smith were awarded the Nobel Prize in Physiology or Medicine in 1978 for their work in developing techniques in sequencing DNA, as the citation stated, "for the discovery of restriction enzymes and their application to problems of molecular genetics." Dr. Alfred Sommer, dean of the Hopkins School of Hygiene and Public Health, has done landmark work with vitamin A that has been credited with saving the lives and sight of millions of children around the world. Among the

Peregrine falcons have taken up residence on the tall Legg Mason Building in downtown Baltimore. Successive pairs have produced many young peregrines, including a bird that made its home on the Chesapeake Bay Bridge. These endangered birds, that almost became extinct when the chemical DDT made their egg shells so thin that theycrushed before they could hatch, have made Baltimore's skyscraper and the bridge's tower into modern cliffs, the traditional nesting place of peregrines. Blythe and her four chicks are pictured here.

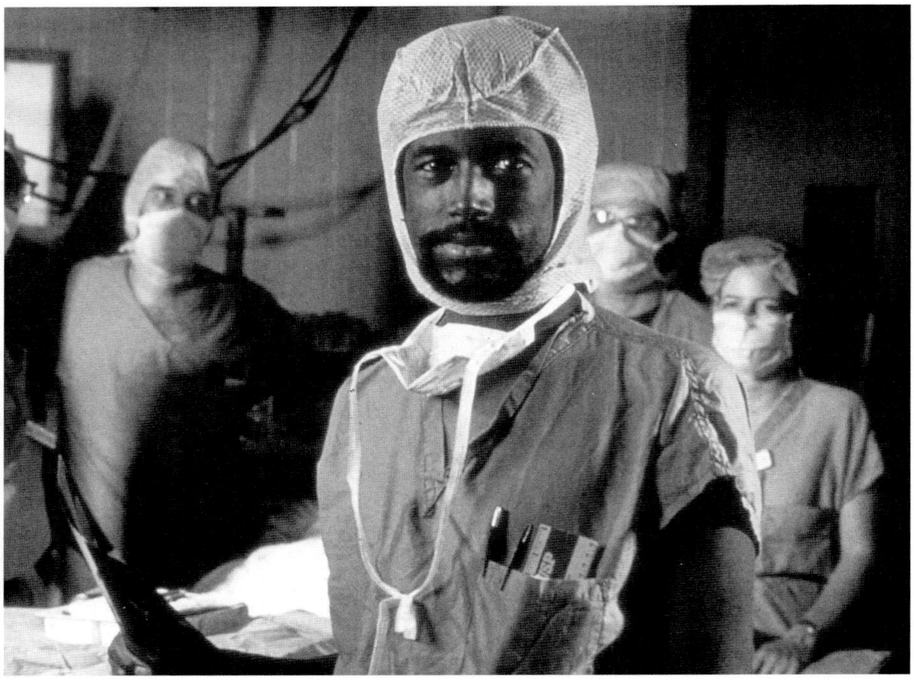

Above:
Dr. Victor McKusick, working at Johns Hopkins, developed the view that hereditary factors in disease are more important than was formerly known and built the framework for locating individual human genes.

Left:
Talented Hopkins surgeons like Dr. Benjamin Carson, pediatric neurosurgeon, have pioneered techniques that result in critical breakthroughs. Dr. Carson received worldwide acclaim when he separated twins conjoined at the head.

many awards he has received is the Albert Lasker Award for Clinical Medical Research. Dr. Victor McKusick, known as the "father of medical genetics," wrote the textbook on heritable disorders. His work led to such procedures as amniocentesis, DNA fingerprinting, gene therapies, and mapping the human genome.

The Baltimore-Washington corridor has become a center for high-tech research, development, and manufacturing. Companies working in computer services, electronics, and telecommunications and research labs in many fields including biotechnology began in Baltimore in the late 20th century. Baltimore is perhaps best known for the Space Telescope Institute, at the Homewood campus of the Johns Hopkins University and operated by a 17-institution consortium, which receives the data from the Hubble Space Telescope. These new high tech industries and research facilities are the key to the economic development of Baltimore and the entire region.

Baltimore in the late 20th century became home to interesting new museums, good theater, fine music, film production, and prize-winning writers. Creativity and the significant generosity of a new generation of philanthropists have made all this possible. New museums include the American Visionary Arts Museum, the Great Blacks in Wax Museum, the Jewish Heritage Center, the Museum of Industry, and Port Discovery, an interactive children's museum. The Baltimore Museum of Art, thanks to Alan and Janet Wurtzburger and Robert and Ryda Levy, added an outdoor sculpture garden and also built a new West Wing for Contemporary Art in 1994. In 1974, the Walters Art Gallery added a modern building and in 1991 the Hackerman House, made possible through the gift of Willard Hackerman whose construction

company has had many city contracts. The arts of China, Japan and Korea are displayed in the restored townhouse. The Maryland Historical Society won nationwide praise and the 1992 award for the best exhibition by the American Association of Museums for its pioneering "Mining the Museum" that interpreted the experience of African and Native Americans. It, too, has expanded physically with the purchase of the old Greyhound bus terminal.

Beginning with Maestro Sergiu Comissiona in 1968, three music directors led the Baltimore Symphony Orchestra to popularity, self-sufficiency, and great musical achievement. David Zinman, who arrived in 1984, led several tours to Europe, the Soviet Union, and Asia. In 1990 Zinman and the BSO, with Yo-Yo Ma performing, won a Grammy in the classical music category. Many Baltimoreans, who felt devastated when Zinman announced his departure, were thrilled during the 1999-2000 season when they heard the orchestra play under the new music director, Maestro Yuri Temirkanov.

Baltimore writers have taken their place among the literary greats at the end of the 20th century. John Barth, a graduate of Johns Hopkins who returned to direct the Writing Seminars there won the National Book Award in 1973 for *Chimera*. Poet and prose write Daniel Mark Epstein won the Prix de Rome for his work. Two Baltimore authors won Pulitzer prizes in 1989: Taylor Branch for *Parting the Waters*, the first of a trilogy about Dr. Martin Luther King and the civil rights movement, and Anne Tyler for her novel *Breathing Lessons*. Author and Baltimore *Sun* staff writer David Simon dealt with another side of life in Baltimore. To write his 1991 book *Homicide: A Year on the Killing Streets*, Simon spent a year with the Baltimore Police Department Homicide unit. Baltimorean Barry Levinson and Tom Fontana produced the Emmy-winning television show based on the novel. In 1993 Simon took another leave of absence from the *Sun*, and joined with Edward Burns, a former Baltimore police officer turned public school teacher, to spend a year doing research for *The Corner: A Year in the Life of an Inner-City Neighborhood* which was published in 1997. This book, made into a movie for HBO directed by Baltimorean Charles Dutton, portrayed life on a drug corner, specifically at Fayette and Monroe Streets in West Baltimore, and the people whose lives were affected by the drug trade. Like *Homicide* this won praise and awards for its realistic and sensitive portrayal of people trying to deal with terrible problems.

Two local filmmakers of national acclaim have set their movies in Baltimore and in recent years residents grew accustomed to seeing large movie production trucks parked on local streets. Barry Levinson filmed *Diner*, *Tin Men*, *Avalon*, and *Liberty Heights* here. He won the Oscar for Best Director in 1989 for *Rain Man*. John Waters produced satiric comedies including *Pink Flamingos*, *Hairspray*, *Cry-Baby*, and *Cecil B. Demented*. The Senator Theater on York Road has been the venue for a number of national premiers, thanks to these local producers. Owner Tom Kiefaber displays paving blocks in front of the Senator for each.

Journalism, important in any city, has retained its high quality in Baltimore. The *Sun* is one of few local newspapers across the country that has maintained its own foreign bureaus. The demise of the rival *News American* in 1986 and of the *Evening Sun* in 1995 brought an end to local competition, but the *City Paper*, a weekly which began publication in 1977, and the *Baltimore Business Journal*, which first came out in 1983, helped fill the gap. Local journalists including Jim Bready, Neil Grauer, and Michael Olesker have published books about the city while *Sun* staffers including Jon Franklin and Alice Steinbach have won Pulitzer prizes for their writing. Dan Rodericks received the American Newspaper Guild's Heywood Brown Award in 1984. Radio journalist

The addition of the Hackerman House has allowed the Walters Art Gallery to display a significant part of its substantial collection of Asian art.

The Meyerhoff Symphony Hall, designed by the architectural firms of Pietro Belluschi and Jung/Brannen Associates, and made possible by the generous gift of Baltimore philanthropist Joseph Meyerhoff, opened in 1982. The excellent acoustics in this 2,443 seat concert hall were developed by the firm of Bolt, Beranek and Newman. The Baltimore Symphony Orchestra, under the direction of Maestro Yuri Temirkanov, offers concerts series here throughout the year.

Right:
Yuri Temirkanov, who began his tenure as Music Director of the Baltimore Symphony Orchestra during the 1999-2000 season, studied violin and viola, graduated from the Leningrad Conservatory, and in 1967 won the prestigious Moscow National Conducting Competition. He has been music director of the Kirov Opera and Ballet and in 2000 serves concurrently as music director of the St. Petersburg Philharmonic.

Marc Steiner, on his popular WJHU talk show, has made vast amounts of information available to listeners across the area and allows people of all political persuasions to talk with the men and women who make policies in the city and state.

Baltimoreans have proven to be loyal fans of local sports teams and athletes. Many have long traditions. The Preakness Stakes at Pimlico Racetrack, which at the end of the 20th century drew huge and rowdy crowds to the infield, and steeplechase races in the spring continue to draw spectators from near and far. Lacrosse has extended its appeal as more schools and colleges field teams. Swimming has drawn fans, especially since Anita Nall in 1992 and Beth Botsford in 1996 brought home gold medals from the Olympics. Both trained at the North Baltimore Aquatic Club in Mt. Washington. Tennis star Pam Shriver, always loyal to Baltimore, began the only tournament that has regularly brought top name players to the city, with proceeds going to charity. Golf's late-20th century popularity has sparked the building of new courses, both public and private, in the hope of satisfying the demands of players and also helping to attract new companies which count golf courses among the desired amenities in any city where they do business.

Football has left Baltimoreans with both wonderful and angry memories in recent decades. Under the ownership of Carroll Rosenbloom, Colts games sold out. Team leaders like Johnny Unitas, Art Donovan, Don Shula, Lenny Moore, Raymond Berry, and Alan Ameche became part of the city's popular mythology. In 1971 the Colts won the Super Bowl, defeating Dallas. Rosenbloom acquired the Los Angeles Rams and Robert Irsay acquired the Colts in a swap in 1972. In 1976, Irsay began to show an interest in moving the team to other cities. This drama ended in the dead of night on March 29, 1984 when the Mayflower moving vans took Irsay's team to Indianapolis. Baltimoreans felt angry and betrayed. They cheered somewhat half-heartedly for the Washington Redskins and then for the Canadian Football League Stallions until 1996 when Art Modell brought the Cleveland Browns to Baltimore where, after a vote of the fans, they were renamed the Ravens. Mayor Kurt Schmoke, the former quarterback from City College, was particularly pleased. Businessman John Moag was the dealmaker that made things work.

Baltimore baseball has been more consistent. The Orioles, whose attendance had been lower than that of the Colts, grew in talent and popularity during the closing decades of the 20th century. They won the World Series in 1970 and 1983, when their attendance topped 2,000,000 for the first time. Several generations of players captured the local imagination and drew a loyal following. Jim Palmer, Boog Powell, and Brooks Robinson stayed in Baltimore after they retired and in 2000 are still active in the community. Frank Robinson went on to become manager of the Orioles and was named Manager of the Year by the Baseball Writers' Association and the national wire services in 1989. Robinson managed some of the new generation of baseball heroes that included Cal Ripken and Eddie Murray who were joined by locally popular Brady Anderson, Harold Baines, Raphael Palmiero, and B. J. Surhoff. There was a scare that the Orioles might move out of town, but that did not materialize. Longtime owner Jerry Hoffberger sold the team in 1979 to Washington lawyer Edward Bennett Williams, who promised not to relocate. After Williams' death in 1988, Eli Jacobs bought the franchise. The fear of losing the team finally ended when Baltimore lawyer Peter Angelos bought the Orioles in 1993. A new baseball stadium, called Orioles Park at Camden Yards, opened on April 6, 1992. Designed to be an intimate space like the parks of earlier years, the ballpark was instantly popular. When the 1993 All-Star game was held there, visitors spent $30 million in six days.

Barry Levinson, who grew up in the Park Heights, has portrayed that neighborhood in his popular films.

Anne Tyler sets many of her novels in Baltimore. The film adaptation of her novel The Accidental Tourist *won two Oscars in 1989.*

Local artist Greg Otto is known for his colorful portrayals of familiar Baltimore scenes. He is one of a number of artists in the city's growing art community

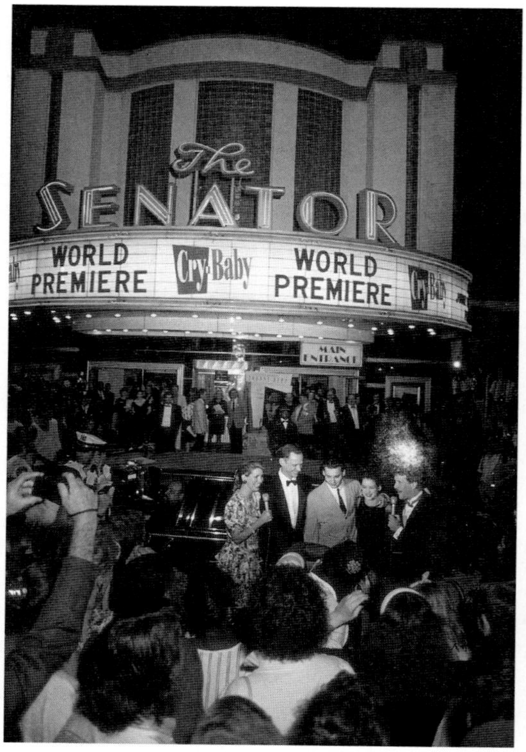

John Waters' loyalty to Baltimore has resulted in world premiers at the Senator Theater on York Road. Here, Waters and others appear for the opening of Cry Baby.

Above: The cast of "Homicide" became a part of the Baltimore community. Members frequented Fells Point restaurants and bars and participated in fundraisers for local organizations.

Baltimore Renaissance 1970-2000

It is clear that the years 1970 to 2000 brought countless changes to Baltimore. Many reflect national trends while some are purely local. One very important change is that power has been spread more broadly. Women and African Americans in 2000 regularly hold high government and civic positions and are leaders in professional and business fields. Newcomers to the city have added a new dimension to the ethnic and religious diversity that has been Baltimore's tradition. The fabulously successful Inner Harbor and growing revival of several city neighborhoods have brought visual beauty and economic growth to the once grimy old industrial city. The city's economy, no longer dominated by manufacturing, includes medicine, high technology, education, and tourism among its mainstays. Increasing recognition of regional interdependence has resulted in cooperative programs in a variety of areas. Public transit has once again begun to connect the city and the surrounding region. Baltimore, like most American cities, takes complex problems from the 20th century into the 21st century. Among these are an under-performing public school system, poverty, drug use, crime, and environmental pollution. These have no easy or quick answers. The need for greater cooperation in dealing with urban problems and physical sprawl continues. Despite continuing challenges, most residents would say that Baltimore is a better place in 2000 than it was in 1970. Baltimoreans, once defensive about their city, now can brag about their hometown. Baltimore has become more than "Charm City," more than a "City of Neighborhoods," more than the "City That Reads." It is, in many ways, a proud and joyous city. All of Baltimore's citizens and leaders in 2000 hope to make it also the city that works.

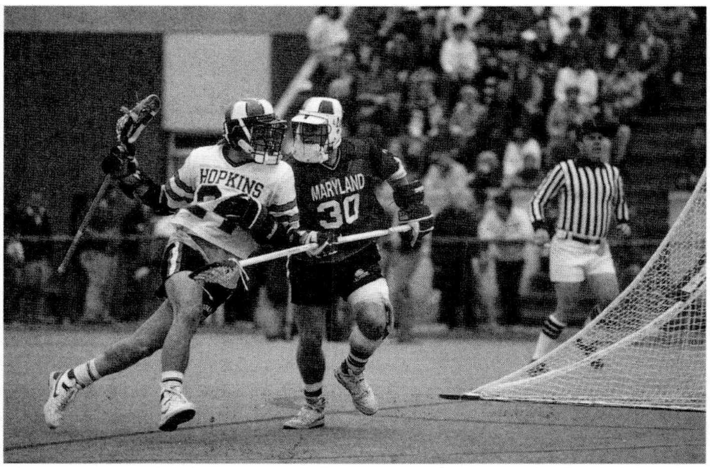

Lacrosse is an established Baltimore tradition. Rivalries among local schools and colleges bring out enthusiastic spectators. Many Marylanders would like it to be made the state's official sport.

Pam Shriver, tennis champion, is an active participant in the civic life of the city.

Baltimoreans and visitors have enjoyed racing at Pimlico Race Course since 1870. It is home to the Preakness Stakes, the second jewel of the Triple Crown.

Cal Ripken is a local hero, celebrated for his participation in the community, his work ethic, and his achievements. He holds the record for the most consecutive games played in major league baseball: 2632. In September, 1995, when he surpassed Lou Gehrig's record by playing game 2131, all Baltimore celebrated.

Locals and visitors alike love Camden Yards, the home of the Baltimore Orioles. An intimate stadium, the spectators can see from every seat. A visit to the vending area is like a stroll on the boardwalk in Ocean City.

Home of the Baltimore Ravens, Baltimore's new PSINet Stadium, with almost 70,000 seats, opened in 1998.

Chronicles of Leadership

VII

Personal accounts of perseverance, ambition, sacrifice, survival, and success are an integral part of the history of Baltimore, "the Port." On the following pages are found the stories of those who envisioned a world port and worked for its reality. Here also are the personal histories of men and women who built Baltimore's factories, financial institutions, warehouses, and ships. Baltimore is the story of the men who determined the conformation of her streets, shipped her goods to foreign ports, and participated in revolutions in transportation and industry.

Intricately woven in the fabric of Baltimore City are the lives of individuals with vision and a special fascination for the future. When Baltimore was still a town, a handful of men saw and realized the capabilities of "the Basin," Baltimore's historical mudflat that was transformed into one of the world's most important and lively ports. As Baltimore's ship traffic increased, so evolved the many goods and services required to accommodate the international exchange of goods.

Many of those who committed their talents and energy to the growth of Baltimore's business community first sailed into the Chesapeake Bay making for the Port of Baltimore. They came from England, Ireland, Germany, France, Russia, Italy, and hundreds of other European countries in search of opportunity.

Many of the enterprises you will read about extended their roots into Baltimore soil when much of the land bordering the city consisted of rural estates and farms. At one time almost all important business and industry were within easy walking distance. The streets were cobblestone. Horse-drawn carriages were the major form of transportation.

The growth of Baltimore is also a story of humble beginnings. Time after time the same tale is told: "We began in a little basement room . . . one desk, one chair . . . ." Yet, massive buildings were erected along Baltimore's streets; factories rose in corn fields; impressive structures were built to evidence the strength of financial institutions; the city's skyline was transformed.

An early Baltimore retailer once wrote: "Baltimore and Progress are synonymous terms." Baltimore industries are proud of their reputation for progressiveness. Companies boast of their willingness to innovate, to modernize, to be the first: the first dental school in the world, the first branch bank, the first asphalt mixer, the first one-story warehouse, the first computer. The growth of Baltimore is founded on the stories of enterprising men and women who quietly and without fanfare revolutionized entire industries.

Baltimore firms are equally proud of the men and women who, through loyalty and hard work, helped the city grow and flourish. Baltimore business leaders rarely take personal credit for their firm's accomplishments. Rather, they cite good fortune in being associated with dedicated and inspired employees and take pride in providing a work environment which encourages, recognizes, and rewards individual achievement.

Many of the firms which first opened their doors of business in Baltimore now claim the city as headquarters for national and international trade. Other companies, realizing Baltimore's future was strong, opened plants or branch offices, bringing new and talented people to share in the city's growth and development.

With the success of enterprise in Baltimore came a commitment to the community that helped make it possible. Corporate contributions to Baltimore's charitable, cultural, civic, religious, and educational organizations have enabled the city's residents to realize multi-faceted and meaningful lives. Philanthropic endeavor continues to be an essential component of Baltimore's business community. Countless dollars are matched with long hours of volunteer effort.

There is a special feeling in Baltimore. The people who work there love their city. They've worked hard and have truly earned the right to boast: "Baltimore Is Best."

Accreditation Board for Engineering and Technology, Inc.

With dozens of institutions of higher education in the Baltimore area and over 5,000 nationwide, quality assurance of those institutions and the educational programs they offer is crucial to parents, students, and employers. The Accreditation Board for Engineering and Technology (ABET), headquartered in Baltimore, Maryland provides that quality assurance for engineering, engineering technology, engineering-related, and soon, computer science programs at over 500 colleges and universities across the country. In addition, ABET has evaluated over 70 engineering educational programs in various countries outside the United States, deeming them "substantially equivalent" to ABET accredited programs in the U.S.

ABET originally began as the Engineer's Council for Professional Development (ECPD) and was formed on October 3, 1932 in Manhattan, New York. Several organizations representing practicing and professional engineers founded ECPD to ensure the quality of the engineering profession and engineering education. The ECPD was governed by a strong commitment to the overall development of the engineer's career from pre-college guidance to post-graduate professional training. The organization also focused heavily on establishing an educational accreditation system.

In 1980, the ECPD, renamed the Accreditation Board of Engineering and Technology (ABET), began a new tradition of solely concentrating on accreditation which is a non-governmental process certifying that an institution or program meets a set of criteria ensuring educational quality. Accreditation is an on-going process; each program is reviewed at least once every six years. The process requires institutions to develop plans for continuous improvement, conduct an extensive internal review of their programs and then submit to an external, peer review to certify that their programs meet the standards set by the profession for entry-level practice. Students, employers, and the public greatly benefit from the value accreditation offers. ABET-accredited disciplines allow prospective students to easily identify high-quality educational programs. Graduates from these programs are better-educated, possess practical skills related to the profession, and are equipped to enter the workforce. Employers who hire graduates from ABET-accredited programs gain qualified employees who are proficient and able to make contributions that improve the standard of living and society as a whole. Currently, ABET accredits some 2,300 engineering, engineering technology, and engineering-related educational programs. In 1997, the organization expanded its mission to include the accreditation of applied science programs, such as computer science.

ABET is a federation of 30 professional engineering and technical societies. Representatives from these societies, who are practicing professionals from industry and academe, form the body of ABET. Industry and academic involvement are important in the accreditation process. Together the 1,500 volunteers develop criteria, make assessments, and determine final accreditation decisions. The active participation of practicing professionals allows accreditation to reflect standards set by the profession itself. This approach provides a better-prepared graduate that ultimately translates into a valuable employee. Many dedicated volunteers administer ABET's activities.

Over the years, ABET has become an international leader in assuring quality engineering education. The organization conducts educational consultancy visits and works closely with agencies in other countries to assist them in developing accreditation systems of their own.

ABET has entered into a number of mutual recognition agreements (MRA) with accrediting organizations in Australia, Canada, Ireland, Hong Kong, New Zealand, South Africa, and the United Kingdom. These agreements recognize that the accreditation systems are comparable to ABET accreditation. Graduates from these programs in member countries are prepared to practice engineering at the professional level.

ABET also provides another important service to the engineering community, credentials evaluation. The Engineering Credentials Evaluation International (ECEI) division of ABET evaluates the academic credentials of individuals who have received an engineering degree from a college or university located outside of the U.S. State licensure boards, as well as employers, graduate schools, and engineering societies use the information provided by this service.

The ABET national headquarters is located in the historic Candler Building, 111 Market Place, Baltimore.

Since its inception, ABET has responded to new challenges as an opportunity for growth and greater service to its constituents. ABET has a strong and solid history; the organization has endured the rapid changes in engineering and technology of the 20th century while continually cultivating an efficient and effective accreditation system. The organization looks forward to meeting the challenges of advancing engineering, technology, applied science, and computing education in the 21st century.

With this forward vision, the ABET leadership constructed a strategy to propel the organization into the new century. After more than a year in development, on November 1, 1997, the ABET Board of Directors adopted the ABET Strategic Plan. ABET's vision is clear and states, *"ABET will provide world leadership to assure quality and stimulate innovation in engineering, technology, and applied science education."*

The national headquarters of ABET has resided in Baltimore since 1994. The relocation of ABET headquarters to this area was very much appropriate given Maryland's strong and long-standing history as a center for science and engineering. The organization hosts many year-round activities that serve as a focal point in attracting individuals to the city. ABET is located in the historic Candler Building that overlooks Baltimore's scenic Inner Harbor. The Candler Building, named after Asa G. Candler, the inventor of Coca-Cola, was once a Coca-Cola bottling company. It has been a landmark in Baltimore since 1908. Undergoing extensive renovations during 1987-88, the building now houses several professional offices.

Throughout its existence, ABET/ECPD has committed itself to quality in engineering, technology, and engineering-related education. The organization continues to implement new initiatives to broaden and enhance its efforts and its influence in higher education quality assurance. ABET's current activities, along with its future vision, will continue to build upon its rich legacy.

Ajilon

The view from Ajilon's corporate headquarters in Towson, Maryland overlooks the Baltimore County Courthouse, county government offices, law offices, small businesses, shops, and churches that line downtown Towson's tidy streets. With its rich history, dynamic present, and promising future, it's a place where Ajilon, a leading provider of information technology (IT) services, feels right at home.

Ajilon's Towson roots date back to 1978, when a husband and wife team and their partner founded Comp-u-Staff. By 1982, Comp-u-Staff had grown from three to 35 employees, with offices in Towson and Harrisburg. Until its Washington, D.C. office opened later in 1982, a Comp-u-Staff van transported six traveling IT consultants to serve Capitol-area clients. The company continued to grow and acquire other IT firms, including a Detroit-based company that was founded in 1969. By 1991, Comp-u-Staff was doing business as Adia Information Technologies.

Roy Haggerty, Ajilon president and CEO.

Ajilon assumed its current moniker in 1996. Tasked with developing a permanent identity for the organization, distinguished by its ability to grow phenomenally while remaining client-focused, an executive team hit upon the word "agile." After some "wordsmithing", Ajilon was born.

Today, Ajilon is the industry leader of IT staffing services with over 30 years of experience, $1.6 billion in revenues and over 15,000 employees internationally. Approximately 150 human resources, communications, training and administration, MIS, and financial professionals staff Ajilon's Towson headquarters. Its national district offices feature delivery teams comprised of district managers, account managers, technical recruiters and administrators who provide client and consultant support. Ajilon has offices in the United States, United Kingdom, Canada and Australia.

Ajilon's clients range from large multinationals, to mid-size corporations and public employers and represent a variety of industries including manufacturing, finance, communications, health, transportation and insurance. In addition to supplemental IT staffing, Ajilon offers several managed services, with responsibility for a complete project. Managed services include eBusiness solutions, systems transformation, functional outsourcing, systems security, IT management, man-

Ajilon consultants at the client site.

Ajilon consultants at the client site.

aged maintenance services, business contingency planning and software testing and quality assurance. Ajilon has recently added executive level IT placement to its full line of services.

Roy Haggerty, president and CEO of Ajilon since 1990, has led the company through a decade that has seen its size more than double. He is a strong advocate of retaining consultants and helping them to build successful careers, and was Ajilon's driving force behind providing eligible consultants with health, dental, vision and life insurance, a flexible spending account, disability programs, tuition assistance, a 401(k) program, on-line training, paid leave and bonuses/comp time. Consultants regularly cite Ajilon's benefits and the sense of stability they provide, combined with the variety of IT responsibilities offered through Ajilon's short- and long-term assignments, as reasons for their satisfaction with Ajilon.

It is Ajilon's employee focus—through full benefits packages, efficient external and internal customer service, thorough employee orientation and continued educational opportunities—that is a key to its success. That same benevolent corporate culture led Baltimore County Executive Dutch Ruppersberger to commend Ajilon's local district in 1998 for its volunteer efforts with the Baltimore County Department of Health's (DOH's) Women's Cancer Protection Program (WCPP). The WCPP provides free medical services to underprivileged women. When the DOH approached Ajilon for assistance in developing an automated system for WCPP patient records, Ajilon provided a team of six consultants to conduct the work *pro bono* so as not to use funds that would directly benefit qualified WCPP participants.

The WCPP and Ajilon's other clients appreciate Ajilon's IT expertise, which frees their internal IT resources to pursue strategic initiatives. Ajilon is equally adept at pursuing organizations' strategic IT initiatives in project management arrangements, thus freeing internal resources for the rigors of day-to-day systems management.

For example, the Internet has brought a new dimension to doing business, and Ajilon's clients are increasingly seeking the tools and guidance to compete in today's eBusiness world. Ajilon completely manages this type of strategic initiative, from holding initial client meetings to maintaining eBusiness solutions, and every task in between. While Ajilon's consultants manage the eBusiness project initiative, its clients' internal IT staffs are free to address daily systems issues.

As clients grow more sophisticated in their IT objectives, the demand for Ajilon's project management expertise via its managed services is increasing. This trend contrasts with the supplemental staffing requests of most clients in the past. Other changes in the IT landscape include a tapering boom period of IT industry growth, as clients' IT vendor lists have been honed to include only the very best. To compete, IT firms must ensure that their consultants possess not only technical prowess, but also project management and business acumen.

It is an exciting time for IT services firms such as Ajilon. Rapid technological developments, new ways of leveraging the Internet and a savvy client base ensure healthy competition and client-focused service delivery. Ajilon looks forward to a future dedicated to providing its Baltimore and international clients with IT solutions for today's business challenges.

American Port Services, Inc.

American Port Services (AMPORTS) is the largest car processing business in the United States, with more than 30 years of experience, innovation, and quality performance in the industry. Formerly known as Hoblemann Port Services, Benicia Industries, and Crown Auto Processing, operations were consolidated under a single name in 1996, in keeping with a plan for continued growth in global transportation logistics.

AMPORTS processes export and import vehicles at four major East and West Coast ports: Baltimore, Maryland; Benicia, California; Brunswick, Georgia; and Jacksonville, Florida; and at a newly-opened car servicing center in Zeebrugge, Belgium. AMPORTS also operates, manages, and develops airports, fixed-based operations (FBOs) and other aviation-related facilities via an aviation management subsidiary acquired in 1997 from Johnson Controls, Inc.

All seaport locations provide features that are essential for fast, high-quality, safe, and efficient vehicle processing. These include streamlined on/off pier loading; well-lit, high-security storage areas; state-of-the art facilities; and equipment for all car servicing and preparation tasks. Each of the terminals also provides complete distribution services, including rail loading and unloading, marine damage surveys, pre-shipment inspection, and staging for shipboard loading and inland transportation.

The company now enjoys an industry-wide distinction for having some of the finest facilities and groundbreaking technologies for vehicle processing and computerized inventory and control systems globally.

The then Rudolph Hoblemann Company served as customs broker/freight forwarders for Volkswagen Beetles brought into ports along the East Coast. Cars were individually hoisted from cargo holds and slung onto the docks, an operation prone to damage. Volkswagen directed Hoblemann to fix any problems, thus beginning the car processing business.

Model 2000 Chrysler cars being loaded on a modern car ship. Today, several thousand vehicles can be loaded or unloaded in a day's time on huge ships capable of handling in excess of 5,000 cars and trucks.

The company was born out of necessity in the late 1950s, when Volkswagens (the beloved "Bug") began arriving in the United States, later swelling to hundreds of thousands of vehicles arriving per year in the 1970s. Volkswagen's agent in the United States, R.G. Hoblemann, was asked to care for and repair, if necessary, the cars arriving in Baltimore. From this beginning grew the combined AMPORTS enterprise, which now operates bi-coastally and internationally.

The intervening years saw many changes in organization and ownership. In 1996, Hobelmann and its subsidiary Crown Auto Processing were acquired by American Port Services of California, which financed the acquisition via a stock offering on the Lon-

Highly efficient conveyor-based, assembly-line systems move cars through detailed inspection processes and the application of protective coatings. Such methods speed vehicle flow and minimize damage.

don Exchange. The company's name then became American Port Services. In July 1997, American Port Services acquired the airport management business of Johnson Controls World Services, Inc., and this aviation arm currently operates facilities at 10 airports in the United States. At the turn of the 21st century, the combined AMPORTS enterprises now are owned by Associated British Ports, PLC, which operates 23 ports in England, including Southampton, Grimsby, and Immingham.

Modern, Technologically Advanced Facilities: Facilities and logistics at all ports are organized and equipped to meet the demands of just-in-time conscious manufacturers. Once vehicles arrive, they are processed and shipped with efficiency and minimum delay. High-security facilities also are available for long- or medium-term storage until dealers request shipment. Each of the ports provides a full range of processing services using skilled, well-trained personnel and employing the latest technology.

In keeping with the sensitivity and responsiveness to customer needs, APS employs the latest radio frequency bar-code technology to track all vehicles entering and leaving the terminals, as well as identifying a vehicle's exact status and location in the facility. With such systems, a complete rundown on a vehicle's exact status can be provided upon a customer's request, day or night, around the world.

Finally, each facility also has earned and maintains the rigorous certificate of the International Office of Standards (ISO 9000) Certification. This internationally-recognized benchmark of quality is awarded only after passing a strict audit of every phase of operations.

Computer based inventory, processing, and billing systems form the AMPORTS operational backbone. With upwards of 20,000 vehicles on-site at terminals in various states of preparation for shipping or trucking, computer tracking enables any unit to be found readily, and full processing and billing using paperless methods

American Port Services, Inc. - The Aviation Group

As part of a bold expansion plan designed to broaden its business horizons into other transportation businesses, American Port Services, Inc., (dba: AMPORTS) acquired the airport and aviation division of Johnson Controls, Inc. in August of 1997. With this acquisition came not only a strategic penetration into an important niche business, but a business with a rich history of leadership and accomplishment in the airport management and aircraft handling arenas.

The roots of AMPORTS' aviation practice can be traced back to the late 1920s claiming its rightful place as a direct descendent of the historic airline, Pan American World Airways, Inc. During the fledgling days of commercial aviation, the design and construction as well as the business of operating airports as a transportation mode was only beginning to evolve. The introduction of scheduled air service initially to Cuba and eventually deeper into the Latin and Pacific regions, necessitated that Pan Am build and operate its own system of airports to support its rapidly expanding route network. Later, throughout the war years, Pan Am's special skills in the fields of airport design, operation and management proved instrumental in the eventual construction of more than 50 airfields in over 15 countries on behalf of the U.S. Government.

The concept of engaging a third party operator to manage an owner's airport first gained a material foothold in 1946 when Pan Am was awarded a contract to operate and manage Roberts International Airport for the Liberian Government in West Africa. Subsequently, through the advent of other successive airport management appointments, Pan Am quickly amassed a reputation as the spawning industry's leading innovator.

The Late 1920s marked the beginning of Pan Am's airport management credential, which today, is an integral part of AMPORTS' services portfolio.

Operating as a division of AMPORTS, the company has taken full advantage of its acquisition of Pan Am's original airport management group.

Leveraging its success during a period of financial uncertainty, Pan Am divested itself of its services organization (Pan Am World Services, Inc, which included its airport management division) to Johnson Controls, Inc. (JCI) in 1989. For Johnson Controls, a Milwaukee-based, Fortune 500 manufacturing and services organization, this acquisition served as the pivotal step toward its emergence as a world-class technical and facility management services provider. The new Johnson Controls World Service Inc., organization quickly grew to over 10,000 service employees in over 39 countries, and placed Johnson Controls in a unique position to stake its claim as the unquestioned leader in contract services.

The years that followed after Johnson Controls acquired Pan Am's services arm were punctuated by great prosperity and substantive growth. However, in an effort to focus upon its core strengths as a commercial and government services provider, Johnson Controls re-aligned its services business and, in doing so, sold its airport and aviation practice to Baltimore-based American Port Services, Inc. (AMPORTS). The acquisition by AMPORTS was consummated in July of 1997 and added a new dimension to the company's already existing transportation businesses.

Operating as a division of AMPORTS, the company has taken full advantage of its acquisition of Pan Am's original airport management group. With several new contracts added to its stable of prominent airports and fixed base operations, AMPORTS has strategically positioned itself to continue its tradition of delivering quality services to a diverse group of maritime and aviation customers.

AMPORTS' aviation pedigree is, thus, both impressive and comprehensive in every respect. Its menu of services range from total airport management to providing specialized facilities management for airline passenger and cargo terminals. Moreover, its aviation capabilities include aircraft fueling, airline ground handling and passenger services, hangar services and a host of defined aviation-related customer services. Today, AMPORTS' geographic sphere of operations includes airport management contracts and airport fixed base operations (FBOs) throughout the eastern seaboard of the United States.

John E. Harms Jr. and Associates, Inc.

John E. Harms Jr., a native of Hagerstown, Maryland, graduated from The Johns Hopkins University with a Bachelor of Engineering degree in Civil Engineering, in 1943.

After serving in World War II in the South Pacific, John initiated his engineering career with the Baltimore firm of Whitman, Requardt and Associates. Twelve years later, in 1955 he founded the firm of John E. Harms Jr. and Associates, Inc. (Harms & Associates). John is registered as a professional engineer in Maryland, Delaware, and the District of Columbia. In 1986, Maryland Governor Harry Hughes appointed him to the Board of Registration for Professional Engineers, where he served until 1998.

The initial location of Harms and Associates was at Greenway and Business Route 3 in Glen Burnie. In 1962, the firm moved to its present location in Pasadena, Maryland. In 1973, the office complex expanded by adding a second floor to the main building. In 1992, the main building was again expanded to house the present staff of 75. In June 1996 a satellite office was established in Frederick, Maryland.

Long-time employee and vice president Ed Lowman was appointed as president in 1991, managing the daily operations, while John Harms remains chairman of the board and "chief consultant" to the business operation. Their corresponding business and management philosophies foster the successful and compatible relationship that sets the tone for the firm's operations.

Harms and Associates provides services in the disciplines of planning, landscape, architecture, ecology, environmental engineering, development engineering, surveying, and inspection. Its staff members serve on many local committees and participate in several community activities. The goal of the firm is to be "service oriented." This goal is best met with a "strong project manager" system, wherein project managers have broad authority and related responsibilities.

Harms and Lowman.

Some of Harms and Associates' early engineering projects were the major developments of Maryland City, Sun Valley, and Southgate. Among larger, early municipal sector projects were the design, stakeout, and inspection of the Cox Creek and Broadneck Wastewater Systems, College Parkway, Maryland Route 4 in Calvert County and the geodetic survey control for the initial Anne Arundel County "Overall Mapping" Project. The firm also served as "town engineer" for several small towns in Maryland.

Other projects of note include the first order control for the entire Baltimore Light Rail and the Rights of Way surveys for the southern leg from Glen Burnie to Baltimore; design of Fallston Sewers for Harford County and the National Institute of Health Treatment Facilities; and ongoing environmental assessments, wetlands delineation, wetlands mitigation design, wetlands monitoring, and stream restoration design for the Maryland State Highway Administration.

Other large private sector projects are Shipley's Choice, Chesterfield, National Business Park, expansion of the Annapolis Mall, Annapolis Exchange, Piney Orchard, and The Arundel Mills.

Harms building.

Atlas Container Corporation

A Tour Guide's Visit To A Very Uncommon Box Company In Baltimore, Maryland: The road is narrow and curls through the southern Maryland foliage. The first thing you notice is the tower, white, shimmering steel looming 150 feet in autumn sunlight. Then you see the word ATLAS in the distance, painted in six-foot tall sky blue letters across the face of a 120,000 gallon steel bubble floating on top of the tower.

It's your first visit to Atlas Container in Severn, Maryland and all you know about the company is that it has somehow balanced itself between the new economy and the old one. You walk in the front door and two things strike you.

Most people crossing the lobby are dressed casually. Everyone walks fast. Some are even running. You detect an unusual urgency in the office. You sense that whatever products or services are made, they must be produced quickly and delivered the same day or next day. As you wait to meet the owners, you feel a high-energy, heavy, adrenaline rush as people move around you. You are guessing that workload and time are inversely proportional. You listen—the air is stirring—a collective whispering that says, "Let's do it now, let's do it today."

Before long—you will learn that nothing takes long at Atlas—someone comes to greet you. She is smiling and the smile appears warm and genuine. Which makes you wonder if these people are moving fast and also having fun. As you are led past the reception area you, too, are walking quickly.

Where there are offices, doors are open. People, sitting at desks and tables studying computer screens lean forward in sprint-ready position. Most of the space is divided into cubicles—a blue, angular maze twisting through a big room. As you walk through the office, you notice the walls. There is an encyclopedic display of information covering the walls. Line graphs and pie charts measure machine run speeds and set up times. Sales and unit volume, waste and downtime have been calculated in bold day-glow bar graphs. A balance sheet and cash flow analysis hang over a potted hydrangea. Columns of numbers on an income statement indicate actual weekly performance and month-to-date projections. It is obvious that anyone walking through the office has access to the company's financial story. Which makes you wonder. How many people actually pay attention to the numbers or really know what they mean?

The founders and new owners of Atlas Container. (l-r) PeteTaylor, Don Fleegle, Peter Centenari and Paul Centenari.

You are introduced to the two owners and you notice they are young, animated and happen to be brothers. You begin to detect something unusual about them. Beneath the open shirt collars and casual clothing, there is a restless intensity. They did not grow up making boxes and even after a decade in the business, they are not typical of the industry. They will not talk to you at length about product design or print graphics. You hear very little from them about their equipment versatility or machine process and capability. They will acknowledge that these details are vital to operating their business. But what distinguishes their intensity is the passion they have for the growth of their business and the development of the people who work for Atlas.

Peter and Paul Centenari bought Atlas Container in 1988. The two brothers made the unlikely transition into the box business after spending several years in the investment banking field. Even as bankers, they shared an incipient desire to buy a business that would produce something tangible. In early 1987, while living in Denver, Colorado, they closed their start-up finance company and began searching for an acquisition.

At first, Peter and Paul could not agree on which industries to focus their search effort. They did decide to target local or regional businesses. They also agreed to search for companies without geographical restriction. If necessary, they would leave Denver and move wherever the business took them. Throughout 1987, they traveled around the country and met with owners of small companies. They went to Santa Fe to talk to a flower grower. In St. Louis, they met with a document storage company. Back in Denver, they toured a steel tank fabricator and talked to owners who produced plastic injection molding products, plastic bags and computerized thermostats. Thirty companies in 21 states; 11 different industries.

In early 1988, they began negotiating for a gourmet cheesecake company

in Denver. Just before purchasing the business, they realized that baking was as much art as science. Cheesecakes, however, led Peter and Paul to corrugated boxes. While learning about making cheesecakes, they discovered that baked goods were shipped in disposable corrugated boxes. They quickly discovered that most products are packaged and shipped in corrugated boxes.

They sent 500 letters to box companies across the country and spoke to everyone who received a letter. Another two road trips produced meetings with 25 box companies. Negotiations with several owners resulted in stalemate. Peter and Paul continued their search until May 1988, when they discovered the Atlas Container Corporation in Baltimore.

Atlas Container was started in 1968 by Pete Taylor, Don Fleegle and a third owner. In the early years, the company operated from the basement of a restaurant in Baltimore celebrated for its shrimp sandwiches. At the time, Atlas acquired its primary raw material—corrugated sheets—from fully-integrated paper companies. Trucks delivering the sheets were unloaded by hand and converted over two small machines into boxes, die cut boxes, mailing folders and trays. By the mid-'70s the owners needed a larger building and moved the company into a 50,000 square foot facility. By 1988, with 35 employees and 250 customers throughout Maryland and Washington, D.C., Atlas had become one of the leading converters of corrugated paper boxes in Baltimore. But after 20 years of profitable growth, the founders believed they had reached a plateau. They agreed to sell their business and began searching for a buyer.

In the middle of the night in late November 1988, Pete Taylor and Don Fleegle sold Atlas Container to Peter and Paul Centenari. The brothers returned to Denver to celebrate Thanksgiving and make arrangements for their move to the East Coast. Two weeks later, with a newfound interest in the moving boxes that contained their possessions and propelled by a mixture of inspiration and trepidation, Peter and Paul left Colorado to run a corrugated box company in Baltimore, Maryland.

Between 1989 and 1992, as the Centenaris learned about making boxes, they struggled to maintain the business. The effect of an economic recession drove sales revenues down and made it difficult for the company to pay down bank debts and meet financial covenants. For a long time, they worried about the survival of the company. In spite of the company's financial problems and because of the recession's impact on other businesses, the brothers were able to acquire two small companies that made boxes in

Atlas Container's manufacturing plant in Severn, Maryland.

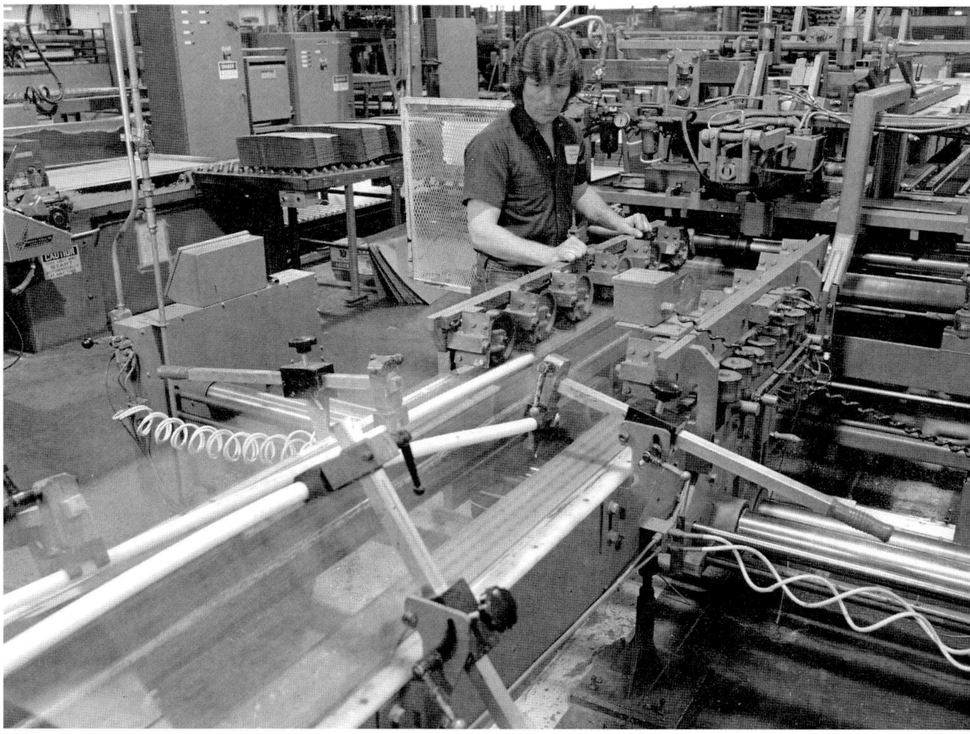

An Atlas stockholder oversees production.

Baltimore. In early 1993, Peter and Paul acquired the Maryland division of a large Canadian paper company and moved their business, including equipment and people into the new facility.

Overnight, everything about Atlas Container quadrupled. Equipment capacity, customer base, sales revenue and debt load grew four-fold from the previous day. The new building, located in Severn, Maryland, eight minutes from Baltimore's airport, contained 200,000 square feet. The acquisition also signified a backward step in integration as the company, using corrugation equipment, began manufacturing its own primary raw material. Over the next three years, the new owners continued to build their business and the organization. And though their employment agreements had long since expired, Pete and Don continued working for Atlas.

In 1996, as part of a major initiative to distribute stock to Atlas employees, the owners constructed an 800 square foot, onsite learning center. They made training classes in basic accounting and finance mandatory for everyone in the organization. After 12 months of financial training, Atlas shut down operations, and everyone convened in the new learning center. For the first time in 27 years the company opened its books to the organization.

Diversified products highlight Atlas' manufacturing capabilities and allow the company to distinguish itself in a very competitive industry.

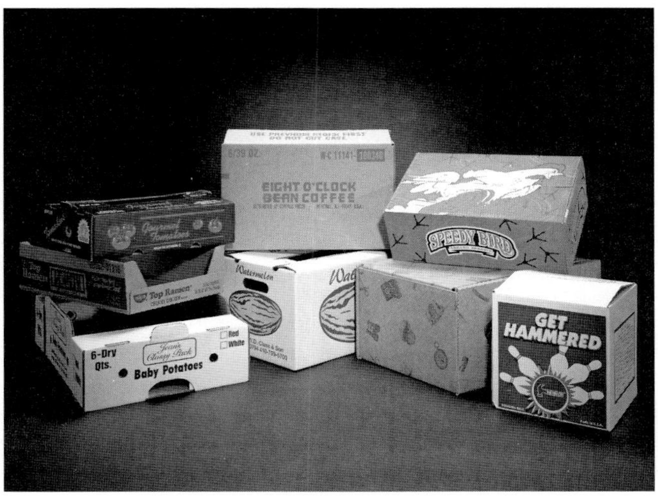

Financial training and company-wide review of monthly financial performance continued over the next three years. In February 2000, Peter and Paul sold stock to more than 100 people at Atlas Container.

You drive away from Atlas Container, the celestial bubble receding in autumn space. You are thinking about the company—the founders who began 30 years ago with just an idea, the new owners who reinvented themselves from bankers to box makers, and the company's passion for explosive growth and an uncommon commitment to the organization.

You think about the things the new owners did not or could not change. The company still manufactures brown boxes. It continues to provide the same quick-turn service to many of the same customers who have been buying boxes from Atlas since the late-'60s. In the plant and office, many of the people have been with Atlas since the beginning or stayed with the company after each acquisition. Several owners of other companies Atlas has acquired come to work every day. And Pete and Don, though their work schedule is abbreviated, still come to the office.

Yet, there have been many important changes. New technology and equipment continually replace the old. An open book management process that allows 220 individuals access to the numbers. A performance story that tells of 20 percent growth in sales, profit and shareholder value every year over the last 10 years. And a stock offering that created ownership for half the people at Atlas.

The water tower is gone from view. You will remember Atlas Container. You have discovered a company where people have raised the level of their game. They are competing as new economy players in an old economy stadium.

iSky, Inc.

Since 1984, Sky Alland Research, Inc. has been a mainstay of Baltimore's growing high-technology marketplace. The fledgling research firm, founded by the late Schuyler Alland and housed in the Johns Hopkins School of Continuing Education building, got its beginning by conducting telephone-based customer satisfaction surveys of automobile owners on behalf of individual dealers in the Baltimore and Washington D.C. areas. The firm soon partnered with some of the world's top automobile manufacturers and moved into other industries where individual customer and prospect management is critical for success.

Schuyler Alland was a master of introducing late-breaking technologies to the customer retention mix. His philosophy was threefold. First, is that inter/intranet technology facilitates a broader array of customer communication options, including telephone, fax and such online customer support vehicles as e-mail, live text chat and voice-over Internet Protocol. Second, is that data warehousing allows these technologies to maintain a comprehensive customer history. And third, is that this data mining enables the company to organize and process its findings to generate sophisticated customer profiling reports to help companies accurately forecast and influence customer behavior.

Richard Hebert, president and CEO of iSky, Inc.

Sky Alland Research, Inc. housed in the Johns Hopkins School of Continuing Education building.

In 1995 Richard Hebert was named president and CEO of Sky Alland Research Inc., and immediately helped reshape the company's vision. Mr. Hebert saw the Internet as the perfect marketing and sales support medium, and soon opened the nation's first web-based customer service center. But that was just the beginning.

In November 1999, after nearly 16 years of service, Sky Alland Research, Inc. officially changed its name to *i*SKY, Inc. in a bid to highlight its Internet strategy and its desire to be the top provider of outsourced, real-time customer care for the e-commerce industry. Despite the name change, the same company today continues to carry on the philosophy first imbued by Schuyler Alland, that quality customer care isn't just important, it's essential—and is almost always the difference between success and failure. No one knows this like *i*SKY, which has built its business on taking care of its customers' customers.

As no two businesses are alike, *i*SKY customer care consultants consider each customer relationship individually. They help determine their customers' needs, design programs to meet those needs, and coordinate and manage their implementation. The bottom line is that *i*SKY solutions get results, including lower costs, greater profitability and increased customer loyalty.

It is no surprise, then, the growing number of Fortune 1,000 companies which outsource their customer care to *i*SKY, whose client roster includes the likes of Audi, BMW, Harley- Davidson, Owens Corning, and Blue Cross and Blue Shield. One facet of *i*SKY's service is that it can ferret out sources of customer dissatisfaction, thereby enhancing overall customer service and creating brand loyalty.

No description of *i*SKY would be complete without mention of its record of community involvement. In an effort to maintain a well-educated employee base, *i*SKY has long been a financial supporter of the University of Baltimore, with Rich Hebert presently serving on the board of advisors for the Robert G. Merrick School of Business. *i*SKY employees also help the community by supporting various non-profit and local civic programs.

The Baltimore Sun

The Baltimore Sun's proud tradition began with the publication of its first issue on May 17, 1837.The paper's founder was Rhode Island-born printer Arunah S. Abell, who came into town full of confidence and introduced a penny paper during a time when Baltimore had six dailies selling for six cents a copy. A pioneer in independent journalism, Abell begen the tradition of in-depth, independent news coverage that has informed *The Sun* all through its history.

Abell was innovative in newsgathering, too, using everything from carrier pigeon and the Pony Express to the telegraph and the railroad to get the news. Under Abells' leadership, *The Sun* furthered the cooperative newsgathering process that was the forerunner of the Associated Press.

From 1910 to 1995, The Baltimore Sun Company published both *The Sun* and *The Evening Sun*, which H.L. Mencken helped found. Mencken's career with the two papers spanned forty years as reporter, columnist, critic and editorial writer. The "Sage of Baltimore," as he was known, gained wide recognition as an outrageous iconoclast, extravagant humorist and consummate craftsman of language.

Until *The Sun's* purchase by Times Mirror in 1986, the newspaper was privately owned by the A. S. Abell Company. The Tribune Company acquired *The Sun* in 2000.

The Baltimore Sun's *new newsroom, viewed from the copy desk. The newsroom was part of a major renovation to downtown headquarters.*

A pressman adjusts the controls on a press at Sun Park, The Sun's *state-of-the-art printing facility. The 376,000 square-foot plant is located in South Baltimore.*

Today, *The Sun*, serving Baltimore and five contiguous counties, is Maryland's largest daily metropolitan newspaper. It dominates its market, has a stable base of loyal customers and is an important part of the fabric of life of Greater Baltimore and beyond.

The Sun entered the 21st century with extensive renovations to its downtown Baltimore headquarters, just a 10-minute walk from the city's famous Inner Harbor and other tourist attractions.

In addition to downtown headquarters, *The Sun* has a state-of-the-art printing facility in South Baltimore, reflective of its national reputation for printing excellence. It also has five foreign bureaus, a Washington, D.C., bureau, a State House bureau in the state capital of Annapolis and four suburban bureaus. In total, *The Sun* employs about 1,800 people, more than 400 of them journalists.

Since its founding, *The Sun* has provided the Baltimore region with quality journalsim. Affirming the newspaper's enduring reputation for excellence, the *Columbia Journalism Review*, one of the country's most respected magazines for journalism professionals, named *The Sun* one of the top ten newspapers in America in 1999. The same year, the Society for News Design named the paper one of the 17 "World's Best Designed Newspapers."

The Sun's journalistic excellence has been recognized with 14 Pulitzer Prizes, including back-to-back awards in 1997 and 1998. The 1998 Pulitzer for investigative reporting went to Gary Cohn and Will Englund for their four-part series "The Shipbreakers." As a result of the series on the little-known industry of salvaging surplus ships, the U.S. House of Representatives convened hearings to examine the practices of the industry, and the U.S. Navy halted plans to send ships to the Third World for scrapping.

The Sun's reputation for outstanding public service journalism grew in 1999 with the "Boot Camps" series, which followed some of Maryland's toughest

The Sun is committed to improving reading performanceof Baltimore-area children through its Reading by 9 initiative. Major program components include ongoing articles on childhood literacy issues. This photo appeared in The Sun *with an article on reading incentives.*

juvenile delinquents as they went though one of the state's highly-acclaimed boot camps. The revelations about abuses set off state and federal probes and earned *The Sun* the George Polk Award and the Robert F. Kennedy Award.

The Sun has always responded to readers' changing needs. In 1998, *The Sun* redesigned and added a variety of new Sunday feature sections focusing on exciting, magazine-style design and reporting and fast-paced "news-you-can-use" content. Among these is the Travel section, which in 2000 earned *The Sun* a first-place gold award for best travel section from the Society of American Travel Writers Foundation.

While providing in-depth coverage of state, national and international news, *The Sun* has expanded local coverage dramatically. Since 1992, the paper has published four different editions six days a week, with zoned editorial and advertising in the local section in three of the most competitive counties. In 2000, *The Sun* expanded local coverage in the Howard County edition, creating a successful model for other demographically desirable and competitive counties in its market.

In addition to publishing *The Sun*, The Baltimore Sun Company also owns The Baltimore Sun Community Newspapers. These papers consist of *The Aegis*, a 35,000 paid circulation twice-a-week newspaper in one of the market's fastest growing counties, and the publications of Patuxent Publishing, which *The Sun* acquired in 1997. Patuxent Publishing is made up of 13 local weekly newspapers and other publications in the Greater Baltimore area.

In 1996, *The Baltimore Sun* developed Alliance Media, designed to create or acquire publications in key categories. Publications include *Jubilee*, targeting the African American family with positive stories about the community from the perspective of local African American writers and photographers, *Fifty Plus, Maryland Family* and *Ooh Baby*.

The Sun added its Web site, SunSpot, in 1996. SunSpot attracts both extended *Sun* readers and a new online audience. Known as Maryland's online community, SunSpot strives to be the dominant local news, information and classified site for the Baltimore metropolitan market.

As Maryland's major metropolitan newspaper, *The Sun* is committed to improving the quality of life in the communities it serves. In 1997, *The Sun* launched Reading by 9, a multifaceted, long-term initiative to improve the reading performance of Baltimore-area children. This comprehensive community service program seeks to inspire a measurable increase in the percentage of nine-year-olds who are able to read at, or above, third-grade level.

The program's main components are news and editorial coverage of childhood literacy issues, an employee volunteer tutoring program in area schools and regular Reading by 9 features for children to enjoy on their own or with an adult. These interactive features were expanded and packaged in March 2000 in a weekly "Just for Kids" section.

Reading by 9 has received numerous prestigious national awards, including the Scripps Howard Foundation National Journalism Award, the Society of Professional Journalists Award for Public Service, the James K. Batten Award for Excellence in Civic Journalism and the Conference Board's Best in Class Award.

In addition to this single major initiative, the company has a strong Newspaper in Education program that provides newspapers and teaching supplements to classrooms. *The Sun also* supports the community through various charitable contributions and sponsorships. It is proud to help advance a wide range of education, arts and culture, civic, health and human services programs.

The first article in "The Shipbreakers" series that earned a 1998 Pulitzer Prize for investigate reporting. The Sun's *14 Pulitzer Prizes and the distinction, in 1999, of being named one of the top ten newspapers in America by* the Columbia Journalism Review *reflect the paper's journalistic excellence.*

THE SUN

Sunday

Dec. 7, 1941:

NAVY 39, ARMY 7

THE SHIPBREAKERS

Scrapping ships, sacrificing men

Orioles, Anderson agree on contract

Voters may get lever on slots

Search for TWA answers moves here

Bond Transfer Co., Inc.

In 1934, with one truck and a dream, William "Elmer" Constantine, Sr. founded Liberty Transfer Company, Inc. His garage was the trunk of his car and his office was his kitchen table. His wife Margaret Constantine, did all of his paperwork.

During the early years a trucker needed authority to transport goods from one state to another. He bought the "rights" to transport paperboard for Chesapeake Paperboard Co. (his first client) to New York and Pennsylvania, with restrictions on his delivery destinations. They were in business for the life of Liberty Transfer. Chesapeake considered Liberty Transfer a goodwill ambassador to its customers, a tradition that continues today with Bond Transfer Company, Inc.

World War II put a stop to Liberty's progress, as drivers, truck parts and gasoline were hard to come by during that time. By now Elmer had five trucks, but only three were operational.

During summer vacations, William "Buddy" E. Constantine Jr. helped his Dad maintain the trucks, doing everything he could to keep them moving. After his discharge from the Army Buddy joined the business full time, and worked out of a real garage in Locust Point in Baltimore, Maryland.

The youngest son, Robert "Bob" M. Constantine, joined the business working in the office and moving trucks around the yard.

Around 1948, William E. Constantine Jr. (Buddy) purchased a company with rights of his own, Bond Transfer Company, Inc. They are still in operation today. This gave Elmer and Buddy access to more areas, and helped both businesses grow.

In 1975, William "Elmer" Constantine Sr. retired and moved to Florida, taking a well-deserved vacation. His son Robert became CEO of Liberty Transfer and his son William Jr. became CEO of Bond Transfer.

Liberty ceased operation in 1980 and all efforts turned to expanding Bond Transfer Company, Inc.

William and Robert worked together in the office. They were joined by Robert's sons Douglas L. and Donald S. Constantine, with William's daughter Joyce A. (Constantine) Pinder and son William "Bill" Constantine III working part-time after school and on weekends. The terminal in Edison, New Jersey, is currently operated by Robert's son Timothy.

Prior to 1980 and the Era of Deregulation, Bond Transfer served only a small number of accounts. Since then, Bond has broadened its scope of operation and makes its service available to many more customers. New and old customers still receive the personalized service that William Sr. offered when he first started his business.

Wm. E. Constantine Jr. in 1947 with Federal truck and first shop.

Wm. E. Constantine Sr.'s first office in 1945.

From a one truck, one-man operation the company has grown to include 100 tractors, 325 dry van trailers, six flat beds and over 125 employees.

For over 64 years, Liberty Transfer and Bond Transfer had operated out of the same small neighborhood in Locust Point, Maryland near Fort McHenry. As the business grew larger so did the need for additional space. The business moved three times, all in the Locust Point, where they began.

The second garage they occupied from 1956 to 1979 began as a church

From left to right: Wm. E. Constatine Jr. and Robert M. Constantine.

Above:
Taken at Fort McHenry in Baltimore, MD.

over 100 years ago, and had since been a store, photo studio and garage by the time it was purchased by Liberty and Bond. Sadly, there were no larger quarters to be had, so Bond moved to Anne Arundel County, Maryland. The move came about in 1998, commemorating Bond's 50th anniversary; the company moved from a one and a third acre facility to an 11-acre complex of offices, and a garage with a trailer repair shop with plenty of yard space.

Elmer's dream of having his sons follow him into the trucking business has more than come true. Along with his two sons, five grandchildren and one great-grandson in the business, there are many more great-grandchildren waiting in the wings.

The grandchildren and great-grandson founded a new business of their own in 1997, Bond Logistics, LLC, which serves all 50 states and Canada. With this new business, both Bond Transfer and Bond Logistics are doing very well.

Elmer's family is dedicated to keeping his dream alive and well. They are aware that few businesses ever make it to the third generation. Family and business have grown up together; all involved know that none of them could run the business alone. They are definitely a team, just as they were raised to be. Their forefather, William "Elmer" Constantine Sr. would be proud.

Below:
Left to right front row: William E. Constantine III (son), VP; Joyce Pinder (daughter), secretary and treasurer; Donald Constantine (nephew), VP; and Douglas Constantine (nephew), VP. Back row: William E. Constantine Jr. (president), Timmy Constantine (nephew), VP.

Bryn Mawr School

In 1884, five talented, visionary women embarked on an educational rebellion to create a preparatory school in Baltimore where girls could benefit from the same educational challenges offered to boys of their generation.

Among the school's five founders, M. Carey Thomas, dean and later president of Bryn Mawr College, and Mary Elizabeth Garrett, an astute businesswoman and philanthropist, most clearly left their mark on the character of the school. Bryn Mawr has striven over the last century to do justice to these women's pioneering ideas. Then and now, Bryn Mawr remains committed to providing the educational preparation girls and young women need to lead lives of consequence.

Bryn Mawr opened its doors in 1885 as one of the first, solely college-preparatory schools for girls in the United States. The school was intended to serve as a feeder school for Bryn Mawr College in the suburbs of Philadelphia. For many years, students could not graduate from Bryn Mawr School without first passing the rigorous entrance exam to attend Bryn Mawr College.

For the first five years, the school was housed in a three-story building downtown on Eutaw Street. At the time, only a handful of students attended the school with eight faculty members. The curriculum was daring and liberal for its time, including both modern and classical languages, English, history, math, the latest scientific theories, and a focus on physical education, which was almost unheard of for girls of that generation.

Bryn Mawr School's basketball team. Circa 1908—1909. Courtesy, Edith Hamilton Library Archives, Bryn Mawr School

Indoor classroom scene of Primary II at Cathedral Street. Circa 1924. Courtesy, Edith Hamilton Library Archives, Bryn Mawr School

From its inception, the school was committed not only to developing girls' and young women's intellectual abilities, but also their physical abilities; exercise was an integral part of the educational regimen. When Bryn Mawr moved to a larger space on Cathedral and Preston Streets, the new building featured a well-equipped gym with a swimming pool, a rowing machine, an indoor running track, ropes, and rings. In 1890, Bryn Mawr strengthened its commitment to physical education and athletics when Dr. Kate Campbell Hurd joined the school's staff as the first resident doctor in a private school in the United States. Dr. Hurd also served as the head of the Athletic Department. Today, over 50 percent of students in the Upper School play junior varsity and varsity sports, while all students participate in either interscholastic sports or other activities.

In 1893, Bryn Mawr's founders played a major role in gaining admission for women to The Johns Hopkins University School of Medicine. Approached for a large gift, Mary Elizabeth Garrett promised $100,000 to the Medical School if women were guaranteed admission. The university ultimately agreed to admit women on the same terms as men, and at Mary Garrett's request, to raise the academic standards for admission generally so the university would not risk being judged as academically inferior because of its female medical students.

In 1896, Edith Hamilton, a bright, forward-looking young woman, became the first formally appointed headmistress of Bryn Mawr School. At the time, she was only 29 years old and a recent graduate of the first class of Bryn Mawr College. She led the school for 26 years and infused the rigorous academic program with the humanistic and classic ideals for which she was known. Today, Edith Hamilton is recognized and celebrated as a renowned classicist, educator, and the author of well-known texts on Greek mythology, including *The Greek Way* and *Mythology*.

In 1926, physical education teacher

Bryn Mawr School's field hockey team. Circa 1926. Courtesy, Edith Hamilton Library Archives, Bryn Mawr School

Rosabelle Sinclair created the first girls' lacrosse program in the country at Bryn Mawr. In 1992, Sinclair became the first woman to be inducted into the Lacrosse Hall of Fame for introducing women's lacrosse in the United States.

Bryn Mawr was one of the early independent schools in Baltimore to become integrated. Headmistress Katharine Van Bibber was instrumental in helping Bryn Mawr achieve the historic decision in 1962 to become integrated, thus transforming the school's identity and shaping its future direction as a truly diverse community. In 1988, Bryn Mawr School was selected as one of eight pilot schools for a multicultural assessment sponsored by the National Association of Independent Schools.

Primary recess at Cathedral Street. Early 1900s. Courtesy, Edith Hamilton Library Archives, Bryn Mawr School

The Lower School complex of three buildings was completed in 1971. Marcel Breuer, world-renowned architect and designer of the Whitney Museum in New York and the Paris headquarters of UNESCO, designed the Lower School complex serving grades K/T-5. The late Edith Ferry Hooper, president of Bryn Mawr's Board of Trustees at the time and a lifelong philanthropist to the arts, was responsible for engaging the Bauhaus architect in the project. The buildings, connected by walkways for continuity, are sunk slightly below ground, with walls that jog to give variety in the open classroom light.

In 1977, Bryn Mawr led the way by pioneering the provision of quality day care with the opening of the Bryn Mawr Little School, a year-round, full-day early childhood center. Today, Bryn Mawr Little School, which is located on the school's campus, has a staff of 21 professionals who teach and care for 137 children.

Bryn Mawr School's campus has a number of notable buildings. The school's Edith Hamilton Library was renovated in 1992, and is among the finest pre-college, on-line libraries in the state. In 1992, the Centennial Hall Lobby and Dance Studio were selected from among dozens of projects for top honors from the Baltimore Chapter of the American Institute of Architects. The Dance Studio won a Grand Design Award in 1992. Five years later, the Lower School Science Center also won a Grand Design Award. And, in 1999, the school's Admissions Cottage won a Grand Design Award as well as other prestigious American Institute of Architects' awards, establishing it as a leading model of "green" design and construction. These award winners were all designed by the local architectural firm of Cho, Wilks & Benn (currently Cho Benn Holback + Associates).

In 1998, Bryn Mawr School initiated a bold, new program to support development and integration of a broad spectrum of environmental initiatives across the campus. A central aspect of the initiatives is an integrated sustainability plan involving all aspects of the school: its campus, buildings (both old and new), curriculum, internal constituencies, and the broader community. Bryn Mawr's commitment to the environment over the next century will be guided by a formal Campus Master Plan that will include a plan for the future of the school's buildings and grounds consonant with its vision of providing an excellent education for young women.

The future of Bryn Mawr School, its students and graduates, holds extraordinary promise. While the school continues transforming, anticipating the educational preparation girls and young women will need to thrive in their lives and careers, Bryn Mawr's mission remains constant: to give each girl the ability, confidence, resilience, and courage to choose her own direction in life and then to pursue it.

Today, Bryn Mawr's accomplished faculty, strong college-preparatory curriculum, and exceptional learning environment are keeping the school's founders' ideals alive by helping each girl pursue her dreams and achieve her very best. Strong relationships between teachers and students nurture a passion for excellence and learning in each girl, preparing her to be a confident leader in the new millennium. Courtesy, David W. Harp

J.K. Cabinet, Inc.

On September 12, 1935 James E. Kundratic was born in the small town of Sterling, Pennsylvania. In the late 1940s James' family moved to a rural portion of Baltimore. When the war broke out in 1941, the family moved into the city of Baltimore. James started his first years of grammar school in the city. After grammar school he moved on to a general vocational school, where he studied woodworking. He graduated in June 1952, at the age of 16. After graduation James went to work for a printing company; he was not able to do woodwork yet, as he was not 18. Then in Fall 1953, James went on to work in a three-man cabinet shop, where he still remembers lumber being delivered by horse and wagon from Horstmeier Lumber Company of Baltimore. James continued to work there until September 1955, when he enlisted into the Marine Corps. While in the Marines James had an 18-month tour of duty in Japan, during which he had the honor of being awarded Marine of the Month, of the first Marine air wing. James then returned to the United States in January 1958, and was discharged at Marine Corp Air Station in Cherry Point, North Carolina.

After his discharge James returned to Baltimore and to work for a cabinet shop. In March 1959, while working for the cabinet shop, James started a small woodworking shop in the basement of his home. James continued to work for the cabinet shop during the day; after work he would work in the basement in his own wood shop until the early hours of the morning. In 1963 the company that he was employed with went out of business. Without a full-time job he transformed his basement woodshop into a full-time business, known as J.K Cabinet Co. Along with the name of the new company came a new name for James. People now knew him as J.K.

James Kundratic with store fixtures.

Within four years word of mouth amongst several designers had developed enough of a customer base for J.K. Cabinet Company that it was able to move the shop out of J.K.'s home to a small 1,200 square foot shop in Baltimore City. In only one year J.K. Cabinet Company moved again, this time to a shop 3,000 square feet in size, and added a full-time employee.

The early customers of J.K. Cabinet were mostly custom built-ins and furniture for residential homes. As the business grew it added custom store fixtures to its product line. In 1965 James bought an old cigar manufacturing building in the Fells Point area of Baltimore City, which added a total of 15,000 square feet and a work force of five employees. Overseeing and managing the office was James' wife Marylou Kundratic, who was also raising five sons at the time.

Shortly after moving into this building, J.K. came in contact with an up-and-coming retail company known as Merry-Go-Round. For the next seven years J.K. Cabinet experi-

One of the first commercial pieces produced by J.K.

Finished product store fixtures.

enced much of its growth due to becoming the exclusive fixture manufacturer for the rapidly-expanding Merry-Go-Round Enterprises nationwide retail chain. Other Maryland-based retail chains J.K. Cabinet constructed fixtures for during this time were Tuerkes Leather Goods, Hahn Shoes, and Philipsborne.

In 1972 the business leased 40,000 square feet from the Crown Industrial Park, its present location. In the 28 years since, it has added an additional 80,000 square feet of manufacturing and warehouse space for a total of nearly 120,000 square feet and employs 60 workers at this location.

The machinery that was used in the beginning consisted of basic woodworking tools. Two of the original machines are still owned by J.K. as memorabilia of the early years and still run today, though they are not used. As time went on and the needs of its customers grew, J.K. used more sophisticated machines and introduced computerized equipment.

At one time or another during the past 40 years, all five of J.K. and Marylou's sons have worked at J.K. Cabinet. There are still three sons employed at this date. Due to a serious accident to J.K. in 1991, daily operations and management of the business were taken over by James' son Ken Kundratic. Although James is still involved in running the cabinet shop his capacity has changed to a more limited consultant position.

Along with J.K.'s involvement with J.K. Cabinet he owns an active dairy farm in Pennsylvania. J.K. also organizes a farm show, which displays and demonstrates historical farm machinery. These farm shows are a way to give back to the community, and to give children as well as adults an informative, yet fun look at farming in the early 1800s and 1900s. With the help of his sons, J.K. puts on two or three shows a year; he also puts on shows for other organizations, free of charge. Some of the items used are a team of oxen, horses and mules, and a 1914 Fick steam engine, along with various other tractors and farm equipment.

The future of J.K. Cabinet, Inc. holds promise as the booming economic growth of the country encourages more expansions of retail chains. The company continues to meet the changing demands of the market and continues producing the quality custom work for which it has been known for over 40 years.

James would like to thank his family for all the support given to him over the past 40 years, especially Mary Lou Kundratic and his five sons. J.K. would also like to thank the loyal business people of Baltimore who have encouraged him to produce quality work in Baltimore City.

1971 picture of Marylou Kundratic and their five sons.

Calvert School

Founded in 1896 by the parents of four Baltimore children, Calvert School began its journey as a small German kindergarten, located on the third floor of the home of Elizabeth and Isaac H. Dixon. Today, Calvert School is an independent co-educational elementary school, enrolling approximately 380 students in grades pre-kindergarten through six and over 17,000 students in grades pre-kindergarten through eight in its Home Instruction Department. Though much has changed in the years since those four students climbed the steps to their third floor schoolroom, Calvert has remained true to the educational philosophy and spirit begun over a century ago.

An intellectual interest in preschool or kindergarten was at the forefront of education in 1896 when Henry M. Thomas, Jr., Robert Abel, William T. Dixon, and Robert W. Williams began their schooling in the Dixon's house at 823 Park Avenue in Baltimore. A brainchild of German educator Friederich Froebel, the kindergarten concept emphasized physical, intellectual, and moral development in children, ages three through seven.

1899 photo including the original 4 students from the German Kindergarten on Park Avenue.

Froebel believed that children had distinct periods of readiness for certain stages of learning, and that instruction should be based on these developmental increments in an orderly manner. Most of all, instruction should be presented in such a way as to stimulate the child's imagination and enthusiasm to learn, with the teacher acting as guide. In this regard, Fraulein Schürmann, a graduate of the Froebel Institute in Berlin, was hired as the first teacher for the little kindergarten on Park Avenue. The following year, 1897, this kindergarten became known as the "Boys' and Girls' Primary School" and opened with 15 children in new facilities over Croft and Conlyn's drugstore at 110 West Madison Street. It is interesting to note that these initial classes were taught entirely in German.

In 1899, the Board of Trustees hired Virgil Mores Hillyer as the School's first head master. Hillyer's vision shaped the School's basic program, and his philosophy and methods remain the standard as Calvert enters into its second century. Though only 24 years old, Virgil Hillyer was sure in his direction of the new school, and on March 3, 1900, Hillyer presented to the Board of Trustees a set of 24 "distinctive features" which set out the educational standards he planned to implement. His overriding theory was that an elementary school education should concentrate on the mastery of the fundamentals of reading, writing, spelling, and arithmetic. At the same time he emphasized the importance of each child maturing into a well-informed person solidly grounded in the cultural

Croft and Conlyn's Drug Store becomes the school site in 1897.

Eighth Age (2nd Grade) classroom in 1912.

Calvert's football team in 1938, Classes of 1938-40.

heritage of art, astronomy, history, geography, geology, botany, and poetry. Over the years, a great deal has been said and written about the Calvert School philosophy of teaching and what has often been termed "the Calvert method." While the founders were aware of and interested in the most modern educational theories, they were committed to the value of tradition and classical scholarship; their goal being to combine of the best of each.

In April of 1899, the school was legally incorporated as "Calvert Primary School of Baltimore City." The permanent name, later shortened to Calvert School, was one of the first suggestions made by the new head master. Calvert, the family name for the Lords Baltimore, was deemed an appropriate name for a Maryland school and the colors of the Calvert family, black and gold, were adopted as the school's colors.

By 1901, Calvert enrolled over 100 students and made a necessary move to a larger space at 10 West Chase Street, which consisted of three floors and a roof garden for outdoor activities. Twenty-three years later, in 1924, Calvert School relocated to its present site at 105 Tuscany Road and erected a school building in the shape of an E, appropriately, for Education.

The years since have produced remarkable growth. The Luetkemeyer Planetarium was added in 1979. Its 20-foot dome provides for the projection of 1,100 stars and for the study of the solar system, the constellations, and the universe. In 1983, the school's fifth Head Master, Merrill S. Hall III, was appointed, and within a year the school entered its first capital campaign. In 1986, the Luetkemeyer wing was completed, adding classrooms, a new gym, and a cafeteria. In the past decade, Calvert entered into curriculum reform partnerships with inner-city schools which gained national and international attention. One of the first independent schools in Maryland to implement state-of-the-art technology for educational purposes, Calvert initiated an innovative laptop program for fifth and sixth grade students in 1999. Most recently, Calvert School has announced its plans to establish a new middle school by adding a seventh and eighth grade, to which it will bring the same strengths and traditions it has brought to its lower school for over a hundred years.

First Head Master, Virgil M. Hillyer.

Lunch on the Roof Garden 1903. Also used for Physical Education.

The Chimes, Inc.

The history of The Chimes is the history of thousands of individuals in many different places. In Virginia, Rob lived most of his life in a state training center. In Israel at the age of one, Or was left unable to speak, sit, crawl or stand through complications after surgery for a congenital heart defect. And in Maryland, the unpredictable emotions and inappropriate behavior of 12-year old Michael denied him his dream of attending a public middle school.

With help from the organization known as The Chimes, Rob, Or and Michael broke through the barriers that kept them from achieving their dreams. For over 50 years The Chimes has worked to unlock the human potential of people with mental retardation and other barriers to independent living. This leading not-for-profit agency is based in Baltimore, Maryland and serves the needs of more than 4,500 children, adults and senior citizens in Maryland, Virginia, the District of Columbia, Delaware, Pennsylvania, California and Israel.

The philosophy that guides The Chimes is a simple one, based on the belief that every individual has the right to develop to his or her fullest potential no matter how many barriers stand in the way. Chief Executive Officer Terry Allen Perl puts it another way, "Our job is, first, to provide the expertise, services, and supports that will help people reach their potential; second to promote feelings of personal integrity, dignity, and self worth; and third, to champion the right to make informed choices." He notes that the mission of the organization has remained steadfast, despite an enormous expansion of services in its 53 years. "Although we continue to grow and change to meet the needs of the people we serve, two constants remain: our refusal to accept conventional wisdom about their limitations and our insistence on their right to a full life."

What eventually grew into The Chimes began when founder Frances Bacon and a group of other Baltimore parents started a school for their children who had moderate mental retardation. In 1947 they established the School of The Chimes in space provided by Baltimore's Episcopal Church of the Redeemer. A reminder of the church's generosity lives on in the organization's name. "The Chimes" is the name inspired by the message of hope for the children from the bells of the church on North Charles Street.

Over the past decade, The Chimes has secured a number of large government set-aside contracts for workers with disabilities. These include the provision of custodial services for the Baltimore/Washington International Airport.

For the next 28 years, the school program grew from five children to more than 70 by 1975, the year when special education programs became mandatory in public schools. As the children grew, so did the services and opportunities offered grow. In 1961, The Chimes Activity Center was created for post-school-age adults with mental retardation needing continued training and instruction. Pre-vocational training was also introduced into the curriculum and in the late 1960s, a work training center was opened, the forerunner of Chimes Vocational Services.

"As the first students graduated from the School of the Chimes, it became apparent that some would need ongoing support for their continued growth and to facilitate their integration into the community. We've worked diligently over the years to meet these challenges. Today, The Chimes is so much more than just a school," notes Perl.

Creating residential options for individuals based on their differing needs became the focus of The Chimes during the 1970s. Curtis Hall, the first community-based residential alternative to state institutions in Maryland, opened in 1971. In response to the increasing demand for services, Terry Allen Perl became The Chimes' first executive director in 1973. The first group home was opened in 1974.

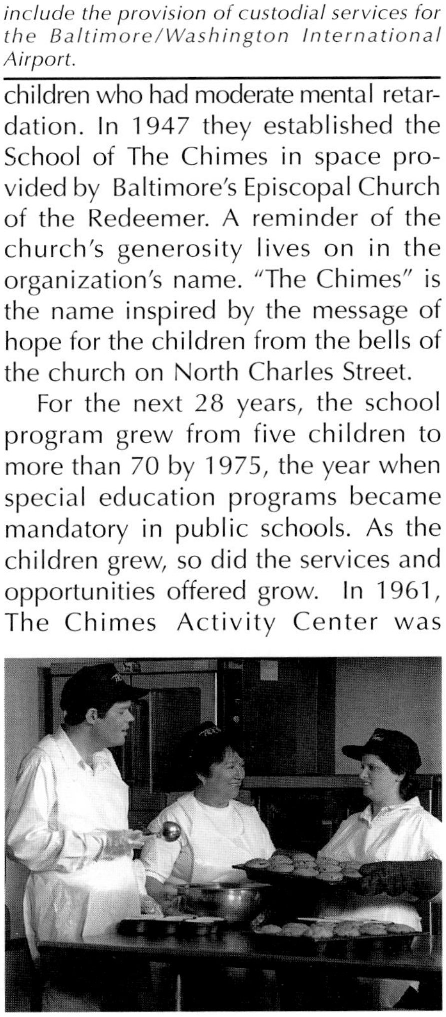

The world of work includes the satisfaction of making something, as these cooks-in-training are learning at the Milford Mill Center in Baltimore. This is where a lot of Chimes careers begin.

Today, Stacy's computer keyboard shows the alphabet. Tomorrow, it might show numbers, hours, or pictures of coins or dollar bills—giving her a foundation of essential lifelong skills and a greater range of choices as she grows up.

The Chimes kept growing throughout the 1980s, now with an emphasis on innovative employment options for adults with disabilities. A 56,000 square-foot facility opened in Baltimore on Milford Mill Road to provide training and employment opportunities. Local businesses began contracting through this center-based work facility, receiving needed services and affording work opportunities to many capable people with disabilities.

The Chimes continued to focus on community integration by expanding residential options as well as developing new employment choices. What had begun as a school in the corner of a church continued to flourish; more group homes and individual apartments with different levels of supervision were added, homes were modified to meet the needs of people with the most severe disabilities; and supported employment was expanded. Eventually the organization that began as a parents' group became the largest provider of community-based residential services for children and adults in Maryland.

Throughout the 1990s, The Chimes continued moving people into residences in the community, with services tailored to accommodate a wide range of age groups and specific needs. Intervals, a licensed medical day-care facility and residential provider serving individuals with complex medical needs merged with The Chimes complementing the broad range of services provided by The Chimes in Maryland.

The Chimes also reached out beyond the local community to establish affiliates in other states and overseas. At the request of the Government of Israel, the affiliate Chimes/Israel was created to operate in Tel Aviv, Herzliya and the Sharon Valley. Chimes/Delaware was established at the request of the State to provide residential and vocational programs for adults with autism, Prader-Willi syndrome, and other specials needs. WORK, Incorporated in California merged with The Chimes and offers vocational training, community employment opportunities, center-based work, and residential services and supports. Chimes/District of Columbia was created to secure and oversee government contracts to employ an expanded group of people with disabilities. Nearly 1,000 people with disabilities have jobs in the community through this Chimes affiliate. Among the many work sites is the Baltimore/Washington International Airport where custodial services are provided 24 hours a day, seven days a week, the Social Security Headquarters, and the Library of Congress.

In 2000, Holcomb Behavioral Health Systems, a provider of comprehensive services for adults with mental illness, drug and alcohol addiction in Pennsylvania and Delaware, joined The Chimes family of services marking Chimes entry into the mental health field, an excellent fit with the organization's other programs.

With the recent development of a new five-year strategic plan, The Chimes board of directors continues to guide the organization's growth in four areas: developing the board of directors to become even more effective, to attract influential members, to set priorities that are clear and to motivate members to fulfill their roles and responsibilities, developing business opportunities to broaden the organization's ability to meet the wider needs of more populations without lowering its excellent standards of service, developing a work environment that will attract and retain staff who share the values of The Chimes, and increasing public awareness of the organization's international leadership reputation.

For thousands of people with disabilities and barriers to independent living, The Chimes continues to help each individual surmount those barriers in search of his or her fullest potential. Through the intervention of The Chimes, Rob now lives in the community in a five-person group home and works in the community. Through The Chimes early childhood program for intensive sensory training and therapy, Or walks, talks and brightens all the lives around her with her smile. And as for Michael, after three years of structured programs in The Chimes School, he fulfilled his dream of entering public school, and has since joined ROTC.

In over 30 locations, through its board of directors, staff, corporate and community volunteers, and the financial support of countless donors, The Chimes continues to create choice and develop the broad spectrum of alternatives that allows individuals with barriers to independent living to realize their dreams.

The Chimes is usually a successful matchmaker. Good times, like the birthday party for one of the residents of Margolis House, are typical.

Colliers Pinkard

In the early 1920s, Walter Clyde Pinkard began his real estate career selling farmland in Hartford County for the Caughy-Hearn firm. In 1922, he opened W.C. Pinkard & Co., a small real estate office in Baltimore concentrating on rural and residential real estate. The first office was located at 12 East Lexington Street with the phone number Plaza 2-4285, an exchange that has survived as the company's main telephone number for over 78 years. Mr. Pinkard's concentration was in selling and appraising homes and apartments in the city and the neighborhoods of Guilford and Roland Park as well as in the farmland surrounding Baltimore. Revenue during these early years averaged $1,200 a month and a typical home sold between $10,000 and $20,000 with a commission to W.C. Pinkard equal to 5 percent of the transaction value.

During the difficult depression years, Pinkard served as agent for the Penn Mutual Life Insurance Co. and was responsible for running "Kernan's $1,000,000 Enterprise"—the Maryland Theater, the Auditorium Theater and Kernan's Hotel. His services included bringing national acts, like Ethel Barrymore, to his stage. He eventually negotiated the sale of these properties, which had fallen victim to the demise of vaudeville. The Auditorium is now the Mayfair and the Congress Hotel was once part of the Kernan theatrical empire.

Walter C. Pinkard & Co. was instrumental in the formation of the Governmental Efficiency and Economic Commission, which flourished under Baltimore's Mayor Jackson. He also served as president of the Real Estate Board of Baltimore (now the Greater Baltimore Board of Realtors) in 1940 and 1941 and was instrumental in originating the first multiple-listing service in the Baltimore area.

A graduate of Princeton, Walter Devier Pinkard joined his father's firm in 1945 after his discharge with the rank of major in the U.S. Army's field artillery. Walter D. Pinkard quickly became active in the Baltimore business community, serving the Junior Association of Commerce, the Mortgage Bankers Association, and the Citizen's Planning and Housing Association. In 1946, he was named a member of the board of directors of the Real Estate Board of Baltimore. He was regional chapter president and a national director of the Society of Industrial Realtors and was chairman of the board and chief executive officer of W.C. Pinkard. & Co. until 1975.

With the Baltimore office under the capable management of his son, who

Walter Clyde Pinkard founded W.C. Pinkard & Co. in 1922, specializing in the selling and appraising of rural and reesidential real estate in the city and the neighborhoods of Guilford and Roland Park, as well as in the farmlands surrounding Baltimore.

Wally Pinkard, president since 1982, was forward thinking from the start, resulting in consistent growth and diversification for the firm.

was instrumental in focusing the firm's activities on the areas of commercial and industrial real estate, Walter C. Pinkard was able to pursue his greatest interest, rural real estate. He opened a branch office in Easton, Maryland, which was active during the 1950s and 1960s.

In the 1940s, W.C. Pinkard & Co. moved its offices to Redwood Street, the majority of which were in the First National Bank Building, keeping the Plaza 2-4285 phone number. In the mid-'60s, the firm broke into the office market downtown with the leasing assignment for its own building. Not long thereafter, Walter D. Pinkard persuaded the Campbell family to construct the first speculative office buildings in Towson, the Alex Brown and the Mercantile Buildings, both leased by Pinkard. Pinkard convinced his long time friend, Henry Knott, to let him develop the Baltimore Washington Industrial Park, which became the first of many successful industrial developments for the Knott family.

In 1958, Philip C. Iglehart joined the company and played a major role in its evolution into one of the state's leading commercial and industrial realty concerns. Mr. Iglehart was elected president of the company in 1975 and became the first non-family stockholder in the firm's history.

1975 marked the year that Walter D. Pinkard, Jr. (Wally) joined the family firm after studying at Harvard Business School and Yale. Within two years of Pinkard's arrival the company was bolstered by the hiring of three individuals who would go on to become early principals in the firm. Two of those individuals, Dennis P. Malone and David R. Frederick, remain with the firm today.

With significant growth of commercial development in the early 1980s that witnessed the delivery of over two million square feet of office space in the Inner Harbor alone, the competitive landscape for real estate in Baltimore had changed. There was an explosion in the number of licensed commercial real estate brokers in Baltimore and branch offices of national real estate companies began appearing in the Baltimore marketplace. Margins were squeezed and investment bankers and accounting firms were competing for a slice of the real estate advisory services pie.

In 1982, Wally Pinkard was elected president of the firm. He was forward thinking from the start, resulting in consistent growth and diversification for the firm. Within his first year as president, the firm launched the appraisal, consulting and investment sales departments and, for the first time, opened up ownership of the firm to its key professionals resulting in over 50 percent of the firm's ownership vested in people outside of the Pinkard

Walter D. Pinkard Sr. was chairman of the board and chief executive officer of W.C. Pinkard and Co. until 1975.

family. The firm continued its growth with the expansion of its market research group and the development of in-house databases long before such became a commodity item. Pinkard was the first real estate services firm in the mid-Atlantic to put a computer on everyone's desk. Pinkard believed in committing the capital necessary to stay on the leading edge of the competition. In 1983, the Columbia office was opened because the firm saw the corridor between Baltimore and Washington, D.C. as a major growth area. While it took over five years for that office to become profitable, it allowed Pinkard to secure an early foothold in what has proven to be one of the hottest growth areas in the mid-Atlantic. An office in Towson, MD was opened to service the northern suburbs during this time frame.

In 1984, Wally Pinkard took the firm to a new level by joining Colliers International Property Consultants, a corporation of independently-owned commercial real estate firms committed to delivering superior real estate services. Colliers is one of the world's leading providers of real estate advisory and transactional services with over 250 offices in 52 countries. In 1999, the collective worldwide revenue of Colliers was more than $870 million. By 1994, W.C. Pinkard & Co. had changed its trading name to Colliers Pinkard and the firm's principals began playing leadership roles within the global Colliers organization. The affiliation with Colliers International has proved to be an important business decision for the firm, providing the capability to execute assignments for clients globally. A deliberate strategy to develop corporate services capabilities has allowed for the growth of service work outside of Baltimore where in an average year, Pinkard professionals handle between 150 and 200 assignments outside the local market.

In 1987, Gregory C. Pinkard, one of the four sons of Walter D. Pinkard Sr., joined the firm as downtown operations manager in the property management department and joined the approximately 20 principals in the firm. The property management department, which he oversees, is charged with servicing in excess of seven million square feet of real estate for clients that include the Bank of America, Northrop Grumman, Penn Mutual and LaSalle Advisors.

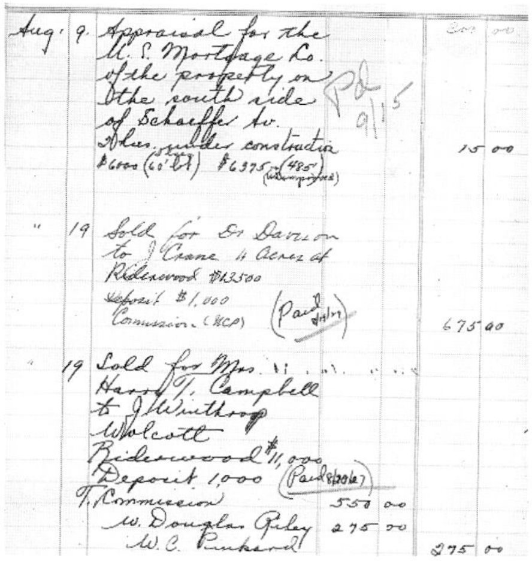

A general ledger page from 1927. Homes sales averaged $10,000 to $12,000 and average monthly sales revenue to W.C. Pinkard and Co. was $1,200 based on a 5% commission fee.

During the last decade of the 20th century, the firm has acted increasingly like a real estate-based management consulting firm. Colliers Pinkard has concentrated on developing advisory relationship business with institutions, organizations and corporations that need ongoing, real estate problem-solving expertise. The firm views its approach as distinctly different from the transaction-driven brokerage business of many real estate companies and one that requires exceptional leadership talent. One example of this leadership can be seen in Jamie Smith, who headed the growth of the Columbia office as well as the expansion of services outside of the immediate geographic area. In a few instances, outside leadership has been recruited to the firm, as happened in 1994, when Colliers Pinkard hired David M. Gillece to bolster consulting activities and the corporate services department, which he now directs.

In a strategic move to provide more growth for the firm and under the leadership of principal David R. Frederick, Colliers Pinkard purchased the Colliers firm in Charlotte, NC to gain a foothold in this important financial center. Colliers Pinkard also bought a leasing and management company in Charlotte with accounts throughout North and South Carolina and in Norfolk, VA. In December 1999, Colliers Pinkard opened an office in the rapidly-growing high-tech hub of Raleigh, NC. Both Charlotte and Raleigh represent opportunities that will be an important part of the firm's growth strategy. At the close of the century, the firm's annual transactional business totaled over $700 million, a far cry from its $20 million level 25 years ago.

Like his father and his grandfather before him, Walter D. Pinkard Jr. is extremely involved in civic organizations. At the turn of the century he is chairman of the board of the Baltimore Community Foundation; member of the executive committee of the board of trustees of Johns Hopkins University; member of the board of trustees for Johns Hopkins Medicine; chairman of the National Council for Johns Hopkins Nursing; co-chairman of Robert Wood Johnson Foundation's Safe & Sound program board; vice chairman and treasurer of the Greater Baltimore Alliance; member of the board of directors of the France Merrick Foundations; board member of the Maryland Business Roundtable for Education; trustee of Gilman School; member of the Downtown Management District Authority; and a trustee for the Leonard and Helen R. Stulman Charitable Foundation, Inc.

Currently headquartered at 100 Light Street, and still with the same telephone number it has had since 1922, Colliers Pinkard's professionals bring a unique perspective to problem solving, calling upon diversity of expertise from consulting to sales, from valuation to management. Corporations such as T. Rowe Price, Deutsche Banc Alex. Brown, Legg Mason, Black & Decker, IBM, and Procter & Gamble have all benefited from the strong foundation and presence of Colliers Pinkard in the Baltimore community and beyond.

Kaestner Company

The KAESTNER COMPANY chronicle begins with Ernest August Kaestner's birth in the city of Baltimore in 1858. Although little is known of his childhood, the entrepreneurial fires were kindled early. By the age of 22, he had established E.A. KAESTNER, "tinner" at 70 N. High Street. Over the next 10 years, Ernest amassed property at the same rate as he did businesses. He appears in the 1880—1890 City Directory, often at multiple locations, as a roofer, a tinner, a manufacturer of stoves and maker of milk cans.

1891 proved an eventful year for this growing company. Ernest was applying his skills as a tinner to design and make tin utensils for the fledgling milk plants and dairy farmers. His talents were directed to the transportation of milk from farm to city, and the United States patent he was granted that year was for a latching device to prevent spillage as the milk was hauled to the dairy by horse and wagon. It still graces the walls of the present KAESTNER COMPANY. That year also found the company at its new location, 516 N. Calvert Street. Next to City Dairy and across from the Calvert Street station of the "Ma & Pa" railroad proved an ideal site for expansion and growth. Farmers would come to town and stop in to place orders and pick up supplies. There the Company remained and grew for the next 58 years, through the death of its founder, the Great Baltimore Fire, the Great Depression, and two World Wars.

Ernest died on May 6, 1897, leaving the future of the business in the hands of his wife Louisa and his 14-year-old son J. George Kaestner. All five sons would join the business by 1911. Under George's leadership, which continued until his death in 1943, the company expanded and doubled their manufacturing area. The payroll ledger from May 12, 1916 details 23 employees working six-nine hour days per week for a munificent total payroll of $271.40. As the younger brothers came of age, they joined the company—Ernest, Robert, Benjamin and Albert each played an important role in production, engineering and office management.

J. George Kaestner (hand on hip) at Farmers Week Show in Baltimore November 28, 1910.

As the years tumbled into decades, once again the firm metamorphosed, this time into E.A. KAESTNER CO., Stainless Steel Fabricators. The third male generation of Kaestners, Benjamin Jr., John, and Albert Jr., began joining the firm after the Second World War. The fire of 1949, which destroyed the Calvert Street location, encouraged a move to the outskirts of the city into a large, freestanding building on Pulaski Highway.

No business can survive a century without reinventing itself periodically. Once again, in 1995, Albert C. Kaestner Jr., then the sole owner of the firm, joined in partnership with Donald S. Good, a valued, long-time employee, to share the responsibility of changing the company's direction. Today KAESTNER COMPANY supplies a broad customer base comprised of food, dairy, pharmaceutical, beverage, and cosmetic industries with complete sanitary, stainless steel processing systems. The partnership is continuing to concentrate on retaining the good business values and practices of the past, augmented by the best technology of the future, to ensure that this strong, viable company continues into the next century.

The founder Ernest August Kaestner's sons, (left to right): Albert, Robert, Ernest, George, and Benjamin.

Comcast Cablevision

As Baltimore County continues to grow in the new century and advance in the areas of technology and education, Comcast Cable will grow with it and continue as the region's largest provider of broadband cable communications networks and content. Comcast has been a mainstay in Baltimore County since 1984, and the company's Baltimore County cable system serves as a model for telecommunications systems across the United States.

Comcast Corporation is based in Philadelphia, Pennsylvania, and is the third largest cable operator in the United States, providing service in 26 states and 1,020 communities. The company's consolidated and affiliated cable operations will serve nearly 8.2 million customers, and its annual revenue as of 1998 is $5.1 billion. Comcast has come a long way from the company's start with a small cable system serving 1,200 homes in Tupelo, Mississippi, in 1963.

Comcast came to Baltimore County in 1984 after the purchase of Cal Tech, which at that time was the cable service provider in the County. The system quickly grew and flourished under the Comcast name and today there are more than 300,000 Comcast customers in the Baltimore Metropolitan Area. Comcast has grown from offering simple, analog cable service to providing its customers with the latest technological advancements available on the market. The 1990s have seen Comcast begin offering customers the opportunity to access the Internet via cable modems and watch TV in a new way through the use of fiber optic technology.

"The Comcast credo states that we will be the company to look to first for the communications products and services that connect people to what's important in their lives," said Doug Sansom, vice president and general manager of Comcast's Baltimore Metropolitan Area Systems. "As technology develops and new advancements enable us to offer premium services to customers, we will be the company to put these products on the market so that Comcast customers in Baltimore County always have the most state-of-the-art telecommunications services at their finger tips."

Comcast Cable's Baltimore metropolitan area headquarters located at 8031 Corporate Drive in White Marsh, Maryland, in Baltimore County.

In December 1995, Comcast selected Baltimore County as the first market in the nation to unveil its Comcast @Home ultra high-speed Internet service. This breakthrough service uses hybrid-fiber coaxial cable infrastructure, a cable modem and the use of the @Home network's high-speed national backbone. This premium network and technology allows Comcast to offer unparalleled speed to the users of its Internet service.

Cable modems are able to provide lightning-fast digital access to the Internet that facilitate downloading information over 100 times faster than a traditional dial-up modem. These faster speeds allow Comcast @Home customers to more thoroughly enjoy multimedia content, which includes real-time video, audio clips and 3-D virtual reality images over the Internet. Comcast also provides an Internet guide that features a menu of local community content in addition to the vast Internet content already available. Local content in Baltimore County can be found on the World Wide Web at www.inbaltimore.com.

Comcast also uses its Web content capabilities to provide children with educational sites on the Internet. Comcast created and currently manages a site called OnlineSchoolyard.com, an award-winning K-12 Web site featuring links to over 500 of the best education sites on the Internet for students and educators. The site was launched in 1997 and is complete with graphics, animation, video and audio designed specially for young students.

"There is so much content available on the Internet that it is very difficult for parents and young students to determine whether a site is giving factual information that could be used in a report or homework assignment,"

Doug Sansom, VP and GM of Comcast's Baltimore metropolitan area systems, reviews data at the company's head end in White Marsh, Maryland.

Two Comcast employees monitor Comcast service through the use of advanced computer technology.

said Sansom. "The OnlineSchoolyard.com site provides links to numerous educational resources including homework help and content assistance. It really takes the uncertainty out of using the World Wide Web as a research tool."

Comcast made perhaps its most significant technological advancement in Baltimore County in July 1998 when the company launched Comcast Digital Cable. Baltimore County was one of the first jurisdictions in the United States that received Comcast Digital Cable. This state-of-the-art service offers customers up to 200 channels of programming choices with a crystal clear digital picture and CD quality sound. Comcast Digital Cable provides customers with premium movie channels including multiple screens of HBO, Cinemax, Showtime and other great channels.

Comcast Digital Cable's on-screen interactive program guide (IPG) allows users to search for shows by time, title, channel, category or alphabetically to more easily find programming. In addition, the IPG also provides parental lockouts for more mature programming and offers reminders of programming start times for viewers. Comcast Digital service does not require a special television for digital reception or a lengthy installation process.

One trait of Comcast Corporation is its effort to play a large role in the communities that it serves, and Baltimore County is no different. Comcast was the largest corporate philanthropist in the Baltimore metropolitan area in 1999 according to the Baltimore Business Journal. Comcast contributed over $8.5 million to various non-profit, educational, civic and charitable organizations in the area. Comcast will continue building great corporate partnerships into the next decade with organizations such as the Cystic Fibrosis Foundation, March of Dimes and Towson University, to name just a few.

A Comcast systems engineer works to ensure the quality of the Comcast Cable systems' more than 3,700 miles of fiber that bring the finest in telecommunications services to Baltimore County residents.

Education has always been at the forefront of Comcast's philanthropic efforts in Baltimore County, and many of the company's most-acclaimed programs have enhanced education. In 1992, Comcast launched its Student Achievement Awards in Baltimore County, awarding a $1,000 scholarship to a student in every Baltimore County public high school each year. Comcast has contributed over $200,000 to this program in schools across Maryland since its inception in 1992. The Comcast Student Achievement Awards Program has helped over 200 students in Baltimore County alone manage the rising cost of a college education.

Although Comcast has proved to be a strong community advocate in a multitude of areas, its greatest charitable program might be the Comcast "High Speed Education Connection." This program resulted in Comcast wiring every school in Baltimore County with the Comcast @Home ultra high-speed Internet service at no cost to the schools. This project resulted in over 160 schools in Baltimore County being wired for the Comcast @Home service at a cost of millions of dollars to the company.

A Comcast technician monitors the cable system through the company's head end at its Baltimore metropolitan area headquarters.

"No one can put a price on educating our children and playing an active role in the community," said Sansom. "Comcast will continue being a strong corporate partner to the citizens of Baltimore County, and students will still be able to look to us first for the educational resources that will give them an added advantage in the computer-driven economy and eliminate the Digital Divide in Baltimore County."

The Community College of Baltimore County

"It feels like home," said a 49-year-old working mom and member of The Community College of Baltimore County (CCBC) Class of 2000. That sentiment has kept students of all ages, backgrounds and ambitions returning to CCBC since the college first opened its doors in 1957 in Catonsville and Essex, and in 1971 in Dundalk.

Although much has changed since the former tri-college system began educating students more than 40 years ago, CCBC still prides itself on educating all people interested in advancing themselves. CCBC, restructured through state legislation on October 1, 1998 as a single college, multi-campus institution, has a rich history that embraces change, celebrates student success and parallels the county's own growth.

This foundation has positioned the college prominently in the new millennium as the area's number one provider of undergraduate education and workforce training. In fact, CCBC now enrolls more than half of all county residents attending undergraduate college. Its Division of Continuing Education and Economic Development is a leading partner for business and industry, serving over 225 companies annually with customized employee development training. This leadership recently earned the college international recognition by the League for Innovation in the Community College as one of only 12 Vanguard Learning Colleges for its outstanding record of achievement in learning-centered education, and the Baltimore Business Journal's top ranking in its *Book of Lists 2000* as the number one provider of technology training.

Under the leadership of Chancellor Irving Pressley McPhail, CCBC has re-invented its mission to meet the challenges and opportunities of the 21st century. The college is leading a learning college revolution which places learning first and provides relevant experiences for learners any place, any time, and any way. CCBC students go beyond the traditional place-bound, time-bound, method-bound classroom with courses offered online, on television, in distance learning labs, through weekend college and at convenient neighborhood extension centers. In short, CCBC delivers an innovative learning environment to its students.

"When CCBC began its journey toward becoming the nation's premier, learning-centered, single college, multi-campus public college in 1998, we recognized that education had changed and it was essential to redefine how we think of higher education," said Dr. McPhail.

One of the most obvious change agents is technology. Technology has not only restructured how we work and how we play; it is rapidly changing how we learn. Responsive to this techno-surge, CCBC has built a powerhouse of technology to expand learning options.

Faculty train themselves in electronic instruction strategies through innovative programs such as the Virtual Academy. As a result, the college is able to engage and motivate a new generation of "visual" learners who have grown up with MTV and the Internet. Aviation management students on the Catonsville Campus experience all axes of flight using the only flight simulator of its kind at a Maryland community college and the only one in the Baltimore-metropolitan area that can simulate 12 different airplane profiles. CCBC Essex veterinary technology students see and talk with students in the classroom at Carroll Community College via distance learning. Cadets at the Dundalk Campus, which houses the Baltimore County Police Academy, use video technology to role-play situations they may encounter on patrol. Each year, more than 100 recruits enjoy such specialized training as CCBC students.

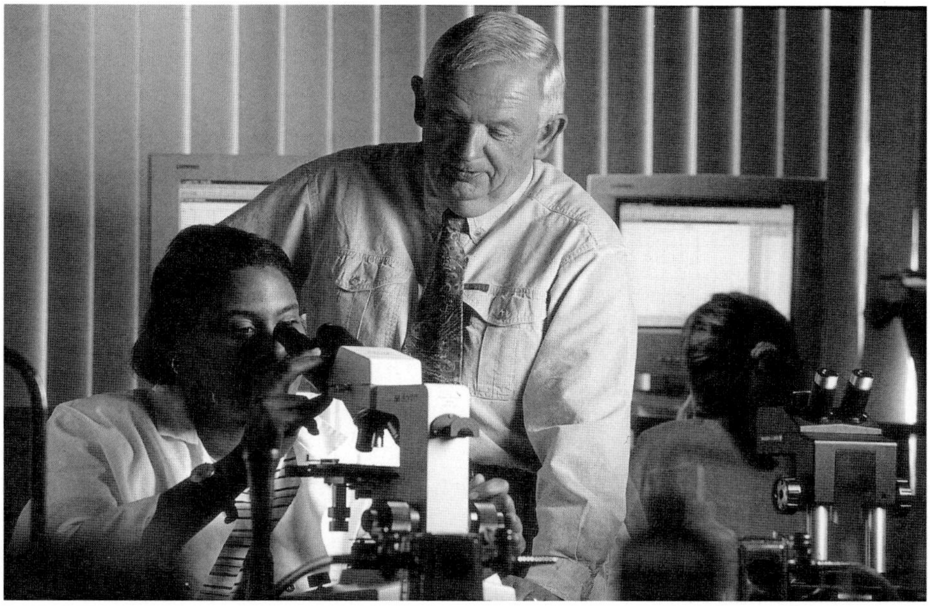

CCBC makes optimal use of technology to enhance student learning in over 60 degree options.

While making optimal use of technology in the classroom, CCBC has responded to emerging technologies and changes in the local economy by introducing such career programs as biotechnology and Internet and multimedia technology. Located in an area that is ranked among the nation's leading health care and manufacturing industries, the college is also expanding its corporate and four-year college and university connections. Surgical tech program graduates are sponsored by The Johns Hopkins Medical Institutions and St. Joseph's Hospital. Bethlehem Steel workers prepare for production start-up of the company's steel mill facility at the college's nearby Dundalk Campus. Dislocated and

The 19th century mansion of the Knapp family estate is the center of CCBC's scenic Catonsville campus.

current workers train for high-tech jobs in computer-aided design and computer automated manufacturing through CCBC's $1 million grant-funded CAD/CAM 2000 project. The project is a collaboration with local manufacturers and several Baltimore County agencies designed to attract and retain a skilled workforce. It is also worth noting that CCBC's Occupational Training Center successfully places some 82 percent of all students who enter the program in career-track positions annually, from geriatric nursing assistants to specialties in computer systems technology.

CCBC boasts a comprehensive network of learning centers, conveniently located throughout Baltimore County. Its three main campuses, Catonsville, Dundalk and Essex, provide a vital educational, economic and cultural resource to the local communities which they serve.

The Catonsville Campus, located in southwest suburban Baltimore on a 130-acre historic estate, features the picturesque Hilton Mansion, dating back to the 1800s, and a planetarium which welcomes thousands of visitors each year. The Dundalk Campus is known for its internationally-recognized theater and impressive art gallery exhibits. Its popular horticulture program also attracts landscape professionals and gardening enthusiasts alike. The Essex Campus is noted for its allied health programs and dance department performances. Students complete clinical training within walking distance at adjacent Franklin Square Hospital.

In addition to the main campuses, the college's two largest extension centers in Owings Mills and Hunt Valley serve as higher education hubs for the booming population in the north and northwest county corridor. These full-service centers, which offer credit, continuing education and corporate contract courses, are located in the major areas of expansion in Baltimore County's Year 2000 development plan. A growing population of Russian immigrants are also enrolled in the English for Speakers of Other Languages (ESOL) program at CCBC Owings Mills.

With its strong community ties firmly established, CCBC will continue building upon the unique successes of its diverse students. As yet another returning adult student observed, "CCBC embraces everyone, yet revolves around the individual."

It is this student-centered focus, responsive to the emerging demands of the 21st century, that has made CCBC Baltimore's leading choice in learning options.

Davis Instruments

While Davis Instruments dates its history in Baltimore back to 1912, the leading manufacturer, distributor and calibrator of test, measurement, control and calibration instruments originated more than 150 years earlier in Derby, England.

In 1756, John Davis founded a business to make instruments used in coal mining. These included anemometers, a meteorological tool that measures air velocity and can be used to detect potentially dangerous changes in air flow below ground. To this day, Davis Anemometers are used to measure the movement of air in every coal mine in the United States.

In 1779, John's nephew Gabriel Davis succeeded him as head of the company. Under his leadership, Davis of Derby added new products, manufacturing optical, surveying and mathematical instruments, as well as additional meteorological instruments such as manometers (for measuring air pressure) and hygrometers (for humidity). Davis Instruments still makes weather-related instruments.

Gabriel was succeeded by his brother Henry, and Henry by his sons Edward and Herbert.

Herbert had his eyes on America. He moved to Baltimore and, in 1912, established a branch office selling the products made in England. In 1928 he broke away, incorporating his own independent firm as Davis Instruments of Baltimore, Maryland, Inc. Davis Instruments manufactured then, and now, many of the same products as Davis of Derby. Davis of Derby, however, is no longer in the instrumentation business.

During the 1940s, Davis Instruments joined in the war effort, manufacturing ammunition cases.

The company remained in the Davis family until 1971, when after the death of Alfred Davis, Martha Davis sold it for $91,000 to Maurice Rudow and Warren Klawans. They continued to make the world famous anemometer, and revenues grew to $850,000 a year.

In 1985, Lee Rudow took over the firm's day-to-day operations. His vision was to diversify the product offering. Capitalizing on Davis' centuries-long reputation for quality, he embarked into distribution, specializing in test, measurement and control products.

His first catalog was 20 pages long and Davis supported it with an inside sales team that fielded calls from around the country.

By 1988, The Davis Catalog of Test, Measurement and Control Instruments had over 350 pages and was well on its way to being recognized as the comprehensive source for instrumentation. Lee Rudow became president of Davis Instruments and, as that decade ended, the staff totaled more than 50 and annual sales reached $10 million. Operations moved to Seton Business Park in northwest Baltimore.

Over the next decade, most American manufacturers adopted Davis *Instruments' Sourcebook* as the place to fill their instrument needs. With its reputation as a one-stop source for industrial instrumentation, the publication became Davis' primary marketing tool. The company added sales operations in Ohio, North Carolina, New Jersey and Virginia, and distributors in more than 22 countries, including Korea, Indonesia, Singapore, Hong Kong, Thailand, Australia, New Zealand, Brazil, Mexico, Chile, Peru, and Argentina.

Founder John Davis in Derb, England, 1756.

By the mid-'90s, company sales hit $30 million, and the company again diversified. This time, it added calibration and asset management services, with its goal to provide the highest quality precision calibrations to the industrial marketplace. Davis Calibration Laboratory earned ISO 9002 certification, and in 1998 began marketing its capabilities to the Fortune 500. To supplement its Baltimore laboratory, Davis launched a fleet of mobile calibration vehicles, serving companies in almost every state on their sites. By the end of the decade, it occupied a 35,000-square-foot building in Seton Business Park and was doing business with nearly every company on *Fortune* magazine's list.

Davis Instruments workshop in 1893.

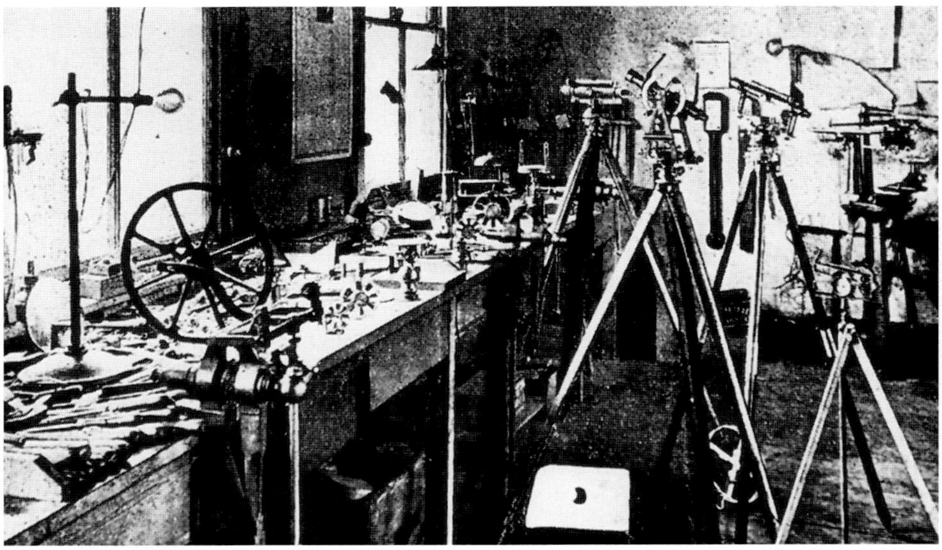

World class calibration services performed in state-of-the-art Davis Calibration Laboratory.

Also in 1998, Davis Instruments stepped into e-commerce. Its Web site, davisontheweb.com, features thousands of items with secure on-line ordering.

In 1999, JPB Enterprises, a private investment holding company based in Columbia, Maryland, purchased Davis Instruments.

JPBE is owned and run by former W.R. Grace president and CEO J.P. Bolduc. Its principal activities include acquiring and operating middle-market manufacturing companies; acquiring and developing real estate properties; and investing seed and expansion capital for start-up or high-growth companies.

"In Davis, we have found a high-growth company with superior management and market position," Bolduc said at the time of the acquisition. "It has experienced tremendous organic growth in recent years in both its distribution and calibration businesses that, we believe, will serve as an excellent platform to grow, expand and acquire strategically."

Rudow said the resources provided by JPBE, both financial and professional, would "allow us to aggressively establish ourselves as the dominant player in the instrumentation sales and service market."

Going into 2000, the Davis Sourcebook's 1,100 pages offered more than 25,000 products from over 400 premiere manufacturers, including Davis itself. The company sold to more than 60,000 customers in over 80 countries.

As 2000 progressed, Davis Instruments continued to add services and software for the new millennium. Following are additional accomplishments:

- It achieved A2LA certification, the industry's highest quality standard.
- It developed a powerful program for tracking and storing customer data. Registered as DATA (Davis Asset Tracking Advantage), the software offers the ability to search, view and print certification documents. It also allows customers to track the status of their assets as Davis Calibration processes them.
- It opened a new X-ray Calibration Laboratory in Baltimore.
- Other new capabilities including microware, fiberoptics, and high-precision pressure calibrations. Davis Calibration is one of only three laboratories in the United States that can calibrate pressure to 40,000 pounds per square inch.

Looking forward, Davis Industries plans to consolidate the fragmented calibration service industry. It will partner with several Fortune 500 companies to offer its asset management and procurement services, while promoting its unique and highly-skilled services.

The company's philosophy is to deliver more than is expected every day, differentiating itself by rewarding achievement and encouraging autonomy at every level.

Rudow attributes Davis' success to its ability to adapt to the ever-changing needs of the marketplace: The customer provides the need; Davis Instruments provides the total solution.

"We focus on the things that differentiate us from the rest of the market," he says. "We go the extra mile, and embrace change as a means of survival. We have a great team of leaders that moves the hearts of everyone within the organization, creating the future growth platforms and energizing the staff to its greatest potential.

"Since we expanded into calibration and service, we've opened nearly 1,000 accounts in these areas. Our record there is the source of our greatest pride. In an industry that turns over an average of 30 percent of its acc-ounts annually, we haven't lost a single customer."

Year 2000 Leadership: Seated-Mitchell Paige, controller; Lee Rudow, president/CEO; Michele Boeri, director of human resources. Standing-Jay Clark, vice president business development; Cliff Ambrose, director calibration services; Eric Weiner, vice president sales, marketing and information technologies.

Euler American Credit Indemnity Company

What happens when a company's customer can't pay for the product it received? The company located at 100 East Pratt Street has been answering that question for business customers for 107 years. By providing business credit insurance on domestic and export accounts receivables, EULER American Credit Indemnity Company (formerly American Credit Indemnity), guarantees payment on those unpaid accounts.

Founded in New Orleans, Louisiana in 1893, EULER ACI is North America's oldest and largest credit insurer. The company, which moved its headquarters to Baltimore in 1940, has weathered major economic fluctuations, recessions, the Great Depression, two World Wars, changes in regulatory and bankruptcy laws, and advances in technology, to continue providing protection against credit losses to businesses.

During the 1830s, William Haskin of New York was an early proponent of credit insurance, but it wasn't until 1862 that the concept of business credit insurance was finally actualized, when the London Guarantee and Accident Company, Ltd. began writing credit insurance in the British Isles. That same company opened a department in the United States in 1892. One year later the American Credit Indemnity Company of New York was organized, an outgrowth of the earlier ACI of New Orleans (headquartered in St. Louis, Missouri).

The economic panic of 1893-95 was a risky time for the fledgling industry and credit insurance losses paid out exceeded premiums written during the panic. However, several young companies survived that panic, along with the silver-campaign depression of 1896-97. "Through the efforts of a few foresighted and determined persons, the writing of credit insurance was not abandoned, although the field faced one of its blackest eras," recalls former ACI executive vice-president J.L. McCauley.

As the United States entered a new phase of rapidly expanding businesses, new inventions and increased production at the turn of the century, deferred payment credit began to grow in volume. ACI introduced a loss-prevention service in 1913, permitting policyholders to draw drafts on debtors. Policyholders sent the drafts to the company, which in turn presented them to the banks for collection. This effective practice was soon followed by the establishment of ACI's solid service department.

Euler ACI's headquarters in Baltimore. Photo by Amy Jones

ACI endured the severe economic climate brought about by the stock market crash of 1929, but times were tough. Claims adjusters were required to call in before writing a loss payment draft to ascertain whether sufficient premium dollars had been received and deposited that day to cover the loss payments. In 1930, ACI wrote $2,500,000 in

gross premiums. As the economic depression deepened, the volume continued to drop. Recovery did not begin until 1940, and the premium volume in that year was a mere $1,800,000.

ACI's major expansion and growth occurred after June 30, 1936, when Commercial Credit Company of Baltimore acquired 49,965 shares of the outstanding 50,000 shares. Commercial Credit Company was founded by A.E. Duncan, an ACI agent from Louisville, Kentucky who transferred to Baltimore sometime around 1908. He left ACI in 1912, and with three other entrepreneurs, founded Commercial Credit Company.

Under its new ownership the company grew steadily during the next three decades, opening new territories throughout the United States and Canada. By the early 1950s, ACI had 155 agents and managers in approximately 23 departments in North America. For many decades agents received a monthly "draw" chargeable against future commissions. It was not unusual for a new agent to take three to five years of production commissions to work the debit balance down to zero.

In the early 1940s, a $150-month draw was typical and a top producer with an annual volume of $100,000 was considered quite successful. When an agent secured a new policy with a premium of $10,000, the agent received a special invitation to bring the new policyholder to Baltimore to process the application.

In the 1950s, ACI expanded its policy offerings to its business customers. Premium volume grew 84 percent during the 1950s; home office training classes were expanded and field agency departments were merged. In 1968, after ACI was purchased by Control Data Corporation, product lines were expanded. A major factor in the growth rate of 184 percent from 1960 to 1970 was a strong marketing effort by ACI's home office management in Baltimore, along with increased incentives for agents. By 1987, gross premiums written totaled $53,400,000. In 1988, ACI was purchased by Dun & Bradstreet, one of the world's leaders in providing business information to companies.

From 1996, when EULER acquired a 50 percent interest in ACI, the company increased its total premium income from $74 million to an estimated $127 million in 2000, a 70 percent growth rate over that period reflecting the demand for the product.

In 1998, the Paris-based EULER Group, which is the world's largest group specializing in credit insurance, became the sole shareholder of ACI. The EULER Group provides coverage on sales to 160 countries around the world. On July 6, 1999, ACI changed its name to EULER ACI to reflect its closer alignment with EULER and its global network of subsidiaries with approximately 3,500 employees worldwide.

"The EULER Group's affiliation has strengthened ACI's global coverage and risk management capabilities," says Doug Brunner, president and chief executive officer since October 1996. "Under the EULER Group's experienced leadership, we earned a Standard & Poor's rating of AA+, a testament to our financial strength. EULER ACI currently covers more than $125 billion in sales around the world, and we anticipate continued development and expansion."

Approximately 150 employees now work at the Baltimore office, where the underwriting office for U.S. customers is located. EULER ACI's Canadian department has localized underwriting staff in Toronto and Montreal. Additionally, there are risk management offices in San Francisco, Miami and Mexico City. The company's underwriters comprehensively rank industries and companies according to a detailed array of performance parameters.

With the opening of a Latin American risk management office in Mexico City in 1999, EULER ACI now offers business credit insurance throughout North America with 35 sales and service offices and more than 300 employees. Its products and services are also distributed through an expanding channel of insurance brokers and banks.

ACI's well-developed risk management division carefully monitors the company's insured exposure diversification by industry, geography and creditor. In addition, the extensive claims management department includes a loss mitigation staff whose early intervention substantially improves the cash flow of EULER ACI's policyholders.

"Thanks to our partnership with EULER, as well as recent technological advances that include an online service option for our customers, we've been able to expand and develop our business beyond the borders of North America," says Brunner. "Our agents represent the preeminent business credit insurance distribution system in North America—they're the best at what they do."

Doug Brunner, president and CEO.

P. Flanigan & Sons, Inc.

Young Patrick Flanigan, native of County Armaugh, Ireland, arrived in Baltimore in 1880. His life's work, and that of his descendants, is intricately bound to the history of an expanding port city. It is also the story of a man with vision and a fascination with the future. Today, this heritage has become an essential part of the philosophy of P. Flanigan & Sons, Incorporated, where Patrick's great-grandson, Pierce J. Flanigan, III, serves as president of one of the most venerable firms in the construction industry.

Five years after his arrival, Patrick Flanigan founded P. Flanigan & Sons, which paved many of Baltimore's cobblestone streets. Soon after, he started his "great venture" —constructing a private sewer line beneath Charles Street. Businesses were soon paying to hook into "Patrick Flanigan's Sewer," which, now owned by the City, remains in operable condition.

Patrick, who was skilled with explosives, assisted the city fire marshal during the Great Baltimore Fire of 1904 by demolishing buildings to create a firebreak. The Baltimore Courthouse was to be the keystone of the project, and Flanigan prepared the building for demolition. However, a Supreme Court judge ordered the dynamite removed, and the courthouse escaped demolition, and later, through extraordinary efforts, the fire.

Patrick Flanigan on right, paving Cross Country Boulevard, circa 1910.

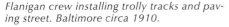

Flanigan crew installing trolly tracks and paving street. Baltimore circa 1910.

During the rebuilding and expansion of Baltimore following the fire, Patrick was among an influential group that installed a two-pipe system beneath city streets: one for storm water, another for sanitary drainage. (Baltimore was one of the first cities in the nation to put this novel concept into practice.)

Bituminous paving was introduced in 1910, and Flanigan was one of its early proponents. The mayor and city council were persuaded to try this "new-fangled" asphalt paving, and once again P. Flanigan & Sons returned to the task of paving Baltimore's streets.

During World War I, the company contributed by building much of the site work for Aberdeen Proving Grounds and Fort Meade.

In the 1920s, Packard and Mack trucks were purchased to replace 200 mules and horses. A steam-driven concrete mixer, pulled by a mule team, allowed the addition of concrete street paving.

The Great Depression almost destroyed the business, but it bounced

back in World War II by working at Bainbridge Naval Training Center and at Bethlehem Steel Fairfield Works.

1n 1981, the firm replaced its asphalt batch plants with a modern computer-controlled drum mixing plant. This improved quality while increasing production by four times. The company expanded into the larger market of repaving the Beltway and the Interstate highways, as well as the runways at BWI airport. It remains a pioneer in the production of improved products including P401 Airport Mix and polymer modified Superpave Highway mixes.

In 1998, the National Quality Initiative recognized the firm's paving on the Baltimore Beltway at Reisterstown Road to Charles Street with a Gold Level Award.

The Baltimore Asphalt Paving Company, a competitor since 1921, which had been acquired by a large British conglomerate in 1989, was purchased in 1997. This added a second identical asphalt plant and a dozen new crews.

Flanigan crew paving Cross Country Boulevard. Baltimore circa 1910.

Friends School of Baltimore

Friends School of Baltimore, an independent, coeducational Quaker day school for students from age four through grade 12, provides an academic environment enriched by the Quaker values of equality, community, truth, simplicity and peaceful resolution of conflict. The School's handsome 34-acre campus in north Baltimore provides the ideal setting for students to learn, discover their natural gifts and build a foundation of ethical standards and concerns. Graduates leave the School prepared to meet life's challenges with a solid base of knowledge, a questioning spirit and an awareness of their individual potential and responsibilities as world citizens.

The Park Avenue Friends School faculty, 1914-1915.

Friends, the oldest school in Baltimore, was founded in 1784 by members of the Baltimore Monthly Meeting of the Religious Society of Friends. They sought to provide their children with a "guarded education"—one that could inculcate not only arithmetic, reading and writing, but also the spiritual insight necessary to lead a life based on ethical and moral values. Classes were first held in the Aisquith Street Meetinghouse in the East Baltimore community of Old Town. The School relocated to the Lombard Street Meetinghouse in the 1840s, and in the early 1900s to a new building adjacent to the Park Avenue Meetinghouse in Bolton Hill. In 1925, Friends purchased 26 acres at 5114 North Charles Street in the Homeland community and began building its Primary School. The Intermediate School soon followed, and by 1936 the entire school population was located at its new campus. Enrollment increased from 15 students in early 1800 to 150 in 1900, to its present 1,000.

Initially, classes were taught in two Gothic-style stone buildings that are still in use today. During the next six decades, the School added facilities to meet the needs of its growing population, including separate Pre-Primary and Middle School facilities, a gymnasium complex with tennis courts and five full playing fields, a major Lower School addition, a music education wing and a dance studio. A 1996 capital campaign significantly expanded computer technology and capabilities in each division, providing campus-wide access to the Internet, enhanced on-line libraries and skills training for students, faculty and staff.

Though the School was separately incorporated as an independent institution in 1973, it retains its strong ties with area Friends meetings, especially Stony Run Meeting. All students at Friends attend Meeting for Worship on a regular basis. Based on the Quaker tradition of silent waiting, this shared religious experience gives participants an opportunity to quietly "center" and express their inner thoughts in an atmosphere of trust and mutual respect. Students and alumni frequently recall experiences with classmates during Meeting for Worship as some of the most profound and nurturing of their formative years.

Each division's curriculum is designed to instill a love of learning by fostering students' critical thinking skills and encouraging them to seek creative methods for solving problems. One example of this is the Lower School's "I to I" conflict resolution program, in which children are encouraged to use "I" statements, e.g., "I

The football squad, Homeland campus, 1932.

feel...I want...I need...." to help them identify their feelings and articulate them in a non-accusatory way. Using the techniques taught in the program, even very young children can learn to peacefully deal with conflict.

In addition to a broad range of challenging academic subjects, all students participate in fine arts and physical education courses. Music is a staple in the daily lives of students. In the Lower School, students gain exposure to instrumental music by trying out different instruments in a group setting. By the time they reach the Upper School, many students achieve a high level of proficiency in a variety of performance ensembles, from chamber choir to jazz. The School's visual arts and drama programs, also offered at all levels, encourage self-expression and help students develop confidence. Each year, an all-School art show features works from the entire student body—from rudimentary clay figures created by Pre-K students to an exhibit of black-and-white prints presented by Upper School photography students.

Friends School's community service program encourages students, from a very early age, to look beyond themselves and form connections with others. The program begins in the Pre-Primary and builds across all grades and divisions. By the time students reach the Middle School, they become comfortable with the concept of service learning and enjoy participating in weekly volunteer activities at a number of local agencies, such as soup kitchens and nursing homes. Upper School students must complete a minimum of 50 hours of off-campus service; many go well beyond that requirement. After-school clubs such as the Hunger Committee and Prison Committee cultivate interest in causes that have been of historical importance to Quakers.

Because the School is located on a single sprawling campus, Friends students enjoy the considerable advantage of structured cross-divisional interaction. During the annual Earth Day celebration in April, for instance, older and younger students work side-by-side, cleaning up the campus and surrounding neighborhood, and planting trees and flowers. Thanksgiving Convocation is another shared experience, during which the entire School community joins together for song and reflection.

Young students walk with their teacher past the Lower School, one of the original Gothic-style buildings on the Homewood campus.

Baltimore Monthly Meeting of Friends, Stony Run Meetinghouse is located adjacent to the Friends School campus.

Friends School is led by its eighth head, Jon M. Harris, and a 26-member board of trustees. The School recently completed an ambitious strategic plan for the next 10 years. Entitled "Vision and Action," the plan calls for a number of bold initiatives, including the creation of a strategic development plan and a master plan to determine facility needs.

While changes have necessarily occurred to meet evolving needs over the past 200-plus years, the Quaker focus has never varied. As W. Byron Forbush, II, a 1947 graduate of Friends School and its headmaster from 1960 to 1998, noted in Dean Esslinger's 1983 history of the School, *Friends for Two Hundred Years,* "Friends has provided unusual leadership in the local independent school setting. Most significantly, it has had the capacity to adapt itself to the changing nature of the world around it. Although its form may have changed throughout its 200-year history, its substance has remained constant."

General Motors Truck Group

Assembling automobiles and trucks is not new to the Baltimore area. On October 16, 1934, Baltimore's Mayor Jackson and Chevrolet representative E.A. Nimnicht broke ground for a new Chevrolet and Fisher Body assembly plant on Broening Highway in the southeast section of Baltimore. The plant was designed to produce 80,000 cars and trucks a year.

This enormous undertaking was completed in record time. On March 11, 1935, the first day of truck production, three trucks were built. On March 26, 1935, 12 passenger cars were built. The new plant produced a total of 24,885 passenger cars and 6,627 trucks during its first model year. About 2,500 people, many of whom had worked on the construction of the plant, were employed during the plant's first year of operation.

In 1935, the original Baltimore General Motors plant occupied 45.7 acres on Broening Highway.

The original plant site covered 45.7 acres and consisted of five buildings, six railroad sidings, driveways, walks, test roads, and a parking lot for employees' cars. The principal unit was the assembly building, which covered 13.5 acres of floor space. Chevrolet occupied two-thirds of the building, and Fisher Body one-third.

Car and truck production was interrupted in early 1942, when the plant was converted to wartime activities. The Chevrolet portion of the plant operated as a military parts depot where parts were received, processed, and packaged for shipment around the world. The Fisher Body plant became part of the Eastern Aircraft Division of General Motors Corporation and was assigned the task of assembling fuselages for Grumman carrier-based aircraft.

In August 1945, immediately following the end of the war, the plant was reconverted to automobile and truck production. By 1949, after 11 years of car and truck production, 1,000,000 units had been assembled at the Baltimore plant.

Today, Baltimore workers proudly assemble the Chevrolet Astro van.

Although Chevrolet cars and trucks have represented the largest portion of the Baltimore plant's production, other car lines have also been manufactured. The versatility of the plant was tested in 1964 when Buicks, Chevrolets, Oldsmobiles, and Pontiacs were assembled one after another on the same passenger car line. In the ensuing years, the number of car lines produced has changed several times. GMCTruck and Coach Division shared Baltimore's truck production as early as the 1947 model year.

A major change occurred in 1968 when the Baltimore plant's two separate General Motors units, Fisher Body Division and Chevrolet Motor Division, were unified under the administration of the General Motors Assembly Division.

On May 24, 1978, with many of Baltimore's business and civic leaders present, Robert K. Bates, plant manager, and Baltimore Mayor William Donald Schaefer drove the plant's eight-millionth vehicle off the assembly line.

The GM Baltimore Assembly Plant sits on 182 acres with 3.1 million square feet of building floor space.

By 1979, the Baltimore General Motors Assembly Division plant site had increased to more than 160 acres with nearly 2.5 million square feet of building floor space. The plant employed nearly 7,000 employees at this point.

The Baltimore plant saw its last car produced on March 31, 1984. The plant began a retooling process in preparation for its current products, the Chevrolet Astro and GMC Safari mid-size vans.

The plant was now a part of the General Motors Truck and Bus Group and began production of the new vans in August 1984. More recently, the plant became part of the General Motors Truck Group, continuing to build Astros and Safaris.

Currently, the plant and its surrounding buildings sit on 182 acres, with 3.1 million square feet of floor space in the assembly building. In 2000, Baltimore Assembly built its 12 millionth vehicle since opening in 1935. Nearly 1,500 employees from all over the Baltimore area work today to continue the plant's 65-year tradition of building quality vehicles for its customers.

The GMC Safari mid-sized van.

General Physics Corporation (GP)

Much like the Baltimore area itself, General Physics (GP) has evolved considerably over the years. This evolution was driven partially by advances in technology, but more importantly, it was driven by customer demand for high quality services.

The principal operating subsidiary of GP Strategies Corporation, a NYSE listed company (GPX), GP is a performance improvement company providing engineering, technical services, training, and consulting for the specific needs of its clients. Programs have been developed for service managers and executives, engineers, sales associates, plant operators, the maintenance and purchasing workforces and information technology professionals in the public and private sectors in the United States, Canada, United Kingdom, Malaysia, Colombia, Brazil and Mexico.

As a global leader in technical and business skills improvement, GP develops training programs by focusing on people, processes, and technology. By objectively analyzing production and business processes, GP can determine where the opportunities for performance improvement reside and develop the best solution to achieve measurable improvement in an organization's performance, cost management and compliance objectives.

Headquartered in Columbia, Maryland, and founded in 1966 by two physicists, GP originally provided technical services to the Navy Submarine Nuclear Power Program in the areas of operation, safety and training. In the 1970s, GP experienced a decade of great growth, and the business focus expanded to include services aimed at commercial energy and other government agencies. The 1980s proved to be an exciting time for GP with its expansion into the automotive industry. During this decade, GP made its first public stock offering and was first named to the *Forbes* magazine list of the "200 Best Small Companies in America." Throughout the '90s and beyond, GP has experienced significant and continuous client growth, serving a variety of market sectors including automotive, paper and pulp, food and beverage, energy, metals, process industries, petrochemical, computer and software manufacturers, telecommunications, the Department of Defense and other government agencies.

GP's Worldwide Headquarters in Columbia, MD.

Since the early 1980s, GP has actively supported chemical weapons disposal efforts. GP constructed and now operates the Chemical Demilitarization Training Facility at the Aberdeen Proving Ground. This important facility provides the U.S. Army with a complete spectrum of first-rate training for the more than 10,000 workers involved in the Chemical Stockpile Disposal Program.

Although GP began with a professional staff of six, today it is the largest technical training company in the world, with nearly 2,000 employees, and offices worldwide. This growth has come through acquisitions, partnerships and alliances, but has been driven by the increasing demands of a global marketplace and an expanding client base. GP's client base has expanded to include Fortune 500 companies, manufacturing and process industries, electric power utilities and other commercial and government customers.

GP delivers quality on-site training.

In today's dynamic and fiercely competitive business environment, their clients realize the importance of having the best-trained workforce possible. Their clients recognize that a highly-trained workforce is an absolute necessity as the global marketplace evolves—that a *better* trained workforce can provide the competitive advantage leading to increased earnings and productivity. By providing soft and hard skills training, lean manufacturing practices, plant startup and consulting services, GP is a total solution performance improvement asset to its clients. GP employs top-notch personnel in every industry that it serves, so that real-world knowledge, academic excellence and technical expertise are applied to customers' critical business challenges.

From NASA to the Aberdeen Proving Ground, General Motors to Ford and Chrysler, Coca-Cola to Kraft Foods and Oracle to Microsoft, GP's customer

www.gpworldwide.com

list reads like a *Who's Who of Business and Industry*. But no matter who the client, GP's goal is to help them translate their strategic initiatives for improvement into actions and lasting results, helping these organizations overcome the inertia of change by providing the appropriate human resources and technical assistance they need.

Recognized as the leader in providing performance improvement services to the manufacturing world, GP was chosen as the training partner for the National Association of Manufacturers (NAM) in 1998, and designed the NAM Virtual University (www.namvu.com) as part of the alliance. NAM's 14,000 member companies have come to rely on this training alliance to provide a wide range of services.

GP's services have been recognized through countless awards, including General Motors' 1999 Supplier of the Year and the 1999 Award for Outstanding Human Performance Intervention awarded by the International Society for Performance Improvement (ISPI). GP has received Southwest Bell Corporation's Year 2000 Silver Supplier Partner Award and accolades from the American Society for Training & Development (ASTD).

The evolution of this impressive company continued in the year 2000 with the introduction of its subsidiary, GP e-Learning Technologies, Inc. (GPe). The growing demand for web-based training coupled with GP's balance of leading-edge technology and proven instructional design made the formation of GPe an important addition to GP's offerings. This new subsidiary focuses on training initiatives involving the Internet as a delivery method. As companies look for better, faster and more economical ways to train their global workforce, the Internet has emerged as the tool of the future. GP is using its 34 years of training and technical experience to lead the way.

As GP looks to the future, its success depends upon its ability to continue to attract, retain and integrate customer service and sales people, instructors, engineers, technical specialists and consultants who possess the skills and experience required to meet clients' needs. Rapidly-changing technology allows GP to be innovative as it seeks out the most cost-effective solutions. GP is squarely focused on providing the best available training, consulting, technical services and engineering to a diversity of corporations in the U.S. and around the world.

As technological advances continue and a changing workforce calls for innovative ways to improve performance, the world will undoubtedly look to Maryland and companies like GP to set the standard of excellence.

At GP, "Leading the World to Better Performance" is their mission and commitment. Additional information about GP may be found at www.gpworldwide.com.

GP's customized workforce improvement courses.

J.J. Haines & Company, Inc.

John James Haines was born February 25, 1837 on a farm near Cold Stream in western Virginia. At age 24 he went to war for the South, enlisting on April 15, 1861, and was given the rank of private in Company "A" 2nd Virginia Infantry.

Haines' stint in the Army stretched across four years, during which he advanced in rank to Captain, and ultimately fell into the hands of the Federal Army in 1863. Capt. Haines was taken and held prisoner for two years at Chicago's Camp Douglas and later at Fort Delaware.

In April 1865, as the fighting ended, the Northern guards were conducting poker challenges with the prisoners. The story goes that Haines won $100 in one hand the night of the surrender at Appomatox! Released on June 13, 1865, Captain John James Haines of Company "E" 2nd Virginia Infantry of the Stonewall Brigade, walked home with $800 in gold coins sewn into his belt to start anew...this time in business. He invested his money in a small general store in Upperville, Virginia. Haines was eager and worked hard daily to learn the business.

J.J. Haines saw a need for a woodenware and a wickerware wholesaler.

It was at 27 South Howard Street in Baltimore, that J.J. Haines and his brother-in-law opened Haines and Small in 1874. The new company offered a host of diverse products, some handmade. From woodenware, house furnishings, baskets, tubs and buckets to twine, kegs and wheelbarrows, Haines was known to carry outstanding lines of products for the home. The company had two of the important elements for success: variety of product and an unwavering commitment to customer satisfaction. It was poised to become a thriving business.

John Marston.

After only a few years, Haines purchased two buildings adjacent to 27 South Howard Street. Thirty-five employees handled the "manufactory" while eight capable salesmen traveled throughout the territories of the South. By 1893, the business picked up more Haines family interest as J.J. Haines' son Harvey Lee joined the company. About the same time Casper Taliaferro Marston, a customer of J.J. Haines in Middlesex County, Virginia, came to work for the company. Marston had lost his first wife in a diptheria epidemic, closed his store, and took the steamboat to Baltimore to work for his previous supplier. Casper T. Marston later married J.J. Haines' daughter Imogene. The family legacy would be extended to include Edward H. Gregg, the other son-in-law of J.J. Haines.

On Sunday, February 7, 1904, in the early hours of the morning, a fire ripped through the heart of the city, destroying 150 acres of the business district. For four days the city burned, and 2,500 buildings in 100 city blocks were destroyed. The fire started only one block away from the J.J. Haines facility on 27 South Howard Street, and

Haines' Chattanooga, Tennessee branch in 1948.

Mort Creech, CEO and M. Lee Marston, chairman of the board.

a change in wind direction saved the distribution facility from total ruin.

In January 1909, J.J. Haines & Company was chosen by Armstrong Cork Company to act as one of 12 original distributors of their initial line of linoleum floor coverings. J.J. Haines is the oldest and the only remaining distributor of the original 12 for what is now known as Armstrong World Industries, Inc. It is a union spann-ing wars, revolutions, depressions and boom years, as well as the onslaught on an ever-challenging, ever-evolving technological world.

In the 1920s, Casper Marston began to think about his retirement and realized that he needed someone to take his place. Casper approached his son John to join the company. After serving an apprenticeship, and as the Great Depression began, Marston's eldest son John Haines Marston prepared to take the helm of J.J. Haines & Company. From 1937 forward, business increased steadily for the company. The Depression continued to devour other businesses and industries who were not willing to invest in change or to overhaul their operations, but J.J. Haines & Company grew.

The first branch was opened in September 1935 and was located at 803 West Broad Street in Richmond. The increase in customer satisfaction and sales was a good omen, so plans were laid for additional branches in Norfolk, Goldsboro, Roanoke, and Bristol.

In 1945, Armstrong realized they were better at manufacturing than distribution and turned over their Atlantic distribution facility to J.J. Haines & Company.

On January 1, 1948, J.J. Haines & Company was incorporated and the officers were named as John Haines Marston, president; R.A. Siegel Jr., vice-president; and O. Jackson Marston, secretary-treasurer. The company no longer functioned as a partnership, and the recently incorporated J.J. Haines & Company, Inc. stood posed to enter into a new age of growth. J.J. Haines, through the guidance of John Haines Marston, had successfully made it through two of the hardest decades of the 20th century, the Depression and World War II.

The firm moved in 1950 to a location better suited to the requirements of the modern floor covering distribution business. John Marston searched for months for a location readily accessible to both rail and road transportation; finally he decided upon a site at 4800 East Monument Street (remembered by many as Baltimore's old circus grounds).

Throughout the changes in business, John Haines Marston was grooming his successors Lee Marston and Mort Creech, both great-grandsons of Captain J.J. Haines.

Four generations later, the J.J. Haines legacy can be found in the capable hands of Lee Marston, who serves as current chairman of J.J. Haines & Company, Inc. Lee Marston was raised in the mountains ofVirginia, where he got his strong work ethic from serving water to produce pickers 10 hours a day as a young boy.

To commemorate Haines' 100th anniversary in 1974, 3,500 retail customers were invited to celebrate the milestone. J.J. Haines & Company, Inc. held six separate Broadway-style productions catered with the finest cocktail party and buffet delicacies imaginable. The night was magical and was one that would be talked about for years.

During the same year, John Haines Marston received a well-deserved Man of the Year Award from the Maryland State Floor Covering Association. The award, also known as the Charles F. Vogel Memorial Award, was presented to him for his contributions to the welfare and growth of the industry. The audience was entertained by a rendition of "This is Your Life" by some of John's early business associates.

Five years later, just two days after Christmas, the industry and the company suffered a great loss. John Haines Marston, who was born on October 25, 1903, died at his daughter's home in California after suffering a heart attack. Mr. John, as he was fondly called, was 76 years old.

From the early days, Haines was a pioneer, inventing a delivery system

that would allow his Baltimore store to carry more stock. The J.J. Haines fleet of "red trucks" has created an unparalleled reputation, responsible for delivering over 90 percent of all merchandise sold. The Haines driver is a very important representative of the company to dealers and their customers, arriving at the dealer's location daily, even more frequently than an account executive.

Haines' transportation system, according to Fred Reitz, vice president of ceramics for Baltimore, encompasses roughly 100 drivers for a fleet of 80 trucks who trek 6.5 million miles a year to deliver 3,500 dealers throughout the Mid-Atlantic area. Greg Johnson, vice president of Armstrong sales, who has been with the company since 1986, relates: "Surveys say our drivers and our warehouse fleet get the highest marks. They see our customers more than anyone else, and are our first line of defense, our heroes who make it happen."

Helping customers to be successful has always been of prime importance for Haines and it should be of no surprise that Haines was at the heart of developing Flooring Plus, a national marketing program for independent retailers. "It's our desire to help dealers compete in a fast-paced and ever changing industry," Charlie Parsons, Flooring Plus executive director, points out. "Furthermore, it is our objective to focus on consumer needs and help our members meet those needs, a direction which can escape us in the routine job of managing products and promotions."

As J.J. Haines enters the new millennium, the ideals and traditions forged so many years ago will be ever present throughout the company. The daily pace of business has increased a thousand-fold since Captain Haines first came to Baltimore and opened his wood and willowware wholesale company. Mini-computers and toll-free telephone orders have replaced longhand written entries in dusty ledgers. A fleet of "Big Red" Haines trucks now travels on interstate highways where horse-drawn wagons once bumped slowly down oyster-shell roads.

Over the years, the philosophy of J.J. Haines & Company has remained basically the same. "Our goal has been to be the best floor-covering distributor serving customers in the Mid-Atlantic states—having the best flooring lines, giving a fair return to stockholders, paying a fair wage to associates, and delivering the market for our manufacturers. That has been our basic overall goal. Staying with that has been one of our main strengths. Our other main strength, of course, has been our people—a very strong, dedicated, hardworking group of people. In the final analysis, "Service is what we have to sell."

All branches had these new trucks in 1986.

Von Paris Moving & Storage

Over 100 years later, the Von Paris's name is still highly visable on American highways.

Moving Experience. That, in short, is the story of Baltimore's 11-decade-old Von Paris Moving and Storage. It is the basis for Von Paris being the official mover of the Orioles and Ravens, Baltimore's professional baseball and football franchises, and of the Baltimore Symphony.

Since its founding in 1892 as a general moving service, Von Paris has moved tens of thousands of people. Its client list includes many Fortune 500 companies, a host of media and sports celebrities, and many government officials—including two U.S. presidents. Today, it is the largest mover in Maryland, and one of the largest and oldest in the nation. With a fleet of more than 150 trucks, this "Mover with the Gentle Touch" handles local, long distance and international moves from its offices in Baltimore, Annapolis, and Gaithersburg, Maryland; Alexandria, Virginia; and Washington, DC.

They are a family business with a very bright future. Their mission is to provide customers with the very best service, offering total quality to exceed their expectations. They seek to achieve this goal using the talents of motivated people working together; individuals who are innovative, highly-trained and totally committed to quality. This builds long-term relationships with their customers, and these relationships are the foundation of the company's success.

During the Great Depression, members of the third generation von Paris family became active in the moving and storage business.

The founder of Von Paris Moving was Eligius Von Paris, a German immigrant. He began his work life in the United States at a brewery in East Baltimore. In 1892, he invested his savings in a horse and wagon, and opened a small business helping people move their belongings as their jobs relocated around the city. He also worked for businesses, facilitating their operations.

His entrepreneurial spirit, and that of his descendants, kept Von Paris abreast of developments in the industry. As a pioneer of long-distance relocation, the company was one of the first movers in the country to convert to a motorized fleet, and is a skilled provider of air freight services. Its computerized satellite tracking-system keeps close tabs on all shipments.

The company has provided storage services since its early days, and today keeps customers' goods in specialized temperature-and humidity-controlled facilities. Clients entrust Von Paris with electronic and medical equipment and sensitive artwork, museum pieces and artifacts.

To serve customer needs, Von Paris expanded into record management systems, specializing in moving, storing and managing archival and business records and documents. It maintains full-service record-management centers at its various locations.

Recognizing the scope and importance of this aspect of its business, Von Paris formed, in 1990, Records Management Systems, Inc. and Commercial Relocation Systems, Inc., two wholly-owned subsidiaries.

In 2000, the company added its expertise to that of the nation's number-one family mover, entering an agreement as an agent for United Van Lines.

They have built a successful enterprise on a proud tradition. They are still growing—a vital, well-diversified moving and storage organization, committed to excellence and total-quality service.

The Von Paris "House on Wheels," the firm's first motor van, was featured in the Baltimore Auto Show.

Harbor Court Hotel

Enjoy traditional American Cuisine in Hampton's, the city's only Mobil 4-Star and AAHS Five Star Diamond restaurant.

Although Harbor Court Hotel may be considered quite young by Baltimore standards, its presence in the Inner Harbor has been quite historical. For the last 15 years, Harbor Court Hotel has maintained the distinction of being Baltimore's only luxury hotel and the city's most award-wining property. The Hotel has received The American Academy of Hospitality's coveted Five-Star Diamond Award, numerous Four-Diamond Awards from the American Automobile Association and Four-Star Awards from the Mobil Travel Guide. *Condé Nast Traveler* consistently names the Hotel in its annual Gold List of "The Best Places to Stay in the Whole World" and numerous presidents, heads of state, royalty, and Hollywood and sports stars have selected Harbor Court as their temporary address for accommodations and formal functions.

The 202-room hotel was built during the Inner Harbor's revitalization in the mid-'80s, by Los Angeles financier David H. Murdoch. Upon opening, the subtle beauty of the Hotel was cleverly disguised by Architect Arnold Savrann's brick façade. Visitors who entered the discreet courtyard would be instantly transported to wide-open spaces and intimate alcoves exquisitely decorated by interior designer Joszi Meskan. To complement Savrann's design, Meskan selected a décor that would reflect a sense of history with effortlessly blended styles, while maintaining a sense of Baltimore and the Chesapeake. The end result was a well-traveled sea captain's home complete with mementos from all over the world. Skilled craftsman were brought in to create the delicate details of the Italian marble floors, carved oak paneling, hand-painted wallpaper and ceiling frescoes that would complement Meskan's hand-picked European antiques and tapestries.

Harbor Court's grand staircase greets visitors upon arrival to the state's only Five-Star Diamond property.

For Savrann's magnificent open lobby with its spiral staircase, Meskan utilized an intimate alcove to create a library filled with Asian antiques, 6,500 original leather bound volumes of literature, plush furniture and an immense 18th-century globe.

At the top of the stairs, on the hotel's second floor, Café Brightons emerged. The room's lemon silk moiré walls, delicate frescoed ceiling and botanical theme transported visitors to a fine British country manor conservatory. The room would host not only visitors for breakfast, lunch and dinner daily, but also the city's first traditional afternoon tea.

The Hotel's showcase restaurant, Hampton's, was designed to be a feast for the eyes. From the fruitwood molding and walls covered in salmon moiré to the high ceiling antique mahogany breakfronts, Chinese lacquered screens

Guestrooms offer all the comforts of home and office in an elegant atmosphere.

and overstuffed armchairs, Meskan's décor would only be second to the cuisine served by the hotel's newly appointed four-star chef.

An intimate area nestled between the Hotel's two restaurants became Explorer's Lounge. Inspired by safari legends and adventure lore, hand painted murals, adventure memorabilia and fine antiques joined plush, faux-leopard covered chairs and card tables to offer the perfect setting for live jazz, single malt scotch, rare cognac, fine cigars and classic cocktails.

The remainder of the second floor became the prestigious Whitehall Ballroom. Savrann designed several smaller spaces to surround the ballroom that could be opened for large affairs or closed for intimate celebrations. While the Ballroom would offer guests subtle elegance in the form of grand crystal chandeliers and traditional English breakfronts, the side rooms offered hand-painted wallpaper of the English countryside and towering screen-panels of English ladies in waiting.

The Hotel's large guestrooms offer the same traditional English setting complete with mahogany furniture, fine art and décor in one of three styles. For the 25 specialty suites, four-poster mahogany beds and marble bathrooms were added to complement the room's breathtaking view of the Inner Harbor. The Harbor Court Suite, a two-bedroom suite, also offers a marble wet bar, working fireplace, dining room for 12, three bathrooms and a baby grand piano.

No less care was given to selecting the Hotel's amenities and services. Catering to today's travelers, each room was designed to carefully blend amenities that would meet the technology and comfort needs of each guest. Multiple telephone lines, modems, fax machines and printers carefully mingle with Glycerin French-milled soap, large, plush towels hand-woven in Ireland and oversized robes. A full-service health club featuring sauna, whirlpool, massage and tanning was also integrated into the Hotel's plush surroundings.

To enhance the aesthetic beauty and luxurious amenities of the Hotel, the management handpicked their staff. Led by Maryland's only Les Clefs d'Or concierge, the Hotel's current staff speaks more than 12 languages and offers unparalleled service.

Whether traveling for business or leisure, any Baltimore traveler will tell you that a Harbor Court stay will always be a pleasure.

Enjoy the exotic safari setting of Explorer's Lounge for classic cocktails and the cool sounds of jazz.

The Hoffberger Family

In Baltimore's business history, one family stands out for its involvement in everything from oil and ice to beer and baseball—the Hoffberger family. Now in its seventh generation in Baltimore, the family has pared down its business identity, focusing on just a few closely-held entities, and continues to address Baltimore's civic concerns. Using the generosity of their forefathers as an example, the Hoffbergers today are greatly respected as philanthropists, concentrating their energies on hospitals, universities, education and the arts.

The first Hoffbergers to arrive in Baltimore—Charles, Sarah and their infant son Abraham—landed on Baltimore harbor in 1882, and made a home on Low Street on the east side of the city, along with many other Jewish immigrants. The son of Samuel and Hinda Hoffberger, Charles was born in May 1857 in either Jaslow, Tarnow or Siedliska, Galicia, now Poland. An enterprising man, Charles found employment as an ice and milk dealer, and eventually started his own ice business. By 1900, he had become a naturalized citizen, and could speak, read and write English. His generosity, to a fault, was well known—he often signed notes for newly-arrived immigrants, which was a prerequisite for entry into the United States. At the time of his death in 1907, he was liable for some $30,000 in such notes.

The untimely death of Charles left Sarah, whom he had married in 1880, a widow with seven young children: Abraham, Harry, born in 1883, Michael in 1884, Samuel in 1888, Jack in 1892, Saul in 1895, and Joseph in 1899. There had also been a daughter, Birdie, born in 1890, who died in infancy. Not a lighthearted woman, Sarah continued her husband's ice business, and set upon raising her brood alone. With glorious red-gold hair worn in a soft bun on the top of her head, she dressed in loose coveralls, with the big side pockets filled with change. Her sons delighted in taking a few pennies here and there from those large, if not deep, pockets.

The Hoffberger Brothers: Joseph (1899-1949), Saul (1895-1963), Samuel (1888-1961), Harry (1883-1940), Jack (1892-1963), Michael (1884-1949), and Abe (1882-1941)

In the early years following her husband's death, Sarah and some of her sons sold cheese, milk, butter, bundles of wood, and buckets of coal out of a store in their home, which was always open. As they grew older, each son would own a horse and wagon that he used to deliver ice, wood, and coal. Sarah, who possessed a limited reading ability, excelled in finances, and used the money earned from the store to support her family, distributing it among her sons according to marital status. Like her husband, Sarah was a generous woman—she looked after the waves of immigrants that lived in her neighborhood. If a family ran out of coal, a horse-drawn wagon filled with provisions was sent out within the hour. Her donations were always sent anonymously, and grew in size as her company prospered.

In 1916, the majority of the family, including Abe and Jack and their wives, Sarah, and the two youngest boys, Saul and Joe, moved to 407 Aisquith Street. In 1922, the family moved en masse to four neighboring houses on Springdale Avenue, where Sarah's grandchildren played their favorite game, "kick the can." Brother Mike lived around the corner on Carlisle Avenue. Springdale became a family playground and meeting-place, and forever knit the entire family together. All of the houses were of equal size (even if the families were not), and a Japanese maple was planted in the front yard of each. Sarah's egalitarian philosophy remained intact as her sons became men and raised their families—there was an understanding among the brothers that they would all drive cars of equal value, and the purchase of extravagant items like fur coats for the wives was discouraged. Competition among the brothers was eliminated, and all seven families were able to present themselves to the community equally.

After Sarah's death in 1925, the Hoffberger brothers, who had named their business the C. Hoffberger Company to honor their father, acquired an old brewery on North Gay Street and converted it to an ice plant. This gave the brothers a modern facility to manufacture block ice. The ice business, which would eventually grow to five ice plants, was run by brother Jack and had three components: private retail, wholesale, and commercial retail sales.

The C. Hoffberger Company also incorporated fuel oil, which was newly being used for heat. This new business was run first by Harry Hoffberger and then by his brother Saul, and finally by Charlie Hoffberger, Harry's son. Fuel oil storage facilities were built at the waterfront and inland terminal on Linwood Avenue, and the business was run out of the family's three-story office building on Monument and Forest Streets. Saul, who was friendly with executives from the Baltimore & Ohio and Pennsylvania Railroad companies, negotiated a right of way, allowing him to run a pipeline parallel to the railroad tracks running from the pier at Clinton Street to the inland terminal on Linwood Avenue. Tankers were used to deliver oil to the coal and oil yard on Braddish and Erdman Avenues. In the early 1940s, this storage yard burned, destroying the property and a fleet of C. Hoffberger trucks. Because the Hoffberger family was respected in the community and among its competitors, and perhaps because those were gentler times, all of C. Hoffberger's competitors pooled their resources, and provided oil to C. Hoffberger customers until the company was back on its feet. The C. Hoffberger Oil Company would be sold to Gulf Oil in 1957, but the name still remains in use today.

On May 16, 1928, the Hoffbergers incorporated Merchants Terminal Corporation, a cold storage warehousing company. The following month, Merchants merged in a share exchange with the C. Hoffberger Company, which was capitalized with $1.1 million, raised by an issuance of Sinking Fund Gold Bonds by Alex Brown and

The first coal truck, 1915.

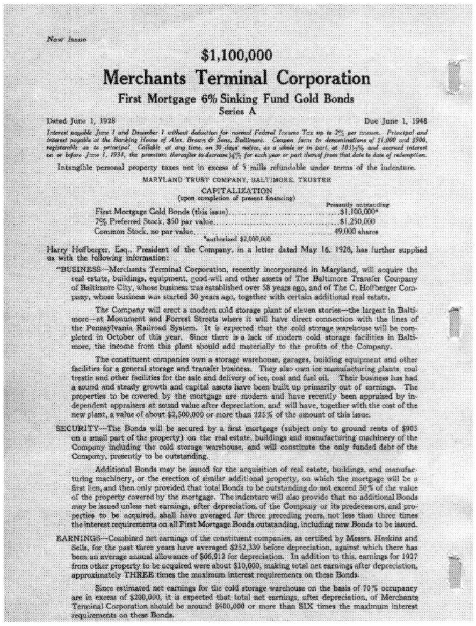

New Issue

$1,100,000

Merchants Terminal Corporation

First Mortgage 6% Sinking Fund Gold Bonds

Series A

Dated June 1, 1928 — Due June 1, 1948

Interest payable June 1 and December 1 without deduction for normal Federal Income Tax up to 2% per annum. Principal and interest payable at the Banking House of Alex. Brown & Sons, Baltimore. Coupon form in denominations of $1,000 and $500, registerable as to principal. Callable at any time, on 30 days' notice, as a whole or in part, at 103½% and accrued interest on or before June 1, 1934, the premium thereafter to decrease ¼% for each year or part thereof from that date to date of redemption.

Intangible personal property taxes not in excess of 5 mills refundable under terms of the indenture.

MARYLAND TRUST COMPANY, BALTIMORE, TRUSTEE

CAPITALIZATION
(upon completion of present financing)

	Presently outstanding
First Mortgage Gold Bonds (this issue)	$1,100,000*
7% Preferred Stock, $50 par value	$1,250,000
Common Stock, no par value	49,000 shares

*authorized $2,000,000

Harry Hoffberger, Esq., President of the Company, in a letter dated May 16, 1928, has further supplied us with the following information:

"BUSINESS—Merchants Terminal Corporation, recently incorporated in Maryland, will acquire the real estate, buildings, equipment, good-will and other assets of The Baltimore Transfer Company of Baltimore City, whose business was established over 58 years ago, and of The C. Hoffberger Company, whose business was started 30 years ago, together with certain additional real estate.

The Company will erect a modern cold storage plant of eleven stories—the largest in Baltimore—at Monument and Forrest Streets where it will have direct connection with the lines of the Pennsylvania Railroad System. It is expected that the cold storage warehouse will be completed in October of this year. Since there is a lack of modern cold storage facilities in Baltimore, the income from this plant should add materially to the profits of the Company.

The constituent companies own a storage warehouse, garages, building equipment and other facilities for a general storage and transfer business. They also own ice manufacturing plants, coal trestle and other facilities for the sale and delivery of ice, coal and fuel oil. Their business has had a sound and steady growth and capital assets have been built up primarily out of earnings. The properties to be covered by the mortgage are modern and have recently been appraised by independent appraisers at sound value after depreciation, and will have, together with the cost of the new plant, a value of about $2,500,000 or more than 225% of the amount of this issue.

SECURITY—The Bonds will be secured by a first mortgage (subject only to ground rents of $905 on a small part of the property) on the real estate, buildings and manufacturing machinery of the Company including the cold storage warehouse, and will constitute the only funded debt of the Company, presently to be outstanding.

Additional Bonds may be issued for the acquisition of real estate, buildings, and manufacturing machinery, or the erection of similar additional property, on which the mortgage will be a first lien, and then only provided that total Bonds to be outstanding do not exceed 50% of the value of the property covered by the mortgage. The indenture will also provide that no additional Bonds may be issued unless net earnings, after depreciation, of the Company or its predecessors, and properties to be acquired, shall have averaged for three preceding years, not less than three times the interest requirements on all First Mortgage Bonds outstanding, including new Bonds to be issued.

EARNINGS—Combined net earnings of the constituent companies, as certified by Messrs. Haskins and Sells, for the past three years have averaged $252,330 before depreciation, against which there has been an average annual allowance of $66,912 for depreciation. In addition to this, earnings for 1927 from other property to be acquired were about $10,000, making total net earnings after depreciation, approximately THREE times the maximum interest requirements on these Bonds.

Since estimated net earnings for the cold storage warehouse on the basis of 70% occupancy are in excess of $200,000, it is expected that total net earnings, after depreciation, of Merchants Terminal Corporation should be around $400,000 or more than SIX times the maximum interest requirements on these Bonds.

The bond issued by Alex Brown & Sons to finance the organization of Merchants Terminal Corporation in 1928.

Sons. Brother Harry Hoffberger, the unofficial architect of the family, built a huge 11-story, refrigerated warehouse, the largest in the state at that time, next door to the offices of the C. Hoffberger Company. Harry's daughter Clara Lebovitz, was quoted as saying her father had "built the warehouse for the future." While this particular warehouse did not survive forever—its doors were closed in 1989 in favor of more efficient facilities—the business grew considerably, and today includes 13-million cubic feet of cold storage space in three separate facilities in Maryland and is the state's largest refrigerated warehousing company. The company, now the family's chief business, was led after Harry by Saul, followed by Harry's son Charlie Hoffberger, until his death in 1997. Harry Halpert, the great-grandson of Harry Hoffberger, oversees the company today.

In June 1928, Merchants Terminal also acquired the Baltimore Transfer Company. At one time the Pennsylvania Railroad had purchased a one-third interest in Baltimore Transfer, enabling the railroad to set delivery costs, delivering part by railroad and part by truck. However, once Baltimore Transfer became a successful company, it was viewed as a competitor of the Pennsylvania Railroad, and Merchants Terminal repurchased the one-third interest. Two years later, Merchants Terminal acquired Motor Freight Express, which was incorporated, and was capitalized with $85,000. Bertram Hoffberger, Jack's eldest son ran the trucking company, one of the first interstate routes of which was to York, Pennsylvania. As Motor Freight Express grew, it acquired a number of trucking companies which owned terminals in Lancaster, Harrisburg, Reading, and Johnstown. Baltimore Transfer Company and Motor Freight Express were merged shortly after WWII under the name of Motor Freight Express, the name chosen for its grand, rather than provincial sounding, name. The newly-consolidated Motor Freight Express, the second oldest privately-owned trucking company in the United Stares, grew rapidly through the 1970s. However, when the government deregulated the trucking industry, the company was forced to declare bankruptcy, a fate shared by 50 percent of the companies in that industry.

Other businesses were purchased during the period that followed prohibition. Pompeian Olive Oil was bought out of bankruptcy and was operated by the family, ultimately by Stanley Hoffberger, the youngest of Jack's three sons, prior to its sale in the 1970s. The Solarine Metal Polish Company, Laco Shampoo Company, and Abbotts Bitters Company, subsidiaries of Pompeian, were also acquired. The Hoffberger, Krieger and Eliasberg families together purchased the Gunther Brewing Company (which would eventually be sold to the Hamm Brewing Company), and the Hoffbergers acquired the National Brewery, which was owned by the O-W Corporation (O-W being the initials of one of its founders). The O-W Corporation name was later changed to the National Brewing Company.

Under the leadership of Saul Hoffberger, the National Brewing Company's first president, the famous little one-eyed man with the big mustache, Mr. Boh, was created as a marketing tool, and would go on to become a Baltimore icon. The Company also created National Premium beer, which as a new product, was exempt from price controls during World War II. After the war, Sam Hoffberger's son Jerold returned from the Army, and became president of the brewery. Under Jerold, the brewery prospered and expanded with the acquisition of breweries in Florida, Detroit, and Arizona. The slogan "From the Chesapeake Bay, Land of Pleasant Living" created a sense of pride in the Baltimore area among drinkers of "Natty Boh." When WMAR-TV opened for business, the National Brewing Company was its first client.

It was during the Hoffberger family's ownership of the National Brewing Company that a relationship developed with the Baltimore Orioles. Jerold Hoffberger, who died in 1999, remembered, "It was obvious that there would be tremendous advertising benefits to the brewery if it owned the TV and radio rights to a baseball team in Baltimore." By the time the St. Louis Browns came to Baltimore in 1954 and became the Baltimore Orioles, the brewery had purchased a three-year TV and radio contract from the Washington Senators. Zanvyl Krieger, an owner of the new Baltimore team, granted the National Brewing Company an option to buy his interest in the Orioles; by 1965 the family would have majority control of the team. During the Hoffberger family's stewardship of the team, Baltimore became accustomed to a winning baseball tradition. The Orioles won American League pennants in 1966, 1969, 1970, 1971, and 1979 and World Series championships in 1966 and 1970.

After the National Brewing Company was sold to Carling National Breweries, Inc. in 1975 and the Baltimore Orioles were sold to Edward Bennett Williams in 1979, the O-W name was once again used. Now O-W had become a securities investment company, which was developed

with the money from the sale of the brewery and the ball team. In 1988, this company merged with the New York Venture Fund, a publicly-owned mutual fund. Today, this well-respected mutual fund operates as one of a family of mutual funds advised by Davis/Selected Advisors L.P.

While the family has always installed a brother or nephew to oversee each of its companies, they have always trusted a non-family professional to run the business, among them Dawson Farber at the National Brewing Company, Frank Cashen at the Orioles, and Roy Johnson at Merchants Terminal. In addition to these executives, the family has always attracted loyal employees, offering a sense of family and pride to each employee. During the civil rights movement, the National Brewing Company pioneered an open door employment policy. To this day, the average tenure of employment at Merchants Terminal is 14 years. If not for the many thousands of dedicated employees over the years, the family's businesses would not have thrived.

As the family businesses grew, a need for legal counsel became apparent. This job fell on the shoulders of Samuel Hoffberger, who had gone to law school—the only of the seven Hoffberger brothers to graduate high school (many of his siblings went to work before finishing grammar school). Sam also had knowledge of real estate, and oversaw the acquisition of improved commercial properties in Baltimore and unimproved parcels of land surrounding Baltimore City; today the family operates several companies' commercial real estate. Sam also created a trotting track outside of Baltimore known as the Baltimore Trotting Races, Inc. While it did not succeed as a harness track, the land on which it was located was ultimately developed by a company known as BTR Realty, which was partially-owned by the family. BTR, which primarily developed shopping centers, ultimately became a publicly-owned Real Estate Investment Trust, or REIT, known as Mid-Atlantic Realty Trust.

When LeRoy Hoffberger, Jack's middle son graduated from law school in 1950, he joined the firm of Samuel Hoffberger, and eventually became a name partner in his own law firm, Gordon, Feinblatt, Rothman, Hoffberger and Hollander. Like his uncle before him, Roy not only advised the Hoffberger entities on legal and financial matters, as he continues to do today, but also engaged in the acquisition and development of real estate both in and around Baltimore, as well as in Montgomery County, Maryland. LeRoy is currently chairman of Mid-Atlantic Realty Trust and Merchants Terminal Corporation. LeRoy also worked with an associate of Sam's, George Englar, in the development of World Wide Rights, the company that owns the formula and trademark of "Grecian Formula 16," the largest selling men's hair coloring product, which is manufactured and sold in the U.S. and Canada by Combe Incorporated.

As Merchants Terminal and its other subsidiary companies performed well, and the Hoffberger brothers and their sons began to realize the fruits of their labor, a philanthropic organization was created to honor Charles and Sarah's legacy of generosity. In the first meeting of the Hoffberger Brothers' Fund on April 8, 1942, three donations were made: $2,500 to Sinai Hospital, $1,250 to Children's Hospital, and $1,000 to the Red Cross. Over the years, the family's tradition of philanthropy has continued—the Hoffberger Foundation and Hoffberger Family Fund, and members of the family as individuals, have donated time and money to charities throughout Baltimore, the state of Maryland, Israel, and around the world. While this tradition has provided valuable resources to the community, more importantly the Hoffberger Foundation and its mission serve as a glue for the family's legacy.

Today, the Hoffberger family remains for the most part, in Baltimore. A prolific bunch, there are some 100 descendants of Charles and Sarah living in the Baltimore area, many of them considered civic and business leaders. The sense of responsibility and business savvy inherited from their predecessors serves the family and its community well—there are Hoffbergers of all ages serving on the boards of hospitals, museums, educational organizations and religious institutions throughout Baltimore.

Merchants Terminal's newest cold storage facility in Jessup, Maryland.

Martin G. Imbach, Inc.

Martin G. Imbach, Inc. (MGI) is a marine and heavy construction company based in Baltimore. The growth of the company has closely paralleled the development of the Port of Baltimore and the growth of the Chesapeake Bay area. With humble beginnings on the Patapsco River, MGI has grown to become a quality marine contractor throughout the Chesapeake and Delaware Bay regions.

Martin G. Imbach, Inc. has been synonymous with the McGeady family name for over half a century. While originally started by Marty Imbach in 1929, Manus E. McGeady purchased the company in January 1944. The company has been run by succeeding generations of the McGeady family ever since.

Manus Eamonn McGeady bought the Imbach company in 1944, and incorporated as Martin G. Imbach, Inc., to readily identify the new leadership with the existing customer base. Operating out of two basement rooms of the old National Marine Bank (a forerunner of Maryland National Bank), Manus McGeady had seven employees. The original time book is still preserved, and top pay for a piledriverman in 1944 was $1.27 per hour. The firm had a small yard in the South Locust Point area and one steam-powered, wooden-hulled floating derrick crane. With many active piers in the port, service and repair work was the mainstay of early operations.

Throughout the late 1940s and 1950s MGI built the strong reputation for quality work and customer service that remains today. In addition to a core of service customers, MGI took on new construction projects around the harbor. The initial improvement of the Light Street Pier area (current location of the Maryland Science Center and Harborplace) was performed by MGI in 1952. Manus took on a partner, and the company grew slowly, expanding its personnel and equipment. The mainstay of the workforce was still the steam derrick, updated with modern steel-hulled barges and machinery platforms.

Pier 5/Christopher Columbus Center Baltimore, MD

The late 1950s and early 1960s saw steady progress for the company, including relocation to another yard in the Locust Point area. It was also at this time when Manus' oldest son Eamonn joined the firm due to his father's failing health. Another brother, Xavier, soon joined Eamonn and the two sons bought the shares of the partner in March 1968, thus completely returning the firm to the McGeady family. Soon after, in July 1968, Manus McGeady died. A third brother, Joseph, joined the firm in 1969. In 1971, MGI moved to its current location in the Curtis Bay area of Baltimore. While initially experiencing difficulties, the brothers were able to maintain a solid plan and gain new business. They developed a unique blend of business skills and family loyalty that set the pace of the company for the next 30 years.

MGI's three generations of leaders—M. Eamonn McGeady III, vice president (left) and M. Eamonn McGeady, president (right) with a portrait of Manus E. McGeady, founder

MGI has been involved in almost every major harbor development project since the early 1960s. From the 1960s through the 1990s, MGI helped to build or refurbish many of the piers and marine structures that make up the Inner Harbor of Baltimore and its surrounding area. Some of these projects were: The National Aquarium Marine Mammal Pavilion; Pier 5 and the Christopher Columbus Center; Pier 6 (Music Pavilion); Inner Harbor Piers; Henderson's Wharf; The Anchorage; The Baltimore Museum of Industry; Canton Cove Park; and the Clinton Street bulkheads.

During this time, Eamonn, Xavier, and Joe McGeady became recognized business and community leaders. They have served on numerous business development councils, governmental committees, engineering steering committees, and boards of directors for prominent nonprofit organizations. MGI is a major supporter of the *Pride of Baltimore*, the Living Classrooms Foundation, the *S.S. John W. Brown*, and the Baltimore Museum of Industry. Many family members are also

Manus E. McGeady, founder, Martin G. Imbach, Inc.

prominent leaders of local church, civic, and social organizations.

In addition to the work in Baltimore, MGI also greatly expanded its scope and areas of operations, especially in the latter part of the 1980s and 1990s. Major MGI projects outside of the Baltimore area include the Annapolis City Dock; U.S. Navy Ready Reserve Pier in Newport News, VA; various structures up and down the Potomac River; ferry slip improvements for the Delaware River and Bay Authority; and work for numerous private customers located on the Chesapeake and Delaware Bays. MGI also expanded its areas of expertise to include shore erosion control and land-based pile driving operations.

MGI's workforce and equipment also underwent significant changes during this time. The company hired project superintendents and managers to meet the growing need for more technical work. Additionally, modern computer accounting practices were adopted. The most important change was the switch from steam to diesel driven cranes, and the growing use of hydraulic vibratory pile hammers for installing all types of piles.

With these changes, MGI was positioned as a very capable, technically proficient, customer-oriented marine and heavy construction firm. These strengths have carried the firm forward through numerous challenges and opportunities over the past four decades.

Throughout the decades and the growth of the company, MGI has always relied on two tenets: service to the customer and care of co-workers. MGI's reputation as a quality contractor was built by the hard work of dedicated employees. The needs of customers and employees figure prominently in all decisions. While maintaining good business practices, the firm never loses sight of the "family" orientation that makes MGI a special place to work and a firm that is extremely responsive to customer needs.

The third significant leadership change in the company's history came in 1998, when Eamonn assumed sole ownership of MGI. Eamonn III, oldest son of Eamonn and a third generation family member in the business, is charged with directing the future operations of MGI. The company continues to focus on its core businesses of marine and heavy construction, pile driving, and shore erosion control. MGI has also expanded its capabilities to include design-build and project management services to meet changing customer needs. Modern equipment, well-trained and experienced personnel, and quality-oriented leadership will serve the company well as it moves forward in the coming years.

MGI Steam Derrick-Light Street Baltimore, MD

Joe Corbi's Wholesale Pizza

Joseph Victor Corbi was born in Baltimore, Maryland on December 10, 1944. He attended St. Bernadine's Elementary School and graduated from Calvert Hall College High School in 1962.

Joe learned the pizza business at an early age by working with his father Joe Corbi Sr., founder of Baltimore Pizza Crust Company.

Joe served in the U.S. Navy for two years aboard the U.S.S. Hassayampa. After being discharged, he returned home and worked for Westinghouse. Eventually he went back to Baltimore Pizza Crust Company and became general manager.

Early in the 1980s Joe was diagnosed with Multiple Sclerosis. He left Baltimore Pizza Crust and took a year to rest and deal with his illness. During that time, after much soul-searching, he decided to put his knowledge to work by starting his own business.

Joe Corbi's Wholesale Pizza, Inc. opened its doors on December 5, 1983. It started with a small bakery and store, two employees, Joe and a young man named Ted. Because he had to mix the dough, bake, work the ovens, take care of the store and answer the phones, Joe asked his sister Joan Bell (a former school teacher) to join him in his venture in January 1984. Joe taught her the bakery business and introduced her to the business world. They spent many happy and constructive hours talking about his dreams and expectations. She is still with the company 16 years later and is currently the vice president.

Joe had a keen sense of business. He was very practical, but also very creative in his business and financial management. For the first year and a half Joe and Joan did most of the work together. Baking and packing the crusts, shredding and bagging the cheese, packing the meats using a handmade funnel made by Joe Corbi Sr. and making fresh pizzas to sell in the store. Keeping labor costs down was essential. One of his early resources for labor was the Howard County Vocational School. He was able to employ at a minimal wage, some young culinary students who were happy to work at a job, giving them the experiences they needed in the field they had chosen for their future. He also hired employees from an agency called FIRN. This agency placed people from foreign countries who were unable to work in many jobs because of the language barriers.

Joseph V. Corbi, founder of Joe Corbi Wholesale Pizza, Inc.

There were many times when family members would come to the bakery to lend a hand. Joe's nephew Edward Bell, at age 15, actually helped to build the bakery with the guidance of his grandfather, Joe Corbi Sr. Grandma Corbi also helped when she was needed doing a little bit of many jobs. Joe's oldest son Victor, would come to help at a very young age, exposing him to the business, which would be his father's legacy to him. He is presently working in the marketing end of the business, in a business he loves.

Dealing with companies that were willing to take a chance on him was a gift Joe used wisely. He researched vendors and suppliers thoroughly to get the best price with the best companies, to meet his standards. His relationship with these companies was excellent.

Pizza Kit-1984. First flier, used to promote sales.

Color coded for easy distribution.

Sometimes the balance in the checkbook didn't quite seem to cover the expenses. Joe would say to pay the bills; the money would be there. It always was. The store grew very fast. Its reputation was spread by word of mouth.

Joe's dream was to have schools and non-profit organizations use the pizza in the form of a kit, to raise money for their organizations. He loved the idea of working with families, children and their groups to help them reach their goals. He believed it to be a good, clean way to make a living.

The day the first representative of a non-profit organization (Sharon McClosky) walked in and asked if she could use Joe's pizza crust to raise money, was the beginning of a humble man's dream. That dream grew into a lucrative business, but most of all its success is measured by the good it has done for so many worthwhile organizations and charitable causes. There was never any advertising or solicitations. Once it started, it spread from one group to the next. When asked how they heard about Joe Corbi's, the answer was always by word of mouth.

The first pizza kit consisted of three 12" honeycomb crusts in one plastic bag, a pound of unseasoned cheese and one can of sauce, packed by a company in Hurlock, Maryland. These were put into a plain white box with a stick-on label on the top of the box. The pizza kit today consists of three individually wrapped 12" honeycomb crusts, baked fresh daily in Joe Corbi's bakery, three bags of a special blend of cheeses and three bags of sauce. The sauce, developed by Joe and his mother, is made right in Joe Corbi's plant as well.

Present day flier showing a variety of pizza kits.

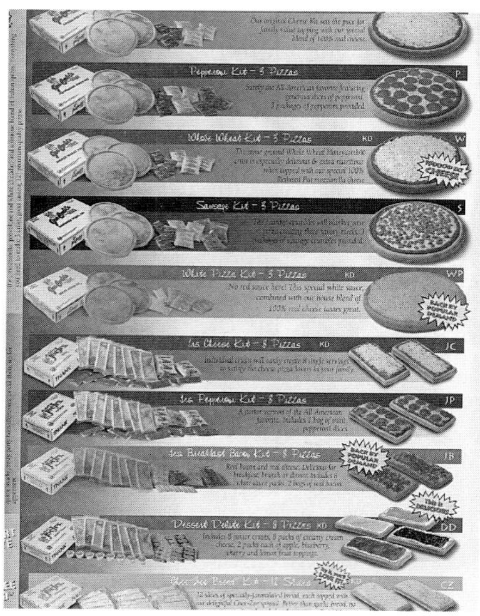

Through the years, Joe has received many awards, humanitarian as well as awards from charitable and non-profit organizations. In 1994 he was chosen as Entrepreneur of the Year.

When Joe realized he would no longer be able to beat his illness and could no longer carry on as head of his company, he began grooming his nephew Rocco Violi, son of his oldest sister Frances Violi, to take on this responsibility. Joe recognized Rocco's abilities as a good businessman and as someone with integrity, who would live up to his standards while keeping the company solid and on the path Joe had chosen. Rocco, as president of Joe Corbi's Wholesale Pizza, Inc. has proven Joe's judgment to be sound.

Joe Corbi passed away on May 20, 1999. He is survived by Victor, Victor's wife Jessica, Alexander and Matther Corbi.

Kelly & Associates Insurance Group, Inc.

It was May 1976 when Frank and Janet Kelly took the first steps of a journey that would transform a "business in the basement" into one of Baltimore's success stories. What is known today as Kelly & Associates Insurance Group, Inc. (KAIG) is one of the Mid-Atlantic region's largest group insurance administrators, brokers and consultants specializing in healthcare. Kelly & Associates has an employee base of more than 120 full time employees and operates from its corporate headquarters in Hunt Valley and three regional satellite offices in Bethesda, Hagerstown and Wilmington, Delaware.

When Frank and Janet Kelly founded the company in May 1976 in the basement of their family home, they had no way of knowing the blessings that were to come.

The business was originally founded as Francis X. Kelly & Associates, Inc. Frank and his wife, Janet, set up shop in the basement of their family's Timonium home. With a $10,000 line of credit, their vision was set in motion. Within the first year Frank brought in a new associate and business partner, Gary Chick, CLU, and changed the company name to Kelly-Chick & Associates, Inc. The company assisted small companies in acquiring affordable health insurance benefits for their employees.

The concept was simple. By pooling small businesses into larger groups through industry, trade or professional associations, they would have access to better benefits at lower rates. It was this innovative response to a need that propelled the company into the small group market.

The Baltimore County Tavern & Restaurant Association, Inc. (BCTRA) was the first association for which Kelly-Chick negotiated. BCTRA's success prompted the Maryland State Licensed Beverage Association's (MSLBA) request to promote BCTRA's plan statewide. Other association endorsements soon followed, including the Restaurant Association of Maryland, the Greater Washington Service Station and Automotive Repair Association and the Maryland Veterinary Medical Association.

Through the years, KAIG relocated to progressively larger facilities reflecting the tremendous growth and success of the company. Today, KAIG operates from its 30,000 square foot corporate headquarters in Hunt Valley and three regional satellite offices in Bethesda, Hagerstown and Wilmington, Delaware.

In 1981 KAIG's growing reputation earned them the opportunity to help renegotiate a new benefit package for the Maryland Motor Truck Association (MMTA). The redesign and marketing of new benefit plans for the MMTA proved to be successful, as demonstrated by a significant increase in member participation. Twenty years later, MMTA is one of KAIG's strongest associations, serving hundreds of its members.

It was in 1985 when Frank and Gary agreed that Frank and the Kelly family would eventually buy the entire business. The buy-out began three years later. Shortly thereafter, Gary retired, remaining a close friend of the Kelly family and a consultant to the business. In 1989 the family crest, with the words "Turris Fortis Mihi Deus" or "God is My Tower of Strength," was adopted as the company logo.

As the business continued to grow, so did Frank's sons, Frank III, John, David and Bryan. After graduating from college, each son joined his father in the family business. Frank's dream came true—working alongside his sons.

Frank III joined full time in 1986 and was named president in 1994. John followed in 1987 and now serves as president and senior consultant of Kelly

Honored in 1999 for their business achievements and leadership, this Kelly family portrait hangs proudly on the "Hall of Fame" wall at the Baltimore County Chamber of Commerce. With this designation of "Business of the Year," Frank Kelly and his company joined the ranks of internationally successful businessman Alonzo Decker of Black & Decker and Buzz McCormick of McCormick Spice. In 1978 Frank was elected to the Maryland State Senate, where he served three terms until 1991. Senator Kelly remains active in the business as chairman and CEO and continues to serve many leadership roles in the community, including chairman of the Shock Trauma Board of Visitors, the Morgan State Board of Regents and chairman of the board of the Baltimore County Community College System. In 1999, the nation's first endowed chair in trauma was named in honor of Senator Francis X. Kelly. All four sons have followed in their parents' footsteps and now hold executive management positions within Kelly & Associates Insurance Group, Inc. Here with their parents, Frank (seated) and Janet, are (from left) Frank III, Bryan, David and John.

Benefit Strategies, the company's direct sales and consulting division. David stepped into the business in 1989 and is now executive vice president of Kelly Benefit Strategies and Bryan Kelly, now vice president of broker sales and marketing, joined his brothers in 1991.

The Kelly sons made a significant impact on the vision, direction and growth of the small family business. In 1992 the Kelly brothers implemented a vision to expand their marketing support and administrative services to and through other independent insurance agents and brokers. They also re-engineered the company's technology to position it for the rapid growth it would experience in the 1990s. Since assuming executive management positions in the early 1990s, the Kelly brothers, working alongside their Dad, have seen the business grow from approximately 1,000 corporate clients to more than 9,000 corporate clients throughout the Mid-Atlantic region. During that period of time, annualized insurance premiums administered and under management grew from approximately $15 million to over $400 million today.

KAIG now works with more than 500 of the region's finest agents and brokers, and its direct sales and marketing division, Kelly Benefit Strategies (KBS), remains a major area of focus for the company. With clients as large as MBNA America Bank and unique as the Baltimore Ravens, KBS offers innovative products and services to meet the diverse needs of its clients.

With a mission statement written in tandem with biblical principles and in harmony with their own personal desire to honor and glorify God, the Kellys are deeply committed to serving the community. From the Fellowship of Christian Athletes' "One Way 2-Play-Drug Free" program and the Penn-Mar Organization's effort to support developmentally disabled adults to various "Welfare to Work" initiatives, KAIG is driven by faith and compassion, to make an impact. Globally, through World Vision, KAIG and its employees sponsor nearly 100 children in the village of Tiya, Ethiopia; they are dedicated to changing the lives of children by strengthening the community in which they live and providing food, clothing, school materials and medicine. While a personal challenge inspired the family's involvement with the Foundation Fighting Blindness, it's about making a difference, here and abroad, that is at the heart of the Kelly family and the people of KAIG.

Frank and Janet count their blessings and recognize that as a result of their strong faith in God and the hard work of their four sons, Kelly & Associates Insurance Group, Inc. has reached heights they never imagined. What began as a vision, now thrives in reality. Kelly & Associates Insurance Group, Inc. proudly celebrates its 25th anniversary here in Baltimore.

KAIG's commitment to staying on the cutting edge of technology has been a driving force of the tremendous growth the company has experienced over the last few years. It's the flexibility of their systems and reputation for excellence that have made KAIG a leader in the industry.

Lacy Foundries, LLC

In 1865 five men from Ireland sailed over to the States to establish an iron foundry in Baltimore, MD, in a section called FellsPoint.

The business struggled. James J. Lacy, the businessman of the group, bought out the others. He made some changes; the business turned around and started to blossom.

Today the foundry is in its fifth generation of Lacys. Each Lacy is making a name for himself.

James J. Lacy started the Iron Foundry, which originally supplied household metal products, machinery cylinders for steam engines, ornamental iron fronts for buildings, and water pipe for the growing needs of Baltimore. It also provided cast kettles and separation pans to the Shot Tower. In time, the number of molders grew to 18 total. Their efforts included protecting the foundry roofs against airborne burning debris during the Great Baltimore Fire of 1904.

After James J Lacy's death in 1906 his son Joseph J. took over the foundry, soon adding a bronze foundry. The first World War kept the iron foundry busy casting steam cylinders, pistons, and propellers for "liberty ships," and the bronze foundry busy making bearings and marine fittings.

The business passed on to the third generation in 1924. James J. Lacy dropped out of Loyola College, where he once scored a remarkable 74 points in a basketball game, in order to take his father's place at the plant. World War II gave the company another boost producing parts for ship repairs and operating seven days a week, 24 hours per day. Following the war, water and gas utility covers were major products and most are still in place along many Baltimore streets. Third generation James also found time for Maryland politics. He served as city fire commissioner and later was elected comptroller of the state of Maryland in 1948. Before his sudden death in 1950, it was rumored that he would run for governor.

In 1935 they poured one of the largest castings, it was a 32,000 pound cast iron cylinder.

Outside view if the foundry, early 1900s.

Joseph J. Lacy had been a freshman at Loyola College when his father died. His mother Rose Lacy would come down the plant to oversee the books and operations. Rose was active in the operations from 1950-1957. She died in 1957, one year after Joseph joined the foundry. After graduation and a stint in the Coast Guard, he learned the family business by working a short time in each department. During his stewardship the foundry was modernized,

In 1910, some of the employees and family outside the Foundry.

a complete pattern shop capability added, new casting processes perfected, and a broader customer based established. To serve this expanded market Joseph purchased the Pennsylvania Bronze Foundry of Harrisburg, PA in 1973. He invested money in the foundry operation, improving its efficiency and productivity, which paid off.

Joseph J. Lacy Jr. followed in his father's footsteps, by working in the different departments of the foundry. However, rather than succeeding his father as the other Lacys had, he happily joined his dad and developed an even stronger bond with him.

On April 13, 1988, two weeks after "young" Joe's fourth child was born, a seven-alarm fire swept through Thames & Block streets. A block-long lumber and an oil company both burned to the ground. Fifty-five gallon drums of oil exploded throughout the night and sparks hitting the brass foundry caught and burnt that to the ground. The iron foundry had been crippled but resumed operations within six weeks. The pattern and office were not hurt at all. Decisions had to be made quickly in order to resume operations. The owners deliberated, asking themselves, "Is it time now to close the operation, or do we start it up again?"

Development was beginning again in the area and there was no room for a smoke stack industry. But it was in their blood; once a foundryman always a foundryman. "Old Joe" took care of the Baltimore operations while "Young Joe" merged the brass work in Balto to the Harrisburg operation, and ran that plant. Today Lacy's is still in the casting business and has added an impregnation process along with an ingot warehouse. As for a sixth generation, there are plenty; it's simply a matter of ensuring that they love what they would be doing.

"I would like to take this opportunity to thank my dad for giving me that chance to run the family business," adds Young Joe. "I love working and still learning from you, Dad, and will always cherish our strong bond in the family business."

"Young" Joe Lacy and "Old" Joe Lacy, 4th and 5th generations.

LB&B Associates Inc.

If there's any area of an organization that needs support and management, LB&B provides it. The diversified services company has grown from its beginnings as a small, woman-owned, disadvantaged business in 1992 to a $65-million, woman-owned, disadvantaged business today.

At the beginning, president and chief executive officer Lily A. Liang Brandon had two partners and four employees, three of whom worked part time. One of the two partners, Mr. Frederick (Rick) Franz, is still involved in the company as a senior vice president and partner. The numbers grew when LB&B won its first contract, assisting a company in completion of their contracts. LB&B placed that firm's employees onto its own payroll; some of those individuals continued on with LB&B after the process was finished. As the result of this effort, a manufacturing division was established in the company, providing logistics support, manufacturing, assembly, and installation services. This division assembles, troubleshoots, and tests electronic components used in communications equipment and mass memory storage devices, and performs other manufacturing work, as well.

LB&B continued to add employees as it won service contracts through competitive bidding. By 2000, it had approximately 1,000 people on its staff, many at client facilities in 20 states and the District of Columbia.

Lily A. Liang Brandon, president & CEO

"Our goal is to be involved in as many areas of support for our customers as possible," Ms. Brandon said from the company's headquarters in Columbia. "Through a partnering relationship with our customers, employees, vendors, and subcontractors, we provide high-quality and cost-effective services. Our personnel are customer-oriented, and our top priority is *customer satisfaction.*"

LB&B's success in achieving this satisfaction is evident in ratings it receives from clients, which include a number of U.S. government agencies. The National Aeronautics and Space Administration (NASA), for example, gave LB&B a 95 percent rating on its first semi-annual review on a new contract. This was one of the highest awards ever given by the customer on the first rating period. "This was the result of us doing what we say we'll do," says Ms. Brandon.

Among LB&B's past and current federal clients are: all five branches of the armed forces; the cabinet-level departments of Agriculture, Commerce, Health and Human Services (HHS), Interior, Justice, State, and Transportation; the General Services Administration (GSA); Federal Emergency Management Agency (FEMA); Federal Bureau of Investigation (FBI); Internal Revenue Services (IRS); Health Care Financing Administration (HCFA); National Oceanographic and Atmospheric Administration (NOAA); Environmental Protection Agency (EPA); Fish and Wildlife Services; and Bureau of the Census.

Its list of non-federal clients includes Lockheed Martin, Johnson Controls, S-3 Technologies, LCC, Ericsson, Allied Management of Texas, Lord Fairfax Community College, and Southwest Virginia Higher Education Center.

Agricultural Research Service, USDA

The services LB&B provides cover all phases of operations, maintenance, and support services. LB&B established itself early in its history in the facilities services industry. Company associates manage sites across the nation, totaling over 30 million square feet of space. They provide operations, maintenance, commercial facility management, mechanical maintenance, facility repair and alterations, custodial services, landscaping, and grounds services. Some of these facilities, including federal buildings and U.S. courthouses, date to the early part of the 20th century, while others are state-of-the-art buildings for which LB&B took responsibility while they were still under construction.

In carrying out operations and maintenance contracts for the Army, Navy, Marines, Air Force, and Coast Guard, LB&B's staff works on everything from routine real property management to safety and security. They maintain vehicles and utility plants; operate landfills; provide utility services, sew-

age plant operations, and hazardous materials disposal; provide electrical, heating, and air conditioning services; do construction, renovation, alterations, and construction monitoring; and provide housing maintenance, transient aircraft alert services, and warehouse and logistics support.

The company supports training devices across the country. This includes such devices as trainers, simulators, and ranges used for elite military and law enforcement personnel. LB&B's staff has done major modifications and relocations of training devices, and has developed software to enhance their capabilities.

LB&B provides facility operations; emergency services; shop services; reliability-centered maintenance; predictive testing and analysis; electrical and mechanical services; plant engineering; planning; construction monitoring; and quality assurance at NASA's Goddard Space Flight Center (GSFC). It also handles mission support during routine and critical operations at GSFC. Steam, potable water, and sanitary facilities are operated and maintained at the Langley Research Center; propulsion test support is provided to the NASA engineers at the Marshall Space Flight Center (MSFC). MSFC is responsible for testing critical components utilized on the Space Shuttles.

Other crucial facilities at which LB&B is responsible for security and public safety systems, in addition to more routine efforts, include the Plum Island Animal Disease Center (PIADC), the Environmental Science Center at Fort Meade, Maryland, and the NOAA Research Center in Boulder, Colorado. At Plum Island, LB&B staff support the scientists and analysts in a bio-containment facility.

The company specializes in ensuring that fuels are properly handled with no harmful impact on the environment. This includes providing fuel for transportation, operating utility plants, and decontamination facilities.

The LB&B staff supports local educational institutions by providing property management, facilities support, custodial services, and lawn services.

Ms. Brandon was born in Lyon, France, but grew up in Taiwan, the daughter of a government official. Her husband F. Edward Brandon, the chief operating officer of LB&B, has extensive experience in corporate management. Their son F. Edward Brandon Jr. is a major contributor to the company as the senior vice president of technology and administration.

The flight simulators LB&B operates and maintains are used to train military pilots, flight engineers, and weapon systems officers, as well as civil air patrol personnel.

NOAA Research Center and National Weather Service in Boulder, CO.

"We built on our backgrounds and experience," Ms. Brandon says, "and on our conviction that we can do anything we set our minds to. We don't take shortcuts. We seek to retain the responsiveness of a small company, while doing everything possible with our own staff.

"We create an environment where each employee has the opportunity to develop and perform to his or her maximum potential. We encourage them to advance their skills while operating at a level where excellence is the "norm." We empower them to improve and reward them for their contributions. LB&B has assembled some of the finest talent in the service industry, which continues to allow us to expand our horizons. We appreciate our staff's devotion and commitment.

We accept the challenges from our customers, meeting these challenges through the creativity and innovation of our experienced and dedicated staff. With these people, we have the ability to do everything."

Despite its relative youth, LB&B has earned, from a loyal base of demanding clients, a reputation for outstanding services, quality performance, integrity, and ethical business practices.

Lincoln Financial Advisors Corp.

The financial services industry has long been an integral part of the Baltimore business landscape. As the 20th century began taking shape, few companies had made a long-term commitment to the area and its people. Lincoln Financial Advisors traces its roots in the Baltimore area back to 1913. Herman Savage was the first agency head and is credited with recruiting a group of professionals to sell life insurance throughout the Baltimore area, thus beginning a legacy of service and support that still exists today.

From its humble beginning at 10 South Light Street, Lincoln Financial Advisors has grown into the premier financial and estate planning firm in the Baltimore area. The 100-plus Certified Financial Planners, Chartered Life Underwriters, investment advisory representatives and affiliated attorneys and certified public accountants, provide a wide range of financial services for their clients.

Lincoln Financial Advisors has been blessed with strong, stable leadership from the outset. Since 1913, the Baltimore office has had only five chief executive officers. In a time when corporations are in a constant state of flux, it is reassuring to work with a company that values long-term relationships and understands that a sense of history has a place in the new millennium.

The planners, brokers, management and support staff who have dedicated their time and expertise to Lincoln Financial Advisors over these many years reads like a "Who's Who" of Baltimore history. In 1952, R.C. "Pat" O'Connor became the first CEO of the modem era to transition a traditional life insurance agency into a multifaceted financial services organization. Irving Abramovitz assumed leadership in 1962 and piloted Lincoln's Baltimore office to the top of the industry. With his superior business sense and impeccable character, Irving became the architect of what is now Lincoln Financial Advisors. Lincoln Financial Advisors has long been known as a company that gives back to the community. It was Irving Abramovitz who instilled this attitude into the corporate culture.

By the early 1980s the winds of change were blowing throughout the financial services industry. Investments and insurance were being sold side by side. Financial advice was now being sold as a commodity. The information age was revolutionizing the industry. Irving Abramovitz needed to pass the leadership of LFA on to a visionary, someone who could take what had already been built and move to a higher level. The person he chose was James G. Morgan. From 1983 until his retirement in 1996, Jim Morgan was the charismatic mastermind behind Lincoln's dominance in the greater Baltimore

marketplace. His inexhaustible enthusiasm and tireless energy made Lincoln Financial Advisors a known and respected company throughout Maryland. Morgan's penchant for education brought him to raise the bar on the professionals Lincoln hired. Today Lincoln Financial Advisors boasts some of the best-educated professionals in the financial services industry. With over 100 professional designations possessed by Lincoln associates, it is clear that education and knowledge are coveted within the Lincoln family.

In 1996 George L. Buckless, Jr. brought his Rosedale roots and his Washington College education to the helm of Lincoln Financial Advisors. Buckless, like his predecessors, recognized that in business, change is the only constant. He set upon a new course for Lincoln. A course which would take Lincoln into the new world of financial planning. Many throughout the financial services industry questioned the shift in focus since Lincoln had already established itself as a leader in the insurance and pension marketplaces. Buckless recognized that consumers were demanding higher levels of service and expertise than ever before. He surmised that the organizations that meet this need would prevail in the coming millennium. Under his tutelage, Lincoln Financial Advisors greater Baltimore office has grown into a leading provider of financial and estate planning. The high level of sophistication and attention to detail make Lincoln a valuable partner to financial professionals and their clients alike.

Today, from its York Road location in Lutherville, Lincoln Financial Advisors is primed for the challenges of the next century. The founding principles of integrity, honesty, and giving of one's self are as alive today as they were 80 years ago. Character *does* matter and at Lincoln Financial Advisors they are committed to earning their clients' trust and to providing innovative solutions for their clients' financial problems.

In the beginning of the 20th century, Lincoln received permission from the son of Abraham Lincoln to use his father's name and likeness. Since that time, they have worked to live up to the standards set by their namesake.

Loyola Blakefield

Loyola Blakefield, originally called Loyola High School, was established in 1852. Francis Kenrick,the Archbishop of Baltimore, asked the Jesuits to oversee the formation of a school for laymen that would concentrate on the preparatory education needed for the priesthood. The Jesuits were selected because of their acknowledged status as teachers around the world and their unparalleled standard of educational excellence. The goal of this new school was to build new men who were conscious of a religious purpose, self-disciplined, and obedient.Today, LoyolaWakefield's mission remains: *To graduate youngmen who are: Open to Growth, Intellectually Competent, Religious, Loving, and Committed to Justice and Integrity.*

These are the true benchmarks by which Loyola's educational success continues to be measured.

On September 15,1852 Loyola High School and College opened on Holiday Street near Baltimore's City Hall, under the direction of its first president, Fr. John Early, S.J. Quickly outgrowing this space, the college and high school moved to a new building on Calvert and Madison Streets in February 1855. Presently, St. Ignatius Loyola Academy and Center Stage Theatre occupy this site in downtown Baltimore. In 1921, the college split away from the high school and moved to its campus on Charles Street.

In the early 1930s the growing high school set its sites on property north of the city for its new home.And, in 1933, thanks to the financial support of major benefactor George Blake, Loyola purchased the land today known as Blakefield, located on N. Charles Street and Chestnut Avenue in Towson. This scenic property was once owned by Elihu Jackson, Maryland's 43rd governor. The downtown campus closed in 1941, and Loyola High School began its new tradition of being part of Baltimore County. The school's scholastic scope remained relatively unchanged until 1981, when a small middle school was added. Later, in 1988, a sixth grade was also added. And, in recognition of this new middle school level, Loyola High School officially became Loyola Blakefield.

Wheeler Hall, a familiar site from Charles Street.

The original 35 acres has since expanded to its current 60-acre campus. The oldest building, constructed in 1933, is Wheeler Hall. Inscribed over the entrance is, "UT COGNOSCAMUS VERUM DEUM," (So that we may learn about the one true God.) Today, Loyola Blakefield still embodies this spirit.

Most of the original buildings, including the Jackson Mansion, were renovated for various purposes. Another noteworthy building was dedicated in 1934 as a memorial to George & Harriet Blake. Their family coat of arms was inscribed over the entrance to this library-science building as a reminding tribute to the support of this generous family. Over the years, other buildings were added as the school continued to grow.

Most recently, Burke Hall was added in 1996, as the main scholastic building. The Chapel of Our Lady of Montserrat is also located there. In 2000, building and expansion continues with the Student Commons and Athletic Center well on its way to completion. When finished, it will be the center of student life, as well as a gathering ground for Loyola Blakefield men, past, present, and future.

From its beginning, Loyola has concentrated on a rigorous and challenging academic curriculum. Once settled on the Blakefield campus, Loyola enriched the educational experience by adding a newfound enthusiasm for athletics. The spirits of teamwork and cooperation are most easily taught by participation in sports, and the Loyola tradition continues in teaching young men about these qualities. Not long after its start, Loyola's athletic teams, known then as the Loyola Blue and Gold, began a tradition of winning state championships in football and basketball. Later, the name was changed to The Loyola Dons. A Don is a Spanish knight known not only for his courage, but also for his gentlemanly ways. Since one of history's greatest Dons is St. Ignatius Loyola, the name fit the school's Jesuit tradition perfectly. Today, the term applies to all Loyola Blakefield students, not only the athletes.

Loyola Blakefield celebrated its 100th anniversary in 1952, beginning its second century of excellence. This time also signaled the beginning of the Sodality movement, whose rules and practice provided a foundation of charity and generosity to help form its students' strong, Christian-centered personalities. Throughout the '50s and '60s the changes in America and individual life-styles meant unparalleled change for Loyola Blakefield as it kept pace with the times. The one constant that remained was its trademark of educational excellence.

Leading the charge to stay ahead of the rapid changes was then president Fr. Leo Murray, S.J. Loyola shifted the curriculum away from its emphasis on the classics and toward the worlds of math and science. While taking into account a student's need to express his individualism, teachers concentrated on helping him to learn to express himself properly.

By the early 1970s, conventional Blakefield as it had been, was gone. In addition to changes in the curriculum, the sports program continued to flourish. And, despite the many outward changes, Blakefield still retained academic excellence. Graduates still progressed to the finest colleges and universities. The process had been altered, but the product was the same.

With the'80s and'90s now complete, Loyola Blakefield, under the leadership of current president and Loyola graduate Fr. Jack Dennis, S.J., himself a '71 Loyola graduate, looks toward the 21st century with the spirit of Loyola still strongly intact. It scans the horizon in order to predict what young Christian men will need in order to be successful in this new millennium. After almost 150 years of successfully preparing young men to meet life's challenges, Loyola Blakefield remains an integral part of the Maryland educational landscape and a beacon in the Christian tradition.

Xavier Hall, formerly Jackson Hall.

Loyola College in Maryland

As Loyola College in Maryland celebrates the 150th anniversary of its 1852 founding, it can look back on a storied past of growth and accomplishment, and forward to a new era of service to the City of Baltimore and the State of Maryland. Now enrolling 6,000 undergraduate and graduate students from around the world, Loyola has brought recognition and distinction to the region by hewing closely to its essential Jesuit and Catholic mission: teaching men and women of character and competence to learn, lead and serve in a diverse and changing world.

At no time has this been more evident—nor more necessary—than in the closing years of the 20th century, a time of sweeping change in higher education and an era of unsurpassed growth in size and stature for Loyola College. In a global economy that places a spiraling demand on knowledge management, the need for education has assumed a critical role. Loyola has—through inspired leadership, careful planning, judicious risk-taking and commitment to its founding vision—positioned itself for continued success. Its emphasis on the Jesuit ideal of developing critical thinking skills, the ability to communicate through both the spoken and written word, and the acknowledgment that ethical behavior and a responsibility to others is the hallmark of the truly educated person, will continue to sustain the institution and its students. As society seeks to harness the power of the information age and to infuse this exciting new paradigm with meaning, Loyola's central education values will play an important part in preparing men and women for leadership.

Loyola College's Evergreen Campus, circa 1922, shortly after the College purchased the property along Coldspring Lane and completed the construction of Beatty Hall.

The Charles Street entrance to Loyola's campus. The stone piers remain intact today.

Founded in 1852 by John Early, S.J. and eight other Jesuits, Loyola College in Maryland was the first college in the United States to bear the name of St. Ignatius Loyola, a Spanish nobleman who underwent religious conversion in the 15th century and founded the Society of Jesus, an order of Catholic priests that quickly assumed the intellectual vanguard of the Church. The New World proved fertile ground for the mission of the Society, and Loyola became the ninth institution founded in the burgeoning urban centers of the United States. Today, there are 28 Jesuit colleges and universities in the United States.

Jesuit institutions initially provided education for the sons of immigrants,

Early science classes were held in the Garrett mansion, the original building on the Evergreen campus.

offering a means to join the growing middle class and an anchor for service to the underprivileged. Loyola embraced this mission, as well: Father Early and his Jesuit conferees opened Loyola's doors to the young Catholic laity of Baltimore—and also to a wider circle of non-Catholics—who sought liberal education without the commitment to joining the priesthood. Less than a year later, the College petitioned the Maryland Legislature for a charter, and on April 13, 1853, the Associated Professors of Loyola College in the City of Baltimore was incorporated. The charter permitted the granting of university-level degrees.

The College's first "campus" was a modest house on Holliday Street in downtown Baltimore, near the present-day site of City Hall. In 1855, spurred by growing enrollments, Loyola relocated to a larger facility on Calvert Street in the City's historic Mount Vernon neighborhood; today, Center Stage and St. Ignatius Church occupy the space once utilized by Loyola College.

The early years were characterized by steady growth and occasional setbacks as the fledgling institution fought to maintain enrollments, faculty and, as always, financial stability, particularly during the years of the American Civil War. However, the period was marked by the emergence of a quality that has become a part of the fabric of Loyola's history: an uncanny ability to adapt to changing circumstance without losing sight of the founding mission. This quality has enabled the College time and again to draw on a strong foundation, while remaining open to new opportunities.

One such opportunity presented itself shortly after the First World War. College-level classes had been suspended at Loyola due to conscription, leaving only the high school (which had been a part of Loyola's operation since its founding) intact. Following the Armistice the College re-opened, and realized that it must secure accreditation in order to remain viable. Accrediting agencies, however, looked askance at colleges with direct connections to secondary schools, and so Loyola sought to separate the two entities and began seeking a new campus. Through diligence and the support of benefactor George Carrell Jenkins, the College moved in 1921 to its present Evergreen campus in the Guilford neighborhood of North Baltimore. The original 20-acre site has grown to over 90 acres today, with the acquisition of neighboring properties.

The Evergreen campus has formed the backbone for the development of the modern Loyola. The natural beauty of the site, its strategic location at the corner of Charles Street and Coldspring Lane, and the space it provided ushered in a new era of growth for the College. Enrollments remained strong throughout the 1930s, dipped during the Second World War, and swelled in the years immediately following the War, due in large part to the GI bill. Evening classes for the undergraduate division commenced in 1942, and seven years later Loyola established its graduate division by adding a master's degree program in education. (A graduate degree pro-

The Alumni Memorial Chapel, constructed in 1952, is the spiritual center of Loyola's campus.

gram in business management was added in 1968, followed by graduate programs in speech pathology in 1971 and finance in 1973. Today, the College's list of graduate programs has grown to include 12 masters' and two doctoral programs.) Students—all of whom were male—came and went from Loyola via streetcars, and later by automobile, while construction of classroom buildings, a gymnasium and student center, a library and the stately Alumni Memorial Chapel continued apace, strengthening the collegiate environment and the belief that Loyola's longevity was assured.

Three developments over the past 30 years proved instrumental in defining the present-day Loyola, and led to the remarkable transformation that saw the College change from a local commuter school educating just men to a national and co-educational residential institution:

- Following the deliberations of the Second Vatican Council in the early 1960s, Loyola—like many other Catholic institutions—invited the laity to become Trustees of the College, bringing greater openness to the governance of the College, and greater accountability.
- The establishment of the separate Joseph A. Sellinger, S.J., School of Business and Management in 1980, giving Loyola entrée into the Baltimore business community, and resulting in business alliances that continue to play a crucial role in the College's development.
- Finally, Loyola became coeducational in the undergraduate program with its 1971 merger with Mount Saint Agnes College, a local women's college operated under the auspices of the Sisters of Mercy.

The Humanities Center is the original building on the Evergreen campus, and served for many years as the Jesuit residence before being converted into a classroom and office facility.

Faculty and students have the latest voice, video and data technology at their fingertips in both the classroom and the dorm room.

These changes ultimately led to the decision to add undergraduate student residences and to begin undergraduate recruiting in a wider area, a decision seen as risky at the time but also as necessary to ensure the survival of the College. Once again, changing circumstances dictated bold action. The landscape of higher education in the 1960s and 1970s was evolving: students were more geographically mobile, the competition for a shrinking market more fierce. Local students, long the lifeblood of Loyola's enrollment, no longer provided a completely reliable source for enrollment, and Loyola needed to expand its pool of applicants. Once implemented, the plan succeeded in two ways: regional applications from the mid-Atlantic grew throughout the 1980s and 1990s, and eventually became a national effort. The quality of the students—as measured by class rank, standardized test scores and grade point averages—also increased.

Loyola now enjoys an applicant-to-seat ratio of 8:1, and SAT scores of its matriculating undergraduates exceed 1200. Students represent 36 of the 50 states and several foreign countries, and over 80 percent of undergraduates live on campus. The College is consistently recognized among the most selective in the nation, and has been ranked among the top five comprehensive universities in the North by *U.S. News & World Report* since 1996. Fourteen athletic teams compete at the NCAA Division I level, and the men's and women's lacrosse teams are perennial top-10 contenders. At the graduate level, the College has established itself as the premier provider of professional graduate education in the region, and over 3,000 students each year look to Loyola for education that enriches their careers and the intellectual capital of the Baltimore-Washington area.

As Loyola's student population has grown, so too has its campus. The last years of the 20th century saw the most ambitious campus expansion program in the College's history: a $90 million initiative that strengthened the educa-

the Catholic studies minor are enriching the Catholic educational tradition on campus.

Loyola also is looking to a future of continued partnerships. A sophisticated and ambitious fundraising program provides opportunities for individuals and organizations alike to share in the success that is Loyola College, and to help assure continued attainment of the institution's ambitious goals for the future. The College's 40,000 living alumni enjoy leading roles in their organizations and communities, and have found success in their professional and personal lives; their commitment to their *alma mater* through financial support and as ambassadors for a Jesuit education at Loyola continues to sustain the College. Likewise, collaboration with civic and corporate entities throughout the region will ensure that Loyola remains vital to the Baltimore region for the next 150 years.

The Sellinger School of Business and Management, completed in 2000, seamlessly blends into Loyola's collegiate gothic architecture, and gives the region's premier business school an impressive home of its own for the first time.

tional and residential environment through the addition and expansion of new student residences, classroom and laboratory space, student dining facilities, and student activity space. Also added was a new academic building solely dedicated to the Sellinger School of Business and Management; and a fitness and aquatic center.

Accolades have accrued as Loyola has aggressively, yet deliberately, pursued its strategic goals. The 1994 approval for a chapter of Phi Beta Kappa—an honor for the Arts and Sciences faculty held by fewer than 300 other institutions—complemented the 1988 accreditation of the Sellinger School by the International Association for Management Education (AACSB). In 1999, Loyola celebrated the selection of its first Rhodes Scholar. Active faculty grants have grown by 50 percent since 1997, an indicator of the important role research plays in complementing the high quality of teaching by the faculty. Loyola also has been widely recognized for its active community service programs that send fully two-thirds of its student body into the community for volunteer work with the needy and underserved. Additionally, approximately 20 graduating seniors each year pursue volunteer work with organizations such as the Peace Corps and the Jesuit International Volunteers.

Today, Loyola is looking to a future of continued service and leadership—to its students and to the greater community. An innovative academic enrichment initiative, the Alpha Program, is strengthening the academic experience of entering freshmen, accelerating their development as scholars by pairing them with the most experienced faculty in challenging, seminar-style classes. Loyola's Jesuit Community has established an endowment to support assessment of the Alpha program as well as research into freshman year pedagogy. The Honors Program is expanding to meet the needs of an increasingly talented student body, while new programs such as

The quadrangle provides a gathering point for students and faculty.

Maryland Port Administration

Looking at a map of the eastern seaboard of the United States, it's easy to pick out the huge land rift that formed the Chesapeake Bay. Its strategic geography becomes evident when the bay's Mid-Atlantic position is also considered. For these reasons the bay's location has had far reaching effects on the growth and development of the surrounding land, its inhabitants, and its waterfront.

It is then no wonder that the rise of the Port of Baltimore was propitious from its very beginning. Founded in 1706 by the Maryland Assembly, it preceded even the official establishment of Baltimore Town by 23 years. The port area was laid out on 60 acres on the Middle Branch of the Patapsco River, a naturally deep and accessible harbor.

The 1700s brought developments of historical significance to the fledgling port. In 1750 merchants experimented with exporting flour, bypassing the conventional tobacco crop, and their success heralded commercial ventures to come. During the Revolutionary War, Baltimore ship owners took the opportunity to "write the book" on privateering by outfitting and manning their own craft to pursue enemy merchant ships and capture goods and supplies for the war effort.

During this era the shipbuilding industry burgeoned and seaman architects experimented with ship design. In 1797 one of the largest ships in the country set sail, a 36-gun frigate. The *Constellation* would become famous through its long service and commissions, and renowned as the first ship to be built as a result of a bill signed by President George Washington. Today, a restored version lies at anchor as the centerpiece of Baltimore's Inner Harbor, a designated national historical landmark and a national treasure.

Local shipbuilders at Fell's Point transformed wooden schooners into graceful tall ships that sailed at "a good clip" and could "clip" time from long ocean voyages. These exceptionally fast vessels were dubbed Baltimore Clippers. One of these famed clipper ships, the *Chasseur,* helped to secure the Port's significance early in the War of 1812 when Baltimore once again rallied its privateers into action to assist the U.S. Navy. More than 126 of them operated out of the Port, gaining fame as blockade runners as well as privateers, but the *Chasseur* stood out with a catch of enemy craft that netted more than $3 million in prizes, earning it the title "Pride of Baltimore."

The development of transportation, inland and on sea, as well as the growth of new agricultural markets, spurred the expansion of Baltimore's port as the

Founded in 1706 on the banks of the Patapsco River, the Port of Baltimore has grown to become one of the busiest ports on the east coast of the United States handling nearly 23 million tons of cargo per year.

The Port of Baltimore is the nation's leading port for roll-on/roll-cargo such as trucks, construction and farm equipment. The port also leads the nation in automobile exports.

Industrial Revolution took hold in the United States in the 1800s. The inland location of the Port of Baltimore fortuitously made it the closest port to the developing Midwest heartland of America. As railroads, canals, steam, iron and coal all contributed to turning the U.S. agrarian economy into an urban industrial giant, the destiny of the Port and the town became inexorably intertwined.

The *Chesapeake* operated as the first steamboat in Baltimore in 1813, leading to further expansion of the Port as steam powered the 19th century to a new start. A quarter century later tourism entered the picture as the Old Bay Line was organized to carry both cargo and passengers in its steamships among the scenic inlets and creeks of Chesapeake Bay. Another example of steam's influence on the expansion of the Port came after the Civil War when George S. Brown, president of Alex. Brown & Sons, formed the Baltimore and Havana Steamship Company and started service from Baltimore to Charleston and Havana, succeeding in just a few years to add New Orleans to the route.

A threat to Baltimore's commercial position was posed by the opening of the Erie Canal in 1825, prompting construction of the first U.S. railroad there, the Baltimore and Ohio, begun in 1827. The Baltimore and Susquehanna Railroad was initiated in 1831, stretching north into Pennsylvania and providing the first rail connection between the Port of Baltimore and farmlands to the west.

But the discovery of the importance of mineral elements in soil to the healthy growth of plants created a whole new industry that would spur the expansion of the Port for decades. In1832 fertilizer became the operative word when Peruvian guano arrived for

Seagirt Marine Terminal is the most productive container terminal on the east coast. With superior intermodal connections, the Port's strategic inland location in the heart of the mid-atlantic puts one-third of the nation's households within an overnight truck drive.

the first time by ship in the lucrative nitrate trade. Other raw ingredients in the manufacture of fertilizer were received at the port from Europe, Mexico, and the West Indies, as the Port became the first major manufacturing and distribution center for the industry, developing 27 fertilizer factories and employing more than 280,000 people by 1880.

In 1845 coffee rose as the next product to influence the Port's trade. Fell's Point evolved as a major loading and emptying hub, making the operations of warehouses such as Brown's Wharf and Belt's Wharf essential. These two warehouses are among the largest along the Port and are still in use today.

Next, fish took the lead in product importance in the 1850s, as Baltimore developed into a world leader in the canning industry. Eastern Shore fishermen hauled their catch in schooners to the waterfront, where it was processed and then carried by the railroads overland to the expanding west.

The Baltimore Clippers were still highly prized at mid-century as demands for the fast ships were spurred by the discovery of gold in California in 1848, and later in Australia. The shipbuilders at the Port could not keep up with the requisitions for the slender square-rigged craft which carried both passengers and cargo, and they became bogged down with orders.

The Clippers continued long after the steady, but slower steamships were available, although the steamships eventually eclipsed them. An example was the greatest of all coastal steamship lines formed by the Merchants and Miners Transportation Company. It was chartered in 1852. Yacht-like steamers *Joseph Whitney* and *William Jenkins*, dependable large ships for the time, carried the largest share of the Port's coastwise trade up until World War II.

The Civil War brought the Port's prosperity to a standstill. The railroad and bridge land links were destroyed and port trade and traffic dwindled. But after the conflict, reconstruction came swiftly and many railroads expanded, strengthening inland connections to the port from the north, south and west, and the consequent development of ocean terminals. The "railroad port" was ranked sixth largest in the world by 1876, due in large part to the grain and commodities brought there from the Midwest.

Activity at the Port during the first 50 years of the 20th century was dominated by three significant events: the opening of the Panama Canal, and the two World Wars. The Panama Canal gave the Port an advantage over northern ports to move west-bound tonnage rapidly, and the wars created a demand for the Port's shipbuilding, repair and outfitting operations.

Nearly 300 years after its founding, the Port of Baltimore continues to drive Maryland's economy. The port generates 18,000 direct jobs and some 127,000 jobs in Maryland are related to movement of cargo through Baltimore. Activities of the port generate nearly $290 million in state, county and municipal taxes.

As a result of the port's private enterprise orientation from its infancy, individual businesses, agencies and entrepreneurs all operated at the harbor independently. During the high activity of the war effort, both the inefficiency as well as the potential of the Port became evident, and a plan was developed to keep the Port competitive while providing a managing structure. As a result, The Maryland Port Authority (MPA) was created in 1956 by the Maryland General Assembly.

Today, the Port of Baltimore is one of the busiest ports on the East Coast, handling more than 20 million tons of cargo a year from around the world. It is one of the largest container ports in the country and also excels in the handling of specialized cargoes such as machinery, automobiles, forest products, farm equipment, coal, steel, and aluminum. The Port of Baltimore is the number one port in the country for roll-on/roll-off cargoes and the number one port for automobile exports. The Port is also a huge economic engine for the Maryland economy, generating 18,000 direct jobs and helping to support more than 127,000 jobs in the region.

The Maryland Port Administration, successor to the old Port Authority, has invested aggressively in public port facilities. Many of the families that helped to build the Port in the 18th and 19th centuries still operate thriving private terminals and cargo distribution complexes.

In 1990, the MPA opened Seagirt Marine Terminal, which is regarded as one of the best and fastest container terminals in the country. Using a computerized gate and high-speed cranes, Seagirt has greatly increased the Port's efficiency and cost-effectiveness. A new, state-of-the-art automobile terminal is set to open in 2000.

Situated in the heart of the fourth largest population center in the nation, the inland geography of the Chesapeake Bay, combined with a 21st century rail and road network, continues to foster growth and progress for the Port of Baltimore. With nearly 300 years of innovation, entrepreneurship, and reliable service tucked behind it, The Port of Baltimore has a firm foundation from which to reach and grow into the next millennium. The achievements that brought it to preeminence in world trade foretell of exceptional and competitive shipping services continuing into the future.

Stevenson & Company

Now in its fourth generation of ownership, Stevenson & Company at 1300 Carroll Street is one of Baltimore's oldest family-owned businesses. Current owners Dale and Terry Stevenson are the great-grandsons of founder William Henry Harrison Stevenson, who began the company at 601-607 South Caroline Street in 1870.

The entrepreneurial spirit still runs strong throughout the small company that manufactures custom-built machinery and machine parts. Just like their great-grandfather, grandfather and father before them, the Stevenson brothers thrive on the many challenges that come with the business of creating custom machinery and machine parts, from commercial pizza ovens to metal rings thinner than the thickness of a piece of paper. Creating in metals and plastics, the six-employee company must work to very precise specifications that require careful attention to variables such as temperature and humidity, as well as measurement and tolerances of materials.

"We have to know our capabilities," says Terry. "People call and say, 'Will you build such and such?' From day to day, you never know what you might be making." For instance, Terry recently found himself folding origami airplanes for desk ornaments, something that sounds simple and easy enough for children. Except that the company that ordered them wanted them made not of paper, but of steel. "That's what makes this business exciting," says Terry. "Sometimes we're not sure what we'll build, but we're always ready to give it a try."

Although most of the records from the early days of Stevenson & Company were destroyed in the Great Baltimore Fire of 1906, Dale and Terry have gathered some information about William Henry Harrison Stevenson and the beginning days of the company he founded.

From its inception, Stevenson & Company has concentrated on making a limited type of machinery, designed and built to the customer's specifications for a particular task. "We don't know specifically a lot about what was manufactured in the early days, although we know they manufactured punch presses and paper cutters for the printing industry. We also know that in my great-grandfather's day during the 1800s, Stevenson & Company employed more than 100 workers," notes Terry.

It was only by chance that Dale found out about the punch press designed by his great-grandfather. A customer called in 1985, looking for spare parts for the Stevenson & Company punch press. Dale had never seen a Stevenson & Company punch press, nor had his father, E. Earle Stevenson, who thought *his* father George Melbourne Stevenson might have worked on them. Members of the two later Stevenson generations were surprised to find out that WHH Stevenson had made the press nearly 100 years earlier. Not surprisingly, there were no spare parts available, but Stevenson & Company offered to make the parts and quoted a price. The customer declined, since the price for the part was more than he paid for the press.

Can making machine for crimping the bottoms of cans. Built in the 1900s by Stevenson & Co.

Another direct link to the 19th century is the working model of the manual can-testing machine that the company keeps on hand and occasionally uses. In 1882, Stevenson & Company began manufacturing can-testing machines, invented by Dr. Mann. The early machines were capable of testing 10,000 to 15,000 cans per day. Stevenson & Company steadily improved the

Rotary can tester redesigned to test 60,000 to 65,000 cans per day. Built by Stevenson & Co. in the early 1900s.

can-testing machines, and by 1914 increased capability to 60,000-65,000 cans. Other early manufactured items included machines for washing bottles, slicing pickles, cutting paper and making paintbrushes for the Samuel M. Dell Company.

Like the punch press, the can-testing machine remained in use for decades after its invention. In his early days with Stevenson & Company, Terry remembers manufacturing the manual can-testing machines, crating them up, and sending them off to destinations around the world. Since the machines operate without electricity, there was a high demand from developing countries and remote destinations. "We would box them up in wooden crates, but we had to drill access holes in the crates so the customs inspectors could tell what they were," notes Terry.

In the 1970s, the company was surprised by a request from Libby Foods for a manual can-testing machine after the food giant had switched to automatic assembly-line-testing machinery. The new machinery kept throwing off cans, but couldn't detect where the leaks were coming from. "They would put the cans on our manual can tester, figure out where the problem was, and then correct the assembly line," says Terry.

Founder WHH Stevenson passed the company on to his son George and in 1936 the company moved from South Caroline Street to 130 South Calverton Road. On January 28, 1933, George M. Stevenson and Otto W. Dieffenbach applied for a patent for making "transparent tubes having autogenous welded overlapped reinforcements," or what is known today as the cellophane drinking straw. George was a very curious and enterprising individual who would try his hand at anything, a characteristic that pervades the generations of Stevenson & Company. He was fascinated with the capabilities of a single-piston engine and not only built an automobile that ran, but he also put a single piston-engine in a boat. "He sailed it halfway around the world—until it sank," laughs Terry.

Stevenson & Company survived the Great Depression, and during World War II donated a lot on South Calverton Road to the Baltimore community to grow vegetables in victory gardens. Times were tough in the mid-1900s when work decreased to an all-time low. Each day, George would travel by streetcar to pick up his raw material, work it into a finished product, deliver it to his customer and use that payment to travel on the streetcar the next morning to obtain more raw material. George persevered, working in the company every day until the day he died in 1967. Grandson Terry remembers his desk on the second floor at South Calverton Road as a hub of activity. "We still have his toolbox, and my father's toolbox. When we can't find something, we'll look in 'Pop's toolbox' or 'Dad's toolbox.'"

Two of George's three sons, E. Earle and Carroll, took over the business and in 1964 the company moved to 1331 Cleveland Street. Under Earle and Carroll's ownership, Stevenson & Company diversified into making molds for the plastics industry and machines for the food industry. Throughout the next three decades, the company grew its business of developing manufacturing and specialty machines for the pharmaceutical and food industries. Stevenson & Company began making pizza ovens for the Baltimore Pizza Company in 1964. When Joe Corbi, son of the founder of the Baltimore Pizza Company, started the Joe Corbi Pizza Kit Company, he asked Stevenson & Company to help design and build the conveyor ovens. Stevenson & Company still makes and repairs the pizza ovens for the Company.

In 1986, E. Earle Stevenson owned Stevenson & Company with his two sons, Dale and Terry, the present owners. The Stevenson brothers bought a 4,000-square-foot building on Carroll Street in 1995 and moved the company in 1996 to its present location at 1300 Carroll Street. Terry estimates that approximately 60 percent of the company's

Foot-operated manuel can tester built by Stevenson & Co. in 1882, testing 10,000 to 15,000 cans per day.

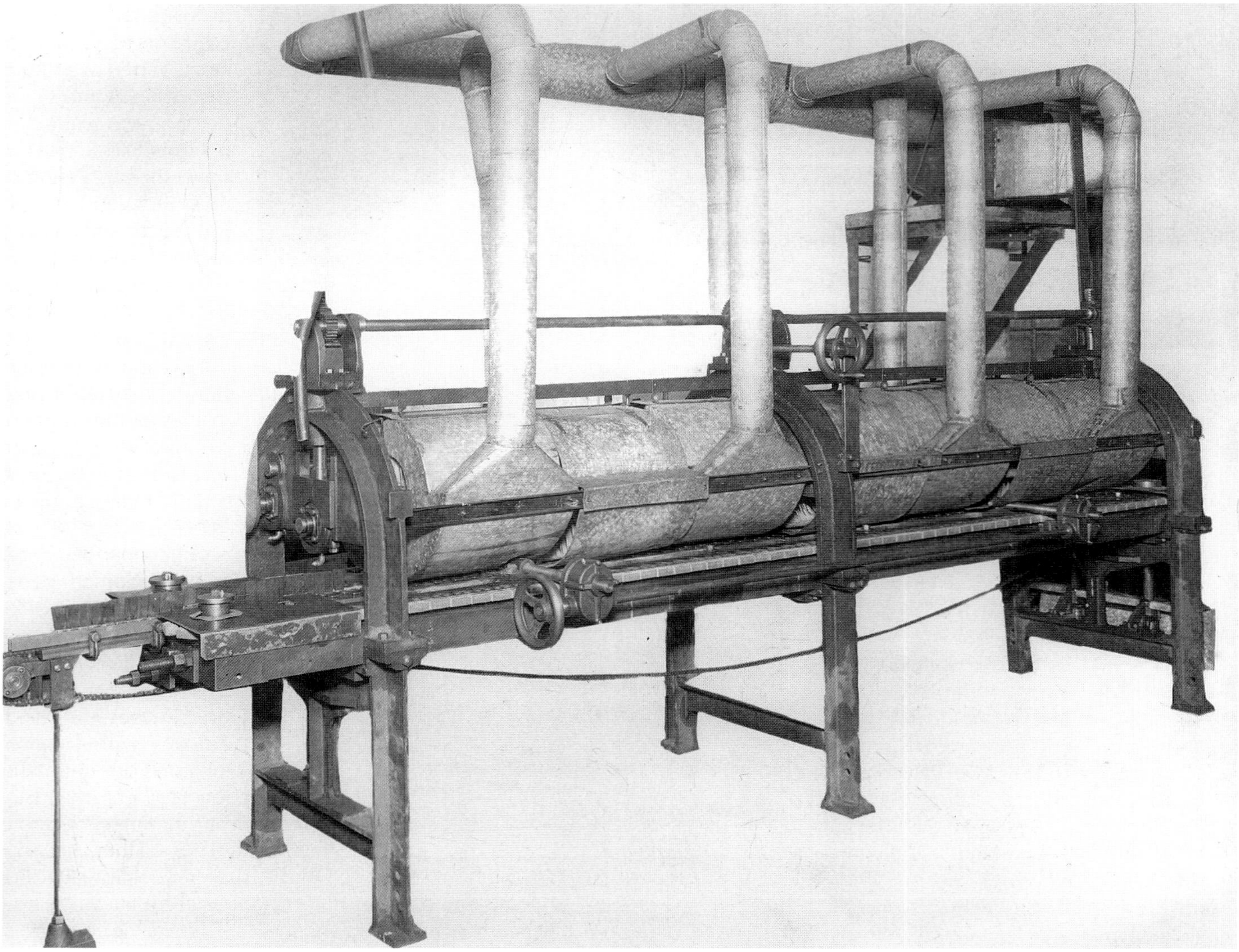

Called the "flagging machine," it is used to taper the ends of paint brushes.

business is now food-related. Stevenson & Company makes machines for the candy industry; the Mary Sue Candy Company is one of its long-time customers. Repairing the molds that manufacture bottles for bottled water is one of the latest additions to the diverse inventory built by Stevenson. As the demand for bottled water increases, this will continue to be an area of growth for Stevenson & Company.

Along with being one of the oldest family-owned businesses in Baltimore, Stevenson & Company also holds the honor of having the oldest, and longest-employed person in the Baltimore area. Francis J. Powder, now semi-retired, began working for George M. Stevenson in 1947. The *Baltimore Business Journal* recently listed the 77-year-old machinist as the oldest and longest-employed person in the publication's *Book of Lists*.

Longevity is also a characteristic of some of Stevenson & Company's customers. "We've worked with some people for more than 50 years," says Terry. With its reputation for innovation and excellence, the company attracts customers through, "...word-of-mouth—the best advertising anyone could have," says Terry. It is only part of the legacy from the generations of Stevensons before them that enables Dale and Terry to move Stevenson & Company into the new millennium.

In addition to developing and building new machinery, the company still repairs and make parts for older machines, many of which are used by printing companies in Baltimore. "We were recently called in to rebuild an old paper cutter," notes Terry. "We make parts for machinery that you can't buy parts for anymore."

His grandfather's toolbox—and the knowledge it represents—is what continues to make Stevenson & Company a success. "It's a real advantage having three generations before us," says Terry. "Our knowledge of the machine industry is what our grandfather learned through trial and error. In 10 minutes, he could show us something that might have taken us years to figure out."

Monumental Life Insurance Company

Colonel George P. Kane, was the first president of Monumental Life Insurance Company. He was later elected mayor of the city of Baltimore.

Colonel George P. Kane, Monumental Life Insurance Company's first president, turned out to be a good risk, despite the fact that he spent part of the Civil War in prison.

Following the Confederate attack on Fort Sumter in 1861, Baltimore was caught in the crossfire between North and South. Colonel Kane, then Baltimore's marshal of police, and Mayor George W. Brown were arrested while trying to restrain angry Baltimore citizens who had ambushed Union troops. Accused of being Southern sympathizers, both men were imprisoned at Fort McHenry.

Released after a short time, Kane was later elected mayor of the city of Baltimore. He also helped build the foundation for what is today one of the oldest, largest and most respected life insurance companies in the country.

Like many successful businesses, Monumental Life grew from humble beginnings. The Maryland General Assembly granted a charter to the Maryland Mutual Life and Fire Insurance Company in 1858. Two years later, the company's board of directors held their first organizational meeting at 91 Second Street, in what is today the 300 block of Water Street. They adopted premium rates from the Mutual Benefit Life Insurance Company of Newark, New Jersey, founded in 1845. The company's first agent was licensed in Texas, Maryland, in 1860.

On January 3, 1862 ..."owing to the unsettled condition of the country"...the young company's directors voted to cease taking risks of life and fire insurance. No more policies were written until 1870, when the word "fire" was deleted from the company's name and it resumed operations as the Mutual Life Insurance Company of Baltimore.

As the country pushed westward, industry and commerce grew, along with the demand for life insurance. The company adapted to European immigration and changing economic and social conditions by opening a German department. In 1873, it also issued what was believed to be the country's first *weekly premium* life insurance policy, to Baltimore resident Valentin Bauscher.

Weekly premium policies—sold and serviced by agents assigned to specific geographic territories—appealed to the city's merchants, manufacturers, small business owners, factory workers, farmers and oystermen. The company's Weekly Premium or Industrial Division grew rapidly; small, paid-weekly policies formed the basis of Monumental Life's business for more than 100 years.

By 1883, a quarter-century after receiving its charter, the company had $1 million of insurance in force. By 1900, that figure had more than doubled, to $2.6 million.

The company survived the Baltimore fire of 1904, and in 1926 moved to its current location at the corner of Charles and Chase Streets. In 1928, with $11 million of assets and $147 million of insurance in force, the company converted from a mutual to a stock life insurance company. Then, in another bold move, it changed its name to reflect its presence and prominence in Baltimore, the "Monumental City," in 1935.

By 1957, Monumental Life had 59 field offices in 12 states and $1 billion of insurance in force. Growth continued at a rapid rate over the next 10 years. In 1967, with $2 billion of insurance in force, construction began on a $3.8 million addition to the company's home office. When completed in 1968, expanded space for Monumental Life and the newly-incorporated Monumental Corporation included the entire 1100 block of Charles Street.

Career agents used premium rate books like this one for over 100 years. The Mutual Life Insurance Company of Baltimore changed its name to Monumental Life in 1935.

Monumental Life moved its home office to Charles and Chase Streets, across from the Belvedere Hotel, in 1926.

The company withstood a hostile takeover attempt in 1978 and headed into the 1980s committed to selling life and health insurance products to meet the final expense and income replacement needs of America's middle income consumers. Though the last paid-weekly policy was sold in 1973, the company's career agents continued to visit policyholders regularly in their homes and businesses to review insurance coverage, meet needs, and if requested, to collect premiums.

In 1986 AEGON Insurance Group, the second largest insurer in The Netherlands, recognized the company's strength, solid performance and potential. Monumental Life and Monumental General, its "sister company" in Baltimore, joined two other insurers—Life Investors of Cedar Rapids, Iowa, and National Old Line of Little Rock, Arkansas—as members of the highly successful AEGON family of insurance companies.

Today, as an AEGON company, Monumental Life Insurance Company belongs to one of the largest and most respected insurance organizations in the world. As a result of acquisitions in 1990, 1992 and 1997, Monumental Life now has assets of $19.7 billion and over $66 billion of insurance in force. It uses three distinct distribution systems—Career Agency, PreNeed and Military—to market its individual life and health insurance products. With more than 2,500 career agents and managers serving over 1,000,000 families from 190 field offices in 22 states, Monumental Life has become an acknowledged leader in the insurance industry's lower and middle income marketplace.

As it nears its 150th birthday in 2008, Monumental Life, like Baltimore, is a "melting pot" of companies, people, cultures and traditions. It has experienced 14 decades of growth and change and served policyholders born in three centuries. Under the leadership of Henry G. Hagan, president and CEO since 1998, Monument Life entered the new millennium focused on the future and committed to its mission of helping American families improve the quality of their lives.

Monumental Life is a member of the AEGON Insurance Group, one of the largest insurance organizations in the world. Its home office in Baltimore now occupies the entire 1100 block of Charles Street.

Morgan State University

Founded as the Centenary Biblical Institute in Baltimore, Maryland in 1867, Morgan State University has always been committed to the broader purpose of providing the best educational opportunities to all of the citizens of the city, state and nation, especially the African-American population. Since its founding nearly a century and a half ago, Morgan State University has evolved into one of the nation's premier minority institutions and one of its finest examples of an urban university closely tied to its communities.

The Centenary Biblical Institute grew out of the visionary efforts of African-American leaders in the Washington Conference of the Methodist Episcopal Church, led by the Sharp Street Church in Baltimore and the white Baltimore Conference of the church to establish an institution of higher education. On December 25, 1866, Bishop Levi Scott convened a group of 13 white leaders with resources to make this dream a reality. There he formed a board of trustees, committed to a budget of $5,000 and charged them to establish an institution. Bishop Scott offered this blessing for their mission: "May God prosper the work of our hands and enable us to do something that shall tell favorably and powerfully on the improvement and elevation of a people long neglected and oppressed."

On April 30, 1867, board member Rev. James H. Brown began a "systematic course of lectures" in the basement of Sharp Street Methodist Episcopal Church, to nine students. On November 27, 1867, at 10:30 a.m., the board filed articles of incorporation establishing the Centenary Biblical Institute as "a body politic and corporate for the education of young men, especially colored, for the ministry of the M.E. Church as shall have been judged by a Quarterly Conference to be divinely called thereto"—with authority to offer diplomas. The first teachers were hired at an annual salary of $150 and the first president, Rev. J. Emory Round, an abolitionist, was appointed at $1,500 per annum.

First permanent site of the Centenary Biblical Institute, corner of Edmondson Avenue and Fulton Avenue, Baltimore, Maryland, 1881.

Enrollment at this small, private institution grew gradually, reaching 20 by the second year. It soon became apparent that, in response to pressures from the community, the Institute should broaden its purpose to include the preparation of teachers, as well as ministers, especially when the school admitted its first female students in 1874.

Thus, the Centenary Biblical Institute amended its charter and established three major divisions: the theological to achieve its original objective, the normal to meet the needs of the growing public school system in Baltimore and the preparatory to increase the pool of students eligible to matriculate in advanced study. It also appointed its first African-American professors in 1877 and established an evening school in 1884 and strove to be a gateway of opportunity for African Americans.

In 1890, with enrollment having increased to 279, the Centenary Biblical Institute changed its name to Morgan College, in honor of Rev. Lyttleton F. Morgan, chairman of the board from 1876-1886, and it applied for and received authority to offer the baccalaureate degree. In 1895, it awarded its first baccalaureate degree to George W.F. McMechen, who three years later graduated from Yale Law School.

The beginning of the 20th century witnessed dramatic change in the academic focus of the institution. In 1902, the College appointed its fourth president, Dr. John Oakley Spencer, the first president of the College with academic, rather than theological, training. During his 35-year tenure—with strong support from board chairpersons Rev. John F. Goucher, Charles W. Baldwin and Judge Morris A. Soper—Morgan enjoyed its first period of prosperity and demonstrable growth in virtually every respect. After a nine-year search for a new location and despite

Morgan's sixth president, Dr. Dwight Oliver Wendell Holmes (8th from left, front row), poses for annual picture with the faculty, 1948.

the angry opposition and legal appeals of its neighbors, Morgan moved to its present location at the corner of Hillen Road and Cold Spring Lane (then Gridon Lane). Existing buildings were renovated; campus development was begun in 1919.

Spencer also brought outstanding faculty to Morgan College, among them published scholars, civic leaders and many African-American educators, and he upgraded the curriculum to replace the academic track with a four-year college preparatory program that was a prerequisite for the collegiate, theological and normal programs of study. He raised the admission standards and implemented a curriculum with broad areas of collegiate study in liberal arts, science, education, home economics and industrial education. A high point of Spencer's leadership was Morgan's successful bid for accreditation by the Middle State Association of Colleges and Secondary Schools in 1925.

Led for 35 years by white religious leaders and for another 35 years by a white academician, in 1937 Morgan welcomed its first African-American president, Dr. Dwight Oliver Wendell Holmes, former Dean of the School of Graduate Studies at Howard University. Holmes's relatively brief 11-year tenure as president marked another critical point in the history and development the College, when the state assumed ownership of and responsibility for Morgan College, committing itself to maintaining and promoting a high-quality institution of higher education for African Americans. On November 9, 1939, Morgan College was officially transferred to the state of Maryland, having been purchased from the Board of Trustees for $225,000.

During the first 10 years of state ownership, Morgan State College gained momentum toward becoming a strong liberal arts institution. The faculty increased in quality and quantity from 30, four of whom held the doctorate, to 85, 25 of whom held the doctorate. A new library and two dormitories for females were added to the physical plant. The student body grew from 752 to 1,595, with significant financial aid available. Most importantly, President Holmes led a campaign to "sure up" the liberal arts focus of the campus, introduced a system of recognizing outstanding student achievement, and implemented the 3.0 grading system. He paved the way for another Howard educator, Dr. Martin David Jenkins, to assume the leadership of the institution on his retirement in 1948.

Professor James E. Lewis poses beside the landmark statue of abolitionist Frederick Douglass, which he sculpted and donated to the universtiy in 1956.

Between 1948 and 1970, under the leadership of Jenkins, Morgan became a nationally-recognized, model liberal arts college and an institution assuming a position of leadership in its community. Jenkins amassed a prodigious group of educators with impressive credentials and outstanding records of scholarship and teaching. He instituted comprehensive changes in the general education curriculum to ensure a common fund of liberal arts knowledge and skills for all students—including required experiences in the arts and humanities, the social and behavioral sciences, the natural sciences, health and physical education, writing, mathematics and contemporary issues. An art gallery and the accumulation of an outstanding collection of African, African-American and European art enhanced the institution's culture, as did a lecture and performance series that brought prominent national and international artists and intellectuals to the campus. Thirteen new buildings were added to the growing campus and an Army ROTC Program to enable

Three Morgan presidents—Dr. King V. Cheek (9th), Dr. Andrew Billingsley (10th) and Dr. Martin D. Jenkins (7th)—pose in 1975 during the inauguration of President Billingsley.

more African Americans to enter the armed forces as commissioned officers, was established with a grant from the Ford Foundation. An Institute for Political Education began to encourage and facilitate African-American involvement in the political life of the city and state, and an Urban Studies Institute to study and address the problems of urban communities in which African Americans had begun to predominate was also established. In 1963 the graduate school reopened, offering master's degrees in several liberal arts areas and in education.

Morgan College in the '50s and '60s became Maryland's other flagship institution. Its graduates set records and broke ground in virtually every aspect of professional life. In state politics they broke the color barriers in the legislature and the courts, and one became the first African-American congressman from Maryland. Alumni and students became political activists, integrating the nearby Northwood Shopping Center and playing a major role in the civil rights movement. They set new records for admittance to graduate schools and won more Fulbright Scholarships than students from almost every public college in the area. In 1969 Morgan was singled out by the Middle States Association of Colleges and Schools as a model liberal arts program and was ranked in a *Newsweek* poll among the top 10 African-American colleges and universities in the country. The track and field team and the football team became legendary, with many of their participants going on to national and international acclaim.

Morgan began to experience its finest hour during the '60s, when its students and graduates broke barriers against integration in virtually every respect. The institution continued extending its legacy of African-American firsts, including the first African-American state senator; judge in the Maryland Court of Appeals; congressman; pitcher in a World Series game; Brigadier General in the Maryland National Guard; state treasurer; winner of the Pulitzer Prize in fiction; and CEO of the National Association for the Advancement of Colored People; among others. Later in the century it was to add other such distinctions as the first Director of Speech Writing for the President of the United States and the Deputy Chief of Staff for Operations and Plans for the U.S. Army, a three-star general.

By the late '60s, nearly 50 percent of its graduate school population was non-African-American. College leaders began a campaign to become a racially integrated, urban-oriented university. That designation came in 1975, five years after the retirement of President Jenkins and after an eight-year interlude of governance by the Maryland Board of Trustees of State College and Universities. Morgan was renamed Morgan State University and granted the authority to offer the doctorate and to focus its programs on the urban community.

In the past several years Morgan has experienced a period of unprecedented growth and development. It is now a sprawling modern campus that will soon include a new Hospitality Management Center (hotel and conference complex). A new Fine Arts Center is under construction, and plans are in motion for a new student center, a graduate center, a communications center, a science research wing, and a new library. These facilities, along with other recent renovations and additions that are state-of-the-art and total over $300 million, position Morgan to offer the latest in educational and research technology to its students and faculty. Recent increases in living accommodations also enable it to house more than 2,000 on-campus students.

Under its current president, Dr. Earl S. Richardson, who chairs the U.S. President's Advisory Commission on Historically Black Colleges and Universities, Morgan has evolved into a university with a strong liberal arts base and major professional schools. It offers 35 undergraduate degree programs, 17 programs leading to the master's degree, and eight doctoral programs leading to the Ph.D., the Ed.D., the D.E., and the Dr.P.H.—

Aerial view of the campus, bordered on the left by Hillen Road in 1970.

Aerial view of the new Carl Murphy Fine Arts Center, under construction on the south campus and scheduled for completion in 2002.

among them the recent addition of Ph.D. programs in business and bioenvironmental science. With well over 33,000 graduates to its credit, Morgan graduates a lion's share of African-Americans in Maryland in virtually every field. It also ranks among the top 20 campuses nationally in baccalaureate degrees awarded to African Americans and continues to produce one of the highest number of Fulbright Scholarships among regional schools.

Morgan takes enormous pride in being a university that is willing to invest in people. In addition to opening its doors to the nation's best-prepared students, it welcomes others who, by traditional measures, have not yet realized or tapped their learning potential. It also takes satisfaction in being concurrently a strong research-based university that has not lost its devotion to teaching. The campus is hospitable to students of all backgrounds, and its faculty is one of the most integrated and international faculties in the state. Students coming to Morgan find an institution and a community of scholars committed to the principle that ordinary people can achieve extraordinary things. The institution promised in the outset to "tell favorably and powerfully on the improvement and elevation of a people long neglected and oppressed," and it remains faithful to that promise.

Below: *Maryland's political leaders pose with President Earl S. Richardson at a Spring 2000 political rally for presidential candidate Al Gore. Left to right: Congressman Ben Cardin, Vice President Gore, President Richardson, Congressman Elijah Cummings, Sentator Barbara McKulski, Governor Parris Glendennign, Lieutenant Governor Kathleen Kennedy Townsend and Senator Paul Sarbanes.*

Municipal Employees Credit Union of Baltimore, Inc.

MECU's corporate offices and the Elmer Bernhardt Headquarters Branch is located at the hub of Baltimore City government across the street from City Hall. Its branches are located in communities where members live and work.

Municipal Employees Credit Union of Baltimore, Inc. (MECU) was organized during the Great Depression when access to financial services was a privilege reserved only for the wealthy. Making ends meet was difficult and City employees often resorted to borrowing money from loan sharks because credit was not available to them.

People paid the loan sharks exorbitant interest rates—as much as 520 percent. It became increasingly difficult to get out of debt and some people even quit their City jobs to collect their pension money so they could pay off the loan sharks. Concerned about the situation, Mayor Howard Jackson and City Payroll Director Elmer Bernhardt decided that a credit union should be formed.

On October 2, 1936, 15 Baltimore City employees each contributed $10 totaling assets of $150, to organize the credit union. For each of them, this $10 investment equaled approximately one week's pay. The purpose of the Credit Union was to free City employees from the high interest rates of these unscrupulous lenders while teaching them to be thrifty. Its purpose is essentially the same today.

From 15 members and $150 in assets, the City employees' credit union grew strong, sound and well-respected. Today MECU serves over 65,000 members and its assets total more than $500 million. MECU is the fourth largest state-chartered credit union in Maryland; and the ninth largest depository institution in Baltimore.

Unlike most financial services providers, a credit union is a wholly member-owned financial cooperative and it is not-for-profit. Members' savings are invested in the form of loans to other members, thereby perpetuating the credit union concept of "people helping people." Earnings after expenses are returned to the member-owners in the form of high paying dividends and interest-bearing savings accounts, low cost consumer loans and mortgages. Additionally, many of the financial services that one would pay for at other institutions, such as checking and ATM services, are free or at minimal cost. For more than 17 consecutive years, MECU has declared a loan interest refund with members receiving a portion of the interest they paid on loans from January to November. It also paid all members an extraordinary dividend on their Share Savings Accounts.

Another unique quality is that a credit union serves a group of people who share a common bond, such as where they live, work or worship. MECU is an occupationally-based credit union serving employees and retirees of Baltimore City and members of their families.

Over the years its headquarters has been at the hub of City government. MECU's first office was located inside the guard station of Baltimore's City Hall. It moved from City Hall to 212 E. Lexington Street in a former fire house; in the early '80s it relocated to its present headquarters building at 401 East Fayette Street across the street from City Hall.

Under the leadership of Chairman Herman Williams Jr. (left) and President and CEO Bert J. Hash Jr., (right) MECU has greatly expanded access to its members by opening three new branch offices in less than a year.

MECU opened its Herman Williams Jr. Fallstaff Branch on Reisterstown Road in October 1999 in the northeast part of the City (pictured). A second branch opened in January 2000 at the Parren J. Mitchell Business Center at the corner of Martin Luther King Boulevard and Saratoga Streets. Its third branch, the John T. O'Mailey Hamilton Park Branch in northeast Baltimore on East Northern Parkway opened in August 2000.

Traditionally, MECU has focused around the unique needs of Baltimore City employees. This is due to the close sponsorship relationship that MECU shares with the City of Baltimore. Over the years, City leaders have been MECU members with many of them having served on the Credit Union's Board of Directors to represent the interests of the members.

MECU has always worked closely with Baltimore City to provide services that meet its members' needs. These innovative services include Pay All Year (PAY) Savings and loan payments designed to assist Baltimore City Public Schools' employees budget for the summer months when they don't receive a regular pay check.

It also offers bi-weekly mortgages that help members build equity faster, pay off mortgages early, and save substantially in interest expense.

To encourage members to "live where they work," MECU developed its "Buy In Baltimore" mortgage loan program. Working hand-in-hand with the homeownership programs offered through the Baltimore City Department of Housing and Community Development, this unique mortgage program offers below-market rates for members who purchase homes in Baltimore City.

Educational workshops and counseling are available for members to receive assistance in managing their family budgets, preparing for home ownership, and managing their use of credit.

The Credit Union is committed to investing in the communities of Baltimore. Since October 1999, Municipal Employees Credit Union of Baltimore, Inc. has opened three branch offices within the Baltimore City limits. The branches are located in neighborhoods where MECU members work and live. This has enabled MECU to fulfill its members' needs more conveniently and efficiently, as well as to provide more jobs in the Baltimore community.

MECU and its employees believe in giving back to the community through volunteer work and charitable contributions. Employees participate in a variety of outreach efforts through the year including adopting a high-risk school, helping to build up underdeveloped neighborhoods, reading to school children, and providing food and clothes to needy families. In the Combined Charities campaign, 98 percent of the staff participated, which was the highest rate of all participating agencies.

MECU's success can largely be attributed its Mission Statement and the business philosophy that surrounds it: "To provide members with high-quality financial services through sound management and innovation."

By striving to create and provide new services that are in keeping with the members' demand, MECU has ensured strong loyalty from its members. By staying member-focused, MECU stays current and abreast of the members' needs, whether product-based, access-oriented, or satisfaction focused. MECU is proud to stay true to its dedication and to the people to whom the credit union belongs—its members.

One of MECU's unique qualities is that there have been only five chairmen of its Board of Directors, the first being its founder, the late Elmer Bernhardt. The other four chairmen continue to serve the Credit Union and include below, (left to right): Charles L. Benton Jr., Harry Deitchman, John T. O'Mailey, and Herman Williams Jr.

O'Conor, Piper & Flynn ERA

O'Conor, Piper & Flynn was founded in October 1984 as a result of the merger of five Maryland-based real estate companies: O'Conor, Flynn & Skirven; Piper & Company; Charles H. Steffey, Inc.; Byrnes, Barroll & Gaines; and Broadbent Realty. Jim O'Conor and Bill Flynn, principals of O'Conor, Flynn & Skirven, together with Jim Piper and John Evans, principals of Piper and Company, became the managing partners of the newly-formed organization. The principals of the three remaining firms assumed various management positions within O'Conor, Piper & Flynn. The business immediately became the most significant real estate entity in Baltimore, gaining national exposure as the largest real estate merger in the nation's history at the time.

Originally, O'Conor, Piper & Flynn (OPF) consisted of 24 offices and 750 sales associates. During the next 16 years more than 40 companies were acquired by OPF, resulting in growth to approximately 2,300 sales associates in 45 offices. In 1984, Metropolitan Baltimore was the company's major market area. Today, that market area has expanded to include the Eastern Shore of Maryland, the northern and southern Delaware resorts, western Maryland, West Virginia and Pennsylvania.

In February 1998, O'Conor, Piper & Flynn became part of a much larger entity when purchased by NRT Incorporated, the world's largest owner of residential real estate firms. As a result of the acquisition, OPF became O'Conor, Piper & Flynn ERA—the largest broker within the ERA network. With the new business alliances and financial opportunities presented by this relationship, continued growth was on the horizon.

In December 1998, NRT Mid-Atlantic Inc. was formed with OPF president and chief executive officer Jim O'Conor taking the helm. OPF immediately became the premier operating company within NRT Mid-Atlantic, Inc., and was soon joined by the Washington, D.C. and Virginia-based Pardoe Real Estate and Pardoe Graham realty firms, as well as the Pennsylvania-based Jack Gaughen Realtor.

Jim Piper, John Evans, Bill Flynn and Jim O'Conor, left to right.

With Jim O'Conor overseeing NRT Mid-Atlantic Inc., John Evans—one of the founding partners, became president of O'Conor, Piper & Flynn ERA, assuming the task of leading the company into the new millenium.

O'Conor, Piper & Flynn ERA is a national leader in real estate technology. From its wide-area communications network spanning three states to the *www.opf.com* website, which highlights more than 6,000 homes for sale, OPF constantly offers agents, buyers, and sellers information upon demand. Additionally, the innovative *Work@nywhere* program gives OPF associates 24-hour access to electronic sales and listing contracts, e-mail and other specialized real estate software from personal computers anywhere. Technological advancements such as Internet marketing, proprietary agent software and digital photography have made the home buying and selling process easy and efficient for all involved.

O'Conor, Piper & Flynn's ever-expanding range of homeownership services has matched this tremendous growth in sales. Fulfilling consumer demand for service, OPF offers an array of client services to satisfy homeowners' needs before, during and after the sale. The AON Home Warranty program protects clients against common household breakdowns. Cendant Mortgage Services provides complete financial packages, including the innovative Phone In/Move In program. Cendant Mobility offers relocation services on a global scale to both corporations and individuals. Title Service brings the settlement process in-house; a full line of insurance products is provided to meet all client's needs; and the Guaranteed Sale Plan allows clients to purchase the home of their choice before they close on the

Above:
State-of-the-art technology enables OPF to offer more services and programs to consumers.

sale of their existing home. Additionally, builder sales; coastal investment and rental services; property management; and the ERA International Collection of Luxury Homes, a marketing program for upper-tier properties, all add to the value of this vertically-integrated real estate company.

OPF Home Services, the newest addition to the service menu, focuses on a tradition of commitment and service to consumers. Leading OPF into the new millennium, Home Services is a one-of-a-kind operation offering specialized attention to OPF's present and past clients, which is supported by a new Customer Service Center, staffed by full-time customer care counselors. With only one call to the Customer Service Center, clients can schedule everything from newspaper delivery to a moving van.

Community service remains a major thrust of this enterprising Baltimore-based company. As sponsors for Harvest for the Hungry, Toys for Tots, House with a Heart and real-time closed captioning of WJZ-TV newscasts, O'Conor Piper & Flynn ERA continues to give back to the communities and people who have made their vision a reality. O'Conor, Piper & Flynn's leadership is active in numerous foundations and on boards for community organizations including Maryland General Hospital; Broadmead Life Care Community; Loyola College; Baltimore Association of Retarded Citizens; Towson University; Sheppard & Enoch Pratt Hospital; First Mariner Bank; the Heart Association; Living Classrooms; and the Cystic Fibrosis Foundation.

Hard work and dedication have earned O'Conor, Piper & Flynn ERA the recognition and reputation of service, community pride and professionalism it enjoys today. Without a doubt, the determination of Jim O'Conor, Bill Flynn, Jim Piper and John Evans—the four competitors turned colleagues—has made their joint effort succeed beyond all expectations and has been at the heart of OPF's accomplishments over the past decade and a half. Ultimately, the wisdom of their innovative business philosophy that links quality customer service with business alliances and technological advances is borne out by the #1 market share held in virtually every market that O'Conor, Piper & Flynn ERA serves.

Below:
John Evans, Jim Piper, and Jim O'Conor award the lucky winner.

Oldfields School

Oldfields School, Maryland's oldest girls' boarding school, is situated on more than 200 acres in Baltimore County. Anna Austen McCulloch founded the school in 1867, when she and her family moved into an old farmhouse on her brother's land in Glencoe, Maryland. Built in the 1700s, the modest, clapboard home still stands as the oldest building at Oldfields, and is affectionately known as "Old House."

Mrs. McCulloch educated the younger members of her family and a few local children in her home. At the start, she did not feel that she was running a formal school; she always claimed she "took a few ladies to educate them." In fact, she was creating the foundation for the philosophy and tradition that Oldfields embraces today.

Oldfields was considered a "country" school by the very nature of its location. Glencoe was then a summer resort area for Baltimoreans seeking fresh, country air. Students walked from the nearby towns on Glencoe Road to the gates of the school. "The little old schoolroom" was equipped with tables and chairs; classes were taught by Mrs. McCulloch and her eldest daughter, Miss Abby. The day began with prompt rising and Devotions before breakfast followed by morning recitation, midday dinner, sewing hour, a daily walk, music hour, supper, and finally, study hour.

While Oldfields was not a church school, Mrs. McCulloch was a founder of Immanuel Episcopal Church, located adjacent to the School. Several local families joined with her to provide the means for building the church in 1870, and Oldfields students attended daily services.

The gates of Oldfields carry its name while Old House bears witness to the School's history.

Students gather around Miss Nan (circa 1910).

By the fall of its second year, Oldfields admitted four local students and four "resident pupils" from Memphis, in addition to the McCulloch family. Mrs. McCulloch never published any advertisements for her school. She said, "My girls are my advertisements."

When she died in 1904, Mrs. McCulloch's second daughter, Anna (known as Miss Nan), became the principal of the School. Miss Nan's brother, the Reverend Duncan McCulloch, served as her co-principal, in addition to his position as rector of Immanuel Church. Ultimately, Reverend McCulloch took the title of head of school, and Miss Nan became known as the resident principal. Under their leadership, Oldfields grew in enrollment and size. An addition was put onto the school building, and in 1912, a gymnasium was built, one of the first at a girls' school south of the Mason- Dixon line.

Miss Nan published the first catalog in 1914, launching the School's first recruitment campaign. She described the intimate, family-like environment, which she believed best served the development of a girl's physical, mental, and spiritual nature. She wrote, "The number of pupils is limited, and effort is made to gain the confidence and affection of the girls and to adapt the teaching to the individual ability and needs of each."

1917 marked the school's 50th anniversary and a period of change at Oldfields and in the world. Women had gained the right to vote, and many were entering the work force. College preparation became an integral part of an Oldfields education, and in 1918, the first diploma was granted.

After serving the School as a chief executive officer, Duncan McCulloch, Jr. became headmaster following his father's death in 1932. Building on his family's legacy, he aimed to increase enrollment and strengthen academics. He designed the curriculum to include a wide variety of studies, sports, and unscheduled recreation. Oldfields became one of the first secondary girls' schools to include chemistry in its program.

Despite its improvements, Oldfields experienced difficulties that were characteristic of many schools at the time. The Depression caused enrollment fluctuation and financial instability. Support came from the Oldfields Association, alumnae and friends, who worked voluntarily to raise funds.

After the outbreak of the war in Europe in 1939, Mr. McCulloch

encouraged student participation in the war effort. Each week included a community service hour for Red Cross work, first-aid training, and civilian volunteer service. An hour of "military drill" and a "Wartime Activity Hour" were set aside for training in civil defense. Resources were scarce, and the girls were required to make sacrifices. Air-raid drills became part of their routine; blackout rules were observed, and the food-rationing coupons limited the menus. Mr. McCulloch maintained morale with trips into Baltimore and Friday night movies. He and Mrs. McCulloch were known as "Ma" and "Pa."

Under the McCulloch's leadership, the School was able to recover from the war, and by the end of Mr. McCulloch's tenure, enrollment was healthy once again.

George S. Nevens, Jr. was appointed headmaster in 1960, making him the first head of school from outside the founding family. An advocate for alternative education, Mr. Nevens supported Oldfields' two-track system, which was designed to challenge students in their areas of strength and support them in areas needing improvement. In 1971, the May Program and Senior Projects were integrated into the course of study, offering opportunities to explore disciplines that could not be provided in the traditional curriculum. Overseas study trips were made available to foreign language students, and courses like creative women in American literature, comparative governments, and filmmaking were offered on campus. The two-track system and May Program continue today.

While changes were being made in the curriculum, the School was also undergoing a considerable building program. During the '60s, a larger gymnasium, new dormitory, student center, headmaster's house, and academic building with a new library were constructed. During Mr. Nevens' tenure, Oldfields' real property increased in value from $340,000 to nearly $5,000,000. He retired in 1976, and Hawley Rogers became headmaster.

Riders in front of Old House (circa 1925) represent the early years of the School's nationally-recognized riding program.

At a time when other small, independent schools were responding to financial difficulties by adding more students or becoming co-educational, Mr. Rogers maintained the single-gender, family-like boarding community that is a hallmark of the Oldfields experience. In 1982, the Board of Trustees capped the enrollment at 180 and limited the percentage of day students to 20 percent of the student population. Oldfields began deliberately seeking a student body that was diverse in nature, and by 1989 was comprised of girls from more than 22 states and 12 foreign countries, representing multiple cultures, religions, and socioeconomic backgrounds.

During his 21 years as headmaster, Mr. Rogers led Oldfields to new levels of financial and academic strength. Endowment was established and facilities were added to support the visual and performing arts, riding, and boarding programs. Oldfields celebrated its 125th anniversary. The academic program flourished and Oldfields became a leader in the integration of technology into its curriculum.

The class of 1998 in front of Old House at Oldfields' traditional outdoor graduation ceremony.

Under the leadership of Head of School Dr. Kathleen Jameson, who arrived in 1997, Oldfields continues to evolve in response to a changing society, while remaining committed to the philosophies and traditions established by Anna McCulloch. The School has undertaken the largest capital campaign in its history with a goal of $21 million. The Largeness of Heart Campaign intends to double endowment, bolster the annual fund, and add academic facilities, including science labs and a new library.

Today, each Oldfields girl is given the opportunity to explore a wide variety of interests in academics supported by state-of-the-art technology. A range of athletics, performing and visual arts, community service and co-curricular activities are available, and the student to faculty ratio is among the lowest in the nation at 4:1.

While Oldfields maintains its status among the top all-girls' boarding schools in the country, the School's history and integrity are never lost. Oldfields is rooted on a campus that has been part of the Baltimore legacy for over 100 years. Within these roots is the work of every teacher, student, and staff member who has passed through the School and affected it in some way.

Sisters of Bon Secours

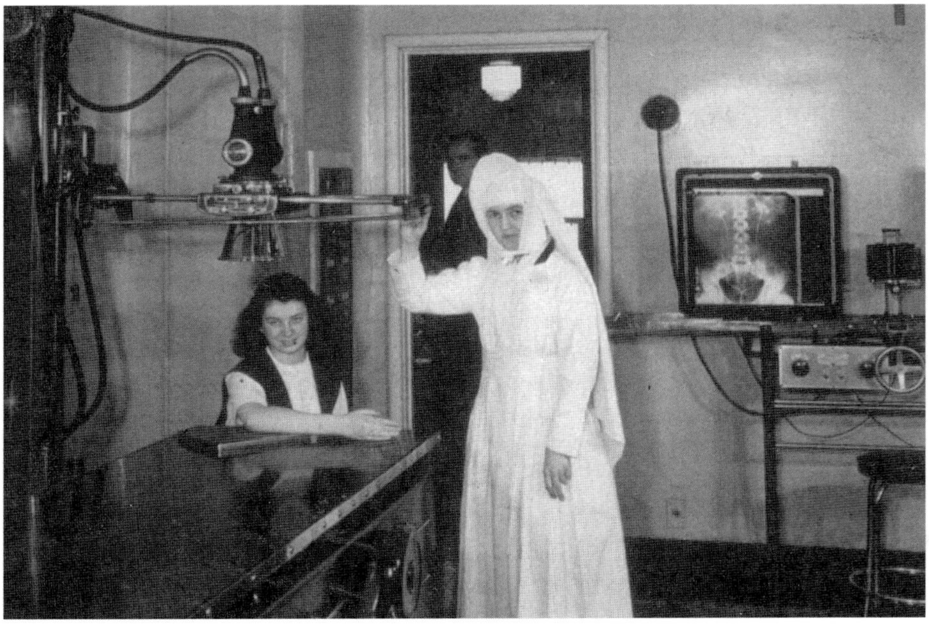

The x-ray room in Bon Secours Hospital in the early 1920s.

The Sisters of Bon Secours began caring for the sick and poor in 1824 in Paris, following the devastation of the French Revolution. Defying the conventions of the times, they left their familiar convents to nurse the sick and dying in their own homes, bringing the message that, "There is a God who loves you." Bon Secours means *good help,* and the Sisters' purpose was and is to bring compassionate care to the sick and dying. In 1870 an English-speaking Sister was asked to care for an American honeymooner from Baltimore, Mrs. Whedbe, who was taken seriously ill while visiting abroad. The Whedbes came home to tout the wonderful care received from the Sisters and requested Bishop Gibbons to invite the Sisters to the United States. In 1881 three Sisters arrived in Baltimore and established their first convent in West Baltimore, the site of the present day Bon Secours Hospital.

The Bon Secours Sister with her black bag and her fluted cap was a familiar figure in the streets of Baltimore. Unaccompanied, and trusting in God, she went out at all hours, day and night, to the homes of the poor and sick. Her black bag contained all that was necessary in the sick room, as well as many items that may have been needed by the family. This bag was looked upon with wonder by the poor, for it contained so many things they needed.

There are many important dates in the history of the Sisters of Bon Secours, many of which show the innovative spirit of this group of religious women.

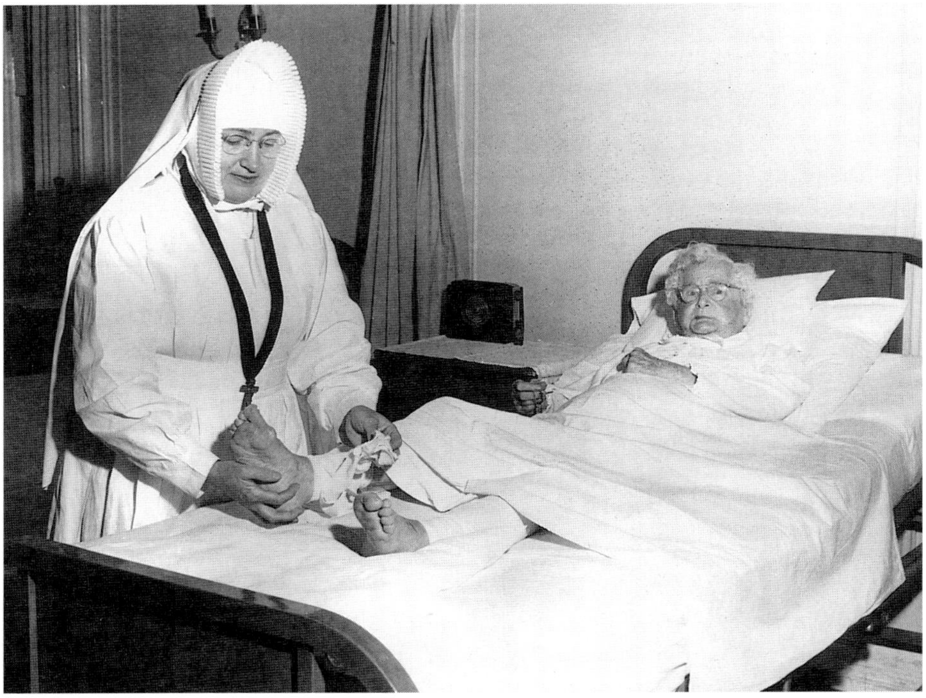

Sr. St. Constance changing a wound dressing for a patient in the 1950s.

In 1907, the Sisters established the first day nursery in Baltimore in St. Martins Parish. This day nursery remained in operation until 1958. In 1912, the Sisters opened their first Novitiate in Baltimore, which was moved in 1965 to Marriottsville, Maryland, along with their Provincial House.

In 1919 the Sisters of Bon Secours opened their first hospital in the United States, on West Baltimore Street. The hospital building was a gift from Mr. and Mrs. George C. Jenkins, whose family had been cared for in their home by the Sisters. In 1921 the Sisters opened the Bon Secours School of Nursing in Baltimore and graduated the first class in 1925. The last class graduated in 1970. In 1933 a new, three-story maternity wing opened, and in 1958 a five-story addition was built, making Bon Secours Hospital one of the largest Catholic hospitals in Baltimore at that time.

Many of those served by Bon Secours today have seen their "American Dream" crumble to a nightmare, and life become a struggle to survive. The hospital stands just two blocks from what David Simon and Edward Burns refer to in their social documentary,

The Sisters of Bon Secours receive WJZ's signature Gold 13 Salute from Channel 13's weatherman Bob Turk (l). Sisters shown (Front row l. to r.) Sr. Mary Cabrini Bonnet, Sr. Urban Auer, Sr. Mary Magdalen Condry. (Back row l. to r.) Sr. Rose Marie Jasinski, Sr. Mary Rita Nangle, Sr. Julia Marie Grimes, Sr. Alice Talone, Sr. Anne Lutz.

The Corner, as a ghetto overrun with drug dealers and crime. The hospital has had for many years a wide variety of outreach programs in the community, including drug treatment, alcohol abuse programs, health clinics and community centers.

Bon Secours Hospital formed its first Community Advisory Board in 1958 when the Sisters renewed their commitment to stay in the inner city. The Sisters of Bon Secours and Bon Secours Baltimore Health System continue today to be an integral part of an under-served community with an expanded and renovated hospital building, renal dialysis centers, a women's resource center, senior housing, and support services.

On the Liberty Village Campus, the former site of Liberty Medical Center (Liberty Medical Center joined Bon Secours Baltimore Health System in 1996), Bon Secours sponsors the Urban Medical Institute, a community-based facility dedicated to improving the health of its communities; the Community Institute of Behavioral Services, a state-licensed outpatient mental health clinic, and the Community Healthcare Network, a primary care network with close to 200 physicians and 40 primary care sites. Over 300 applications have been received to date for the 84-unit senior housing complex being built on the Liberty Village Campus. The hospital and its outreach programs serve a predominately African American population. People of all faiths are welcomed at all Bon Secours facilities and programs.

For many years after the opening of Bon Secours Hospital the Sisters directed the care of the patients. The spirit of Bon Secours was later extended through the hands of committed nurses and others that joined the staff. The Sisters communicated their philosophy of kindly care to all who shared their work. They appointed their first lay administrator in 1970, who said, *"Bon Secours is not the typical hospital one finds in the country today. Running a hospital in the inner city has to rank among the fine arts.... The needs of the community must be met. We must learn to thrive on minimal amounts of money, and yet we must produce a maximum amount of care."*

Though times have changed and the delivery of health care has become much more complex, the Sisters of Bon Secours' mission is the same, to be a sign of compassion, healing and liberation. Today, the Sisters carry forth their ministry of healing in a variety of health and healing professions in hospitals, primary care centers, home health agencies, and nursing homes. Sisters of Bon Secours can also be found as health care leaders, parish nurses, patient advocates, community organizers and chaplains—all addressing the wounds of a hurting society.

By creating the Bon Secours Health System in 1983, an integrated national health system, the Sisters ensure that care will be available and accessible to those in need well into the future. Today the Sisters of Bon Secours, USA have health care facilities in Michigan, New York, New Jersey, Pennsylvania, Maryland, Virginia, Kentucky, South Carolina and Florida and employ over 27,000 people. They also have a website located at bonsecours.org.

The Sisters' vision extends beyond themselves to their associate community who support Bon Secours' healing mission. Others may also be touched by the Bon Secours values through Bon Secours Spiritual Center in Marriottsville, which provides an atmosphere of renewal and contemplation to people of all faiths and is available for spiritual and professional meetings.

In 1999 the Sisters of Bon Secours celebrated their 175th Jubilee, recognizing the vitality of the original and continuing mission of the Sisters. "Our Charism of healing, compassion and liberation is as relevant and as needed today as it was in 1824," says Sr. Anne Marie Mack, current president of the Sisters of Bon Secours, USA. *The Sisters of Bon Secours...good help to those in need since 1881.*

Sr. Rose Marie Jasinki and Sr. Mary Rita Nangle in West Baltimore, chat with neigborhood child.

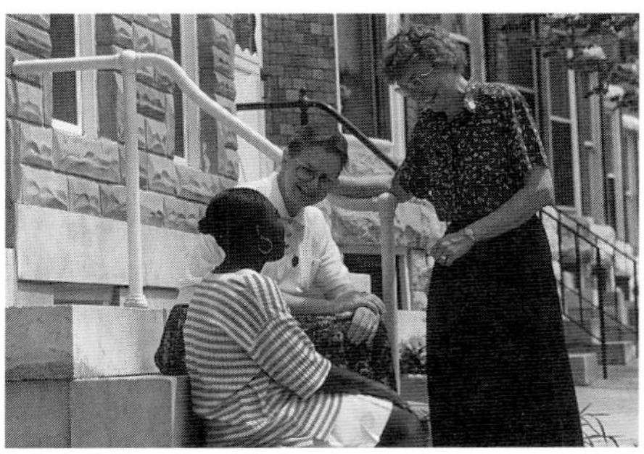

Unilever Home & Personal Care - USA

For the many passersby on Holabird Avenue, the main artery through the Dundalk/Canton section of Baltimore, the Unilever Home & Personal Care-USA/Lever Brothers plant is a landmark. And for the multitude of people who travel Interstate 95 on trips north or south, the sprawling structure is a familiar reminder that they are passing through East Baltimore's industrial section...just an exit away from the Harbor Tunnel.

Located on the site of an old dairy farm, the original plant was a single building erected in June 1925 and operated by the Gold Dust Corporation. In 1936 the facility was sold to Hecker Products Corporation for the production of powders, scouring cleaners and soap. Lever Brothers purchased the plant in 1938. The sign out front remained Lever Brothers until 1997, when the parent company, Unilever, united Lever Brothers with Chesebrough Pond's and Helene Curtis to form Unilever Home & Personal Care-USA. The strong heritage remains.

Lever Brothers was originally established in Warrington, England by brothers William and James Lever, sons of a wholesale grocer. *Sunlight,* pure laundry soap, was their first product, and it was an immediate success in Britain. *Lifebuoy* bar soap was introduced in 1894. Their business in the United States began in 1895, when William Lever opened a sales office in New York. The company expanded its sales structure with offices in New York, Philadelphia, Chicago, Kansas City and San Francisco in 1919. That same year the first granulated laundry soap, *Rinso,* was introduced. The home washing machine had skyrocketed in popularity and signaled the eventual end of washboard scrubbing. *Rinso,* in turn, eliminated the housewife's chore of cutting bar soap into chips for the wash. The introduction of *Lux* soap in 1926 set a precedent in soap making. It was the first white, milled, perfumed soap to be made and sold in America at a popular price. In a few years it was the largest selling beauty soap in the country.

Over the years, the original building erected in 1925 has been modernized and the site expanded into a large manufacturing complex.

When Lever Brothers purchased the Baltimore facility, they began installing equipment to manufacture *Lux* toilet soap, *Lifebuoy, Lux* flakes and *Rinso.* The Baltimore plant's first entry in the detergent field was *Breeze,* which was introduced in 1947 and manufactured as a dish washing detergent, followed a year later by *Surf,* a heavy duty laundry detergent.

Main entrance to the Unilever Home & Personal Care-USA/Lever Brothers plant on Holabird Avenue.

The Baltimore Lever Brothers plant scored a number of firsts in new product development. In 1955, the "milder than soap" beauty bar, *Dove,* was introduced. One year later, *Wisk*, an all-purpose, heavy-duty liquid detergent, hit the market. The acquisition of the "*all*" brand in the late-'50s was another important addition to the port-

folio of products manufactured at the Baltimore site. With numerous formulation enhancements and packaging improvements since, all of these products are still manufactured at the Baltimore facility. Today, the total national volume of Unilever's laundry detergents and much of the national volume of bar soaps are manufactured at the Baltimore plant.

To remain competitive, the Baltimore plant strives for continuous improvement, with a steady state of upgrades in all areas. With the latest technology in process controls and highspeed, automated packaging machinery, the plant has kept pace with the needs of the market. The products produced have changed as well to keep up with the changing household and personal care needs of families. The original five-story building has been modernized and the site expanded into a large manufacturing complex, including a mammoth warehouse & distribution center, large enough to fit five football fields. As the demand for the products has grown, so has the capability and capacity of the operations at the Baltimore plant.

The Baltimore plant has been a trendsetter in work practices and employee recognition. In 1920, Lever employees and their families were given company-paid group life insurance, one of the first such plans in American industry. In 1940 its Quarter Century Club, for employees with 25+ years of service, was established with an initial membership of four. Today the club has a membership of 737, of which 45 are active employees and 692 are retirees. In 1945 Baltimore employees received Lever's first pension plan, which was then regarded as very progressive. The company's Profit Sharing and Investment Plan was offered to employees in 1952, and a Tuition Refund Program was established in 1957. Many safety programs have been instituted over the years, including a 1977 compulsory, total-eye protection program. In 1986 several retirees established the Lever Brothers Retirees' Association. The group gets together throughout the year for social events and work projects. The plant currently has 500 employees; the factory workers are members of the International Chemical Workers Union, and the lab workers belong to the Teamsters.

Susan Flanigan is shown working on the Wisk® *production line.*

Through charitable donations, Unilever supports such organizations as the Johns Hopkins Children's Center, United Way of Central Maryland, and Family Crisis Center of Baltimore County. Unilever has donated to and partnered with local educational institutions, such as Southeast Middle School, Sollers Point/Southeastern Technical High School, and Dundalk Community College. The Baltimore plant began a new annual program in 1999 as corporate sponsor for Baltimore County Schools, of the Science Screen Report for Kids, a videotape series that focuses on recent developments in science, technology and engineering. in addition, the Unilever employees participate in food and clothing drives with their "Adopt A Family" programs. In 1996 the plant's commitment to the local community was honored with the receipt of the Mayor's Business Recognition Award for outstanding service.

Unilever also recognizes the importance of environmental initiatives. The plant was a corporate sponsor of TreeMendous Maryland, a statewide conservation program. Unilever participated in the Project C-Wrap, a wetlands conservation and environmental education project for Baltimore-area schools. In addition, employees have volunteered for projects with the National Park Foundation at Fort McHenry to promote recycling, and a cleanup project at Gwynn's Falls Park.

Unilever will continue its efforts to be a good neighbor to Baltimore and an asset to the Dundalk community.

Products manufactured at the Baltimore plant include Wisk®, all®, *and* Surf® *laundry detergents, and* Dove® *and* Caress® *beauty bars.*

M.S. Willett, Inc.

Willett cap lining machine, circa 1950.

M. S. Willett, Inc. designs and builds high quality tools and dies used to produce metal stampings and assemblies. A metal stamping is an object produced from flat or rolled sheet metal. It is the most ambiguous form of formed or shaped metals. Examples range from watch components and food or drink cans, to automotive parts.

Moses Showell Willett founded the firm in 1929. Mose, as he was known, was born on the Eastern Shore in Berlin, Maryland, however he grew up in Baltimore.

In the 1920s, after serving his apprenticeship as a tool and die maker, Mose worked for a number of Baltimore-area can making companies. At that time, Baltimore was a can making center, due to its location near the head of the Chesapeake Bay and an extensive water transportation system all along the Bay.

In late 1929, after the Wall Street market crash, Mose Willett was approached by the owner of Columbia Specialty Company to take over the operation of his machine shop and run it as an independent business. Columbia Specialty produced primarily closures, screw caps, and slip fit cans. Mose invited his son-in-law Stuart "Mac" McCaughey and his daughter Edna McCaughey to join him.

The first customers Willett had, other than Columbia, were the Liberty Can and Sign Company, now a division of J.L. Clark of Rockford, Illinois, and the closure division of the Armstrong Cork Company. Clark is still an important Willett customer.

When World War II came along, Willett purchased its own facility—a building near Johns Hopkins Hospital at 1913-19 Ashland Avenue. Willett made many tools, including water canteens, ammunition belts, mess kits, gas mask canisters and c-ration cans.

In 1947, Moses Willett retired from management of the company. He remained an advisor/consultant. Mac McCaughey, his son-in-law, took over the operation of Willett.

Once Mac became president, he launched Willett into the metal stamping business. Willett was principally a metal stamper of metal hardware for inexpensive furniture and kitchen dinette sets. The tool and die department was active with metal packaging dies and special machines.

By 1960, the firm moved to a new suburban facility in Cockeysville about 10 miles north of Baltimore. This pattern of growth continued as Willett expanded its engineering capabilities, apprentice training and plant facilities in response to the ever-increasing demand for its products and services. It was during the 1960s that the Willett Transfer was developed.

Willett High Speed Horizontal Transfer System to produce wine bottle capsules, circa 1980s.

Willett High Speed Turnkey System with five sets of tooling to produce automotive heat exchange components, circa 1990s.

J.L. Clark Company, a leading producer of packaging for the spice industry, came to Willett needing to economically produce steel tops for spice cans. The tops were perforated and contained a plastic disc which was rotated in order to pour the spice. Willett developed the method of transferring these can ends from die station to die station using cam-activated mechanisms mounted to the die set. These systems were operated at 110 strokes-per-minute and were faster than anything available.

On July 2, 1965, Moses S. Willett passed away.

In 1957, Stuart and Edna's only son, John McCaughey, joined the firm, after graduating from the Georgia Institute of Technology (Georgia Tech) with a Bachelor of Science (Industrial Engineering). John McCaughey worked his way up from an engineering position to company president in 1974.

In the 1970s Willett found new markets for its high-speed in-press transfer system. The first application involved the transfer of automobile engine rocker arms through a die that performed secondary operations after the basic part has been formed in a progressive die. Willett designed and built systems used for the complete production of automobile engine rocker arms. At one point, 90 percent of all rocker arms made in North America were made in Willett transfers.

Willett also built an integrated three press system to produce one piece aluminum and brass door knobs for the Kwikset Lock Company, then a division of USM.

On October 22, 1983, Mac McCaughey passed away. He had continued to remain active as an advisor to the company until his final months.

In the 1980s Willett's Production Group brought in new metal stamping business and became an indispensable part of Willett. The Production Group took over manufacturing of the majority of stampings that Black & Decker was manufacturing at their Hampstead, Maryland plant. Well over 1,000 dies were delivered to Willett. Harley-Davidson approached Willett for a similar program and over 700 dies were absorbed. Willett is now the principal supplier of sheet metal parts to Harley-Davidson.

In the late 1980s Willett entered into a technology agreement with National Steel (now known as Weirton), giving Willett the exclusive rights to tool certain types of steel safety fold easy open ends.

Willett also developed a number of new transfers, including Willett Quick Change Transfer (WQC), Customizer, Technotransfer, Transrobot and Servo Transfer.

In the 1990s Willett delivered its first production machine used to make steel easy-open can ends which contained the unique Weirton Steel Triple Fold Safety Edge Technology. The first end was used for corned beef. Willett retains exclusive rights to manufacture Weirton-style non-round steel triple fold ends.

With the Weirton Triple Fold Safety End Technology a proven success, Willett set upon a course to capitalize upon that as well as its unique feed bar system used in transferring can ends. The first, and to date most outstanding success, has been with various types of meat can ends. These have been tooled for Glud & Marstrand, now Scandinavia's largest manufacturer of three piece cans.

Parallel to the promotion of its equipment to the can making industry, Willett increased its efforts to sell transfers and tooling to general industry, particularly automotive.

On October 3, 1998, Edna McCaughey passed away. With her passing the last of the three founders of the company was gone. The spirit of these three founders lives on at Willett—a spirit that is dedicated to hard work, resulting in customer satisfaction!

In 1999 Willett was ISO9001 certified. In April 2000, Willett added a third location to its facilities in Cockeysville, Maryland and invested $2 million in state-of-the-art computers and machinery.

Willett remains committed to producing quality products that meet or exceed their customers' expectations.

A Timeline of Baltimore's History

1608 Captain John Smith sailed up the Chesapeake Bay and recorded the first description of the area that would become Baltimore, then a hunting ground for local American Indians.

1634 The *Ark* and the *Dove* landed at St, Mary's City, bringing the first European and African settlers to Maryland.

1649 Maryland passed the Toleration Act, the first religious freedom law in the American colonies, guaranteeing freedom of worship for all Christians, but not non-Christians.

1663 Alexander Mountenay patented land along Harford Run, where Central Avenue now is located.

1715 Maryland's Colonial Assembly authorized the convening of a court to serve the growing number of residents in Baltimore County and set four yearly sessions for the court.

1729 Baltimore County citizens petitioned the Assembly to establish a town to ease the process of exporting tobacco and importing goods from elsewhere. The new town's first commissioners bought 60 acres of land along the Patapsco River from Daniel and Charles Carroll.

1732 Jones's Town, a tract of 10 acres sometimes called Old Town, was established along the Jones Falls.

1745 The merger of Baltimore Town and Old Town enlarged the original Baltimore Town.

1752 First census of Baltimore Town listed thirty names of early settlers. First census of Baltimore County enumerated free whites, white servants, free blacks, and slaves.

1763 Fells Point was established as a town and quickly became a major shipbuilding center.

1765 The Stamp Act led to protests against the first direct tax levied on the colonies by England.

1773 Baltimore annexed Fells Point.

1773 William Goddard began publication of Baltimore's first newspaper, *The Maryland Journal and Baltimore Advertiser.*

1775 Maryland revolutionary leaders who began to govern the colony through the Maryland Provincial Convention sent delegates to the Second Continental Congress in Philadelphia. Fighting between American and British troops broke out in New England.

1776 Second Continental Congress declared independence from England and the new Maryland constitution set up a government for the independent state.

1781 The Revolution ended when the British surrendered at Yorktown, Virginia. Maryland became an independent state.

1789 The new United States Constitution became the law of the land.

1789 The Baltimore Society for Promoting the Abolition of Slavery was founded.

1797 Baltimore City held its first elections under the new city charter. James Calhoun was elected Baltimore's first mayor.

1810 Free African Americans outnumbered slaves in Baltimore.

1812 The War of 1812 began.

1814 In the Battle of Baltimore, General Samuel Smith led local soldiers and civilians in an important victory over the British. Francis Scott Key wrote the words to *The Star Spangled Banner* during the bombardment of Fort McHenry.

1818 Baltimore City annexed 13 square miles of land from Baltimore County.

1820s *The Genius of Universal Emancipation*, the nation's first exclusively anti-slavery newspaper, was published in Baltimore.

1826 A new law allowed Jews to vote in Maryland for the first time.

1828 The Baltimore & Ohio Railroad was incorporated. The tracks reached Wheeling on the Ohio River in 1853.

1829 Baltimore opened its first public schools, two for boys and two for girls. Approximately three percent of all eligible children attended. Only white children were eligible.

1840 Baltimore's first public high school, which became Baltimore City College, opened.

1840-1860 Immigrants from Germany and Ireland came to Baltimore.

1860 Just before the Civil War, 90 percent of Baltimore's black population was free.

1860 Druid Hill Park opened on the outskirts of the city.

1861 The first deaths of the Civil War occurred in Baltimore when the Massachusetts 6th Regiment marched through the city from the President Street Station to Camden Station en route to Washington, D.C.

1861-1865 When the Civil War broke out, Union troops occupied Baltimore to insure the city's loyalty to the Union. Troops from Baltimore fought for both the North and the South.

1864 Maryland's new constitution ended slavery in Baltimore and throughout the state.

1865 The Civil War ended when Confederate General Robert E. Lee surrendered to General Ulysses S. Grant at Appomattox Courthouse in Virginia.

1867 Centenary Biblical Institute, which became Morgan State University, opened.

1870 African Americans voted in Baltimore for the first time since 1810.

1870 Pimlico Race Course opened.

1870s to 1910s Immigrants from southern and eastern Europe settled in Baltimore.

1872 Baltimore's first league-franchise baseball team, the Lord Baltimores, began playing at Newington Park.

1876 The Johns Hopkins University opened for male students.

1879 The first interclub lacrosse game was played in Baltimore.

1885 Baltimoreans founded the Reform League to spearhead efforts to improve the city.

1885 The Women's College of Baltimore, later renamed for its benefactor John

Goucher, offered classes for female students, some taught by Hopkins faculty.
1886 The Enoch Pratt Free Library opened to make books available to everyone.
1888 Baltimore City annexed 23 square miles of land and added 38,000 people.
1889 The Johns Hopkins Hospital opened. The Medical School, which accepted both male and female students, followed in 1893.
1890 Harry Cummings, a Republican and the first African American elected to public office in Baltimore, won a seat on the City Council.
1895 Reformers won in the Baltimore City elections.
1900 Baltimore ranked 3rd in the nation with $130 million in foreign trade.
1902 School attendance became compulsory for children aged 8 to 12 in Baltimore.
1904 A fire that broke out in the Hurst Drygoods Company burned much of downtown Baltimore.
1916 The Baltimore Symphony Orchestra was founded as a branch of the municipal government. It became independent in 1942.
1917-1918 As the United States fought in World War I, soldiers and sailors from Baltimore served in the military, and Baltimore industries manufactured large amounts of war supplies.
1918 Baltimore added over 50 square miles of land when it annexed parts of Baltimore County and Anne Arundel County. A law passed after World War II forbade further annexations.
1919 After the Volstead Act was passed by the United States Congress, Baltimore Mayor Howard Jackson refused to appropriate any local money to enforce Prohibition. Baltimore was known as a "wet" city.
1920 The 19th Amendment to the United States Constitution gave women the right to vote. For the first time in history, all adult citizens in Maryland could vote.
1929 The Baltimore Museum of Art opened at Wyman Park.
1930 The Baltimore Trust Company was the first local bank to close its doors as the effects of the Great Depression were felt.
1933 Approximately 20 percent of Baltimore's workers were unemployed.
1941-1945 As the United States fought in World War II, Baltimoreans served in the Army and Navy. Baltimore industries, including ship and aircraft building, supplied the Armed Forces.
1947 Commercial television broadcasting began in Baltimore.
1949 Memorial Stadium opened, with one level of seats, in North Baltimore.
1950 Baltimorean Alger Hiss was sentenced for perjury, one of many episodes in a post-World War II Red Scare.
1950 According to the United States census, Baltimore's population stood at its historically highest number.
1950 Friendship International Airport, now the Baltimore Washington International Airport, opened for commercial flights.
1953 The National Football League Colts began to play in Baltimore.
1954 The Baltimore Orioles, formerly the St. Louis Browns, began to play baseball in Baltimore.
1954 The first African Americans were elected to the Maryland General Assembly from West Baltimore.
1954 Following the Brown v. Board of Education decision in the United States Supreme Court, public schools in Baltimore began to desegregate.
1954 The Baltimore-Washington Parkway opened, making the drive between the two cities shorter.
1955 Business leaders organized the Greater Baltimore Committee to work to revitalize the downtown in West Baltimore.
1957 The Baltimore Harbor Tunnel opened.
1959 Highway I-83 connected Baltimore and Harrisburg, PA.
1960-2000 Baltimore showed a population loss with each census taken.
1960-2000 New immigrants from Asia, the Caribbean and Central America added to the city's ethnic and linguistic diversity.
1961 Ground was broken for Charles Center.
1962 The Baltimore Beltway and the Jones Falls Expressway opened, providing fast roads for commuter traffic.
1968 Riots in Baltimore followed the assassination of Dr. Martin Luther King.
1970 The first Earth Day marked the beginning of the modern environmental movement in Baltimore and elsewhere.
1970 The Baltimore City Fair brought crowds back into downtown Baltimore.
1977 The World Trade center opened on the northeast corner of the Inner Harbor.
1979 The Baltimore Convention Center opened, marking the beginning of a large convention business for the city.
1980 Harborplace opened, drawing large crowds to downtown Baltimore.
1981 The National Aquarium in Baltimore opened and quickly became the city's largest single tourist attraction.
1984 The Baltimore Colts packed up and moved out of town in the dark of night, leaving Baltimoreans angry and disappointed.
1992 Orioles Park at Camden yards opened and became another major attraction downtown.
1998 PSINet Stadium opened as the new home for the Baltimore Ravens, the city's new National Football League team.
1999 Baltimore had over 40,000 vacant homes and an annual murder rate at more than 300.
2000 Baltimore celebrated the 20th anniversary of Harborplace with fireworks and a party.

Selected Readings

Andrews, Matthew Page. *The Fountain Inn*. New York, Rich R. Smith, 1948.

Arnett, Earl, Robert Brugger, and Edward C. Papenfuse. *A New Guide to the Old Line State*. Baltimore: The Johns Hopkins University Press in association with the Maryland State Archives, 1999.

Baker, Jean H. Ambivalent Americans: *The Know Nothing Party in Maryland. Baltimore,* The Johns Hopkins University Press, 1977.

Baker, Jean H. *The Politics of Continuity*. Baltimore, The Johns Hopkins University Press, 1973.

Baltimore: *Two Hundredth Anniversary, 1729-1929.* Baltimore, The Baltimore Municipal Journal, 1929.

Barker, Charles Albro. T*he Background of the Revolution in Maryland, New* Haven: Yale University Press, 1940.

Bedini, Silvio, *The Life of Benjamin Banneker: The First African American Man of Science*. 2nd edition. Baltimore: The Maryland Historical Society, 1999.

Beirne, Francis F. *The Amiable Baltimoreans*. New York, Dutton, 1951.

Beirne, Francis F. *St. Paul's Parish Baltimore*. Baltimore, St. Paul's Parish, 1967.

Blum, Isidor. *The Jews of Baltimore*. Historical Review Publishing Company, Baltimore, 1910.

Bready, James H. *Baseball in Baltimore: The First 100 Years.* Baltimore: The Johns Hopkins University Press, 1998

Bready, James H. *The Home Team*. Baltimore: Baltimore Baseball Club, 1979 (3rd ed.).

Brooks, Neal And Eric Rockel. *A History of Baltimore County.* Towson, MD: Friends of the Towson Library, 1979.

Brown, George William. *Baltimore and the Nineteenth of April, 1861*. Baltimore: N. Murray, 1887.

Browne, Gary L. *Baltimore in the Nation*, 1789-1861. Chapel Hill: University of North Carolina Press, 1980.

Brugger, Robert J. *Maryland: A Middle Temperament, 1634-1980*. Baltimore: The Johns Hopkins University Press in association with the Maryland Historical Society, 1988.

Chapelle, Suzanne E., *et al. Maryland: A History of Its People*. Baltimore: The Johns Hopkins University Press, 1986

Coyle, Wilbur F. *The Mayors of Baltimore*. Baltimore: The Baltimore Municipal Journal, 1919.

Crooks, James B. *Politics and Progress: The Rise of Urban Progressivism in Baltimore, 1895 to 1911*. Baton Rouge: Louisiana State University Press, 1968.

Cunz, Dieter. *The Maryland Germans*. Princeton: Princeton University Press, 1948.

Dehler, Katharine B. *The Thomas Jencks-Gladding House*. Baltimore: Bodine and Associates, 1968.

Dorsey, John, *et al.* A Guide to Baltimore Architecture. Centreville, MD: Cornell Maritime Press, 1997.

Eddis, William. *Letters from America*. Ed. Aubrey C. Land. Cambridge: Harvard University Press, 1969.

Farrar, Hayward. *The Baltimore Afro-American, 1892-1950.* Westport, CT: Greenwood Press, 1998.

Fee, Elizabeth, Linda Shopes, and Linda Zeidman. *The Baltimore Book*. Philadelphia: Temple University Press, 1991.

Fields, Barbara Jean. *Slavery and Freedom on the Middle Ground: Maryland during the Nineteenth Century.* New Haven: Yale University Press. 1985.

Fein, Isaac M. *The Making of an American Jewish Community*. Philadelphia: The Jewish Publication Society of America, 1971.

First Records of Baltimore Town and Jones Town, 1729-1797. Mayor and City Council of Baltimore, 1905.

Grauer, Neil A., *Baltimore: Jewel of the Chesapeake.* Chatsworth, CA: Windsor Publications, 1991.

Griffith, Thomas W. *Annals of Baltimore*. Baltimore, 1824 (printed by William Wooddy).

Gurn, Joseph. *Charles Carroll of Carrollton, 1737-1832.* New York: P.J. Kenedy and Sons, 1932.

Hall, Clayton Colman. *Baltimore: Its History and Its People.* New York: Lewis Historical Publishing Co., 1912.

Hayward, Mary Ellen, *et al. The Baltimore Rowhouse*. Princeton: Architectural Press, 1999.

Hirschfeld, Charles. *Baltimore, 1870-1900*. Baltimore: The Johns Hopkins University Press, 1941.

Hoffman, Ronald. *A Spirit of Dissension: Economics, Politics, and The Revolution in Maryland*. Baltimore: The Johns Hopkins University Press, 1973.

Janvier, Meredith. *Baltimore in the Eighties and Nineties.* Baltimore: H.G. Roebuck and Son, 1933.

Johnston, William. *William and Henry Walters, The Reticent Collectors*. Baltimore: The Johns Hopkins University Press in association with the Walters Art Gallery, 1999.

Kelly, Jacques. *Peabody Heights to Charles Village.* Baltimore: The Equitable Trust Co., 1976.

Kenny, Hamill. *The Origin and Meaning of the Indian Place Names of Maryland*. Baltimore: Waverly Press, 1961.

King, Thomson. *Consolidated of Baltimore*. Baltimore, 1950 (published by the Consolidated Gas Electric Light and Power Company of Baltimore).

Lucas, Fielding. *Picture of Baltimore*. Baltimore: A.T. Francis, printer, 1832.

Manakee, Harold R. *Indians of Early Maryland*. Baltimore: Maryland Historical Society, 1959.

—— *Maryland in the Civil War.* Baltimore: Maryland Historical Society, 1961.

Maryland Gazette. Annapolis, 1745- passim.

Maryland Journal and Baltimore Advertiser. Baltimore, 1773-passim.

May, Alonzo. *May's Dramatic Encyclopedia*. Baltimore, 1904.

Merrill, Philip and Uluaipou-O-Malo Aiono. *Baltimore*. Charleston, SC: Arcadia Publishing, 1999.

Olson, Sherry. *Baltimore: The Building of an American City.* 2nd edition. Baltimore: The Johns Hopkins University Press, 1997.

Orser, W. Edward. *Blockbusting in Baltimore: The Edmondson Village Story.* Lexington: University Press of

Kentucky, 1997.
Owens, Hamilton. *Baltimore on the Chesapeake*, Garden City: Doubleday, Doran and Co., 1941.
Phillips, Christopher. *Freedom's Port: The African American Community in Baltimore, 1790-1860.* Urbana: University of Illinois Press, 1997.
Preston, Dickson. *Young Frederick Douglass: The Maryland Years.* Baltimore: The Johns Hopkins University Press, 1980.
Quarles, Benjamin. *The Negro in the American Revolution.* New York: Norton, 1961.
Renzulli, L. Marx, Jr. *Maryland: The Federalist Years.* Rutherford, New Jersey: Fairleigh Dickinson University Press, 1972.
Rukert, Norman. *The Fells Point Story.* Baltimore: Bodine and Associates, 1976.
Rusk, David. *Baltimore Unbound: Creating a Greater Baltimore Region for the Twenty-First Century.* Baltimore: The Johns Hopkins University Press in association with the Abell Foundation, 1995.
Scharf, J. Thomas. *The Chronicles of Baltimore.* Baltimore: Turnbull Brothers, 1874.
—— *History of Baltimore City and County.* Philadelphia: Louis H. Everts, 1881.
Semmes, Raphael. *Captains and Mariners of Early Maryland.* Baltimore: Johns Hopkins University Press, 1931.
Shivers, Frank. *Bolton Hill.* Baltimore: The Equitable Trust Co., 1978.
Sioussat, Annie Leakin. *Old Baltimore.* New York: MacMillan, 1931.
Skaggs, David Curtis. *Roots of Maryland Democracy 1753-1776.* Westport, Conn.: Greenwood Press, 1973.
Skidmore, Howard. *The Story So Far, Sesquicentennial of the Baltimore and Ohio Railroad, 1827-1977.* Baltimore, 1977.
Smith, C. Fraser. *William Donald Schaefer: A Political Biography.* Baltimore: The Johns Hopkins University Press, 1999.
Smith, Ellen Hart. *Charles Carroll of Carrollton.* New York: Russell and Russell, 1942.
Steffen, Charles. *The Mechanics of Baltimore: Workers and Politics in the Age of Revolution, 1763-1812.* Urbana: University of Illinois Press, 1984.
Stevens, Barbara M. *Homeland: History and Heritage.* Baltimore, 1976.
Thom, Helen Hopkins. *Johns Hopkins: A Silhouette. Baltimore:* Johns Hopkins University Press, 1929.
Travers, Paul. *The Patapsco: Baltimore's River of History.* Centreville, MD: Tidewater Publishers, 1990.
Wagandt, Charles Lewis. *The Mighty Revolution: Negro Emancipation in Maryland, 1862-1864.* Baltimore: The Johns Hopkins University Press, 1964.
Walsh, Richard, and Lloyd Fox, William. *Maryland: A History, 1632-1974.* Baltimore: Maryland Historical Society, 1974.
Weekley, Carolyn, and Colwill, Stiles T. *Joshua Johnson: Free man and Early American Portrait Painter.* Baltimore: The Maryland Historical Society, 1987.
Williams, Harold. *History of the Hibernian Society of Baltimore, 1803-1957.* Baltimore: Hibernian Society of Baltimore, 1957.
——*The Baltimore Sun, 1837-1987.* Baltimore: The Johns Hopkins University Press, 1987.
Wright, James M. *The Free Negro in Maryland, 1634-1860.* New York: Octagon Books, 1971 (1st ed., 1921).

Scholarly articles from the *Maryland Historical Magazine* cover a wide range of subjects in local history and are an extremely valuable source. Articles from the Baltimore *Sun*, the *News American* archives, and *Baltimore Magazine* are also good sources.

Index

Chronicles of Leadership Index

General Index

Page numbers for illustrations are printed in italics.

Illustration Credits

Abell Foundation: 233 top left
Afro-American Newspapers: 183 top left, 195 center, 195 bottom, 201 top, 207 top, 209 bottom
Alan Mason Chesney Medical Archives of the Johns Hopkins Medical Institutions: 249 bottom, 249 top right
Babe Ruth Museum: 133
Baltimore and Ohio Railroad Museum: 82 left, 82 right, 83 right, 83 bottom, 118, 119, 147 bottom, 151, 155, 157 bottom, 159 top, 175 center, 205 bottom
Baltimore County Public Library: 151
Baltimore Friends School: 239 center
Baltimore Hebrew Congregation: 187 bottom right
Baltimore Magazine: 253 bottom right, 254 bottom right, Photo by David Colwell,
Baltimore Neighborhood Heritage Project: 153 bottom, 183 bottom, 189 bottom left
Baltimore News American: 183 top left, 207 bottom left, 209 bottom
Baltimore Orioles: 209 top, 255 bottom, 255 top right
Baltimore Public Schools: 165 left, 177 bottom right
Baltimore Sun: 159 bottom, 167 top right, 177 left, 187 bottom left, 195 top left, 197 top, 197 left, 201 bottom, 205 top, 207 top, 207 bottom right, 210, 211 top left, 211 top right, 211center, 213 top, 213 bottom
Baltimore Symphony Orchestra: 251 bottom right
Blackstone Studios, Inc.: 189 top
Bragg, Arthur 166
Brown, Marie Scott: 143 top
Bryn Mawr School: 141 top
Chapelle, Suzanne Ellery Greene: 233 top left, 243 bottom, 253 top right
Chesapeake Bay Foundation: 245 top, 247 top
Clarke, Mary Pat: 239 top center
Cummings, Harry Jr. and Louise Dorcas, daughter of Harry Cummings: 167 top left, 167 top center, 169 top left, 169 top right
Ehlers, Brenda: 187 center
Enoch Pratt Free Library: 9, 21 top, 21 bottom, 37 right, 41 left, 41 right, 55 bottom right, 61 top right, 61 bottom right, 71 bottom, 83 left, 91 bottom, 109, 111, 121 top, 121 center, 125 top, 134, 135 top right, 137 top right, 165 right, 191 bottom left, 191bottom right
Evans, Middleton: 230, 233 bottom, 235 top, 235 bottom left, 235 bottom right, 237 top, 237 right, 239, top, 241 bottom, 243 center, 243 top, 245 bottom, 249 right, 249 top left, 251 bottom left, 251, top, 245 bottom, 251 top 253 top right,253 bottom left, 254 bottom left, 255 top left, 256,back cover
Fisk University Archives: 96
Goucher College: 183 top right
Hollie, Donna Tyler: 177
Housing Authority of Baltimore: Photo by A. Jay McCullough, 238, Photo by A. Jay McCullough, 239 bottom right
Jaramillo, Alain: 187 top, 211 bottom, 213 center,
Johns Hopkins University Archives: 139 top, 139 center, 139 bottom
Lemon, Jessie Fitzgerald: 200
Library Company of the Baltimore Bar: 87 bottom right
Maryland Department of Business & Economic Development, Photos by Dennis Roos: 228 top, 228 bottom, 229 top, 229 bottom
Maryland Historical Society: Front cover, Frontispiece vi, 3 top, 3 center, 3 bottom, 5 top right, 5 top left, 5 bottom right, 5 bottom left, 7 top, 7 center, 7 bottom, 11 top, 11 bottom left, 11 bottom right, 13, 14, 15, 17, 19 left,19 center, 19 right, 21 center, 23 top left, 23 top right, 23 bottom, 25 top, 25 bottom left, 25 bottom right, 26 top, 26 bottom, 27, 29, 30, 33 top, 33 bottom, 35, 37 left, 41 bottom, 41 right, 43 top left, 43 center left, 43 bottom left, 43 right, 45 left, 45 top right, 45 bottom right, 47 top, 47 bottom, 49 top, 53 left, 53 right 55 top, 57 top, 57 bottom left, 59 bottom, 59 top right, 59 center, 67 top right, 70 top, 70 bottom, 71 top, 71 center, 72, 75 top, 75 bottom, 77 left, 79 bottom, 81, 85, 87 top, 89, 91 top, 93 bottom, 95 top, 95 bottom left, 95 bottom right, 97, 99 top, 99 bottom, 101, 102, 103, 107, 115 bottom, 115 top, 121 bottom, 123 bottom, 125 bottom, 126, 128, 129 top, 129 bottom, 130, 131 top, 131 center, 131 bottom, 135 bottom,137 top left, 137 bottom, 141 bottom left, 141 bottom right,143 bottom, 145 top, 147 top left, 147 top right,149 top, 150 top, 152 top, 154, 157 top, 161 right, 175 top, 175 bottom, 178, 180, 185, 189 center, 191 top, 193, 203 top, 203 bottom right, 203 bottom left
Maryland State Archives: 233 top center, 236
Mencken, Leroy: 197 right
Morgan State University Office of Public Relations: 241 top right
National Aquarium in Baltimore: 247 center - Photo by Fred Pahl, 247 bottom - Photo by Joe McSharry
National Association for the Advancement of Colored People (NAACP): 241 top center
Office of Senator Barbara Mikulski: 239 bottom right
Office of Senator Paul Sarbanes: 239 top right
Office of the City Council President: 240
Office of the Mayor: 241
Random House: 253 top center
Schmoke, Kurt: 237 bottom
University of Maryland, Baltimore County: 149 bottom right, 150 bottom, 163, 179 top, 179 center
University of Maryland Medical School: 55 bottom left
Waldek, Alfred: 153, 189 bottom right
Young, Raymond: 61 left, 63 top, 167

Baltimore

Baltimore

An Illustrated History

By Suzanne Ellery Greene Chapelle

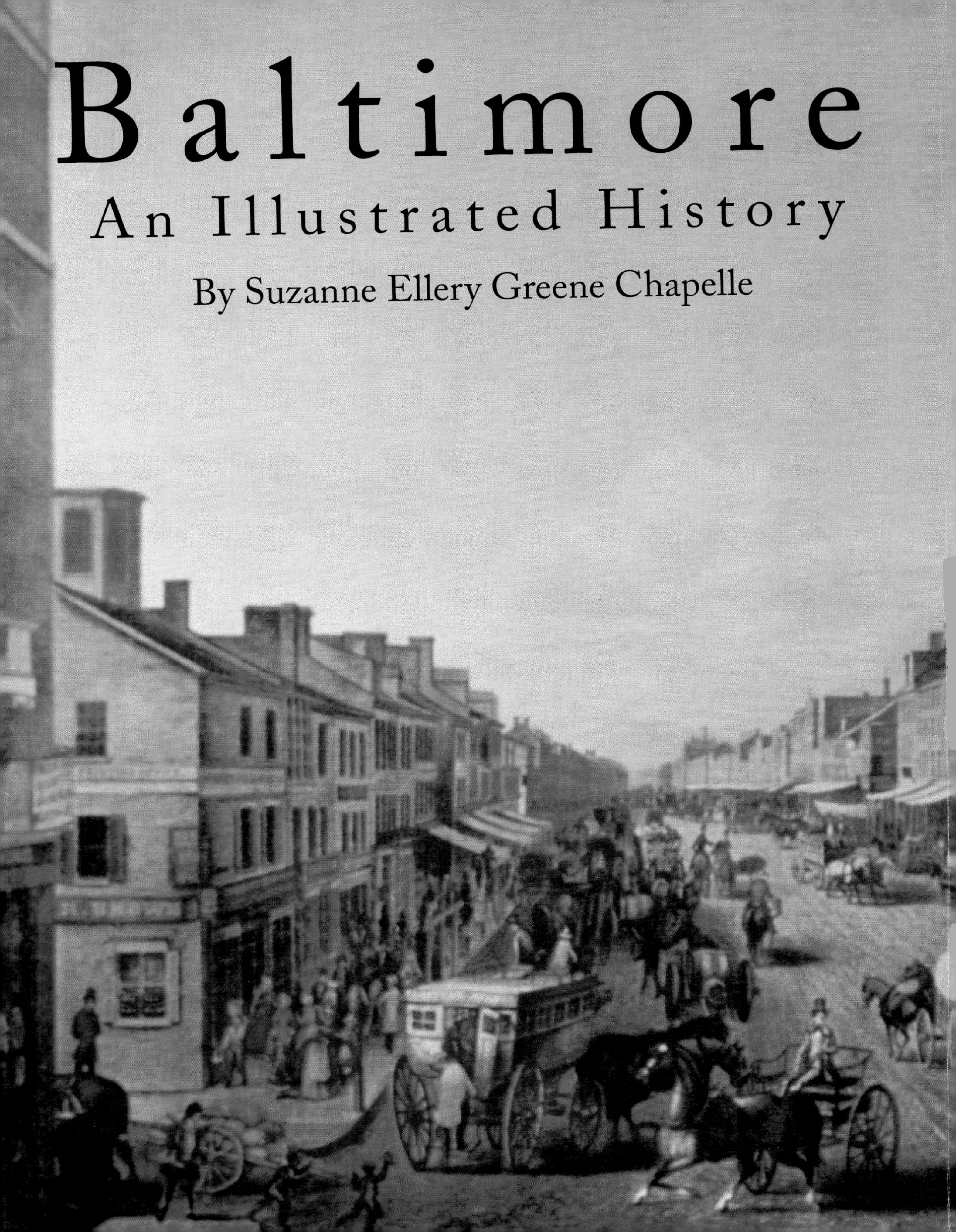